THE RESOURCE
BOOK OF
JEWISH MUSIC

Recent Titles in the Music Reference Collection

Series Advisers: Donald L. Hixon
                     Adrienne Fried Block

Music for Oboe, Oboe D'Amore, and English Horn: A Bibliography of Materials at the Library of Congress
Compiled by Virginia Snodgrass Gifford

A Bibliography of Nineteenth-Century American Piano Music: With Location Sources and Composer Biography-Index
John Gillespie and Anna Gillespie

THE RESOURCE BOOK OF JEWISH MUSIC

A Bibliographical and Topical Guide to the Book and Journal Literature and Program Materials

Compiled by
IRENE HESKES

Music Reference Collection, Number 3

Greenwood Press
Westport, Connecticut • London, England

Library of Congress Cataloging in Publication Data

Heskes, Irene.
    The resource book of Jewish music.

    (Music reference collection, 0736-7740 ; no. 3)
    Includes indexes.
    1. Jews—Music—Bibliography.   2. Music—Bibliography.
I. Title.   II. Series.
ML128.J4H48   1985   016.7817 '2924   84-22435
ISBN 0-313-23251-2 (lib. bdg.)

Library of Congress Catalog Card Number: 84-22435
ISBN: 0-313-23251-2
ISSN: 0736-7740

First published in 1985

Greenwood Press
A division of Congressional Information Service, Inc.
88 Post Road West
Westport, Connecticut 06881

Printed in the United States of America

10 9 8 7 6 5 4 3 2 1

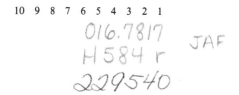

Contents

Preface

There is a Jewish saying that the world was created for the sake of music. Truly a universal human expression, it transcends time and place, affording pleasure, inspiration, and spiritual reflection. No wonder that early passages of the Bible refer to Jubal, master craftsman of the musicians. The Jews have fashioned their music into a heritage corollary to traditions, customs, and history. Viable for each generation wherever settled, this Jewish musical patrimony has pervaded synagogue, home, and wayside of everyday life; and, unconfined by barriers of language, social isolation, or religious difference, it has related to the musical mainstream in often noteworthy ways. Intimately bound up with ideological concepts and with the continuity of a people, Jewish music is Judaism become transparent through melody.

The purpose of this book is to provide a bibliographic tool for the examination of Jewish music. Prepared as an annotated roster of published English textual resources, it is intended to serve reference needs of musicians, scholars, and the general public. More than a source of information, this bibliography also can constitute a portal to less than familiar materials which are eminently suitable for further research endeavors, study projects, or musical performances.

Inasmuch as the value of a resource depends upon the accessibility of its contents, this collection has been shaped for use with several means of approach. All of the entries, together with their individual imprint data and annotations, have been placed into a consecutive numerical order; and index referral is by the particular number assigned to an entry. None of the listings are duplicated, except in a few instances where an article has been cited again among issues of a Jewish music periodical. In the main, however, citations appear only once—whether in descriptions of serial publications or under any of the other classifications.

The entries also have been placed within context of the types of publications: reference works; books and monographs; articles; periodicals; instruction manuals; music collections; and dance materials. These categories have been further refined into subdivisions, in order to facilitate location of appropriate matter here and to serve as guidance aid to location of full publications at libraries and archives. For each of those sixteen specifically titled sections—the entries have been placed alphabetically, according to the last names of authors, editors, or compilers. Thus, access points to this entire bibliographic roster are by number, genre, and alphabetical order.

Imprint data for each entry includes the following information: author/editor/compiler; translator; complete title of work; edition—place, publisher, date, pagination, and added matter. Multiple editions are indicated. Dimensions are not given. For articles, details specify periodical as to name, volume, date, and source, along with the title and author of the particular work and its own pagination. This basic description is extended with an annotative delineation for every entry—in terms of essential subject area covered, range of content, and manner of treatment; along with some additional comments about author/editor/compiler. Remarks are not evaluative, but rather devised to aid in assessment of use as a reference source. Annotations vary in length and substance, as warranted.

Selection of materials for inclusion in this bibliography was based upon a broad overview of Jewish music comprising Bible, history, religion, folk-expression, scholarship, musicianship, education, and sociological developments from all over the world, from ancient times to the contemporary era. Each entry was sought out, examined, and annotated by this compiler, and thereby verified as to content, relevance and reasonable availability. This search was concluded in the spring of 1984.

The roster of literature materials has been restricted to English-language publications, or any matter with English abstracts. The music collections have *romanized* texts. The term romanized refers to the representation of Yiddish, Hebrew, and other foreign languages in Roman alphabetic characters. This method is generally used by Jewish publishers to facilitate proper pronunciation. As a rule, such transliterations are consistent. However, where alternative spellings have appeared, all versions are given.

Certain types of materials have been purposely omitted from this bibliography: standard biographical reference works and most biographies, inasmuch as these may not have a direct relevance to musical Judaica; book reviews, as duplications of the books that are already among listings; pieces in newspapers and popular magazines; community and organization bulletins; texts on recording jackets; concert program notes; publicity brochures; dissertations; fiction; unavailable and obsolete items; and that which is patently erroneous or scurrilous in nature.

An extensive topical index for this bibliography provides additional access to the 1,220 entries, in terms of subjects. Index referrals are by the number assigned to an entry. Many of the indexed topics are cross-referenced to other index listings so as to enlarge upon or clarify materials and terminologies. Perusal of this topical reservoir affords a survey of the array of information, defining the field and covering such areas as: historical periods; different traditions, branches and folk customs; world-wide developments; the Jewish calendar year of observances; comparative studies of liturgical music—Jewish, Christian, and Moslem; synagogue music and musicians; folksongs in many languages; ancient and modern Israel; diverse and dynamic expressions in America; women's music; children and schools; hymnology. The index listings for instrumental and vocal scores, and for recordings, serve to supplement entries for catalogues of Jewish music publishers and should be consulted by those seeking ideas for program planning. Also highlighted here are various special collections and archives.

Further means of access to all of the materials in the book is the index of authors. This roster also serves as a bibliographical listing for the many notable scholars and writers who have treated subjects related to Jewish music. Another topical amplification is the glossary of Judaica, which has been prepared as an explanatory key to various Jewish terms of expression. Eighty-six different items are defined and briefly discussed. Scanning these materials is recommended for general information as well as resource aid in use of the bibliography.

Finally, a list of abbreviations interprets the imprint data, and also constitutes a roster of organizational groups. The process of identification/location/examination/documentation/organization for this bibliography has been long and exhaustive, yet an exciting and educational experience for me. Along the way the book emerged as somewhat different in form and approach than envisioned in earlier plans. Often, this work seemed to take on its own life-force and even impose demands. As it progressed, the very multitude of the publications commanded by turns interest, satisfaction, and then inspiration.

During the course of this project, I have been sustained by the generous help and warm encouragement of many colleagues in the fields of music and Judaica. I wish to express my gratitude to the following libraries and librarians: Brown University Library (Providence, R.I.)—Rosemary L. Cullen, curator of the Harris Special Collections; Gratz College, Tyson Jewish Music Library (Philadelphia, Penn.)—Shalom Altman, music director, and his staff; Haifa Music Museum and AMLI Music Library (Haifa, Israel)—Moshe Gorali and Nina Benzoor, directors; Hebrew Union College—Jewish Institute of Religion, Klau Libraries—Herbert C. Zafren, chief of libraries (Cincinnati, Ohio) and Philip E. Miller, librarian of the Klau Branch in New York, N.Y., and staffs; Hebrew University Library, Music Division (Jerusalem, Israel)—Israel Adler, Bathja Bayer, and Lea Shalem, librarians and research scholars; Israel Institute for Sacred Music,

Archives (Jerusalem, Israel)—Avigdor Herzog, director of research; Jewish Theological Seminary of America, General Library and Special Collection of the Cantors Institute (New York, N.Y.)—Menahem Schmelzer, chief librarian, and Herman Dicker and staff, as well as Morton Leifman, director of the Cantors Institute; Library of Congress (Washington, D.C.), Music Division—library staff, and Jewish Division—librarian Myron Weinstein and staff; New York Public Library (NYPL) at 42nd Street (New York, N.Y.), Jewish Division—Leonard Gold, librarian, and staff; NYPL at Lincoln Center (New York, N.Y.), Dance Collection—library staff, and Music Research Division—Frank Campbell, librarian, and staff—with particular thanks to Susan T. Sommer, librarian of Special Music Collections and Richard Jackson, librarian of American Music Collection for their generous consultation assistance and valuable ideas; Tel Aviv University Library, Music Division (Tel Aviv, Israel)—Hanock Avenary, scholar and educator; Union Theological Seminary Library (New York, N.Y.)—Richard C. Spoor, chief librarian, and Seth Kasten, reference librarian; Yeshiva University, General Library and Special Collection of the Cantorial Training Institute (New York, N.Y.)—Frederic S. Baum, chief librarian, and Stanley Klein, reference librarian, as well as Macy Nulman of the Cantorial Department and Mitchell Serels of the Sephardic Studies Department; YIVO-Institute for Jewish Research, Library (New York, N.Y.)—Dina Abramowicz, librarian; Glascow University Library (Glascow, Scotland)—Sheila Craik, assistant librarian.

For opportunities to examine their archives, I am indebted to these organizations and their staffs: American Guild of Organists—Brian Murray; Board of Jewish Education of Chicago—David Politzer; Board of Education of New York—Richard Neumann; Cantors Assembly of America—Leonard Wasser; Central Conference of American Rabbis—Elliot L. Stevens; Jewish Education Services of North America—Shimon Frost, director; Leo Baeck Institute—Fred Grubel, director; United Synagogue of America—Morton K. Seigel director.

Many publishers have been helpful: Ashbourne, Charles Davidson; Israel Music Institute, William Elias; Israeli Music Publications, Peter Gradenwitz and Robert Kleiman; Jewish Publication Society of America; KTAV, Bernard Scharfstein; Oxford University Press; Tara, Velvel Pasternak; Transcontinental/UAHC, Judith Tischler.

Other colleagues have led me to special materials: Helen Ephros; Jack Gottlieb; Tzipora Jochsberger; Judith Karzen; Joseph Mlotek; Ruth Rubin; Shirley Singer; Johanna Spector; Eric Werner; and Max Wohlberg.

My special thanks to music editor and scholar Kurt Stone for his recommendations in structuring this bibliography, and to Marilyn Brownstein, acquisitions editor of Greenwood Press, for her enthusiastic interest and abiding support over the many months.

Most of all, I am beholden to my husband for his constant reassurance and patience, and especially for his technical partnership in the preparation and computerized development of the book.

This work is respectfully dedicated to all bibliographers. Their labors are acts of faith in the future.

Abbreviations

AAJE	American Association for Jewish Education		c	circa
			CAA	Cantors Assembly of America
ACC	American Conference of Cantors		CCA	Cantorial Council of America
ACLS	American Council of Learned Societies		CCAR	Central Conference of American Rabbis
ACUM	Authors, Composers and Music Publishers in Israel		CJC	Canadian Jewish Congress
			comp(s)	compiler(s), compiled
AGO	American Guild of Organists		CTI	Cantorial Training Institute
AICF	American Israel Cultural Foundation		CYCO	Congress for Yiddish Culture Organization
AJ Com	American Jewish Committee			
AJ Cong	American Jewish Congress		d	died
AJHS	American Jewish Historical Society			
			ed(s)	editor(s), edited, edition
AMLI	Americans for a Library in Israel		ed bd	editorial board
			enl ed	enlarged edition
AMS	American Musicological Society		ex	example
AOS	American Oriental Society		GTM	Guild of Temple Musicians
arr(s)	arranger(s), arranged			
ASI	Arnold Schoenberg Institute		Heb	Hebrew
			HUC	Hebrew Union College
ASJM	American Society for Jewish Music			
			IAML	International Association of Music Libraries
AZYF	American Zionist Youth Foundation		ICL	Israel Composers League
			IFMC	International Folk Music Council
b	born			
BCE	Before the Common Era		IISM	Israel Institute for Sacred Music
BJE	Board/Bureau of Jewish Education		illus	illustrated, illustration
			IMI	Israel Music Institute

IMP	Israel(i) Music Publications		NYPL	New York Public Library
IMS	International Musicological Society		orig ed	original edition
incl	including, inclusive		p,pp	page, pages
intro	introduction, introductory		pbk ed	paperback edition
ISM	Institute for Sacred Music (Israel)		pl	plural
			pt(s)	part(s)
			pub	published, publication, publisher
JBC(A)	Jewish Book Council (of America)			
JDC	Joint Distribution Committee		RAA	Rabbinical Assembly of America
JEC	Jewish Education Committee		repr	reprint
JHS	Jewish Historical Society		rev	revised,, revision
JIR	Jewish Institute of Religion		RILM	International Repertory of Music Literature
JLMSA	Jewish Liturgical Music Society of America		RISM	International Inventory of Music Sources
JMC(A)	Jewish Music Council (of America)		RMA	Royal Music Association
JMCAA	Jewish Ministers Cantors Association of America		SATB	Soprano, Alto, Tenor, Bass
			SMP	Sacred Music Press
JMRC	Jewish Music Research Center (Israel)		suppl	supplement
JNUL	Jewish National and University Library (Israel)		TAU	Tel Aviv University
			TMP	Transcontinental Music Publications
JPSA	Jewish Publication Society of America		trans	translated, translation
JTSA	Jewish Theological Seminary of America		UAHC	Union of American Hebrew Congregations
JWB	Jewish Welfare Board		Univ.	University
			UPTA	United Parents and Teachers Association
LC	Library of Congress			
LCI	League of Composers in Israel		vol(s)	volume(s)
MLA	Music Library Association		WCJMP	World Centre for Jewish Music (Palestine)
MTNA	Music Teachers National Association		WCO	Workmen's Circle Organization
NCJE	National Council for Jewish Education		WJC	World Jewish Congress
NCJW	National Council of Jewish Women		WUJS	World Union of Jewish Studies
n d	no date		WZO	World Zionist Organization
NFTB	National Federation of Temple Brotherhoods		Yid	Yiddish
NFTS	National Federation of Temple Sisterhoods		YIVO	Yiddish Institute for Jewish Research
NFTY	National Federation of Temple Youth		YKUF	Yiddish Cultural Organization
NJRC	National Jewish Resource Center		ZOA	Zionist Organization of America
no(s)	number(s)			
n p	not paginated			

THE RESOURCE
BOOK OF
JEWISH MUSIC

1.
Reference Works

A. Encyclopedias and Dictionaries:
    Entries on Jewish Music

1
Book of Jewish Knowledge. **NATHAN AUSUBEL, ed.** New York:
Crown, 1964; xi,540pp, illus.
    See entries - *Baal Tefillah*, p.30; *Hazzan*, pp.91-6;
    Folk Music and Dance, pp.162-8; Hymns of the Synagogue,
    pp.220-1; Music: Ancient Jewish, pp.306-7; Music in the
    Temple, pp.307-8; Musical Accents, pp.308-9; Musical
    Instruments of Bible, 309-11; *Zemirot*, pp.525-6. Other
    authors not indicated. Facsimiles and photographs.

2
Columbia Encyclopedia. **WILLIAM BRIDGWATER and ELIZABETH J.
SHERWOOD, eds.** New York: Columbia Univ. Press, 1950; vi,
2,203pp., illus.
    See entry - Jewish Music, p.1,010. General survey from
    Biblical era, through synagogue liturgical developments
    to more recent times.

3
Concise Encyclopedia of Jewish Music. **MACY NULMAN ed.** New
York: McGraw-Hill, 1975; xii,176pp., illus., music.
    Alphabetically arranged roster of names, titles, terms,
    subjects and other relevant entries on Jewish music.
    Brief annotations, explanations and definitions. Compre-
    hensive information on traditional Jewish liturgical
    music and its special terminologies. Data carried up to
    1960. Supplemented with chronological table of "High-
    lights in the History of Jewish Music." Facsimiles,
    photographs, music examples and source notes. Prepared
    by cantor and music educator Macy (Moshe) Nulman, head
    of Cantorial Training Institute at Yeshiva Univ.

4
Concise Oxford History of Music. GERALD ABRAHAM, ed. London,Eng.:Oxford Univ. Press,1979; xviii,968pp.,illus.,music.
    See entries - Part 1: Music In the Old Testament, pp.37-
    40; (Hebrew Music and) Early Christian Music, pp.50-2.
    Authors not given. Information on Salomone Rossi (c.1565
    -c.1628) included on pp.329-30, 335. Consult index for
    other relevant topics.
5
Dictionary of the Bible. JAMES HASTINGS and JOHN A. SELBIE
eds. Edinburgh,Scot./New York:T.Clark/C. Scribners, 1909;
4vols., illus.
    See entries - vol.3: Music and Musical Instruments,
    p.456; Nature of Hebrew Music, p.457. Both by G. Millar.
    Attention to references in Bible itself. Facsimiles.
6
Dictionary of the Bible. JOHN L. McKENZIE, ed. Milwaukee:
Brucie, 1965; xviii, 954pp.+ plates, illus.
    See entry - Music, pp.593-4. Author not given. Bible
    references cited. Facsimiles.
7
Dictionary of the Bible: Second Edition. FREDERICK C.
GRANT and H.H. ROWLEY, eds. Edinburgh,Scot./New York: T.
Clark/C.Scribners, 1963; xvi, 1,059pp.+ plates, illus.
    See entry - Music and Musical Instruments, by A.W.
    Streane and R.A. Barclay, pp.680-2. Biblical refer-
    ences to music. Facsimiles.
8
*Dictionary Catalog of the Jewish Collection - Reference De-
partment, N.Y.P.L.* Editorial Committee, eds. Boston:G.K.
Hall, 1960; 14vols. *First Supplement.* Boston:G.K. Hall,
1975; 8vols.
    Catalog - see entries - vol.4: Folk Music and Folk
    Songs, pp.3,114-22. vol.8: Music and Musicians,
    pp.6,422-31. vol.10: Synagogue Music, pp.8,737-47.
    Supplement - see entries - vol.2: Folk Music and Folk
    Songs, pp.564-7. vol.4: Music, Musical Instruments and
    Musicians, pp.530-7. vol.6: Synagogue Music, pp.101-9.
    Photocopies of index cards for library holdings on
    literature, music collections, hymnals and scores.
9
*Dictionary Catalog of the Music Collection at Boston Public
Library.* PHILIP J. McNIFF and Editorial Committee, eds.
Boston:G.K. Hall, 1972; 20vols.
    See entry - vol.9: Music:Jewish, pp.280-93. Photocopies
    of index cards for library holdings on literature, music
    collections, hymnals and scores.
10
*Dictionary Catalogue of the Klau Library of H.U.C.-J.I.R.,
Cincinnati.* HERBERT C. ZAFREN and Editorial Committee, eds.
Boston: G.K. Hall, 1964; 32vols.
    See entry - vol.18: Music (category), pp.334-509. Photo-
    copies of index cards for complete library collection of
    music holdings - literature, scores and sheet music, and
    various anthologies. Publications in English, French,
    German, Hebrew, Latin, Russian, Spanish, Yiddish. Also,

includes unpublished papers, journalistic materials and
archival items. Note: The Eduard Birnbaum Collection of
Jewish Music is housed at this library in Cincinnati.
11
Dictionary of Religious Knowledge. **LYMAN ABBOTT and T.J.
CONANT, eds.** New York:Harper, 1875; xv, 1,074pp., illus.
See entry - Music and Musical Instruments, pp.667-71.
Author not given. Biblical era music references and rise
of early synagogue liturgical chants. Facsimiles.
12
Encyclopedia of the Arts. **DAGOBERT G. RUNES and HARRY G.
SHRICKEL, eds.** New York:Philosophical Library, 1946; ix,
1,064pp., illus., music.
See entry - Jewish Music, by Abraham W. Binder, pp.520-
7. Survey of wide range of topics on this subject area.
Facsimiles and musical examples.
13
Encyclopedia Biblica: A Critical Dictionary of the Bible.
T.K. CHEYNE and J. SUTHERLAND BLACK, eds. repr.ed. New
York:Macmillan,1913;4vols.(orig.ed. New York:Macmillan,1902)
See entry - vol.3: Music, by J.D. Prince, pp.3,225-43.
Biblical references to music, musicians and musical in-
struments, and consideration of Temple service music.
Facsimiles, music examples and source notes.
14
Encyclopedia Dictionary of Religion. **PAUL KEVIN MEAGHER,
THOMAS C. O'BRIEN and CONSUELO MARIS AHERNE, eds.** Wash.,
D.C.:Corpus, 1978; 3vols., illus.
See entry - vol.2: Jewish Music, by P.J. Hennessey,
pp.1,891-2. Outline of topic. Facsimiles.
15
Encyclopedia of Jewish Knowledge. **JACOB DE HAAS and Editorial Committee, eds.** New York:Behrman,1934;xv,686pp.,illus.
See entry - Music, by Abraham Zebi Idelsohn, pp.374-5.
Brief informative essay with source notes. Also consult
index of book for other relevant information.
16
Encyclopedia of the Jewish Religion. **R.J. ZWI WERBLOWSKY
and GEOFFREY WIGODER, eds.** Jerusalem,Isr.:Massada Press,
1966; vii,415pp., illus.
See entries - Accents (Cantillation), pp.10-1; Cantor
and Cantorial Music, pp.79-80; Liturgy, pp.240-1; Music,
pp.276-7; Organ, p.292; *Zemirot*, p.413. Authors not
given. Brief but informative items. Facsimiles.
17
Encyclopaedia Judaica. **CECIL ROTH and GEOFFREY WIGODER,
eds.** Jerusalem,Isr./New York:Keter/Macmillan, 1971-1972;
16vols., illus., music.
See entries - vol.4: Bible,In the Arts - Music, by
Bathja Bayer, pp.937-8. vol.5: Cantillation, by Bathja
Bayer, pp.127-9; Dance, by Dvora Lapson, Selma Jeanne
Cohen and Yohanan Boehm, pp.1,262-74. vol.6: Folklore -
Folk Song, by Dov Noy, pp.1,384-8. vol.7: Guglielmo
Ebreo da Pesaro, by Cecil Roth and Walter Sorell,
pp.969-70; Hassidism - The Place of Music in Hassidic
Thought, by Andre Hajdu and Yaacov Mazor, pp.1,421-32;

Hatikvah, by Bathja Bayer, pp.1,470-2; *Hazzan*, by
Herman Kieval and Simon Marcus, pp.1,542-52. vol.9:
Israel — Music and Dance In, by Yohanan Boehm, pp.996-
1,020. vol.10: *Kol Nidre*, by Bathja Bayer, pp.1,166-9.
vol.11: Masoretic Accents — Musical Rendition, by Avigdor Herzog, pp.1,098-111. vol.12: Music, by Bathja Bayer, Hanoch Avenary and Yohanan Boehm, pp.554-678; Musicians, by Bathja Bayer, pp.678-715; *Nusah* (Liturgical
Melody), by Hanoch Avenary, pp.1,283-4; Obadiah, the
Norman Proselyte, by Israel Adler, pp.1,306-8. vol.13:
Psalms, Book of — In Music, by Bathja Bayer and Hanoch
Avenary, pp.1,327-34; *Purim*, by Louis Jacobs, pp.1,390
-5; *Purim-Shpil* (Holiday Plays), by Chone Shmeruk,
pp.1,396-404. vol.14: Salomone Rossi, by Edith Gerson-
Kiwi, pp.318-20; *Shofar*, by Albert Lewis, pp.1,442-7.
vol.15: Suesskind von Trimberg, by Godfrey E. Silverman,
pp.483-4; Theater — Jews in Musical, by Harvey Cooper,
pp.1,059-60. vol.16: Yemen — Musical Tradition, by
Johanna Spector, pp.749-50 and 756-9; *Yigdal* (Hymn of
Praise), by Aaron Rothkoff and Bathja Bayer, pp.833-5;
Zemirot (Liturgical Songs), by Ernst D. Goldschmidt,
pp.987-9. Also consult guideline materials and index
roster in vol.1 for other relevant entries, including
Jewish liturgical terms, hymn titles, specific Biblical
instruments, varous calendar observances and commemorations, and names of particular composers, performers,
scholars, educators and communal leaders. Facsimiles,
photographs, musical examples and comparative tables,
sources and bibliographic references. Hebrew romanized.
  18
Encyclopedia of Music in Canada. **HELLMUT KALLMANN, GILLES
POTVIN and KENNETH WINTERS, eds.** Toronto,Ont.:Toronto Univ.
Press, 1981; xxix, 1,076pp., illus., music.
    See entries — Jewish Cantors, by Ben Steinberg, p.476;
    Jewish Music Month, by Rhoda Resnick, p.476; Jewish Re-
    ligious Music, by Ben Steinberg, pp.476-7; The Jew: Mu-
    sic and Musicians, by Hellmut Kallmann and Mabel Laine,
    pp.477-8. Also consult index for other relevant topics.
  19
*Encyclopedia of Religion and Ethics.***JAMES HASTINGS, JOHN
A. SELBIE and LOUIS H. GRAY, eds.** repr.eds. New York: C.
Scribners, 1970/1955; 13vols., illus. (orig.ed. New York:
C. Scribners, 1908-1927).
    See entries — vol.9: Music: Hebrew, by George Wauchope
    Stewart, pp.39-43; Music: Jewish, by Francis Lyon Cohen,
    pp.51-2. Stewart treats Bible music, musical instruments
    and musicians. Cohen briefly covers topic of synagogue
    music, including chant, cantillation and hymnody. Fac-
    similes and source notes.
  20
Encyclopedia of Zionism and Israel. **RAPHAEL PATAI, ed.**
New York:Herzl Press/McGraw-Hill, 1971; 2vols., illus.
    See entry — vol.2: Music in Israel, by Peter Gradenwitz,
    pp.816-8. Survey of contemporary musical scene, noting
    composers, performers and organizations. Photographs.

21

Funk and Wagnall's Illustrated Encyclopedia of Music.
NORMA H. DICKEY, ed. New York:Funk and Wagnall's, 1980;
288pp., illus., music.
　　See entry — Jewish Music, pp.128-9. No author given.
　　General view of topic.

22

*General History of Music, from the Earliest Times to the
Present Period; to Which is Prefixed, a Dissertation on the
Music of the Ancients.* **CHARLES BURNEY.** repr.ed. **FRANK
MERCER, ed.** London,Eng.:Foulis/New York:Harcourt, 1935;
2vols., illus., music. (orig.ed. London,Eng.:Burney, 1776-
1789; 4vols., illus., music)
　　See entry — vol.1(1776): The History of Hebrew Music,
　　pp.217-52. Exposition on: music, musicians and musical
　　instruments as cited in Bible; participation of women in
　　music of Biblical era; musical terminology in Psalms;
　　music of Levites and Temple services; musical meanings
　　of such terms as *Lamenatseah* and *Selah*; music during
　　Babylonian Captivity, Second Commonwealth, Roman occu-
　　pation and Maccabean era. Facsimiles, tables, musical
　　examples and source notes. Fascinating essay in this
　　monumental work by Charles Burney (1726-1814).

23

Grove Dictionary of Music and Musicians:5th Edition. **ERIC
WALTER BLOM, ed.** New York:St. Martin's Press, 1955; 9vols.,
illus., music. [repr.eds.1961,1973,1975] *Supplement.* **ERIC
WALTER BLOM and DENIS STEVENS, eds.** New York:St. Martin's
Press,1961;493pp.(*Grove Dictionary:4th Edition.* HENRY COPE
COLLES, ed. London,Eng./New York:Macmillan, 1940; 5vols.+
suppl.vol., illus., music. *Grove Dictionary:3rd Edition.*
HENRY COPE COLLES, ed. London,Eng./New York:Macmillan, 1927;
5vols., illus., music. *Grove Dictionary:2nd Edition.* JOHN
ALEXANDER FULLER-MAITLAND, ed. Phila.:T.Presser, 1918-1920;
5vols.+suppl.vol., illus., music. *Grove Dictionary.* [repr.
ed. 1900] orig.ed. GEORGE GROVE and JOHN ALEXANDER FULLER-
MAITLAND, eds. London,Eng.:George Grove, 1878-1890; 4vols.,
illus., music.)
　　Monumental music reference publication planned and pro-
　　duced by George Grove (1820-1900) with editorial associ-
　　ation of J.A. Fuller-Maitland (1856-1936), and carried
　　forward in subsequently revised editions by H.C. Colles
　　(1879-1943) and Eric W. Blom (1888-1959).
　　See entries — vol.2: Church — Music of the Early, by
　　Eric Werner, pp.283-91 (origins, relationship to early
　　synagogue liturgical music, parallel developments).
　　vol.3: Folk Music — Jewish, by Edith Gerson-Kiwi, pp.304
　　-13 (Oriental/Near Eastern, Sephardic/Ladino, Ashkenazic
　　European/East European/Yiddish, Hebrew/Israeli). vol.4:
　　Hebrew Music, by Peter Gradenwitz, p.214; Israel, by
　　Peter Gradenwitz, pp.555-7; Jewish (Liturgical) Music,
　　by Eric Werner, pp.615-36 (Bible, Temple — musicians and
　　instruments, chant, cantillation, hymnology, early syna-
　　gogue and church music, various Jewish traditions of
　　Diaspora, 19th and 20th century developments); Jews In
　　Music, by Peter Gradenwitz, p.637. vol.6: Palestine, by

Peter Gradenwitz, pp.505-6. vol.7: *Shofar*, by D.J.
Blaikley, p.763. vol.8: Syrian Music, by Henry George
Farmer, pp.251-8 (Biblical/ancient origins, forms and
terminologies). Also consult other entries - names of
composers, performers, scholars and educators - for additional information. Among contributors on topics of
relevance to Jewish music: Nathan Broder; Carl Engel;
Henry George Farmer; Edith Gerson-Kiwi; Peter Gradenwitz; John Stainer; Egon Wellesz; and, Eric Werner. Facsimiles, photographs, musical examples and comparative
tables, source notes and bibliographic references. See
Supplement (errata and additions) entries: Folk Music-
Jewish, p.154; Hebrew Music, p.217; Jewish Music and
Jews In Music, p.237; and *Shofar*, p.407. See in early
editions of *Grove Dictionary* - vol.2: Hebrew Music, by
Arthur M. Friedlander, pp.594-9.

24
Harper's Bible Dictionary. **MADELEINE S. MILLER and J. LANE
MILLER, eds.** repr.ed. New York:Harper and Row,1973;ix,853pp
+ plates,illus. (orig.ed. New York:Harper and Row, 1952)
See entry - Music and Musical Instruments, pp. 466-70.
Author not given. Treatment of Biblical references and
interpretations. Facsimiles and photographs.

25
Harvard Dictionary of Music. **WILLI APEL ed.** rev.ed. Cambridge,Mass.:Harvard Univ. Press,1969; xi,935pp., illus.
(orig.ed. Cambridge,Mass.:Harvard Univ. Press, 1944;
ix,829pp., illus.)
See entry - Jewish Music, by Willi Apel, in rev.ed.
pp.444-7, and in orig.ed. pp.378-83. Survey of topic,
with source notes.

26
Harvard University Library Catalogue of Hebrew Books. **Editorial Committee, eds.** Cambridge, Mass.:Harvard Univ. Press
1968; 6vols. ***Supplement.*** Cambridge,Mass.:Harvard Univ.
Press, 1972; 3vols.
Catalogue - see entry - vol.3: Music and Musical Instruments, pp.432-3. *Supplement* - see entry - vol.1:
Hymns and Liturgical Music, pp.89-118. Photocopies of
index cards for library holdings of literature, music
collections, hymnals and scores.

27
Historia Judaica. **GUIDO KISCH, ed.** New York: Kisch/
Schocken, 1938-1961; 23vols., illus.
See entry - vol.6 (1944): Prolegomena to a Bibliography
of Jewish Music, by Eric Werner, pp.175-88. Critical
description of musical documentations and published resources on the topic, in historio-chronological order
from Biblical era to recent times. Source notes. Note:
This material was reprinted, with some modifications, as
an introductory essay: "Prolegomenon," pp.1-36 for volume of collected articles: *Contributions to a Historical Study of Jewish Music*, edited by Eric Werner.
(New York:KTAV, 1976; vi,287pp.)

28
Interpreter's Dictionary of the Bible. GEORGE ARTHUR
BUTTRICK, ed. New York/Nashville:Abingdon Press, 1962;
4vols., illus., music.
     See entries - vol.3: Music; Musical Instruments, both by
     Eric Werner, pp. 457-76. Concise informative treatment
     of topics. In addition to Biblical materials, includes
     discussion of developmental rise of synagogue music and
     its relationship with growth of church liturgical chant.
     Explanations of Hebrew terminologies, as well as various
     interpretations by leading rabbinical figures of early
     Common Era. Source references, comparative tables, fac-
     similes, photographs and musical examples.
29
Jewish Art and Civilization. GEOFFREY WIGODER, ed. New
York:Walker, 1972; 2vols., illus.
     Encyclopedic collection of 15 studies by various noted
     scholars, considering Jewish art expression from ancient
     times to contemporary era, placed in historical chronol-
     ogy and in geographical perspectives. Includes informa-
     tion on Jewish music as related to "Jewish Art." Consult
     index in vol.2 for topical references in both volumes.
30
Jewish Catalog Series. Phila.:J.P.S.A., 1973-1983;4vols.
*First Jewish Catalog.*RICHARD SIEGEL, MICHAEL STRASSFELD
and SHARON STRASSFELD eds. Phila.:J.P.S.A., 1973; 320pp.,
illus. *Second Jewish Catalog; With Jewish Yellow Pages.*
SHARON STRASSFELD and MICHAEL STRASSFELD, eds. Phila.:J.P.
S.A., 1976; 464pp., illus. *Third Jewish Catalog.* SHARON
STRASSFELD and MICHAEL STRASSFELD, eds. Phila.:J.P.S.A.,
1980; 416pp., illus. *Jewish Kids Catalog.* CHAYA BURSTEIN,
ed. Phila.:J.P.S.A.,1983; 224pp., illus.
     First Jewish Catalog - see: Music, by George Savran,
     pp.211-5. Information on Hassidic, Yiddish and Israeli
     songs. *Second Jewish Catalog* - see: The Arts:Dance, by
     Fred Berk, pp.337-51; The Arts:Choral Music, by Marsha
     Bryan, pp.360-7; The Arts:*Hazzanut* (Cantorial Music),
     by Robert Agus, pp.368-76. *Jewish Yellow Pages* - list
     related to music, p.439. *Third Jewish Catalog* - see
     index for references. *Jewish Kids Catalog* - see: sec-
     tion, Music: Songs and Dances, pp.180-99, which includes
     8 songs, melody lines with guitar symbols, Hebrew and
     Yiddish romanized.
31
Jewish Encyclopedia. JACOB SINGER, ed. repr.ed. New York:
KTAV, 1964; 12vols., illus., music. (orig.ed. New York: Funk
and Wagnall's, 1901-1906)
     See entries - vol.3: Cantillation, by Francis Lyon Cohen
     pp.539-49 (comparative traditions of Biblical chant).
     vol.5: Folksongs, by Alexander Harkavy, p.427 (Ladino
     and Judaeo-German, with only introductory concept of
     Yiddish). vol.6: *Hazzan* (Cantor), by Alois Kaiser and
     Max Schloessinger, pp.284-7; *Hazzanut* (Cantorial Art),
     by Ludwig Blau, pp.132-40 (chanting of prayers). vol.9:
     Music and Musical Instruments, by Wilhelm Nowack and
     Emil G. Hirsch, pp.118-9 (Bible and Temple Era); Music:

Synagogal, by Francis Lyon Cohen, pp.119-35. vol.10:
Psalms, by Emil G. Hirsch and Crawford Howell, pp.142-
51; *Shofar*, by Francis Lyon Cohen and Judah D. Eisenstein, pp.301-10 (various shapes and special sounds).
vol.12: *Yigdal*, by Francis Lyon Cohen, pp.606-10 (significant Jewish hymn in comparative versions). Also see
other entries, such as: terminologies in Jewish music
and liturgical services; titles of prayers and folksongs; Sabbath, High Holy Days and Festivals; Jewish
calendar commemorations; and, life-cycle ceremonials.
Facsimiles, photographs, musical examples and comparative tables, sources and bibliographical references.
32

*Jewish People: Past and Present - Jewish Encyclopedic Hand-
books.* **SHLOMOH F. GELINSKY, ed.** New York:C.Y.C.O., 1946-
1955; 4vols., illus., music.

See entries - vol.3 (1952): Jewish Music, by Abraham W.
Binder, pp.324-76. Survey from Biblical times to 20th
century developments. Consideration of range of synagogal musical traditions, various types of religious and
secular folksongs of Jews throughout world, and aspects
of composition, performance, collection and academic
study. Facsimiles, photographs and musical examples.
vol.4 (1955): Yiddish Culture in the United States, by
Samuel Niger, pp.264-307. Includes references to Yiddish
musical theater earlier in this century, and the folk
operettas of Abraham Goldfaden. Array of photographs.
33

Jewish Yellow Pages. **MAE SCHAFTER ROCKLAND and MICHAEL
AARON ROCKLAND, eds.** New York:Schocken, 1976; 212pp.,illus;
New Jewish Yellow Pages. **MAE SCHAFTER ROCKLAND, ed.** New
York:Schocken, 1980; 271pp. illus.

Jewish Yellow Pages - see: Music, pp.151-9, with facsimiles and photographs. *New Jewish Yellow Pages* -
see: Dance and Music, pp.192-206. Authors not given.
With resources for programs and projects. Also consult
indexes of both volumes for other relevant items.
34

Jews: Their History, Culture and Religion. **LOUIS FINKEL-
STEIN, ed.** repr.eds. Phila.:J.P.S.A., 1960 and 1955;
3vols., illus. (orig.ed. Phila.:J.P.S.A., 1949)

See entry - vol.3: The Jewish Contribution to Music, by
Eric Werner, pp.950-83. Historical survey from Biblical
era and Temple services, through establishment of wide
range of synagogue chant and hymnology, religious and
secular folksong traditions, with rise of cantorial role
and forms of music of services. Influences upon developments in church music - chant, psalmody and hymnology.
Attention to Jewish music styles of Central and Eastern
Europe, as well as Near East, over centuries. Consideration of 19th and 20th century musical expressions of
composers, performers, scholars and writers - in terms
of their Jewish as well as general contributions. Source
notes, comparative tables and music examples.

35
Macmillan Encyclopedia of Music and Musicians. **ALBERT E.
WIER, ed.** New York:Macmillan, 1938; 2,089pp., illus.
    See entry — Jewish Music, pp.898-903. Author not given.
    General outline from Bible era to more recent times.
36
Milon Ha-musika - Music Dictionary. **Editorial Committee,
eds.** Jerusalem,Isr.:Acad. of Hebrew Language,1955; 174pp.
    Dictionary of musical terms in Hebrew, Italian, English,
    French and German.
37
*Miqra'ey Musika: A Collection of Biblical References to
Music in Hebrew, English, French and Spanish.* **SHLOMO HOF-
MAN, ed.** Tel Aviv,Isr.:I.M.I., 1966; 200pp., illus.
    Citation of approximately 1,000 Biblical passages which
    include music in some aspect or form of expression. Text
    printed in all four languages. Biblical materials are
    given in full, placing each musical item into context.
    Indexes for categories of instruments, performers, per-
    formances, functions, rituals, customs, melodies and
    varied usages.
38
New Bible Dictionary. **J.D. DOUGLAS, ed.** London,Eng.:
Inter-Varsity Fellowship,1962;xvi, 1,375pp.+ plates, illus.
    See entry — Music and Musical Instruments, by D.G.
    Stradling, pp.852-6. General discussion. Facsimiles.
39
New Catholic Encyclopedia. **Editorial Committee of Catholic
Univ. of America, eds.** New York:McGraw-Hill, 1967; 15vols.,
illus., music.
    See entry — vol.10: Music:Hebrew, by Edith Gerson-Kiwi,
    pp.91-7. Survey from Biblical era, with references to
    varied traditions of East and West, and into modern
    times. Source notes and musical examples.
40
*New Grove Dictionary of Music and Musicians. [6th Edition
of Grove Dictionary]* **STANLEY SADIE, ed.** London,Eng.:
Macmillan, 1980; 20vols., illus., music.
    Essentially a new compilation, rather than revision or
    enlargement of previous editions of *Grove Dictionary.*
    See entries — vol.4: Cheironomy, by Edith Gerson-Kiwi,
    pp.191-6 (ancient/Egypt, Israel, Byzantine, Roman);
    Chorus — Antiquity and Middle Ages, by James G. Smith,
    pp.342-3; Christian Church — Music of the Early, by
    Christian Hannick, pp.363-71 (origins, Judaic background
    and psalmody). vol.6: Ekphonetic Notation (Cantillation)
    by Gudrun Engberg, pp.100-1. vol.9: Israel (Art, Folk
    and Popular) by Don Harran, Edith Gerson-Kiwi, Gil
    Aldema, and William Elias; Israel Festival, by William
    Elias; Israeli Music Publications, by Peter Gradenwitz,
    p.361; Jerusalem, by Hanoch Avenary and Ury Eppstein,
    pp.608-11; Jewish Music — Liturgical/Secular/Folk, by
    Eric Werner, Edith Gerson-Kiwi, Shlomo Hofman and Israel
    J. Katz (Bible, Temple — musicians and instruments, rise
    and development of synagogue liturgical music — chant,
    cantillation, psalmody, hymnody, religious folksongs,

various Diaspora traditions in religious and secular
musical expression, 19th and 20th century creativity and
expression in Europe, America and Israel). vol.15:
Psalm - Antiquity and Early Christianity, by Eric Werner
pp.320-22. vol.16: Salomone Rossi (Life and Works), by
Iain Fenlon, pp.223-5. vol.17: *Shofar*, by Jeremy
Montagu, pp.261-2. vol.18: Tel Aviv, by William Elias,
pp.645-6. Also consult relevant entries for composers,
performers, scholars, journalists and educators. Fac-
similes, photographs, musical examples and comparative
tables, source notes and bibliographic references. Con-
tributors on Jewish music topics include: Gil Aldema;
Hanoch Avenary; Benjamin Bar-Am; Yohanan Boehm; Joachim
Braun; Dalia Cohen; Yehuda Cohen; William Elias; Ury
Eppstein; Alfred Frankenstein; Miriam Gideon; Peter
Gradenwitz; Edith Gerson-Kiwi; Don Harran; Avigdor
Herzog; Shlomo Hofman; Israel J. Katz; Zvi Keren;
Alexander Ringer; Amnon Shiloah; Johanna Spector; Uri
Toeplitz; and, Eric Werner.

41
New Standard Jewish Encyclopedia. **CECIL ROTH and GEOFFREY
WIGODER, eds.** London,Eng.:W.H. Allen,1975; 2,028pp.,illus.
See entries - Cantor and Cantorial Music, pp.392-4;
Music, pp.1,393-6. Musical examples for both; authors
not given. Also see other brief topical entries on
Jewish music - religious and secular, liturgical and
folk - as well as on Sabbath and calendar holidays.

42
New Westminster Dictionary of the Bible. **HENRY SNYDER
GEHMAN, ed.** Phila.:Westminster,1970;xi, 1,027+plates,illus.
See entry - Music, pp.641-3. References to music in
Bible passages. Author not given. Facsimiles.

43
Oxford Companion to Music:Tenth Edition. **(PERCY A. SCHOLES
orig.ed.)JOHN OWEN WARD, ed.** enl.rev.ed. London,Eng.:Oxford
Univ. Press,1970; lx, 1,189pp.+ plates, illus.,music. (repr.
eds.and orig.ed. London,Eng.:Oxford Univ. Press, 1938-1955)
Tenth Edition - see entry - Jewish Music, by Hanoch
Avenary, pp.538-41. In original *Oxford Companion*, con-
ceived, prepared and edited by scholar Percy A. Scholes
(1877-1957) - see entry - Jewish Music, also by Avenary,
pp.482-6. Brief survey of 9 topical areas, including
cantillation, chant, hymnology and cantorial traditions,
as well as range of Jewish folksong expressions. Music
examples. Consult roster for other relevant subjects.

44
Oxford History of Music. **W.H. HADOW, ed.** repr.ed. London,
Eng.:Oxford Univ. Press, 1929; intro.vol.+6vols., illus.,
music.(orig.ed. London,Eng.:Oxford Univ. Press, 1901-1905)
In *Introductory Volume*, ed. by scholar Percy Clark
Buck (1871-1947) - see entry - Chapter 2: Music of the
Hebrews, by W.O.E. Oesterley, pp.35-65. Treats general
character of ancient Hebrew music, musical instruments,
Biblical and post-Biblical Hebrew song, liturgical music
of the synagogue and Jewish secular musical expression.
Source notes, facsimiles and musical examples.

45
Popular Jewish Encyclopedia. BEN ISAACS and DEBORAH WIGO-
DER, eds. Jerusalem,Isr.:Massada Press,1973; 336pp.,illus.
    See entry - Music:Jewish, pp.218-21. Outline of topic;
    author not given. Facsimiles. Also consult index for
    other relevant subjects.
46
*Resources of American Music History: A Directory of Source
Materials from Colonial times to World War II.* D.W.KRUMMEL,
JEAN GEIL, DORIS J. DYEN, DEANE L. ROOT, eds. Urbana,Ill.:
Illinois Univ. Press.,,1981; 463pp.
    Geographical roster which includes libraries that have
    holdings of Jewish music, either directly or among their
    special collections. Consult index subjects: Hebrew
    Music; Jewish Music; Ladino Music; Yiddish Music.
47
RILM Abstracts of Music Literature. BARRY S. BROOK, ed.
New York:R.I.L.M./I.M.S./I.A.M.L./A.C.L.S., 1967-1978;
12vols.+2cum.index vols.:1967-1971 and 1972-1976. BATHJA
BAYER, ed. - Judaica/Hebraica entries.
    Consult rosters and indexes for following topical cate-
    gories: Folk Dance - Israel; Folk Dance - Jewish; Folk
    Music - Israel; Folk Music - Jewish; Hebrew Music; Hym-
    nology - Jewish; Israel; Music and Liturgy - Jewish.
    Source for materials in foreign languages as well as in
    English. Reference tool of admirable scope.
48
Standard Jewish Encyclopedia. CECIL ROTH, ed. Jerusalem,
Isr.:Massada Press, 1959; 1,980pp., illus., music.
    See entries - Cantor and Cantorial Music, pp.398-400;
    Music, pp.1,375-7. Music examples for both; authors not
    given. Also consult other relevant topics for Sabbath,
    calendar holidays, folk expressions and liturgy.
49
Thompson's International Cyclopedia of Music and Musicians.
BRUCE BOHLE, ed. enl.rev.ed. New York:Dodd,Mead, 1975; xx,
2,511pp.,illus.,music. (repr.eds. London,Eng.:J.M. Dent,
1943-1964;illus.,music;orig.ed. London,Eng.:J.M. Dent, 1939)
    Enlargement of extensive work originally conceived, pre-
    pared and edited by scholar Oscar Thompson (1887-1945).
    In latest edition, see entry - Jewish Music, by Macy
    Nulman, pp.1,118-22. Outline of topic, with special fo-
    cus upon traditional synagogue music - origins, forms,
    melodic qualities and cantorial artistry. References
    also to various types of religious and secular folksong
    expressions. Facsimiles and musical examples.
50
Universal Jewish Encyclopedia. ISAAC LANDMAN, ed. repr.
ed.New York:KTAV, 1969; 10vols.+index vol., illus.,music.
(orig.ed.New York:Universal Encyclopedia, 1939-1942)
    See entries - vol.1: Bible In Music, by David Ewen,
    pp.326-7. vol.2: Cantillation, by Jacob Beimel, pp.14-6;
    Cantor, by Ismar Elbogen, pp.17-8. vol.3: Dance, by
    Dvora Lapson, pp.455-63. vol.4: Folk Songs, by Max Wohl-
    berg, pp.350-5. vol.6: *Kol Nidre*, by Julius Jarecki,
    pp.440-1. vol.8: Music - In the Bible, by Curt Sachs,

pp.46-8; Music - Synagogal, by Jacob Singer, pp.48-54;
Music - Synagogue Music Published in the 19th and 20th
Centuries, by Max Wohlberg, pp.54-5; Musical Instruments, by Simon Cohen, pp.55-6; Musical Organizations
and Jews, by David Ewen, pp.56-66; Musicians - Jewish,
by David Ewen, pp.66-8; Organ, by Caesar Seligmann,
pp.321-2. vol.9: *Purim*, by Max Joseph, pp.36-42; Sabbath, by Ismar Elbogen, Fritz Lamm and Bernard Drachman,
pp.295-9; *Seder*, by Max Joseph, pp.453-6; *Shofar*,
by Max Joseph, pp.524-5. Also consult index volume for
other relevant information. Facsimiles, photographs,
musical examples and comparative tables, source notes
and bibliographic references. Hebrew romanized.

51

Vallentine's Jewish Encyclopedia. ALBERT MONTEFIORE HYAM-
SON and ABRAHAM MAURICE SILBERMANN eds. London,Eng.:Shapero
and Vallentine, 1938; xi,696pp.,illus., music.
See entries - Musical Instruments of the Bible, by
Maurice Bannister, pp.446-7; Music:Jews In, by Gertrude
Azulay, pp.447-50; Music of the Synagogue, by Maurice
Bannister, p.450; *Zemirot*, by Herbert Loewe, p.687.
Facsimiles and musical examples.

52

Who's Who In ACUM: Israeli Music and Musicians. MENASHE
RAVINA and SHLOMO SKOLSKY, eds. Tel Aviv,Isr.:ACUM/I.M.I.,
1965/1966; vii,106pp., illus.
Dictionary reference roster of Israeli music - authors,
composers/arrangers and publishers. Biographical notes
with principal works. Photographs.

B. Bibliographies and Catalogues of Jewish Music

53

ABRAVANEL, CLAUDE and BETTY HIRSHOWITZ, comps. *The Bible
in English Music: William Byrd (1543-1623) and Henry Purcell
(1659-1695) - Bibliographies.* (AMLI Studies in Bibliog.
Series, 1) Haifa, Isr.: Music Museum and AMLI Library, 1970;
32 pp., illus.
Annotated listings in English and Hebrew of each composer's varied musical settings for different portions
of the Old Testament, including psalms.

54

ADLER, ISRAEL, comp. *Hebrew Writings Concerning Music in
Manuscripts and Printed Books from Geonic Times up to 1800.*
(RISM - International Inventory of Music Sources, Series B
ix, vol. 2) Munich, W. Ger.: G. Henle, 1975; lviii, 389 pp.
Inventory catalogue for Jewish musical sources of the
Jewish Music Research Center at Hebrew University. List
serves as bibliographic reference and corpus of 61 texts
(in Hebrew characters for Hebrew, Aramaic and Judeo-
Arabic materials) with 5 additional cross-reference en-
tries. Introduction (in English) covers scope, chrono-

logy, classifications of texts, explanations for entries
as well as sources, lacunae, indices and transliterations. Materials covered are from years 933 to 1800. Descriptions for 66 items include details of contents and
actual text. Editor Adler indicates publication represents state of his research to 1974. General index provides names, subjects and terminologies in alphabetical
sequence. Publication sponsored by International Musicological Society and International Association of Music
Libraries. Facsimile illustrations.

55
ADLER, ISRAEL, comp. *Jewish Music: A Selected List of Ref-
erence Works and Song Collections.* Paris, Fr.: Alliance
Israelite Universelle and A.J.Com. (N.Y.C.), 1959; 15 pp.
     Annotated listing in both English and French texts of 97
     items - literature, liturgy and song collections.

56
ADLER, ISRAEL, comp. *Research Report and Project Cata-
logue.* Jerusalem, Isr.: Jewish Music Research Center at
Hebrew Univ., 1967; 19 pp.
     Since 1964, Research Center has been collecting and
     studying documents related to musical life and tradi-
     tions among historically significant Diaspora Jewish
     communities. Report-catalogue lists and describes cur-
     rently active and proposed projects, notes scholars as-
     sociated with activities, and indicates publications or
     works in preparation.

57
ADLER, ISRAEL and JUDITH COHEN, comps. *A. Z. Idelsohn
Archives at the Jewish National and University Library:
A Catalogue.* (Yuval Monograph Series, 4) Jerusalem, Isr.:
Magnes Press of Hebrew Univ., 1976; 144 pp., illus.
     Annotated listing in English and Hebrew texts of a col-
     lection of 950 diverse papers, study documents, corre-
     spondence and research materials donated to library by
     family of Abraham Zebi Idelsohn (1882-1938). Source of
     new information concerning the "father of modern Jewish
     musicology." Facsimiles and photographs. Consult index.

58
APPLETON, LEWIS, comp. *Bibliography of Jewish Vocal Music.*
New York: J.M.C., 1968; 128 pp.
     Annotated catalogue of solo and choral vocal works, with
     and without instruments, for religious services (Sabbath
     or holidays and festivals), Jewish folksongs in Hebrew
     and Yiddish, music for special occasions including wed-
     dings, and children's selections. Index of publishers.

59
APPLETON, LEWIS, comp. "Bibliography of the Works of A. W.
Binder (1895-1966)." In *Studies in Jewish Music: Collected
Writings of A. W. Binder.* (New York:Bloch, 1971) pp.311-29.
     Annotated listing of wide variety of musical works -
     religious services and secular compositions by Abraham
     Wolf Binder. Index of publishers.

60
AVNI, TZVI, comp. *Catalogue of the Bronislaw Huberman Archives.* Tel Aviv, Isr.: Central Library of Tel Aviv, 1977; 32 pp. illus.

    Listing of collected books, scores and personal docu-
ments of Bronislaw Huberman (1882-1947), noted concert
violinist and founder of the orchestral ensemble which
was to become the Israel Philharmonic Orchestra.

61
BENZOOR, NINA, comp. *Bibliography of Jewish Music Peri-
odicals in Hebrew, Yiddish and Other Languages.* (AMLI
Studies in Music Bibliog. Series, 2) Haifa, Isr.: Haifa
Music Museum and AMLI Library, 1970; 36 pp., illus.

    Some texts in English (most in Hebrew) for annotated
listings of various periodicals. Incomplete roster, but
informative on Israeli materials.

62
BINDER, ABRAHAM WOLF and Committee, comps. *Music for the
Tercentenary: A Bibliography.* New York:J.M.C.,1954; 27pp.

    Annotated listings of Jewish music of American signifi-
cance: vocal solos and choral works; instrumental compositions; song compilations. Publishers index. Prepared
by music educator and communal leader A.W. Binder (1895-
1966) with other members of Jewish Music Council, for
American Jewish tercentenary celebration (1654-1954).

63
BLOCH, SUZANNE, comp. "Catalogue of Ernest Bloch's Works."
In *Ernest Bloch: Creative Spirit - A Program Source Book.*
(New York: J.M.C., 1976) pp. 121-34.

    Prepared for distribution separately by the Ernest Bloch
Society and then included in this program aid. Annotated
listing, classified according to various instruments -
solo and ensemble. Instrumentation data, dates of all
compositions, chronology of works, with an index of publishers. All music of Ernest Bloch (1880-1959).

64
BLOCH, SUZANNE, comp. "Selected Bibliography of Ernest
Bloch." In *Ernest Bloch: Creative Spirit - A Program
Source Book.* (New York: J.M.C., 1976) pp. 117-20.

    Roster of manuscripts, documents and music library
sources. Listing of materials in print about Ernest
Bloch (1880-1959) and his music - reviews, commentaries,
biographical sketches, studies of individual works - in
periodicals, biographical collections and newspapers.

65
BUGATCH, SAMUEL, comp. "Bibliography of Yiddish Folksongs"
In *The Historic Contribution of Russian Jewry to Jewish
Music.* (New York: J.M.C., 1967) pp. 54-72.

    Annotated listing of vocal solo and choral music with
Yiddish texts. Roster by composers or arrangers.

66
BUNIS, DAVID M., comp. *Sephardic Studies: A Research Bibliography.* New York:Garland, 1981; vi,234pp.

    See "Folksong, Folk Poetry and Folk Music," pp.105-24,
for listings in French, Spanish, Ladino (Judezmo), Hebrew, Serbian and English; and, "Ballads," pp.124-38,

for other relevant entries. Includes literature, music collections, individual songs and recordings.

67
COHEN, JUDITH, comp. *Bibliography of the Publications of Eric Werner.* Tel Aviv,Isr.:Tel Aviv Univ. Press, 1968;12pp.
   Listing of works to 1967 (books, articles, reviews and papers) of Eric Werner, notable musicologist special- izing in Jewish music and member of faculty at Tel Aviv University and Hebrew Union College in New York City.

68
COHEN, JUDITH, trans. and ed. *Jewish Musicians at the Court of the Dukes of Mantua (1542-1628): A Bibliography Compiled by Eduard Birnbaum.* (Musicology Documentation and Studies Series, 1) Tel Aviv, Isr.: Tel Aviv Univ. Press, 1975; 52 pp. illus.
   From the collected studies of Jewish music history by Cantor Eduard Birnbaum (1855-1920), an edited and de- tailed listing of the works of Salomone Rossi Ebreo of Mantua (c.1565-c.1628), with geneological table of the Rossi family of musicians.

69
EDELMAN. MARSHA BRYAN, comp. *An Index to Gershon Ephros' Cantorial Anthology.* (*Musica Judaica.* vol. 2, no. 2 — entire issue) New York: A.S.J.M., 1978/79; vi,57pp.
   Guide catalogue, without annotations, for the important six-volume liturgical collection, compiled and edited by Cantor Gershon Ephros (1890-1978).

70
FACULTY, SCHOOL OF SACRED MUSIC: H.U.C.-J.I.R., compilers. "An Annotated Music Bibliography for Sabbath Eve Services." *Journal of C.C.A.R.*,vol.8.(New York:C.C.A.R.,1955),pp.24-29
   Listing for use in services of Reform congregations.

71
FREIDUS, ABRAHAM SOLOMON, comp. "On Jewish Music," in *Se- lected List of Works in New York Public Library Relating to the History of Music.* (New York: N.Y.P.L.Bulletin, vol. 12, 1908) pp. 30-31.
   Brief listing, notable for its early date and for com- piler, A. S. Freidus (1867-1923), dedicated scholar who served as first chief librarian (1897-1923) for Jewish Division of New York Public Library.

72
GALLO, F. ALBERTO. "Philological Works on Musical Trea- tises of the Middle Ages: A Bibliographical Report." *Acta Musicologica*, vol.44, no.1. (Kassel, W. Ger.: I.M.S., 1972) pp.78-101.
   Followed by annotational remarks, rosters of studies on music of Middle Ages, including materials relevant to Jewish music topics. Categories of lists: Early Mid- dle Ages — *Ars Musica. Musica Plana, Mensure Instru- mentorum. Organum:* Late Middle Ages — France, England, Italy, Spain, Central and Eastern Europe; Conclusion — an inventory of the sources. Valuable bibliography.

73
GOLDBERG, IRA, comp. *Bibliography of Instrumental Music of Jewish Interest: In Three Parts.* New York: J.M.C., 1970/71. *Part One*: "Orchestra and Band," 1970; xiv, 80 pp. *Part Two*: "Ensemble and Solo," 1970; xiv, 181 pp. *Part Three*: "Voice With Instruments: Solo/Orchestra," 1971; xiv., 120 pp
> Same introductory essay and index of publishers printed in all three parts. Introduction details method of annotation for the listings, with explanation of terms used. Music is graded and contents include wide range of works and some unusually interesting combinations.

74
GOLDBERG, JANET and Committee, comps. *Music to Wed By: Music for the Jewish Wedding.* New York:Women's League for Conservative Judaism, 1978; 18pp., music.
> Bibliographic resource of appropriate liturgical and secular selections — vocals and instrumentals, scores and recordings — for Jewish wedding ceremonies and celebrations. Annotated listings with sources. Including melody lines for 3 songs. Hebrew and Yiddish romanized.

75
GOODMAN, PHILIP, comp./ed. *Israel Program Resources.* New York:J.W.B., 1972; 94pp.
> "Selected and annotated listings of audio-visual materials, dramatizations, music, books, pamphlets and other aids — issued on occasion of the 25th anniversary of the State of Israel." Prepared by rabbi and editor Philip Goodman, with assistance of various contributors. See section on "Israeli Music" by Irene Heskes, pp.29-34; and materials on "Folk Dances," p.11 and "Musico-Dramatic Works," pp.18-19.

76
GORALI, MOSHE and Committee, comps. *The Old Testament in World Music: A Pictorial Catalogue.* Haifa, Isr.: Haifa Music Museum and AMLI Library, 1976; 144 pp., illus.
> With English text, souvenir brochure-catalogue for an exhibition prepared by Haifa Music Museum for international touring display in Europe and America. Photographs and facsimiles of materials assembled. Christian and Jewish liturgical arrays, artifacts and artistic representations of Old Testament music and musicians. Roster of examples of operas, oratorios and dramas, folksongs, vocal and instrumental art music scores. Maps and attractive color plates.

77
GORALI, MOSHE, with BETTY HIRSHOWITZ and TALI TUREL, comps. *The Old Testament in the Works of Johann Sebastian Bach (1685-1758).* (AMLI Studies in Bibliog. Series, 5) Haifa, Isr.: Haifa Music Museum and AMLI Library, 1979;48pp.,illus.
> Annotated listings of Bach's cantatas, motets and other works which set texts from Old Testament passages. Full texts are given in German and Hebrew. Historical data.

78
GORALI, MOSHE and RIVKA WATSON, compilers. *The Old Testament in the Works of George Frideric Handel.* (AMLI Studies in Music Bibliography, 6) Haifa,Isr.: Haifa Music Museum and

AMLI Library, 1982; 44pp., illus., music.
> Texts in English and Hebrew. With background on G.F.
> Handel (1685-1759) and authors of librettos for those
> works of Biblical inspiration. Annotated rosters of the
> oratorios, with performance data. Listing of anthems
> with Old Testament texts. Passages from Old Testament
> used in oratorio "Messiah." Also, Hebrew translation of
> for full text of oratorio "Esther," and Hebrew notations
> for some other oratorio materials. Facsimiles and notes.

79
GOTTLIEB, JACK, comp. *Leonard Bernstein - A Complete Catalogue of His Works.* New York: Amberson Enterprises/Boosey
and Hawkes, 1978; 68 pp, illus.
> Includes classified and chronological listing of music
> and literature by Bernstein, as well as discography and
> bibliography of and by this notable composer-conductor.
> Details given of Bernstein's activities. Index of music
> titles. Prepared in celebration of his 60th birthday
> year. Photographs.

80
GRADENWITZ, PETER, comp. *Paul Ben-Haim - 70th Birthday
Tribute.* Tel Aviv, Isr.: I.M.P., 1967; 28 pp.
> Annotated listing of compositions - vocal and instru-
> mental - by "dean" of Israeli composers, Paul Ben-Haim
> (1897-1984). Some biographical information.

81
GRIMM, CARL HUGO, comp. *A Catalogue of Music for the Synagogue.* Cincinnati: C.C.A.R., 1930; 67pp.
> Annotated listing of hymnals and songbooks for the
> Reform branch of Jewish liturgical observances. Inter-
> esting for view of materials in use at that time.

82
HELLER, JAMES GUTHEIM, comp. "List of Anthems for Choir,"
C.C.A.R. Yearbook, vol.33. (Cincinnati: C.C.A.R., 1923),
pp.479-90.
> Listing prepared for use with adult and children's
> choral groups of Reform congregations.

83
HESKES, IRENE, comp. "Annotated Resource Listings," in
Israeli Music: Program Aid (New York:J.M.C.,1978) pp.15-78.
> Roster of source materials developed as supplement for
> a lecture text: "Song of Exile and Return," by Judith
> K. Eisenstein. Listings include scores, recordings, song
> collections, dance books, libraries and publishers. With
> special section on *Hatikvah* (Israeli anthem) settings.

84
HESKES, IRENE, comp. *The Historic Contribution of Russian
Jewry to Jewish Music:Supplement.*New York:J.M.C.,1968;33pp.
> With biographical essays on two composers: Lazar Weiner
> (1897-1982) and Joseph Yasser (1893-1981). Bibliograph-
> ical listings of works by Weiner and Yasser, as well as
> by other Russian-Jewish musicians of early 20th century
> period in Russia and America. Some references to scores,
> recordings and books.

85
HESKES, IRENE, comp. "Israeli Music," in *Israeli Program
Resources.* (New York: J.W.B., 1972) pp. 29-34.
　　Prepared for celebration of 25th anniversary of State of
　　Israel (established in 1948). Listings given for re-
　　cordings, songbooks, vocal and instrumental collections,
　　music catalogues, Israeli books and periodicals, and
　　sources - publishers and libraries. No annotations.
86
HESKES, IRENE. "Jewish Music Literature." *Jewish Book
Annual*, vol.23. (New York: J.B.C.A., 1965/66), pp.34-41.
　　Survey of books on Jewish music published since end of
　　World War II and available in English text versions in
　　America. Detailed descriptions and discussion of field.
87
HESKES, IRENE, comp. *Music Program Aids:1973.* New York:
J.M.C., 1973; 10 pp.
　　Listings of Jewish music resource materials for use in
　　planning of programs - scores, recordings, song collec-
　　tions and publishers. Some annotations.
88
HESKES, IRENE, comp. "Survey of Jewish Music Books," in
Congress Bi-Weekly, vol. 27, no. 18. (New York: A.J.Cong.,
Dec. 1960) pp. 11-12.
　　Essay style roster of some more recent publications on
　　Jewish music topics, with details of their contents.
89
HORN, DAVID, comp. *The Literature of American Music in
Books and Folk Music Collections; A Fully Annotated Biblio-
graphy.* Metuchen,N.J.:Scarecrow Press, 1977; xiv,556pp.
　　Inclusion of some materials related to Jewish music and
　　topical field subject matter. Consult index.
90
IDELSOHN, ABRAHAM ZEBI, comp. "Collections of and Literature on Synagogue Song (18th and 19th Century)." in *Studies
in Jewish Bibliography and Related Subjects.* (New York:
Alexander Kohut Memorial Foundation, 1929) pp. 388-403.
　　Bibliographic essay by Idelsohn (1882-1938) presents a
　　roster of important liturgical music collections, with
　　descriptive details and perspectives on the field by
　　"father" of modern Jewish musicology. Among liturgists
　　discussed are: Baer, Naumbourg, Sanger, Friedmann and
　　Consolo. Essay included in volume dedicated to memory of
　　an outstanding Jewish scholar and librarian - Abraham
　　Solomon Freidus (1867-1923).
91
KAISER, ALOIS, comp. "Sulzer's Music," *C.C.A.R. Yearbook,*
vol.14, (Cincinnati:C.C.A.R., 1904), pp.237-43.
　　Annotated listing, prepared for celebration 100th anni-
　　versary birth of historically significant Cantor Salomon
　　Sulzer (1804-1890) who served Vienna's largest congre-
　　gation - Seitenstettengasse Shul - and was a significant
　　composer, arranger, collector and innovative cantorial
　　musician. Alois Kaiser (1840-1908) was a European born
　　cantor/music director for Baltimore Reform congregation
　　who in association with William Sparger (1860-1904), the

cantor at Temple Emanu-El in New York City, edited the
first edition of the *Union Hymnal* in 1897. Kaiser's
bibliographic study of Sulzer's works, which was widely
circulated throughout the country at that time, confirms
important liturgical music communication and influence
between America and Europe by late 19th century.
92

KATZ, ISRAEL J., comp. "Abraham Zebi Idelsohn (1882-1938):
A Bibliography of His Collected Writings." *Musica Judaica*,
vol.1 (New York:A.S.J.M., 1975/76), pp.1-32.
    With introductory material and citation of references
    and sources, presentation of chronological roster of
    Idelsohn's publications from 1908 onward — as written in
    German, Yiddish, Hebrew and English texts. Included are
    books, essays and studies, articles, music collections
    and songbook-hymnals. Some descriptive details of items,
    and index to publications in listing.
93

LETHERER, GARY P., comp. "Discography: Ernest Bloch," in
Ernest Bloch: Creative Spirit - A Program Source Book.
(New York: J.M.C., 1976) pp. 107-16.
    Detailed listing of recorded performances on 78 rpm and
    33 1/3 rpm releases of compositions by Ernest Bloch
    (1880-1959). Performers and label information.
94

LICHTENWANGER, WILLIAM and Committee, comps. "Bibliography
of Asiatic Musics: Part iii, Section C — Jews: Ancient and
Modern," in *M.L.A. Notes*, vol. 5, nos. 3 and 4. (Ann Arbor
and Phila.:M.L.A., June 1948/Sept. 1948) pp.354-62/pp.549-56
    Listing covers broad selection of books, articles and
    music collections, in European languages as well as Eng-
    lish and Latin. Roster includes works by leading schol-
    ars, and is set in context of entire bibliographic range
    of Asiatic cultures and of Christian music of that area.
    Materials on Jewish music assume position here within
    ethnological sweep. Items up to 1944 imprint date.
95

LOEWENSTEIN, HERBERT (HANOCH AVENARY), comp. "Notations
of Jewish Music Before 1800," in *Kiryath Sepher,* vol 19.
(Jerusalem, Isr.: Bibliographic Services of Hebrew Univ.,
Jan. 1943) pp. 259-66.
    Annotated roster in English and Hebrew of early Jewish
    music printings 1518-1800.
96

LOEWENSTEIN, HERBERT (HANOCH AVENARY), comp. "The Science
of Music in Jewish Sources of the 10th to 17th Centuries,"
in *Kiryath Sepher*, vol. 21 (Jerusalem, Isr.: Bibliographic
Services of Hebrew Univ., Jan. 1944) pp. 187-92.
    Annotated roster of resource materials on Jewish music
    in various early scholarly writings.
97

MANDELL, ERIC. "A Collector's Random Notes on the Bibliography of Jewish Music." *Fontis Artis Musicae*, vol.10,
nos.1/2. (Kassel, W.Ger.:I.A.M.L., 1963), pp.34-42.
    Critical survey of various types of collections and ros-
    ters of Jewish music: *Bibliography of Music* (New York,

1959) by Alfred Sendrey; Hebrew listings in Israel by
Haifa Music — AMLI Library, Central Music Library of Tel
Aviv, and Hebrew University Library in Jerusalem; some
European and early 20th century American catalogues of
German, Hebrew and Yiddish materials. Eric Mandell, as
collector of a remarkable repository of Jewish music
(which is now housed at Gratz College Library in Philadelphia), reflects upon other collectors and the studies
of A.Z. Idelsohn (1882-1938) and Arno Nadel (1878-1943),
and reports upon his own lifelong activities in field.
    98

MARKS, PAUL F., comp. *Bibliography of Literature Concerning Yemenite-Jewish Music.* (Detroit Studies in Music
Bibliog. Series, 27) Detroit: Information Coordinators,
1973; 50 pp.
    Listing of bibliographic materials covers Yemenite-Jew-
    ish topical areas of anthropology, sociology and history
    in addition to music. Includes primary and secondary
    sources. Introduction and appended selected discography.
    99

MAZOR, YAACOV, ANDRE HAJDU and BATHJA BAYER, comps. "The
Hassidic Dance — *Niggun*: A Study Collection and Its Classificatory Analysis." *YUVAL:Studies of J.M.R.C.*, vol.3.
(Jerusalem,Isr.:Hebrew Univ./Magnes Press, 1974), pp.136-
266, illus., music.
    Extremely detailed bibliographical study. Contents: I.
    Introduction; 1. Form structure of the *Niggun*; 2. Form
    structure of musical section; 3. Modal classification;
    4. Specimen analysis; 5. Classification tables. II. The
    Study Collection, with source data rosters and 250 me-
    lodic examples of materials gathered, transcribed and
    catalogued at National Sound Archives of Jewish National
    and University Library in Jerusalem. Consideration of
    musical criteria for definition and description of Has-
    sidic *Niggun* (wordless religious melody) as vocal im-
    provisational tune and in devotional dance expression.
    Comparative tables and musical illustrations.
    100

MIRON, ISSACHAR, comp. *Music of Israel Today: Annotated
List of Musical Compositions by Israeli Composers.* New
York: J.M.C. and A.-I.C.F., 1963; 134 pp.
    Roster includes information on various composers, their
    works and publication sources.
    101

MLOTEK, ELEANOR GORDON, comp. *A List of 55 Recommended
Yiddish Records: Index of 500 Recorded Songs.* New York:
Workmen's Circle, 1964; 42pp.
    Annotated and descriptive listing of music with Yiddish
    song texts, on L.P. recordings made in America and Is-
    rael. Sources. Yiddish titles romanized.
    102

NEWMAN, JOEL and FRITZ RIKKO, comps. and eds. *Thematic Index of Works of Salamone Rossi (c.1565-c.1628).* New York:
Mercury Music/C.A.A./J.T.S.A., 1973; 113pp., illus., music.
    Thematic index includes translation of various Hebrew
    prefaces to original publication by Rossi (Venice, 1623)

and other editions of Rossi's works. Biographical introduction on Salamone Rossi Ebreo da Mantua. Analyses of
Rossi's music itself. Selected bibiliography and other
data, including title indexes for works. Facsimiles of
early editions. Note: This is "volume 3 - supplement"
for 2-volume publication of music itself as compiled and
edited by Newman and Rikko (New York, 1967).

103
OLITZKY, KERRY and JOEL STEVENS, comps. *An Index to the*
Sound Recordings Collection of the American Jewish Archives
Cincinnati: Archives and H.U.C. Press, 1980; 74 pp.
Listing of over 2,000 items, with some annotations. In-
cluded are Yiddish popular songs, Hebrew liturgical se-
lections, many types of Jewish folksongs, as well as
recordings of works by composers of Jewish lineage.

104
RAVINA, MENASHE, comp. *Who's Who in ACUM (Authors, Com-*
posers and Music Publishers in Israel). Tel Aviv,Isr.:ACUM,
1965/66; 106pp., illus., music.
Biographical notes and rosters of principal works by
many Israeli composers, as well as activities of performers, writers and educators. Compilation prepared by
musician and journalist Menashe Ravina (1899-1968).

105
REIF, STEFAN C., comp. "The Music Title Page," in *Studies*
in Bibliography and Booklore, vol.10, nos. 1/2 (Cincinnati:
H.U.C. Press, Winter 1971/72) pp. 57-61, illus., music.
With a "Postscript" (pp. 62-68) by Herbert Zafren, roster of examples of music iconography in Jewish publications of 17th and 18th centuries. References to some
materials presently in Bodleian Library at Oxford University. Includes information on *Yigdal* hymn (c. 1714)
and facsimiles of other materials as well as footnotes.

106
RODGERS, JONATHAN, comp. "Report on Special Collections,"
in *Studies in Bibliography and Booklore*, vol,.13, nos.1/2.
(Cincinnati: H.U.C. Press, Winter 1980/81) pp. 36-38.
Roster of collections at Klau Library of Hebrew Union
College - Jewish Institute of Religion in Concinnati,
among which are such music materials as song sheets of
earlier eras, sound recordings of various types, and
musical theater memorabilia.

107
RUBIN, RUTH. "Literature on Jewish Music." *Jewish Book*
Annual, vol. 6. (New York: J.B.C.A., 1947/48), pp.64-70.
Review of various publications on subject as well as the
collections of folksongs issued since turn of century.
Details of editions and some reflections on contents.

108
RUBIN, RUTH, comp. "Resource Addenda Section," in *The*
Yiddish Folksong: An Illustrated Lecture. (New York: J.M.C.
1974) pp. 26-34.
Listing includes folksong collections, recordings, performance scores, literature references and publishers or
libraries sources.

109
RUFER, JOSEF, comp. *The Works of Arnold Schoenberg -
A Catalogue of His Compositions, Writings and Paintings.*
trans. from German by Dika Newlin. New York: Free Press of
Glencoe/Crowell Collier, 1963; 203 pp., illus.
    Annotated listings of music, various writings and art
    works — all the creativity of Arnold Schoenberg (1874-
    1951) — with other materials related to his career. In-
    cludes chronological roster of compositions.
110
SEGRE, MARCELLA, comp. *Bibliography of Jewish Music Bib-
liographies.* (AMLI Studies in Bibliog. Series, 3) Haifa,
Isr.: Haifa Music Museum and AMLI Library, 1970; 32 pp.
    Listing in English and Hebrew of 250 items of diverse
    contents and sources, with some annotation information.
111
SENDREY, ALFRED. *Bibliography of Jewish Music.* repr. ed.
Millwood, N.Y.: Kraus Reprint, 1969; xli, 404 pp. (orig. ed.
New York: Columbia Univ. Press, 1951; xli, 404 pp.)
    Catalogue listing of over 10,000 varied types of items
    in literature and music scores up to 1944 imprint date.
    Introduction affords background to this collection, and
    additional introductory essay on "Historical Survey of
    Bibliography of Jewish Music," traces earlier efforts at
    such collections from 16th century to mid-20th century.
    Contents of this work comprised of publications in many
    European languages, and Hebrew, Yiddish, Arabic, as well
    as English texts. Table of abbreviations and appended
    rosters of early biblical and rabbinical sources. Alfred
    Sendrey (1884-1976) based his three subsequently issued
    books of Jewish music history upon information derived
    from many of these entries. This bibliographic volume
    provides a substantial reservoir of resources, notably
    for non-English and European materials. Listings alpha-
    betically organized into topical categories with numeri-
    cal reference guides. Two indexes: Literature and Music.
112
SEROUSSI, EDWIN, comp. "Eduard Birnbaum: A Bibliography."
YUVAL:Studies of J.M.R.C., vol.4. (Jerusalem,Isr.: Hebrew
Univ./Magnes Press, 1982), pp.170-8.
    Compilation prepared as result of project of cataloguing
    of Eduard Birnbaum Collection at H.U.C.-J.I.R. in Cin-
    cinnati, done in 1979-1980, under direction of Israel
    Adler. Preparation of this outline bibliography based
    upon: prior bibliographical article by Eric Werner (*H.
    U.C. Annual*, vol.18, 1943/44; pp.397-428); *Bibliogra-
    phy of Jewish Music* (New York, 1951) by Alfred Sendrey
    (1884-1976); and an inventory which Eduard Birnbaum
    (1855-1920) prepared for his collection of Jewish music.
    This bibliography (topical contents only) is divided in-
    to: 1. Birnbaum's published writings of all types; 2.
    His lectures (in manuscripts); 3. Published materials
    treating Birnbaum's life and work.
113
SHILOAH, AMNON, comp. *The Theory of Music In Arabic Writings (c.900-1900): Descriptive Catalogue of Manuscripts in*

Libraries of Europe and the U.S.A. (RISM - International
Inventory of Music Sources Series, BX) Munich, W. Ger.: G.
Henle, 1979; 512 pp.
     Roster of 341 Arabic texts, translated and annotated.
     Notable scholarly aid for further research in the field.
     114
SHUNAMI, SHLOMO, comp. *A Bibliography of Jewish Bibli-
ographies.* Jerusalem, Isr.: Magnes Press of Hebrew Univ.,
1965; xxiv, 992 pp.
     See section on "Music," pp. 193-9, which includes some
     English, as well as Hebrew, listings up to 1964.
     115
SHUNAMI, SHLOMO, comp. *Bibliography of Jewish Bibliogra-
phies: Supplement.* Jerusalem,Isr.:Magnes Press of Hebrew
Univ., 1975; xvii,464pp.+16n.p.
     See pp.49-54 and pp.317-8, for entries related to music
     in Hebrew and English texts.
     116
VICTOR, WARNER, comp. *Rare Books from the Eric Mandell
Music Collection, Parts 1 and 2.* Phila.:Music Library of
Gratz College of Jewish Studies,1982/83; 19pp./33pp., illus.
     Detailed descriptions of materials (c.1705-1870) from
     the Eric Mandell Collection of Jewish Music - scores and
     literature - presently housed at library and study fa-
     cilities of music department at Gratz College. Hymnals
     and books - mostly German publications along with few
     from England and America. Part 1 - 36 items; Part 2 -
     26 items, with facsimile illustrations. Prepared for
     library by bibliographer Warner Victor.
     117
WEINREICH URIEL and BEATRICE WEINREICH, comps. *Yiddish
Language and Folklore: Selective Bibliography for Research.*
The Hague: Neth.: Mouton, 1959; 66 pp.
     See: Part Two - section 15 "Folksong and Folk Music -
     a. Bibliography; b. Collections; c. Studies," pp. 46-49.
     Listing, without annotations, for 55 items of different
     types mostly in Yiddish texts.
     118
WEISSER, ALBERT, comp. *Bibliography of Publications and
Other Resources on Jewish Music.* New York: J.M.C., 1969;
6 n.p., 117 pp.
     Revised and enlarged edition based upon 1955 brief com-
     pilation made by Joseph Yasser (1893-1981). Listing of
     wide variety of literature for period 1954-1967, and in-
     cluding full roster of Jewish Music Council publications
     1942-1969. Documentary information with no annotations.
     Albert Weisser (1918-1982), scholar and educator in the
     field, collected helpful array of items which highlight
     growth of Jewish music activities in America after
     World War II. Introductory essays by Yasser and Weisser.
     119
WEISSLER, LENORE E., comp. *Selected List of Material Re-
lating to Hebrew and Israeli Folk Music;and, Brief List of
Material Relating to Yiddish Folk Music.* Wash. D.C.: The
Archive of Folksong, Music Div. at L. of C., 1970; 10 pp.
     Listing on type-script sheets of some resources in the

field of Jewish folksong.
120
WERNER, ERIC, comp. "An Early Compendium of Ashkenazic
Synagogue Music." In *Studies in Bibliography and Booklore,*
vol. 5 - Klau Library Dedication Issue. (Cincinnati: H.U.C.
Press, 1961) pp. 110-21.
  Roster in essay form of liturgical music from Southwest
  Germany of mid 19th century. Basically an overview of
  liturgy collected by Cantor Eduard Birnbaum (1855-1920),
  with special attention here to such acquired materials
  as four volumes compiled c.1862 by M. Levi of Wuettemburg. Eric Werner, notable scholar, writer and educator
  in field of Jewish music, served as consultant-curator
  to Birnbaum collection in Cincinnati before joining
  faculty of Hebrew Union College - Jewish Institute of
  Religion in New York City. Birnbaum Collection contains
  much valuable material and constitutes a substantial
  part of present music section of Klau Library.
121
WERNER, ERIC. *"Prologomena* to a Bibliography of Jewish
Music." *Historica Judaica*, vol.6(New York:1944),pp.175-88.
  Historical and general overview of publications in Jewish music extant at time (1944), prepared by Eric Werner as musicologist and educator in Jewish liturgical
  music. Highlighting of 19th century achievements, and
  significant collection work of Eduard Birnbaum (1855-
  1920) and Abraham Idelsohn (1882-1938). This article
  subsequently was greatly expanded and updated by author
  to serve as introduction for his collection of essays on
  Jewish music by various authors: *Contributions to a
  Historical Study of Jewish Music* (New York, 1976).
122
WERNER, ERIC, comp. "The Tunes of the Haggadah." in
Studies in Bibliography and Booklore, Vol. 7. (Cincinnati:
H.U.C. Press, 1965) pp. 57-83.
  Entire volume devoted to various aspects of topic: "The
  Haggadah: Past and Present." Roster, in essay form, of
  different editions and folksong versions of music in-
  cluded in traditional ritual book (*Haggadah*) of the
  Passover holiday observance of *Seder* (festive special
  home celebration service and meal). Music examples.
123
WOLFSON, ARTHUR, comp. "Section Three: Bibliographic List-
ings,"in *The Cantorial Art.*(New York:J.M.C.,1966)pp.91-112
  Selected roster of modern synagogue music scores and
  cantorial recordings prepared by Cantor Arthur Wolfson
  (1912-1977) who served at Reform congregation Temple
  Emanu-El in New York City.

2.
Books and Monographs
on Jewish Music

124
ADLER, CYRUS. *The Shofar; Its Use and Origin.* Wash.,D.C.:
Smithsonian Institute – U.S. National Museum and U.S. Govt.
Printing Office, pamphlet no. 936, 1894; 20 pp., illus.
   Separate issue of article which originally appeared in
   Proceedings of United States National Museum, vol.16,
   1892, pp. 287-301, plates xlvi-xlix. Cyrus Adler (1863-
   1940), then assistant curator of Oriental Antiquities at
   the Museum, had presented this material in 1889 as a
   paper at a meeting of the American Oriental Society
   (*A.O.S. Journal*, vol.14, 1890). Adler's valuable
   scholarly study treats the ancient Jewish ceremonial
   music instrument – *Shofar* – which still serves a significant ritual purpose for traditional observance of
   High Holy Days synagogue services. Fine illustrations.
125
ADLER, ISRAEL. *Musical Life and Traditions of the Portuguese Jewish Community of Amsterdam in the 18th Century.*
(Yuval Monograph Series, 1) Jerusalem, Isr.: Magnes Press of
Hebrew Univ., 1974; 144 pp., illus., music.
   Publication by musicologist Israel Adler, Director of
   the Jewish Music Research Center at Hebrew University,
   essentially is an English version, revised and enlarged,
   of Part iv of his scholarly work: *La Pratique Musical
   Savante Dans Quelques Communautes Juives en Europe aux
   xvii et xviii Siecles.* (Paris, Fr.: La Haye/Mouton,
   1966.) English volume organized into two sections: literary references and repertoire of synagogue music. Sub-
   topics treated include: survey of music training and
   secular music life among Jews of Low Countries; musical
   practices in synagogue at holidays, special occasions or
   communal events; an inventory of 18th century music
   manuscripts of Amsterdam Jewish community (with thematic
   annotations); consideration of Jewish composers and art
   music of that time. Among appended materials are: alpha-

betical list of literary incipits; facsimiles of music;
English translations and annotations. Hebrew texts romanized. Israel Adler cites manuscripts from the Eduard
Birnbaum Collection of Jewish Music housed in Cincinnati
at Klau Library of H.U.C.-J.I.R. as information source
for this work, and also studies of such scholars as A.Z.
Idelsohn (1882-1938) and Eric Werner. Consult footnotes,
and see index roster for various subjects treated here.

126
AVENARY, HANOCH. *The Ashkenazic Tradition of Biblical
Chant Between 1500 and 1900.* (Music Documentation and
Studies Series, 2) Tel Aviv, Isr.: Tel Aviv Univ. Press,
1978; 87 pp., illus., music.
    Comparative analysis and musical reconstruction of chant
    notations for recitations of biblical texts at various
    religious services during the calendar year, in tradi-
    tions of mid-European Ashkenazic Jews. Hanoch Avenary,
    Israeli scholar, writer and educator, member of music
    faculty at Tel Aviv University, presents his study of
    Jewish cantillation within cultural and historic con-
    texts. Table of organization and appended data afford
    guidance to specific subject areas.

127
AVENARY, HANOCH. *Encounters of East and West in Music; A
Collection of Selected Writings.* Tel Aviv, Isr.: Tel Aviv
Univ. Press, 1979; 207 pp., illus., music.
    Seventeen articles by Hanoch Avenary, all previously
    published in various journals, have been collected into
    one book as a tribute to this scholar-educator by his
    colleagues of the Department of Musicology at Tel Aviv
    University. Materials are organized into four topical
    categories: Musical Instruments - Symbolism and Reality;
    Concept of Mode; Aspects of Synagogue and Church Music;
    and, Jewish Folklore. Appended is a listing of Avenary's
    publications to 1979. Those articles by Avenary which
    originally appeared in English are listed and annotated
    elsewhere in this bibliography. However, the following
    six articles, originally written in Hebrew, Have been
    translated into English for his tribute volume: "Hy-
    draules and Choraules: A Chapter of Music History in
    Jewish Hellenism," (Haifa,Isr.:*Tatzlil*,vol.2;1966);
    "The Experience of Nature and Scenery in the Israeli
    Song," (Tel Aviv,Isr.:*Israeli Music*;1974/75); "The
    Interpretation of Music Notation of Ovadyah (Obadiah)
    the Proselyte," (Haifa,Isr.:*Tatzlil*,vol.14;1974); "The
    Maoz Tsur Tune: New Facts for Its History," (Haifa,
    Isr.:*Tatzlil*,vol.7;1967); "Gentile Songs as a Source
    of Inspiration for Israel Najara," (Jerusalem,Isr.: *The
    Papers:2.* of Fourth World Congress of Jewish Studies;
    1968); and, "Toward an Israeli Design of Music History,"
    (Tel Aviv,Isr.:*Bat Kol*,vol.1;1955).

128
AVENARY, HANOCH. *Hebrew Hymn Tunes; The Rise and Development of a Musical Tradition.* Tel Aviv., Isr.: I.M.I., 1971;
44 pp., illus., music.
    Musicological, historical and literary consideration of

qualities of Jewish hymnology, exploration of varied
types and sources, and annotated study of 15 specific
examples of hymns spanning eight centuries of creativity
in this genre. Melody lines, with poetic texts of the
liturgy, are considered here in two broad categories:
"free rhythm in poetry and music," - 7 hymns; "metric
symmetry and periodic structure of melodies," - 8 hymns.
Hanoch Avenary appends an explanatory roster of Hebrew
terms and list of source references. Music examples are
from Jews of Cairo, Bagdad, Damascus, Yemen, Balkans,
and European Sephardic and Ashkenazic groups, as well as
Hassidic sects of Eastern Europe.

129

AVENARY, HANOCH, ed. *The Hebrew Version of Abu L-Salt's
Treatise on Music.* (Yuval Studies Series, 3) Jerusalem,
Isr.: Hebrew Univ. Press, 1974; 82 pp., illus.

Edited and annotated version of treatise on music by
early Medieval scholar Abu L-Salt (1068-1134). Text reflects thinking among Arabo-Jewish philosophers of that
period. Given here in English and Hebrew. Musicologist
Hanoch Avenary has structured the materials and added
helpful information in his notes.

130

AVENARY, HANOCH. *Studies in the Hebrew, Syrian and Greek
Liturgical Recitative.* Tel Aviv, Isr.: I.M.I., 1963; 47 pp.
illus., music.

Scholarly survey of three branches of religious chant,
outlining stages in development, notation, music style,
and various influences of chants upon European vocal
music expression. In this study, scholar and educator
Hanoch Avenary reflects on relationships between three
traditions as shaped early-on and then, in turn, as
shaping forces of subsequent liturgical as well as
secular music creativity.

131

BAYER, BATHJA. *The Material Relics of Music in Ancient
Palestine and Its Environs; An Archeological Inventory.*
Tel Aviv, Isr.: I.M.I., 1963; 55 pp., illus.

Survey by Israeli scholar Bathja Bayer of 250 archaeological discoveries, with annotated inventory of these
materials, dating from 3,000 B.C.E. to 6th Century. Intriguing aspects of research into music culture of ancient Palestine area viewed in terms of items recovered
through "digs" projects over recent years.

132

BENTWICH, MARGERY. *Thelma Yellin - Pioneer Musician.*
Jerusalem, Isr.: Rubin Mass, 1964; 131 pp., illus.

Biography of English-born Zionist and musician who settled in Palestine in 1920. Thelma Yellin (1895-1959) was
notable concert cellist and music educator. She helped
establish and maintain formal music education facilities
during British Mandate period between the two World Wars
and into early years of State of Israel. Substantial information here on musical activities and leading music
figures of that earlier era.

133
BRAUN. JOACHIM. *Jews in Soviet Music.* (Soviet and East
European Research Papers, 22) Jerusalem, Isr.: Hebrew Univ.
Press, 1977; ii, 92 pp.
> Monograph based upon research of Joachim Braun while at
> Bar Ilan University in Tel Aviv. Topic is introduced in
> broad general manner, highlighting some individuals,
> collected data and specific details of activities. At
> present time, there is limited access to sources of in-
> formation concerning Jewish music in the Soviet Union.
> Nevertheless, the subject of Jewish music creativity and
> Jewish musicians in Old Russia, and now in contemporary
> U.S.S.R., merits further scholarly attention. Braun's
> study serves as preliminary effort. Source notes.

134
BROD, MAX. *Israel's Music.* trans. from German by Toni
Volcani. Tel Aviv,Isr.:Sefer Press,1951;vii, 62pp., illus.
> Subjective essay by Prague-born novelist, librettist and
> journalist Max Brod (1884-1968), who settled in Tel Aviv
> in 1939. Discussion of Israeli composers and their works
> as well as particular trends of music in that country.

135
COHEN, BOAZ. *The Responsum of Maimonides (1135-1204) Concerning Music.* New York: Posy-Shoulson, 1935; 27 pp.
> English translation of tract presented with annotations
> and commentary by scholar-educator Boaz Cohen (1899-
> 1968), who specialized in Medieval rabbinical writings
> and comparative Judaic law. Moses Maimonides - rabbi,
> physician, trader in commerce, writer in Hebrew, Aramaic
> Arabic and Spanish, translator of liturgical texts, com-
> mentator upon Bible, *Talmud* and other sacred writings,
> codifier of Jewish law, ritual and custom, scientist who
> calculated the Jewish calendar - vitally shaped the de-
> velopment of rabbinic Judaism for centuries after his
> time and even influenced theological ideas and practices
> for Christianity and Islam. Though this tract on music
> is brief, the impact of Maimonides' opinions continue to
> affect traditional Jewish practices.

136
COHEN, DALIA and RUTH KATZ. *The Israeli Folk Song: A Meth-
odological Example of Computer Analysis of Monophonic Music.*
(Yuval Monograph Series, 6) Jerusalem, Isr.: Magnes Press
of Hebrew Univ., 1977; 100 pp., illus., music.
> Examination of specific repertoire elements in the field
> of Israeli folksong. Utilizing a computer program, this
> technical study relates both to the music itself and to
> the useful application of new technological equipment
> for musical analysis and research.

137
COHEN, FRANCIS LYON. *The Rise and Development of Synagogue
Music.* London,Eng.:Wertheimer, 1888; 58pp., illus., music.
> Publication of lecture delivered at Anglo-Jewish His-
> torical Exhibit (at Royal Albert Hall, London) on May
> 16, 1887, by musician and writer F.L. Cohen (1862-1934).

138
COHEN, JUDITH, ed. *Proceedings of World Congress on Jewish Music (Jerusalem, 1978).* Tel Aviv,Isr.:Institute for Trans-
lation of Hebrew literature,1982;x,271pp,47n.p.,illus.,music
Summaries and abstracts of papers presented at confer-
ence by international gathering of music scholars. Con-
tents: Eric Werner: "Identity and Character of Jewish
Music." Israel Adler:"Problems in Study of Jewish Music"
Eric Werner:"Impact of Hellenism." Karl-Gustav Fellerer:
"Jewish and Early Christian Chant." Amnon Shiloah: "The
Mediaeval Arab World." Don Harran: "Influence of Hebrew
Accents on Renaissance Music Theory." Peter Gradenwitz:
"18th Century Germany and Viennese Classical Masters."
Bruno Nettl: "Concept of Preservation in Ethnomusicolo-
gy." Simha Arom: "Utopian Proposals for Preservation of
Jewish Traditions." Dalia Cohen and Ruth Katz: "Inscrip-
tion as Transcription." Avner Bahat: "Yemenite Diwan -
Poetry/Chant/Dance." Avigdor Herzog: "Metrical Aspects
of Samaritan Music." Hanoch Avenary: "Contacts Between
Church and Synagogue Music." Dom Jean Claire: "Points de
Contact Entre Repertoires Juifs et Chretiens." Karl-
Gustav Fellerer: "Jewish Elements in Pre-Christian
Chants." Milos Velimirovic:"Byzantine Musical Tradition"
Dalia Cohen: "Comparison Between Eastern and Western
Music." Bathja Bayer: "Early *Mishnah* and Its Cantilla-
tion." Raymond J. Tournay: "Rhythmologie Comparee et
Technique Psalmodique." Max Wohlberg: "Aspects of Ash-
kenazic Hazzanic Recitative." Judith K. Eisenstein:
"Chant in Changing American Synagogue." Mark Slobin:
"Iconography of Jewish-American Sheet Music." Michal
Smoira-Cohen: "Introduction - Folksong in Israel." Ben-
Zion Orgad: "Musical Potential of Hebrew Language."
Joachim Braun: "Jewish National School in Russia." Boris
Schwarz: "Russian and Jewish Musicians of 19th and 20th
Centuries." Shlomo Hofman: "Jewish Petersburg Composers
and Impact on Music Renaissance in Israel." Carl Dahl-
haus: "Patterns of Meyerbeer Criticism." Hans Heinz
Stuckenschmidt: "Schoenberg's *Kol Nidre.*" Hans Keller:
"Can Music of Diaspora Represent Jewish Traditions."
Arieh Sachs: "Art Music as Non-Jewish." Alexander L.
Ringer: "Jewish Music - Old Problems and Dilemmas."
With complete program roster, including musical perform-
ances and performers, and general panel discussants.

139
COHON, ANGIE IRMA. *An Introduction to Jewish Music; In Eight Illustrated Lectures.* Chicago/New York: N.C.J.W.,
1923; 225 pp., illus., music.
Originally prepared by Angie Irma Cohon as a series of
lectures on Jewish music for presentation at women's
organization meetings, this material has value to this
day because texts remain suitable. Excellent musical
examples. Hebrew romanized. Topics: 1. "Introduction to
Jewish Music (An Historical Survey from Biblical Times)"
2. "Traditional Music in the Old Synagogue." 3. "Traditional Music in the Modern Reform Synagogue." 4. "Religious Music in the Jewish Home (Sabbath, Holidays and

Weddings)" 5. "Jewish Folksong — Yiddish, Hebrew, Hassidic." 6. "The Influence of Jewish Music on General World
Music." 7. "The Influence of General World Music on Jewish Music." 8. "Modern Settings of Ancient Themes."
    140

CORNILL. KARL HEINRICH. *Music in the Old Testament.*
trans. from German by Lydia G. Robinson. Chicago, Ill.: Open
Court Publishers, 1909; 25 pp., illus.
    Karl Heinrich Cornill (1854-1920) was professor of Old
    Testament Theology at the University of Breslau. In this
    monograph, he considers a range of biblical references
    to music instruments, musical activities and musicians,
    and Temple ritual uses of music, including citations in
    the Psalms, women and music-making of the biblical era,
    and some aspects of scales and modes. Interesting, if
    dated work, which cites Apocryphal writings in effort to
    tie in materials to music qualities and influences be-
    yond Old Testament era. No index.
    141

EISENSTEIN, JUDITH KAPLAN. *Heritage of Music; The Music
of the Jewish People.* New York: U.A.H.C., 1972; xix,
339pp., illus., music.
    Not a history of Jewish music, but a topical survey in
    28 chapters, affording broad sweep of subjects, ranging
    in geography and time, and covering such areas as: many
    different liturgical traditions of *Ashkenazim, Sephard-
    im* and other groups; folksongs in Yiddish, Ladino and
    Hebrew; music of the *Hassidim*; hymnology and holiday
    melodies; musical reflections of life and communal com-
    memorations; songs of Zionism, Holocaust and American
    immigration. Judith Kaplan Eisenstein — educator, writer
    and composer — presents materials in narrative style,
    with 129 musical selections highlighting varied topics,
    and 81 appropriate photographs. Lists of sources and of
    reference works. Consult roster of music examples and
    index for wide selection of subjects, because chapter
    titles are too general. Hebrew and Yiddish romanized.
    142

ELIAS, WILLIAM. *Ben Zion Orgad.* Tel Aviv, Isr.: I.M.I.,
1981; 19pp., illus.
    Brief biographical study of Israeli composer Ben Zion
    Orgad, with roster of his works and activities.
    143

EVANS, ROBERT HARDING. *An Essay on Music of the Hebrews.*
London,Eng.:John Booth, 1816; 48pp., illus., music.
    "Intended as a preliminary discourse to the Hebrew melo-
    dies which have since been published by Messrs. (John)
    Braham and (Isaac) Nathan." Monograph by English writer
    Robert Harding Evans (fl.early 19th cent.). General
    treatment of music, musicians and musical instruments in
    the Bible, Psalms and Temple of Solomon, synagogue tra-
    ditions and influences upon church music. Facsimiles,
    music examples and sources.
    144

EWEN, DAVID. *Hebrew Music; A Study and an Interpretation.*
New York: Bloch, 1931; 65 pp., illus., music.

David Ewen dedicated this monograph to composer Ernest
Bloch (1880-1959). Nine brief chapter-essays trace the
development of Jewish music from biblical "beginnings"
to the present (1930). Ewen considers then "mew" trends
in composition of secular works of Judaic inspiration
and of liturgical music for the synagogue. No index.

145
FARMER, HENRY GEORGE. *Moses Maimonides (1135-1204) on*
Listening to Music, from the Responsa of Moses Ben Maimon.
(Mediaeval Jewish Tracts on Music Series, 1) Hertford,
Scot.: Farmer, 1941; 21 pp.
    Edited text, with English translation and commentary by
scholar Henry George Farmer (1882-1965), of important
tract by one of the most significant figures in rabbinic
Judaism — a formative philosopher and codifier of Jewish
laws, customs and rituals, whose influence reached out
also to general theological developments during his era.
Maimonides' brief but cogent opinions on music affected
its subsequent expression in Jewish traditional life.

146
FARMER, HENRY GEORGE. *Sa'adyah Gaon (c.892-942) on the*
Influence of Music. London, Eng.: A. Probsthain, 1943:
xi, 109 pp., illus., music.
    Sa'adyah ben Yosif ha-Pitomi was earliest Jewish writer
on the theory of music. Chosen in 928 as *Gaon* (intellectual and spiritual leader) of the leading Rabbinical
Academy at Sura in Mesopotamia, he was a rationalist
theologian and skilled linguist who wrote in Arabic and
Hebrew and left a legacy of studies and responsa. Henry
George Farmer (1882-1965) considers Sa'adyah's tracts on
music in context of Jewish interest at that time in the
theory of music, its origins, modality, ethos and influences. He then traces the impact of Sa'adyah's ideas on
music upon subsequent scholars into the 15th century —
in terms of their various interpretations. Those texts
and commentaries, with summary of their lives and works,
are presented for: Sa'adyah; Al-Kindi; Bar Hiyyah; Ibn
Tibbon; Berakyah; and others. Rosters of names and references. List of technical terms. Subject index.

147
FINESINGER, SOL BARUCH. *Musical Instruments in the Old*
Testament. Baltimore: Finesinger, 1926; 64 pp., illus.
    Discussion of string, wind and percussion instruments as
mentioned in the Bible, together with roster of sources,
references in Judaica, diagrams and comparative tables.
Heavy dependence upon 19th century scholarly writings of
Engel, Cornill, Stainer, F.L. Cohen and early works by
Idelsohn. Quirky but interesting work. No index.

148
FLIEGEL, HYMAN J. *Zavel Zilberts: His Life and Works.* New
York: Bnai Zion Foundation, 1971; 159 pp., illus.
    Biographical tribute to Jewish musician Zavel Zilberts
(1881-1949) who was a composer-arranger, pianist, organist, conductor and music director for synagogues and
Yiddish choral groups in East Europe and America. Zilberts was a well-trained and highly respected musician

who devoted his talents to artistic advancement of Jew-
music — liturgy and folksong.
149

FRIEDLANDER, ARTHUR M. *Facts and Theories Relating to Hebrew Music.* London, Eng.:H. Reeves,1924;16pp.,illus.,music.
Publication of paper delivered at meeting of the Royal
Asiatic Society (July 1923). Includes facsimile of an
early Hebrew manuscript containing neumes. (Obadiah?)
150

FROMM, HERBERT. *On Jewish Music; A Composer's View.* New
York: Fromm, 1978; viii, 173 pp., illus., music.
Collection of articles, reviews and "musings" about
various aspects of Jewish music and musicians. Discussions of secular works, liturgical compositions, trends
in musical creativity over recent years. Herbert Fromm,
composer and organist, has served Reform congregations
as music director and choral conductor. Consult index.
151

GERSON-KIWI, EDITH. *The Legacy of Jewish Music Through the
Ages.* Jerusalem,Isr.: W.Z.O., 1963; 23 pp., illus., music.
General survey essay which was originally prepared for
a music conference in Jerusalem: "East and West in Music," held August 1963. Edith Gerson-Kiwi, leading Israeli musicologist and educator, presents varied aspects
of Jewish music development, and the range of influences
among different traditions. No index.
152

GERSON-KIWI, EDITH. *Migrations and Mutations of the Music:
East and West; Selected Writings.* Tel Aviv, Isr.: Tel Aviv
Univ. Press, 1980; 248 pp., illus., music.
Collection of articles previously published in various
periodicals 1950-1975, and listed with annotations elsewhere in this bibliography. The one-volume collection is
a tribute issue prepared by the Department of Musicology
of Tel Aviv University honoring member of faculty, Edith
Gerson-Kiwi, noted scholar and writer. Materials grouped
in four topical sections: Instruments and Instrumental
Forms; Sacred Chant in Cult and Religion; Theory and
Practice in the Music of the Middle East; and, Music and
Society. Prologue, epilogue and listing of Gerson-Kiwi's
writings to 1980.
153

GRADENWITZ, PETER. *Music of Israel: Composers and Their
Works.* (Arts in Israel Series) Jerusalem,Isr.: Hechalutz/
Jewish Agency, 1952; 107 pp., illus., music.
Survey of trends in creativity and styles of expression
among Israeli composers, with consideration of their
lives, works and with an overview of various musical or-
ganizations. Materials treated date from 1920's onward.
Peter Gradenwitz fled from the nazis in 1936, settling
in Tel Aviv where he formed the Israeli Music Publica-
tions firm and began to edit and issue the works of many
notable composers, among them Paul Ben-Haim (1897-1984),
Uriah Boscovich (1907-1964), Marc Lavry (1903-1967) and
Oedoen Partos (1907-1977). Consult annotated roster of
Israeli musicians, music schools and musical groups.

154

GRADENWITZ, PETER. *The Music of Israel; Its Rise and Growth Through 5,000 Years.* New York: W.W. Norton, 1949; 334 pp., illus., music.

With prologue and epilogue, 12 topical chapters covering a range of Jewish music history from biblical era into centuries of varied musical expression — liturgical and secular — throughout Diaspora areas of Jewish settlement and up to 19th and 20th century world-wide developments. Peter Gradenwitz considers the newer musical creativity in emergent State of Israel. Chronological table of Jewish history and roster of biblical references to music. With study on origins of *Hatikvah.* Also consult index.

155

GRADENWITZ, PETER. *Music and Musicians in Israel; A Comprehensive Guide to Modern Israeli Music.* Tel Aviv, Isr.: I.M.P., 1978; 226 pp., illus., music.

Descriptive information on musical life, institutions, organizations and styles of expression in the State of Israel. Brief biographical studies of sixty composers and their particular types of creativity, considering different groups and trends. Peter Gradenwitz has resided in Israel since 1936, working as writer, music editor and publisher of music by many notable Israeli composers. Consult annotated roster of musicians.

156

HESKES, IRENE. *The Historic Contribution of Russian Jewry to Jewish Music: Supplement.* New York: J.M.C., 1968; 29 pp.

Biographical essays on lives and works of two notable figures in Jewish music who were born in Russia and began their careers there before emigrating to America where they pursued productive musical lives. 1. Pianist, organist, musicologist and educator Joseph Yasser (1893–1981). 2. Composer, conductor, pianist and educator Lazar Weiner (1897–1982). With bibliographic lists and rosters of recordings. Prefatory commentary on Jewish musical expression on Old Russia and then in U.S.S.R., with reflections on influences upon Jewish music and musicians in America during 20th century.

157

HESKES, IRENE, ed. *Studies in Jewish Music; Collected Writings of A.W. Binder.* New York: Bloch, 1971; vii, 355 pp.

Collection of 25 previously published articles by composer, conductor, music director and educator Abraham Wolf Binder (1895–1966). Edited and placed in chronology (1927 to posthumous publications), the materials are of varying lengths and treat many topics: Judaic musical history; synagogue liturgy; Jewish folksong and holiday melodies; Israeli music activities; and, newer trends in creativity in America. Brief prefatory tributes to Binder by colleagues Peter Gradenwitz and Joseph Yasser (1893–1981). An extended biographical introduction by editor Irene Heskes places A.W. Binder and his diversified musical career within the context of 20th century Jewish musical developments. Articles: 1. "*V'shomru:* A Century of Musical Interpretations," pp.51-64 (*Israel*

Abrahams Memorial Volume. Vienna, 1927); 2. "*Hanukkah
in Music*," pp.65-71 (*Hanukkah - The Feast of Lights.*
Phila.,1937); 3. "Some Jewish Contributions to the Art
of Music," pp.72-78 (*Bulletin of Jewish Academy of Arts
and Sciences.* New York, 1937); 4. "Changing Values in
Synagogue Music," pp.79-84 (*Bulletin of Jewish Music
Forum.* New York, 1941); 5. "How Congregations Can be
Made to Sing," pp.85-87 (*Bulletin of Jewish Music Fo-
rum.* New York, 1943); 6. "The Neglect and Need of Jew-
ish Music," pp.88-92 (*The Jewish Center.* New York,
1944); 7. "The Music of the Synagogue; An Historical
Survey," pp.93-96 (*The Diapason.* New York, 1945); 8.
"The Sabbath in Music," pp.97-112 (*Sabbath, the Day of
Delight.* Phila., 1944); 9. "The Spirit of the Sabbath
Eve Service," pp.113-16 (*Summary of Proceedings, Second
Annual Institute on Jewish Liturgical Music.* New York,
1951); 10. "*Purim* in Music," pp.117-28 (*The Purim
Anthology.* Phila., 1949); 11. "Jewish Music; An Ency-
clopedic Survey," pp.129-99 (*Jewish People:Past and
Present.* New York, 1952); 12. "Israel's Choral Music,"
pp.200-02 (*Choral and Organ Guide.* New York, 1952);
13. "Music Education of Israeli Children," pp.203-06
(*Israel:Life and Letters.* Tel Aviv, 1952); 14. "Jewish
Music Movement in America," pp.207-29 (*Jewish Tercentenary Celebration.* New York, 1954); 15. "New Trends in
Synagogue Music," pp.230-35 (*Journal of C.C.A.R.* New
York, 1955); 16. "New Jewish Music Creativity," pp.236-
41 (*The Reconstructionist.* New York, 1956); 17. "Introduction to Cantillation,: pp.242-47 (*Biblical Chant.*
New York, 1959); 18. "The Jewish Liturgical Music Society of America," pp.248-50 (*J.L.M.S.A. Bulletin.* New
York, 1963); 19. "Hassidism," pp.251-54 (*Jewish Folk-
songs.* New York, 1963); 20. "A History of American –
Jewish Hymnody," pp.255-69 (*The Hymn.* New York, 1963);
21. "A Perspective on Synagogue Music in America," pp.
270-76 (*Journal of Church Music.* New York, 1964); 22.
"A Rebirth of Biblical Chant," pp.277-81 (*The Cantorial
Art.* New York, 1966); 23. "Salomon Sulzer's Legacy to
the Cantorate," pp.282-88 (*J.L.M.S.A. Bulletin.* New
York, 1967); 24. "Isaac Offenbach: His Life, Work and
Manuscript Collection," pp.289-303 (*Yearbook of Leo
Baeck Institute.* London, 1969); 25. "The Ideas and
Theories in My Synagogue Compositions," pp.304-10 (un-
published paper prepared in 1964). Concludes with roster
of musical works by A.W. Binder, as compiled by Lewis
Appleton. Also consult index for topics and names.
158
HERZOG, AVIGDOR. *The Intonation of the Pentateuch in the
Heder of Tunis.* Tel Aviv,Isr.:I.M.I., 1963; 16 pp., music.
Presentation and discussion of what author identifies as
"an extra-synagogal version" of a biblical chant pattern
from Tunis, which relates to folklore traditions as well
as folk music and liturgy. Avigdor Herzog is an Israeli
ethnomusicologist and a music educator.

159
HOLDE, ARTUR. *Jews in Music; From the Age of Enlightenment
to the Mid-Twentieth Century.* new enl. ed. prepared by
Irene Heskes. New York: Bloch, 1974; xiv, 366 pp. (orig. ed.
New York: Philosophical Press, 1959; 364 pp.)

Survey of modern developments in Jewish music over the
past two centuries, presented in the perspective of its
outstanding figures. Highlighted are notable and varied
achievements in liturgical and secular musical areas,
with consideration of many individuals: composers, conductors, cantors and other vocal artists, instrumental-
ists, scholars, educators, journalists, publishers and
organizational leaders. For his book, Artur Holde (1885-
1962) developed much of the materials which he had previously contributed as columnist to the German American
Jewish newspaper *Aufbau*. Additional texts in the new
edition include a preface by Irene Heskes which serves
as a brief biographical study of Holde and critique of
his work. Consult index for particular individuals and
subjects treated in this book.

160
IDELSOHN, ABRAHAM ZEBI. *The Distinctive Elements of Jewish
Folksong.* Hartford,Conn: M.T.N.A.,1926; 16pp.,illus.,music.

Separate publication of paper delivered by Abraham Zebi
Idelsohn (1882-1938) at the 1924 conference of the Music
Teachers National Association. Considered are modal elements such as Dorian, Aeolian, Harmonic Minor and an
altered Mixolydian. "If, by folksong, we understand
words and tunes of war and drink, of carnality and jazz,
of the bar-room underworld, then the Jews have no folksongs. Jewish folksong, like Jewish life, nestles in the
shadow of religion." (p.3)

161
IDELSOHN, ABRAHAM ZEBI. *Jewish Music In Its Historical Development.* repr. ed. Westport, Conn.:Greenwood Press, 1981;
xii, 535 pp., illus, music. (repr. pbk. ed. New York:Schock-
en Press, 1956 and 1967; xii, 535 pp., illus., music; repr.
ed. New York: Tudor Press, 1944 and 1948; xii, 535pp.,illus.
music; orig. ed. New York: Henry Holt, 1929; xii, 535 pp.,
illus., music.)

Remains "classic volume" on Jewish music, despite fact
that in fifty years since its original publication, many
scholars have gone beyond Idelsohn's studies in several
topical areas. This pioneer work by A.Z. Idelsohn (1882-
1938) is significant part of scholarly legacy left by
"father" of modern Jewish musicology. Book organized in
two sections: Part One (Chapters 1-16) treats broad area
of "The Song of the Synagogue," in an historical survey
and analysis of liturgical music of various traditions
from biblical era to 20th century. Part Two (Chapters
17-23) examines "Folksong," in terms of numerous forms,
styles and vernacular expressions, concluding with some
considerations of the Jewish modes themselves. All 23
chapters are topically headed as follows: 1. Historical
Survey of Religious and Secular Music in Israel and Its
Neighboring Countries Throughout Biblical and Post-Bib-

lical Ages up to the Destruction of the Second Temple;
2. Semitic-Oriental Song; 3. The Oldest Unrhythmical
Elements of Jewish Song. A: The Modes of the Bible — the
ta'amim (Musical Notation) of the Bible; 4. B: The
Modes of the Prayers; 5. Historical Survey of the Syna-
gogal Song After the Destruction of the Second Temple
Until the Rise of Islam; 6. Rise and Development of the
Precentor and the *Hazzan* from Ancient Times Until the
8th Century; 7. Rhythmical Song in the Oriental and Sephardic Synagogue; 8.Synagogue Song of the *Ashkenazim*;
9. Song of the Synagogue in Eastern Europe up to 18th
Century; 10. Introduction of Harmony and Polyphony into
Synagogue in Italy by Salomone Rossi; 11. Ashkenazic
Song of the Synagogue in 17th and 18th Centuries; 12.
Influence of Reform Movement on Synagogue Song in Be-
ginning of 19th Century; 13. Influence of Moderate Re-
form upon Synagogue Song During 19th Century in Central
and Western Europe; 14. *Hazzanim* and *Hazzanuth* in
Eastern Europe in 19th Century; 15. Synagogue Song in
United States of America; 16. Collections of and Liter-
ature on Synagogue Song; 17. Folksong of the Oriental
Jews; 18. Folksong of the *Ashkenazim*; 19. Hassidic
Song; 20. *Badkhonim* (Merry-Makers) and *Klezmorim*
(Music-Makers) — Song and Singers in Folk Style; 21.
Artistic Endeavors; 22. Jew in General Music; 23. Harmony. Thirty five sets of comparative melodic tables,
and informative chapter notes. Also consult fine index.
162

KANTER, KENNETH AARON. *The Jews on Tin Pan Alley; The
Jewish Contributions to American Popular Music. 1830-1940.*
New York:KTAV, 1982; xii, 226 pp., illus.
Popular-styled narrative includes background on many
notable song-writers, lyricists and publishers. Author
presents intriguing point of view regarding influences
of Jewish music and musicians upon developments in field
of American popular music. Facsimiles of sheet music
covers. Roster of song titles. Consult index for topics.
163

KATZ, ISRAEL J. *Judeo-Spanish Traditional Ballads from
Jerusalem; An Ethnomusicological Study.* vols. 1 and 2.
(Musicological Studies, vol. 23, nos. 1 and 2) Brooklyn,
N.Y.: Institute of Mediaeval Music, 1972; vol. 1 — xi,
205 pp., music; vol. 2 — xvii, 44 pp., music.
Scholarly consideration of Judeo-Spanish *Romancero*,
with particular attention to ballad tunes found during
investigations of folklore traditions in Israel, conducted by author from 1959 to 1961. Sources, texts,
thematic materials and background information. Volume 1
presents historical and musical contexts for materials,
and specific analysis of five particular ballads in collected versions. Appended are bibliography, roster of
published editions of songs and inventory of music examples assembled for this research study. Volume 2 gives
details for various forms of ballads, with locations and
individuals as sources for renditions of melodies. Also
index listing for complete study.

164

LACHMANN, ROBERT. *Jewish Cantillation and Song on the Isle of Djerba.* trans. from German by Clarissa Graves and H. Bentwich-Mayer. Jerusalem, Pal.: Hebrew Univ. Archives of Oriental Music, 1940; 115 pp., illus., music.

Posthumously published work of scholar Robert Lachmann (1892-1939) who had been associated with Department of Oriental Music of Prussian State Library in Berlin, before escaping nazis and settling in Jerusalem in 1935. His field was Arabic and Jewish music of the Near East, and this monograph outlines his studies in 1929 of folk music on the island off the Tunisian shores, Djerba, or "Isle of the Lotus-Eaters," as known in the *Odyssey*. In 20th century, island is home of Berbers and Tunisian Jews. Contents of publication include: introduction with overview of Jewish music of Near East and its component qualities; liturgical cantillation, for range of biblical chants and in analysis; festival songs, in melodic patterns and styles; women's songs, sung in Arabo-Hebrew vernacular; summary remarks with added music examples. For this 1940 edition, tribute foreword given by Judah Leon Magnes (1877-1948), and listing of Lachmann's 38 scholarly articles, a significant roster of studies accomplished in such a brief life-span.

165

LANDMAN, LEO. *The Cantor - An Historical Perspective; The Study of the Origin, Communal Position and Function of the Hazzan.* New York: C.T.I. of Yeshiva Univ., 1972; xv,192 pp.

Scholarly consideration of the traditional liturgical music leadership office of *Hazzan* (cantor) in terms of its historical development, special characteristics and qualifications, training and duties of office, and role in Jewish traditions, rituals and customs. Valuable as study of the cantorial position itself. Consult index for great variety of information and subjects covered.

166

LIPTZIN, SOL. *Eliakum Zunser; Poet of His People.* New York: Behrman House, 1950; 248 pp., illus., music.

Biography of Eliakum Zunser (1840-1913), Jewish minstrel and wedding bard (*badkhen*), writer of folk poetry and songs, in East European ghettos and after 1889 on the Lower East Side of New York City. Social and cultural background of period as well as information on its folk expressions. Vintage photographs. Melody lines with the texts and English translations for 12 Yiddish songs.

167

MARGOLIOUTH, MOSES. *Sacred Minstrelsy; A Lecture on Biblical and Post-Biblical Hebrew Music.* London,Eng.:Westheim, Macintosh and Hunt, 1863; vi,50pp., illus., music.

Discussion of musical references in Bible, especially of Temple and Levites services, with some consideration of development of early synagogue liturgical chants. Study by English rabbinical scholar Moses Margoliouth (fl.19th cent.). Music examples; several melody lines with piano accompaniment. Hebrew romanized.

168
MODDEL, PHILIP. *Joseph Achron.* Tel Aviv, Isr.: I.M.P.,
1966, 80 pp., illus.
Biographical sketch and roster of works by Joseph Achron
(1886-1943), who was associated with a group of Jewish
musicians active in St. Petersburg, Russia. He emigrated
to America after World War I. Included here are writings
by Achron on Jewish music subjects, and there is a foreword by bibliographer Alfred Sendrey (1884-1976).
169
MODDEL, PHILIP. *Max Helfman; A Biographical Sketch.*
Berkeley, Cal.: Magnes Museum, 1974; 90 pp., illus.
Brief biography of synagogue musician – composer, conductor, educator – Max Helfman (1901-1963), with roster
of works and tributes.
170
OESTERLEY, WILLIAM OSCAR EMIL. *The Psalms in the Jewish
Church.* London, Eng.: Skeffington and Son, 1910; x,
267 pp., illus., music.
Knowledgeable work for its time, reflecting serious interest and scholarly investigation of subject, referring
not only to musicological and historical sources but
also to rabbinical, Talmudic and other Judaic resources
for both Sephardic and Ashkenazic congregational traditions. W.O.E. Oesterley (1866-1950) covers in 12 chapters the topical areas of: vocal and instrumental music
among ancient Hebrews; backgrounds and qualities of Temple worship music and of the Psalms; psalmody in early
synagogue services and into more modern synagogue practices; Jewish exegesis of Psalms and usages in private
devotions. Concluding commentary on Psalm 91, an antiphonal celebration of security in God's protection:
"With long life will I satisfy him; and make him to be-
hold My Salvation." Consult index for topics treated.
171
RABINOVITCH, ISRAEL. *Of Jewish Music; Ancient and Modern.*
trans. from Yiddish by Abraham Moses Klein. Montreal, Can.:
Jewish Book Centre/C.J.C., 1952; 321 pp., illus., music.
Personalized but informative collection of essays on
various topics in Jewish music history, activities and
musicians, by Canadian Yiddish journalist Israel Rabin-
vitch (1894-1964). Materials in four sections: historical surveys of different forms of Jewish musical expression; considerations of modern developments in 19th and
20th centuries; Jewish music of continental America in
20th century, in terms of both secular and liturgical
creativity; reflections upon Holocaust musical legacy
and post-World War II music ideas. Consult index.
172
RAVINA, MENASHE. *Organum and the Samaritans.* trans. from
Hebrew by Alan Marbe. Tel Aviv,Isr.:I.M.I.,1963;62pp.,music.
Study of musical elements among dissident pre-rabbinic
Judaic sect, surviving remnants of which reside for most
part in Samaria area of Israel. Organum, a manner of
singing in parallel voices, is part of an ancient tradition, and is discussed here in terms of historical

music practices of Samaritan liturgy. Fine examples.

173
ROSENBLATT, SAMUEL. *Yossele Rosenblatt: The Story of His
Life as Told by His Son.* New York:Farrar, Straus and Young,
1954; ix, 371 pp., illus.
   Popularly styled, but informative, biography of the life
   and musical activities of Cantor Yossele (Joseph) Rosenblatt (1882-1933), whose voice and musical style made
   him one of the leading cantorial artists of the century.
   Cantor Rosenblatt served pulpits and performed Jewish
   liturgical selections and folksongs at public concerts.
   His voice was admired by Enrico Caruso (1873-1921), and
   Rosenblatt declined offers to perform in opera. Numerous
   old recordings preserve some of his vocal artistry. No
   index, but glossary of Jewish terms and discography.

174
ROSOLIO, DAVID. *Music In Israel 1948-1958.* Jerusalem,
Isr.: Ahva Press, 1958; 32 pp., illus., music.
   Summary of music activities, leading composers and edu-
   cational groups during first decade of State of Israel.

175
ROSOWSKY, SOLOMON. *The Cantillation of the Bible: The Five
Books of Moses.* New York: Reconstructionist Press, 1957;
xiv, 669 pp., illus., music.
   Technical study of the cantillations (*Trop*) of the
   Pentateuch (*Torah*) portion of the Bible, as chanted in
   recitation at Sabbath services by Jews of Lithuanian -
   East European Ashkenazic traditions. Scholar - liturgist
   Solomon Rosowsky (1878-1962) presents careful analysis
   of expressive melodic rendition of Holy Scriptures, considering tropal signs, motifs and patterns of performance, based upon his research in East Europe, America
   and Israel. Contents of volume: introductory background
   to cantillation; Part 1 - specific details and data for
   scholarly work; Part 2 - analysis of textual relationships and musical interpretations of tropal signs, or
   accents; and transcriptions of cantillation passages for
   specific verses. Appended materials include: notations,
   linguistics, source references and comparative tables.
   Ample music examples. Two indexes: subjects and names.
   Valuable achievement in this field.

176
ROTHMUELLER, ARON MARKO. *The Music of the Jews: An Historical Appreciation.* trans. from German by H.C. Stevens.
enl.rev.ed. South Brunswick, N.J.: Thomas Yoseloff, 1967;
320pp.,illus.,music.(repr.ed. New York:A.S. Barnes, 1960;
xv,254pp.,illus.,music; orig.ed. New York:Beechhurst,1954)
   Non-technical account of history and development of
   Jewish music by singer, composer and teacher Aron Marko
   Rothmueller. Contents: 27 topical chapters treating liturgical and secular Jewish music, folk and art, as well
   as scholarly and organizational activities. Materials
   arranged into three parts: 1. Earliest times to destruction of Second Temple; 2. Synagogal service and Jewish
   music from 1st to 20th century; and 3 - New Jewish music
   in 19th and 20th centuries. Appendix of "Obscure Expres-

sions Used in the Psalms." Consult index for subjects.
Musical examples. Hebrew and Yiddish texts romanized.
177

RUBIN, RUTH. *Voices of a People; The Story of Yiddish Folksong.* enl. ed. New York: McGraw-Hill, 1973; 558 pp., illus., music. (orig. ed. New York: A.S. Barnes, 1963; 496 pp., illus.)

Lovely collection of poetic lyrics of 150 Yiddish folksongs with background information, compiled, translated
and annotated by folksinger and ethnomusicologist Ruth
Rubin. With a prologue on the "ancestry of Yiddish folksong," materials are arranged and discussed in 17 topical sections: cradle; children's world; love and courtship; marriage; customs and beliefs; merriment; dances;
history and topics; Hassidic melody; literary texts;
poverty, toil and struggle; out of shadows; to America;
to Zion; Soviet Yiddish folksong; struggle to survive -
Holocaust; and, folksong - a universal language. Additional matter includes map of Pale of Jewish settlement in Eastern Europe and linguistic guides. Enlarged
edition (1973) has added melody lines with texts for 54
of folksongs discussed in book. Song roster and index.
178

SALESKI, GDAL. *Famous Musicians of Jewish Origin.* enl.ed.
New York:Bloch, 1949; xvi,716pp.,illus. (orig.ed. *Famous Musicians of a Wandering Race.* New York: Bloch, 1927; xiv, 463pp.,illus.)

Roster of brief biographical sketches - most also with
photographs - for 350 musicians of Jewish lineage. Included are composers, conductors, violinists, cellists,
pianists, singers, educators, scholars, ensembles and
organizations. Compiler Gdal Saleski (1888-1966), composer and cellist, presents impressive roster as his
"answer to anti-semitism." There are surprises and some
inaccuracies - for example, Max Bruch was not Jewish -
and specific criteria for inclusions in various rosters
are unclear. No index. Photographs interesting.
179

SAMINSKY, LAZARE. *Music of the Ghetto and Bible.* repr.
ed. New York: AMS Press, 1980; vii, 261 pp., illus., music.
(orig. ed. New York: Bloch,1934; vii, 261pp.,illus.,music.)

Lazare Saminsky (1882-1959), music director of Temple
Emanu-El in New York City from 1924 to his death, was
composer and collector-arranger of Jewish music. Before
emigrating to America in 1920, he was active among other
Jewish musicians in Russia, collecting and performing
Jewish folksongs of East Europe. Volume is compilation
of Saminsky's writings, arranged by author into seven
topical parts: 1. Song of Zion in Exile (introductory
essay); 2. Hebrew Music - Past and Present (survey of
Jewish music history with consideration of synagogue
music forms, Hassidic melodies, and of Jewish musical
activities early in century by his colleagues in Moscow
and St. Petersburg);3. Hebraic and Judaic Share in Tonal
Art (superiority, according to Saminsky, of Hebrew elements and "inauthenticity" of Yiddish expressions); The

Jews in Music: Problems and Personalities (composers of
Jewish lineage and their works); 5. Synagogue: East and
West (diverse liturgical expressions in Asia, Near East,
Europe and America); 6. Biblical Melody (Jewish cantil-
lation and relationship to early Christian chant); 7.
Jewish Folksong (essentially statement of Saminsky's
position in long-standing polemic with composer, collector-arranger, publisher, journalist Joel Engel (1868-
1927) regarding Hebraic vs. Diaspora-Judaic music). Joel
Engel endorsed Yiddish elements, yet emigrated to Tel
Aviv; Saminsky advocated (p.77) "two repositories of our
hope - synagogue and Land of Israel" and then settled in
New York. Interesting materials here, including citation
of works of Cornill and Ewen on biblical music. Consult
index for subjects treated.

180

SAMINSKY, LAZARE. *Music of Our Day; Essentials and Prophe-*
cies. New York: Crowell, 1932; 315 pp., illus., music.
　　Collected writings by composer-arranger, conductor and
　　music collector Lazare Saminsky (1882-1959). Topics in-
　　clude: American-Jewish composers and their works (Cop-
　　land, Jacobi, BLitzstein, Bloch, etc.); musical ideas of
　　Arnold Schoenberg (1874-1951); Russian-Jewish musicians
　　and their creativity; music of Russian Orient - Georgian
　　Jewish, Caucassian and Armenian.

181

SCHALIT, MICHAEL. *Heinrich Schalit; The Man and His Music.*
Livermore, Cal.: Schalit, 1979; x, 116 pp., illus.
　　Brief biographical summary of life and work of Jewish
　　liturgical music composer Heinrich Schalit (1886-1976).
　　Additional tribute remarks. Listing of all compositions.

182

SECUNDA, VICTORIA. *Bei Mir Bist Du Schoen; Life of Shalom*
Secunda. Weston,Conn.:Magic Circle Press,1982;271pp.,illus.
　　Biography of Shalom Secunda (1894-1974), composer and
　　arranger of music for Yiddish theatricals and for the
　　synagogue services, music director and choral conductor
　　for Jewish organizations and congregations, associated
　　on recordings and in concerts with opera star and cantor
　　Richard Tucker (1914-1975). Information on Yiddish stage
　　musicals from 1920 to more recent times. Secunda wrote a
　　Yiddish song which he sold for a few dollars and only
　　several years later watched it become an international
　　popular favorite. After years of litigation, financial
　　settlement was made. Secunda wrote very many tunes, but
　　never repeated the success of "Bei Mir Bist Du Schoen."

183

SENDREY, ALFRED. *Music In Ancient Israel.* New York:Philo-
sophical Library, 1969; 674 pp., illus., music.
　　Compiler of meritorious *Bibliography of Jewish Music*
　　(New York: Columbia Univ. Press, 1951) Alfred Sendrey
　　(1884-1976) presents here a formidable apparatus of
　　materials arranged into twelve sections, with epilogue,
　　extensive notes, lengthy bibliography, listings of bib-
　　lical and rabbinical references. Though essentially in-
　　corporating scholarly works to 1950, volume nevertheless

constitutes valuable source literature on music for
biblical era and post-biblical Talmudic period (to 5th-
6th centuries). Topical sections: 1. Music of earlier
and of neighboring civilizations; 2. Bible and other
historical sources of Jewish music; 3. Systematic survey
of biblical references to music; 4. Book of Psalms; 5.
Singing in ancient Israel (forms, styles, singers); 6.
Musical instruments; 7. Orchestra (ensemble music); 8.
Dance (forms, styles, dancers); 9. Music instruction;
10. Supernatural power of music; 11. Women in music of
ancient Israel; and, 12. Music organizations. Scriptural
citations include Old and New Testaments and Apocryphal
writings. Rabbinic literature sources cover *Midrash,
Mishnah, Talmud* and other tracts and treatises of that
epoch. Extensive illustrations. Monumental endeavor by
Sendrey to incorporate vast compendium of published
studies, some contradictory to each other, along with
his own commentaries and hypotheses. More anthology than
analytical work, volume is excellent research tool. Consult comprehensive index.

184

SENDREY, ALFRED. *The Music of the Jews in the Diaspora (Up
to 1800): A Contribution to the Social and Cultural History
of the Jews.* Cranbury, N.J.: Thomas Yoseloff/A.S.Barnes,
1970; 483 pp., illus., music.

Narrative history by bibliographer Alfred Sendrey (1884-
1976) of Jewish music as religious and secular communal
cultural expression from beginning of Diaspora until
rise of modern times. Formidable array gathered of
scholarly studies in musical and Judaic history, presented in sociological context, and treating various
geographical areas and different traditions as developed
and practiced over centuries. Consideration of rich texture of Jewish music of that epoch, much of which large-
ly undocumented by general music histories. Discussion
of such topics as: music instruments, singing, dancing -
styles and performers; Jewish music in French and Spanish regions and in Arabic domains; music of *Ashkenazim*
of Central Europe; creation of synagogue liturgy and
hymnology, and development of *Hazzan* and cantorial
office; Jewish art music and folksong of various Ghetto
communities throughout Europe; rise of Hassidic music.
Ample illustrations and music examples. Notes and bibliography. Consult detailed table of contents and extensive index. Valuable resource work.

185

SENDREY, ALFRED. *Music in the Social and Religious Life of
Antiquity.* Cranbury, N.J.: Farleigh Dickinson Univ. Press,
1974; 489 pp., illus.

Bibliographer and musicologist Alfred Sendrey (1884-
1976) was musician and scholar in Europe before emigrating to America in 1940, where he resumed his career.
Volume intended as companion work to his *Music in Ancient Israel* (New York: Philosophical Press, 1969), and
is another impressive reservoir of source materials, now
treating significant sociological, as well as religious,

role of music in antiquity. Consideration of Judaeans in
context of musical influences of other peoples in Asia
Minor and Mediterranean areas in ancient times, through
Greek and Roman eras. Scholarly information gathered by
Sendrey on music expression as social phenomenon from
earliest Judaean history to Temple era and development
of synagogal communal life. Among topics treated: early
Jewish sacred and secular music practices; singing and
and liturgy; Psalms; musical instruments and dance; and,
music of various Judaic sects. Extensive bibliography.
No music analysis. Consult comprehensive index.

186
SENDREY, ALFRED and MILDRED NORTON. *David's Harp; The*
Story of Music in Biblical Times. New York: New American
Library, 1964; 288 pp., illus.
Popularized treatment, in 25 topical chapters, by Alfred
Sendrey (1884-1976), scholar and bibliographer, with
writer Mildred Norton of music in Bible from Patriarchs
(Abraham, Isaac and Jacob) through settlements of tribes
in Cana'an , era of Prophets and Kings, Temple epoch,
Babylonian exile, Second Commonwealth and defeat by Ro-
mans in 70 C.E. Consideration of such topics as: women
in music; music and "superstitions;" dance; influences
of Greek and Roman musical cultures; and, concluding
with Chapter 25 — "The Hebrew Psalms in Christian Liturgy." Presentation of some interesting information in
light manner. Detailed table of contents. No index.

187
SLOBIN, MARK. *A Survey of Early Jewish-American Sheet Mu-*
sic (1898-1921). (Working Papers in Yiddish and East European Jewish Studies, 17) New York: YIVO, 1976; 38pp., music.
Preliminary study of aspects of Yiddish popular song,
as published in sheet music and sold to East European
Jewish immigrants settled on the Lower East Side of New
York City, early in this century. Materials reflective
of years to end of World War I, and of tenement life,
with its economic and social struggles. Analysis of some
particular songs, with texts and melody lines given.

188
SLOBIN, MARK. *Tenement Songs; The Popular Music of the*
Jewish Immigrants. (Music in American Life Series, 21)
Urbana, Ill.:Illinois Univ.Press, 1982; 213pp.,illus.,music.
Ethnological treatment, with historical overview, of
Yiddish folksong and popular song of the immigrant Jews
who came to America from Eastern Europe around turn of
the century, settling generally on the Lower East Side
of New York City. Study of developing styles and modes
of Yiddish mass-music here, as products of theatricals
and reflections of social movements. Selection of some
representative songs, with translation of texts, discussed in terms of era, milieu and special experiences.
Particular iconography of sheet music highlighted with
facsimiles of 30 covers. Aspects of traditional roots of
of Jewish music explored, as well as subsequent creative
influences to and from general American music scene over
later decades. Consult index for many subjects covered.

189
SMOIRA-ROLL, MICHAL. *Folk Song in Israel: An Analysis Attempted.* Tel Aviv, Isr.:I.M.I., 1963; 60 pp., illus.,music.
  Analytical treatment of varied forms and distinctive
  styles of folksong creativity, reflecting modern Zionist
  movement and rise of State of Israel. Music placed in
  context of recent Jewish history and cultural affairs.
190
SOLTES, AVRAHAM. *Off the Willows: The Rebirth of Modern Jewish Music.* New York: Bloch, 1970; 311 pp.
  Collected writings — essays, scripts and sermonettes —
  treating wide variety of topics related to Jewish music
  and musicians of 20th century in Europe, America and
  Israel. Work of rabbi and community leader Avraham
  Soltes (1917-1983). Consult table of contents.
191
STAINER, JOHN. *Music of the Bible: With Some Account of the Development of Modern Musical Instruments from Ancient Times.* FRANCIS W. GALPIN, ed. repr.ed. New York:Da Capo Press, 1970; xii,230pp., illus.,music. (enl.rev.ed. by F.W. GALPIN — London,Eng.:Novello, Ewen, 1914; orig.ed. by JOHN STAINER — London,Eng.:Novello, 1879; 204pp.,illus.,music.)
  A "classic" of its genre, this work first appeared as a
  collection of essays for the English journal *The Bible
  Educator*. John Stainer (1840-1901) was a 19th century
  musicologist who specialized in early music history.
  Francis W. Galpin (1858-1945) added illustrations and
  supplementary notes to shape this widely known edition
  of the book. Introduction covers such topics as "Proba-
  ble Sources of Ancient Hebrew Music." Parts i, ii and
  iii treat musical instruments, while Part iv is devoted
  to vocal music, with consideration of cantillation accent signs and ancient chants. Appendices include: classifications of instruments; Hebrew, Greek and Latin
  names of instruments; biblical passages which mention
  instruments; and, roster of Hebrew cantillation accents.
  Galpin appended a brief essay on "The *Shophar* in the
  Synagogue," pp. 224-26, in which he corrects Carl Engel
  (1818-1882) who had misplaced the terms *Tekiah* and
  Teruah Shebarim for *Shophar* (*Shofar*) sounds. Yet,
  Galpin also notes the debt of information which both he
  and Stainer owe to the work of Engel. In some editions,
  there is frontispiece "Sounding the *Shophar*." Book is
  extraordinary work to this day, and may be treated as a
  companion to the publications of Curt Sachs (1881-1959)
  on musical instruments and music history. Table of contents serves as guide to specific materials treated.
  More than 100 excellent illustrations.
192
STOLNITZ, NATHAN. *Music in Jewish Life.* Toronto, Can.: Stolnitz/C.J.C., 1957; 328 pp., illus.
  Substantially in Yiddish, but with 62 pages of English
  text materials treating in brief essays such topics as:
  music in ritual; musical "bridge" between Israel and
  Diaspora; cantorial music in United States and Canada.

193
TARG, MAX. *The AMLI Story; A Dream Come True.* Evanston,
Ill.: Schori Press, 1976; xii, 89 pp., illus.
　　Tribute volume of historical background, achievements
　　and current activities of a Jewish music organization
　　called "AMLI" – Americans for a Music Library in Israel.
　　Since 1948, it has supplied music instruments to school
　　children in Israel, supported public music libraries in
　　Tel Aviv, Haifa and Jerusalem, established a music con-
　　servatory in Beersheba, and shaped as well as supported
　　the Haifa Music Museum and AMLI Library. Organization
　　was founded by American businessman Max Targ, who has
　　guided its work over the years.

194
TOPEL, JOSEPH. *Some Aspects of Hebrew Cantillation in Rabbinic and Masoretic Literature.* Cincinnati: H.U.C.-J.I.R.
Press, 1962; viii, 159 pp., illus., music.
　　Scholarly study of Jewish literature – various important
　　scriptural commentaries and rabbinical tracts – which
　　refer to liturgical chant and biblical musical recita-
　　tion. Solid background information demonstrating strong
　　connections between music expression and traditional
　　textual interpretations. Consult index.

195
WAGNER, RICHARD. *Judaism in Music.* ed. and trans. from
German by Edwin Evans. London, Eng.: Reeves, 1910; xv,95 pp.
　　English translation, with commentary notes and intro-
　　duction, of infamous essay *"Das Judenthem in Der Musik"*
　　by Richard Wagner (1813-1883). For this edition, part 1
　　is the text which orginally appeared in print in 1850,
　　and presented negative generalizations, along with spe-
　　cific criticisms of Felix Mendelssohn (1809-1847) and
　　Giacomo Meyerbeer (1791-1864); part 2 adds Wagner's own
　　"supplement" for 1869 edition of tract, which amplifies
　　extent of hostility toward Jewish musicians and musical
　　creativity. Concluding remark: "Whether the decadence of
　　our culture can be prevented by forcible expulsion of
　　foreign elements of pernicious character I cannot say;
　　as powers for this purpose are requisite, of the exist-
　　ence of which I am not aware." (p.93) Questions may be
　　raised about motivations of editor-translator and of
　　publication of this work in 1910 in England. During the
　　following decades, many nazi-inspired volumes appeared
　　which attacked and listed for banning, banishment, or
　　worse, Jews in music. Most of those books cited this
　　essay by Wagner as cultural and artistic justification.

196
WEISSER, ALBERT. *The Modern Renaissance of Jewish Music;
Events and Figures, Eastern Europe and America.* repr. ed.
New York: DaCapo Press, 1983; 175 pp., illus., music. (orig.
ed. New York: Bloch, 1954; 175 pp., illus., music.)
　　Musician, educator and scholar Albert Weisser (1918-
　　1982) affords good source of information on seminal in-
　　fluences of leading figures in Jewish music developments
　　early in this century. Part 1: backgrounds, formation
　　and "pioneer" achievements of St. Petersburg Society for

Jewish Folk Music, and its sister group in Moscow, which from 1908 to 1918 flourished in Russia. Part 2: studies of lives and works of six of those early leaders: Joseph Achron (1886-1943), Joel Engel (1868-1927), Michael Gniessin (1883-1957), Alexander Krein (1883-1951), Moses Milner (1886-1953), and Lazare Saminsky (1882-1959). Part 3: some considerations of subsequent (post World War I) developments in America (to 1954). Consult index.
197

WELLHAUSEN, JULIUS. *The Book of Psalms - A New English Translation With Explanatory Notes; And, an Appendix on the Music of the Ancient Hebrews.* trans. from German by Horace Howard Furness (Psalms), John Taylor (Notes) and J.A. Paterson (Appendix). New York: Dodd, Mead, 1898; xii, 237 pp., illus., music.

Scholar and liturgist Julius Wellhausen (1844-1918) discusses each of Psalms, in extensive section of notes, with reflections on their music (pp. 162-216). See appended section "Music of the Ancient Hebrews," (pp. 217-34). In his consideration of *Shofar*, Wellhausen cites scholarship of Cyrus Adler (1863-1940). Excellent collection of illustrations.
198

WERNER, ERIC. *From Generation to Generation; Studies in Jewish Musical Tradition.* New York: A.C.C./H.U.C.-J.I.R., 1968; vii,168pp., illus., music.

Collection of various lectures and writings by scholar and educator Eric Werner, issued in his honor by colleagues in Jewish music and former students (American Conference of Cantors and School of Sacred Music at H.U.C.-J.I.R.). Following range of essay topics presented: Music in the Bible; Musical Instruments in the Bible; Music of Post-Biblical Judaism; Role of Tradition in the Music of the Synagogue; Function of Synagogue Music Today; Ideas and Practices of Liturgical Music; Practical Applications of Jewish Musical Research; Rise and Fall of American Synagogue Music; Salomon Sulzer - Statesman and Pioneer; and, Abraham Zebi Idelsohn - In Memoriam. Excellent compilation of materials. No index.
199

WERNER, ERIC. *Hebrew Music.* (Anthology of Music Series: Collection of Complete Musical Examples Illustrating the History of Music) Cologne, W.Ger.:Arno Volk/London, Eng.: Oxford Univ. Press, 1961; 66 pp., music.

Morphological description of certain elements of Hebrew song and chant by scholar and educator Eric Werner. Consideration of historical continuity and authenticity, structures, notations and performance practices for such topics as: hymns, Psalm tunes, scriptural cantillations and prayer chants. Traditional music examined for Jewish groups of Yemenites, Babylonians, French-Carpentras, Spaniolics (*Sephardim*) and Germanics (*Ashkenazim*). Section of 75 melody lines of prayer tunes, doxologies, melismatic melodies, minstrel and cantorial music, wordless tunes (*Nigunim*) of *Hassidim* (Pietists) and old Hebrew songs. Excellent tables and music examples. With bibliographic roster. Good study resource.

200
WERNER, ERIC. *The Sacred Bridge; The Interdependence of*
Liturgy and Music in Synagogue and Church During the First
Millennium. repr. ed. New York: Da Capo Press, 1979; xx,
618 pp., illus., music. (orig. ed. London, Eng.: Dennis Dob-
son/New York: Columbia Univ. Press, 1959; xx, 618 pp.,
illus., music.)

    Comparative study of music of Jewish and Christian
liturgies by scholar Eric Werner, examining this interdependence up to 10th century. Considered are prayer
texts, orders of services, modality, psalmody, hymnology
and other aspects of devotional expression. Two sections
of 18 topical chapters. Part One: Historic-Liturgical --
1. Jewish Liturgy at the Time of Primitive Christianity;
2. Liturgical and Musical Tracts of the Earliest Christian Community; 3. Scriptural Lesson and its Liturgical
Significance; 4. Musical Tradition of Lessons and Cognate Liturgical Forms; 5. Psalmodic Forms and Their Evolution; 6. Semi-psalmodic and Melismatic Forms in the
Liturgies of Church and Synagogue; 7. Hymns and Cognate
Forms; 8. Liturgical Acclamations; 9. Doxology in Synagogue and Church; 10. Aesthetic and Ethical Evaluation
of Music in Synagogue and Church. Part Two: Musical Comparisons and Studies -- 1. Conflict Between Hellenism
and Judaism in the Music of the Early Christian Church;
2. Origin of the Eight Modes of Music (Octoechos); 3.
Ecphonetic Notation in Judaism and Christianity; 4. Formulas and Cadences of Lesson and Oration; 5. Plain Psalmody; Its Formulas and Intervals; 6. Ornate Psalmody and
Cognate Forms; 7. Music of the Hymnic Forms; 8. Results,
Outlooks, Perspectives. With introductory remarks, glossary of terms and list of scriptural references. Over
200 music illustrations. Much of materials here based
upon studies and published articles by Werner to 1950,
when manuscript for this volume was completed. A brief
foreword by Curt Sachs (1881-1959) links up work of A.Z.
Idelsohn (1882-1938) with scholarship of Eric Werner.
Consult extensive index. Vast compendium of materials
and significant resource in comparative music liturgy.

201
WERNER, ERIC. *The Sacred Bridge; Liturgical Parallels in*
Synagogue and Church. repr.ed. New York: Schocken Books,
1970; xviii, 364 pp.

    Composed of Part One - 10 topical chapters - of original
publication *The Sacred Bridge* (Columbia Univ. Press,
1959) by scholar and educator Eric Werner. Roots and
interdependencies of liturgies of Synagogue and Church
are studied, with attention to such subject areas as:
scriptural cantillation; liturgical chants, modes, forms
and styles; psalmody and hymnology; doxologies; calendar
year of services and liturgical rites. Glossary of terms
and list of scriptural references. Chapter notes and
prefatory materials. Consult substantial index. Valuable
study in comparative liturgical history.

202

WERNER, ERIC. *Three Ages of Musical Thought; Essays on Ethics and Aesthetics.* (Da Capo Music Reprint Series) New York: Da Capo Press, 1981; xi, 372 pp., illus., music.

    With new brief preface by Eric Werner, collection of 17 of his articles previously published in various types of journals from 1941 to 1965. (Note: These articles are listed and annotated separately in this bibliography.) Reprint titles: "The Common Ground in the Chant of Church and Synagogue" (*Musica Sacra*, Rome, 1952); "The Origin of Psalmody" (*H.U.C. Annual*, vol.25, 1954); "The Oldest Sources of Octave and Octoechos" (*Acta Musicologica*, vol.20, 1948); "The Conflict Between Hellenism and Judaism in the Music of the Early Christian Church" (*H.U.C. Annual*, vol.20, 1947); "'If I Speak in the Tongues of Men...' St. Paul's Attitude to Music" (*Journal of A.M.S.*, vol.13, 1960); "Musical Aspects of the Dead Sea Scrolls" (*Musical Quarterly*, vol.43, 1957); "The Philosophy and Theory of Music in Judaeo-Arabic Literature" (*H.U.C. Annual*, vol.16, 1941); "Greek Ideas on Music in Judaeo-Arabic Literature" (*Commonwealth of Music*, 1965); "The Psalmodic Formula *Neannoe* and Its Origin" (*Musical Quarterly*, vol.28, 1942); "Manuscripts of Jewish Music in the Eduard Birnbaum Collection of the Hebrew Union College Library" (*H.U.C. Annual*, vol.18, 1944); "The Role of Tradition in the Music of the Synagogue" (*Judaism*, vol.13, 1964); "The Mathematical Foundation of *Ars Nova*" (H.U.C. Annual, vol.17, 1942/43); "The Last Pythagorean Musician: Johannes Kepler" (*Aspects of Medieval and Renaissance Music*, 1966); "Two Obscure Sources of Reuchlin's *'De Accentibus...Linguae Hebraicae'*" (*Historia Judaica*, vol.16, 1954); "New Light on the Family of Felix Mendelssohn" (*H.U.C. Annual*, vol. 26, 1955); "The Family Letters of Felix Mendelssohn Bartholdy" (*Bulletin of N.Y.P.L.*, vol.65, 1960); "Mendelssohn's Fame and Tragedy" (*Reconstructionist*, vol.25, 1959/60). Valuable compilation of scholarly works available in one volume. No index.

203

WERNER, ERIC. *A Voice Still Heard...The Sacred Songs of the Ashkenazic Jews.* (Leo Baeck Institute Series) Univ. Park, Penn.:Penn. State Univ. Press, 1976; xiii, 350 pp., illus., music.

    Impressive scholarly study by Eric Werner of *Minhag Ashkenaz*, Ashkenazic liturgical traditions, dating from early Rhine Valley Jewish settlements during Roman Era. Ashkenazic customs and culture developed, grew and then spread out geographically throughout Europe over the centuries, despite social, political, religious and economic vicissitudes, flourishing until eve of Holocaust annihilation. Werner presents introductory essays on history and traditions, followed by analysis of four groupings of sacred music: *Missinai* tunes (holy melodies); special prayer chant modes; scriptural cantillation motifs; and *Piyyutim* (old poetic hymnology).

Among musical materials considered are selections for
calendar year of observances, holidays and rituals, for
Kol Nidrei. *Ma'oz Tsur*, tunes of *Seder* (Passover
feast) and Sabbath *Z'miroth* (table songs), as well as
cantorial artistry. Text illustrated with comparative
tables and music examples. Additional extensive section
of music. Detailed notes for each of 13 topical chapters
and glossary of terms. Indexes. Excellent resource.

204
WILEY, LULU RUMSEY. *Bible Music.* New York: Paebar Press,
1945; xv,218pp., illus.,music.

Survey in 13 topically headed chapters, treating such
subjects as: references in Bible to music; biblical
music instruments and musicians; examples of dancing and
singing of biblical period; psalms and their musical
terms; and, women in Bible music. Very general work.

205
WOHLBERG, MAX. *The Music of the Synagogue.* New York: J.M.
C., 1948; 23 pp., music.

Informative monograph by cantor, educator and writer Max
Wohlberg. Survey of varied styles and forms of synagogue
music from biblical times and Temple era to development
of synagogal liturgy. Consideration of cantillations,
prayer chant motifs, sacred melodies and hymns of services, role of *Hazzan* (cantor) and some more recent
developments (to 1948). Good music examples.

3.
Books and Monographs with Information on Jewish Music

A. Collections of Essays on Music by Various Authors

206

ADLER, ISRAEL and BATHJA BAYER, eds. *Proceedings of the 10th International Congress of Music Libraries of IAML/UNES-CO.* (*Fontes Artis Musicae*,Special Edition,vol.22,nos.1/2) Kassel, W.Ger.:Baerenreiter, 1975; 90pp., illus., music.
  Collected abstracts and reports of sessions, with summaries of discussions, details of concerts and exhibits for conference held at Hebrew University in Jerusalem, Aug. 18-24, 1974. Attention also to reports of working committees of IAML. Texts in English, French and German. Special summaries of presentations on music in Israel, including considerations of contemporary composers, scholarly and pedagogical activities, and descriptions of major music traditions of land - Judaism, Islam and Christianity. Music programs included chamber works, choral ensembles, liturgical and folkmusic performances, as well as dramatic opera "Moses and Aaron" by Arnold Schoenberg (1874-1951). Exhibition materials were arranged by Jewish National and University Library and by National Sound Archives of Israel.

207

AVNI, TZVI, EMANUEL AMIRAN and AMI MAAYANI, eds. *Joachim Stutchewsky; On His 85th Birthday.* Tel Aviv, Isr.: AMLI Central Music Library/OR-TAV, 1975; 110pp., illus., music.
  Biographical tribute to violoncellist, music educator and composer Joachim Stutchewsky (1891-1982). Editors have selected and arranged variety of materials, which highlight his many music activities and artistic contributions to musical life in Israel, in Europe where he was born and studied, and in America where he visited to perform and teach. Roster of works and photographs.

208
BLOCH, SUZANNE and IRENE HESKES, eds. *Ernest Bloch: Cre-*
ative Spirit. New York:J.M.C.,1976;xiv,148pp.,illus.,music.
Collection of articles by various authors, treating life
and work of Ernest Bloch (1880-1959). Prefatory essays
by Suzanne Bloch and Irene Heskes. Part One (10 brief
studies) - 1. "Ernest Bloch: A Biography" by Alex Cohen
and Suzanne Bloch, pp. 3-8; 2. "Correspondence: An Ex-
change Between Bloch and Koussevitzky on *Schelomo*",
pp. 9-10; 3. "My Sacred Service" by Ernest Bloch, pp.11-
16; 4. "Two Review Articles on Bloch" by Ernest Newman,
pp. 17-19; 5. "On Ernest Bloch" by Jacob Epstein, p. 20;
6. "A Great Composer at 75" by Olin Downes, pp. 21-23;
7. "Ernest Bloch as Teacher" by Isadore Freed, pp.24-25;
8. "The Story of a Sculpture" by Suzanne Bloch and Ivan
Bloch, pp. 26-28; 9. "A Composer's Vision: Photography
by Ernest Bloch" by Eric Johnson, pp. 29-34; 10. "Bloch
and the Library of Congress" by Carl Engel, pp. 35-36;
Part Two - "Program Notes for Bloch's Compositions (45
Works)" by Suzanne Bloch, pp. 39-103. Part Three - "Discography: Ernest Bloch" by Gary P. Letherer, pp. 107-16;
"Selected Bibliography" by Suzanne Bloch, pp. 117-20;
"Catalogue of Ernest Bloch's Works Listed by the Ernest
Bloch Society," pp. 121-34. Part Four - "How To Use This
Resource Publication" by Irene Heskes, pp. 137-46.
209
BROWN, MALCOLM HAMRICK, ed. *Musorgsky: In Memoriam 1881-*
1981. (Russian Music Studies, 3) Ann Arbor, Mich,: UMI Research Press, 1982; vi, 337 pp., illus., music.
Collection of various studies on life and work of Modest
Petrovich Musorgsky (1839-1881). See "Musorgsky's Interest in Judaica" by Boris Schwarz, pp. 85-94, which discusses several of the composer's works - two songs, two
choral selections, the piano suite "Pictures at an Exhibition" and the biblical scene "Joshua" - where music
motifs of Jewish origin may be discerned. Author particularly cites the inclusion in "Joshua" of a Jewish liturgical theme that Musorgsky heard chanted by some of
his neighbors during *Sukkot* (Tabernacles) holiday.
A Hassidic tune (*Nigun*) was developed for a choral
selection. While on musical tour of Southern Russia in
1879, Musorgsky appears to have attended synagogue services twice in Odessa, noting cantorial and male choir
chants. At that time, the composer also heard some Jewish folksongs during a boat trip. Interesting study.
210
COHEN, JUDITH, ed. *Proceedings of the World Congress on*
Jewish Music, Jerusalem 1978. Jerusalem, Isr.: W.J.C. and
Israel Ministry of Education and Culture,1982; 318pp.,illus.
Publication of abstracts and summaries in English and
Hebrew of 30 lecture papers and several panel discussion
sessions presented at Congress held in Israel July 31 -
Aug. 4, 1978 at Hebrew University. Participating were
musicologists, composers, performers and educators from
many countries. Topics treated Jewish liturgical and se-
cular music - scope of expressions, styles and forms,

traditions and customs, old music and newer creation,
issues of preservation and of performance qualities.
There also were 8 special concert programs as detailed.

211
HESKES, IRENE, ed. *A.W.Binder; His Life and Work.* New
York: J.M.C., 1965; 63pp., illus.
 Publication honoring Abraham Wolf Binder (1895-1966) on
 occasion of his 70th birthday. Biographical sketch by
 Irene Heskes, along with collection of numerous brief
 tribute messages from notable musicians and communal
 leaders. Roster of works and photographs.

212
HESKES, IRENE, ed. *The Cantorial Art.* New York: J.M.C.,
1966; vi, 122 pp.
 Collection of articles treating aspects of cantorial
 music. "Introduction" (essay on historical background
 of cantor) by Irene Heskes, pp.i-iv. Section One (five
 brief articles) - 1. "The Cantor in the Modern Synagogue" by Avraham Soltes, pp.1-10; 2. "The Cantorate:
 Pages from its History" by Max Wohlberg, pp.11-33; 3.
 "The Philosophy of Improvisation" by Joseph Yasser, pp.
 35-52; 4. "A Rebirth of Biblical Chant" by A.W. Binder,
 pp.53-57; 5. "Idelsohn and Ephros: A Continuity in Music
 Collection" by Irene Heskes, pp.59-67. Section Two -
 Descriptive Essays on Three Schools of Cantorial Music:
 1. "Cantorial Training Inst. of Yeshiva Univ." by Karl
 Adler and Macy Nulman, pp.71-74; 2. "Cantors' Inst. of
 Jewish Theol. Sem. of Amer." by Hugo Weisgall, pp.75-79;
 3. "School of Sacred Music of HUC-JIR" by Paul Steinberg, pp.81-88. Section Three - Bibliographic Materials:
 1. "Selective Bibliography of Modern Synagogue Literature" by Arthur Wolfson, pp.91-107; 2. "Selective List
 of Cantorial Recordings" by Irene Heskes, pp.109-12; 3.
 "Sample Programs" by Irene Heskes, pp.115-22.

213
**HESKES, IRENE, ed. *Jewish Music Programs and How to Com-
mission New Works.*** New York: J.M.C., 1978; 142 pp.
 Included with program listings and other resource in-
 formation, collected and reprinted here are 8 brief
 articles on aspects of Jewish music creativity. 1. "The
 Cultural and Creative Approach to Jewish Survival" by
 Joachim Prinz, p.107; 2. "Commission a Jewish Musical
 Work" by Emanuel Green, pp.108-9; 3. "On Jewishness in
 Music" by Joseph Yasser (1893-1981), pp.110-11; 4. "New
 Trends in Synagogue Music" by A.W. Binder (1895-1966),
 pp.112-13; 5. "The Qualities of Jewish Music" by Isadore
 Freed (1900-1960), pp.114-15; 6. "Reflections of a Com-
 poser" by Abraham Ellstein (1907-1963), p.116; 7. "Music
 for the Jewish Dance" by Corinne Chochem, pp.117-9; and,
 8."My Experiences in Jewish Music" by Mario Castelnuovo-
 Tedesco (1895-1968). Also, see "What are the Leadership
 Responsibilities in This Field of Jewish Music" by Irene
 Heskes, pp. 137-41. No index.

214
**HESKES, IRENE and ARTHUR WOLFSON, eds. *The Historic Con-
tribution of Russian Jewry to Jewish Music.*** New York: J.M.

C.. 1967; vi, 80 pp., illus., music.
   Collection of articles and resources related to Jewish
   music developments in Eastern Europe early in this century. Prefatory materials by editors, pp.i-vi; "The Contribution of East European Jewry to the Music of ·the
   Synagogue" by Max Wohlberg, pp.1-6; "The Yiddish Folksong: Its Importance to Jewish Music" by Samuel Bugatch,
   pp. 7-12; "The Hebrew Folksong Society of St. Petersburg: Historical Development" by Avraham Soltes, pp.13-
   27; Roster "Yibneh" Music Publications (eds.), pp.28-29;
   "The Hebrew Folksong Society of St. Petersburg: Ideology
   and Technique" by Joseph Yasser, pp.30-42; Programs of
   St. Petersburg Society (eds.), pp.43-46; "Influence of
   Russian Jews on the Music of Israel" by Issachar Miron,
   pp.47-53; "Bibliography of Yiddish Folksongs" by Samuel
   Bugatch, pp.54-72. Music selections. Publishers index.
   215

HUESCHEN, HEINRICH, ed. *Musicae Scientia Collectanea: G.K.*
Fellerer Festschrift (70th Birthday). Cologne, W. Ger.:
Volk, 1973; 715 pp., illus., music.
   See "An Old Controversy; Aesthetics and Politics in the
   Writings of Mendelssohn and Wagner" by Eric Werner, pp.
   640-60, which reviews some deeply polemical issues , including the infamous essay of Richard Wagner on "Jews
   in Music" (1850/1869), that was cited by anti-semites
   and often quoted by the nazis during the Holocaust Era.
   216

HUGHES, DOM ANSELM, ed. *Early Medieval Music up to 1300.*
(The New Oxford History of Music, vol 2) London, Eng.: Oxford Univ. Press, 1954; xviii, 434 pp., illus., music.
   Topical sections by various authors. For studies which
   include information on Jewish music, see in Part One –
   "Early Christian Music" by Egon Wellesz (1885-1974),
   pp. 1-13; and see in Part Four – "Gregorian Chant" by
   Higinio Angles (1888-1969), pp. 92-127. Also see index.
   217

LaRUE, JAN, ed. *Aspects of Medieval and Renaissance Music-*
A Birthday Offering to Gustave Reese. repr. ed. New York:
Pendragon Press, 1978; xvii,905 pp., illus., music. (orig.
ed. New York:W.W. Norton, 1966; xvii,905 pp., illus., music)
   Collection of scholarly articles published in tribute to
   musicologist and educator Gustave Reese (1899-1977). See
   "King David and His Musicians in Spanish Romanesque
   Sculpture" by Isabel Pope, pp.693-703, for interesting
   biblical arts study. Also, see "The Last Pythagorean
   Musician: Johannes Kepler" by Eric Werner, pp.867-82,
   which is contribution by noted scholar in Jewish music
   and explores linkages of mathematical ideas and musical
   creativity. Consult book index.
   218

MAY, ELIZABETH, ed. *Musics of Many Cultures; An Intro-*
duction. Berkeley and Los Angeles, Cal.: Univ. of Cal.
Press, 1982; 360 pp., illus., music.
   See "On Jewish Music" by Abraham A. Schwadron, pp. 284-
   306, for survey consideration of aspects of Jewish folksong and of traditional liturgical hymnology. Sources,

notes and music illustrations.
219
McCULLOH, JUDITH, ed. *Ethnic Recordings in America: A Neg-*
lected Heritage. (Studies in American Folklife Series, 1)
Wash.,D.C.: American Folklife Canter/Library of Congress,
1982; 269 pp., illus.
> Contributions by musicians and ethnologists. See "Ethnic
> Recordings: An Introduction" by Pekka Gronow, pp.1-50,
> for information on Yiddish recordings in America of the
> 1910's and 1920's, both secular and cantorial, as well
> as data on 78's by label for Jewish folksongs in Hebrew,
> and Ladino (*Judezmo*). Also, see "Commerical Ethnic
> Recordings in the United States" by Richard K. Spotts-
> wood, pp.51-66. Of particular relevance is "Recorded
> Ethnic Music: A Guide to Resources" by Norm Cohen and
> Paul Wells, pp.175-250, which includes a sub-section on
> "Jewish Traditions" pp.220-29 and pp.246-7, with entries
> on Hebrew liturgical music, Hassidic and Zionist songs,
> Yiddish folksongs, Jewish art and theater music, dances,
> Ladino and other miscellaneous items. Rosters of refer-
> ences, and recordings sources. Also consult index.
220
MENDEL, ARTHUR, CURT SACHS and CARROLL PRATT. *Some Aspects*
of Musicology; Three Essays. (American Council of Learned
Societies, Committee on Musicology) New York: Liberal Arts
Press, 1957; 88 pp., illus., music.
> See "The Lore of Non-Western Music" by Curt Sachs, pp.
> 21-48, which treats the array of social, religious, eth-
> nic and artistic aspects of musicological studies in
> Near Eastern area. Sachs ties ethnomusicology to essence
> of human society, past and present. Considerations of
> Judaic music materials. No index for book.
221
PAOLI, DOMENICO and Committee, eds. *Lazare Saminsky; Com-*
poser and Civic Worker. New York:Bloch, 1930; 65pp., illus.
> Collection of 5 brief biographical studies on composer
> and music director Lazare Saminsky (1882-1959), with a
> chronology of life and works (to 1930). Contributors -
> Domenico Paoli, Leigh Henry, Leon Vallas, Leonide Saban-
> eyev and Joseph Yasser - highlight that Saminsky "wishes
> to be a Hebrew composer," compare his work with Ernest
> Bloch (1880-1959), discuss his Russian background and
> collecting of Georgian-Jewish folksongs in South Russia,
> and consider his ideas on "Hebraic and Biblical art."
222
REESE, GUSTAVE and ROSE BRANDEL, eds. *The Commonwealth of*
Music. New York: Free Press/Collier, Macmillan, 1965;
374 pp., illus., music.
> 25 scholarly articles intended as a celebration volume,
> but became memorial tribute book for Curt Sachs (1881-
> 1959), prepared by his colleague Gustave Reese (1899-
> 1977). See "Greek Ideas on Music in Judeo-Arabic Litera-
> ture" by Eric Werner, pp.71-96, which offers intriguing
> information on this topic. Also, see "Women's Songs from
> the Yemen (Jewish and Arabic): Their Tonal Structure and
> Form" by Edith Gerson-Kiwi, pp.97-103, a valuable study

in comparative ethnomusicology. No index for book.

223
ROBERTSON, ALEC and DENIS STEVENS, eds. *Pelican History of
Music: Ancient Forms to Polyphony.* (Pelican Series, 1)
Baltimore, Md.:Penguin Books, 1960; 343 pp., illus., music.
    See Section One — "Non-Western Music" by Peter Crossley-
Holland, pp.13-135, and notably materials on "The Jews,"
pp.104-17, for survey of topic. Also, consult relevant
passages in other sections of book dealing with such
subjects as: plainsong, *Ars Antigua*, and *Ars Nova*.
Use index. Bibliography and discography.

224
VELIMIROVIC, MILOS, ed. *Studies in Eastern Chant*, vol 2.
London, Eng.:Oxford Univ. Press,1971;vii,198pp.,illus.,music
    See "The Origin of the Modes" by David Wulstan, pp. 5-
20, which presents materials relevant to development of
modal patterns and usages in Jewish and other liturgies.
Notes and music illustrations.

225
VELIMIROVIC, MILOS, ed. *Studies in Eastern Chant,* vol. 3.
London, Eng.:Oxford Univ. Press, 1973; 187pp.,illus., music.
    See "Theory and Practice in Liturgical Music of Chris-
tian Arabs in Israel" by Dalia Cohen, pp. 1-50, which
offers valuable information on comparative Near Eastern
Christian chants, as currently practiced in the State
of Israel. Notes and music examples.

226
WELLESZ, EGON, ed. *Ancient and Oriental Music.* (The New
Oxford History of Music Series, 1) London, Eng.:Oxford Univ.
Press, 1957; xxiii, 530 pp., illus., music.
    Eleven topical chapters contributed by various scholars,
several studies of which contain materials relevant to
Jewish music. See Chapter 5 "The Music of Ancient Mesopotamia" by Henry George Farmer (1882-1965), pp.228-54;
and Chapter 6 "The Music of Ancient Egypt" by Henry
George Farmer, pp.255-82. Both chapters offer valuable
background information on rise and development of musics
in that area, including roots of Judaic expression. See
Chapter 7 "Music in the Bible" by Carl H. Kraeling (1897
-1966) and Lucetta Mowry, pp.283-312, which covers music
practices, instruments and terminologies. Of specific
relevance is Chapter 8 "The Music of Post-Biblical Judaism" by Eric Werner, pp.313-35, treating such topics as:
cantillation, chants, synagogue modes and melodies, liturgical poetry and hymnology, as well as an overview in
later periods of the musical traditions of Italian Jews,
Central European Jewry, Sephardic elements and other
materials. Musical illustrations. Also, see Chapter 11
"The Music of Islam" by Henry George Farmer, pp.421-77,
for some interesting correlative information on semitic
musical expression. Bibliographical section for book on
pp.479-503. Brief roster of recordings. Excellent index.

227
WELLESZ, EGON and MILOS VELIMIROVIC, eds. *Studies in
Eastern Chant,* vol. 1. London, Eng.: Oxford Univ. Press,
1966; xvi, 134 pp., illus., music.

See "Greek Ekphonetic Neumes and Masoretic Texts" by
Gudrun Engberg, pp. 37-49, which compares Greek with
Hebrew Ekphonetic systems in reading of scriptural
passages, according to notations for cantillations of
texts. Parallels noted and examined.

228
WERNER, ERIC, ed. *Contributions to a Historical Study of*
Jewish Music. New York:KTAV, 1976; 287 pp., illus., music.
Collection of 12 scholarly studies treating topics in
Jewish music, previously published in various journals
and reprinted in this newly-prepared volume. (Note: As
articles, these materials are also listed and annotated
elsewhere in this bibliography.) "*Prolegomenon*" (as an
introduction for book) by Eric Werner, pp.1-36, presents
an historical survey of musicological studies and publications in field of Jewish music. Articles - 1. "A Geniza Find of Sa'adya's Psalm - Preface and Its Musical Aspects" by Hanoch Avenary (*H.U.C. Annual*, 1968), pp.37-
54; 2. "Hebrew and Oriental Christian Metrical Hymns - A
Comparison" by Eric Werner (*H.U.C. Annual*, 1950), pp.
55-90; 3. "Musical Traditions for the Reading of the
Megillah" by Eduard Birnbaum (1855-1920), translated
here from German (*Allgemeinzeitung des Judenthums*,
1891), pp.91-103; 4. "The Origin of the Eight Modes of
Music (*Octoechos*)" by Eric Werner (*H.U.C. Annual*,
1948), pp.104-48; 5. "The *Kol Nidre* Tune" by Abraham
Zebi Idelsohn (1882-1938) (*H.U.C. Annual*, 1931/32),
pp.149-65; 6. "The Notated Synagogue Chants of the 12th
Century of Obadiah, the Norman Proselyte" by Israel Adler, translated here from French, (*Journal de Musico-*
logie, 1967), pp.166-99; 7. "Parallels Between the Old
French and the Jewish Song" by Abraham Zebi Idelsohn
(*Acta Musicologica*, 1933), pp.200-6; 8. "Jewish Music
in Medieval Spain" by Higinio Angles (1888-1969), translated here from French (*Yuval*, 1968), pp.207-27; 9.
"Franz Schubert as a Composer of Synagogue Music" by Eduard Birnbaum, translated here from German (*Allgemein-*
zeitung des Judenthums, 1898), pp.228-40; 10. "Gustave
Mahler and Arnold Schoenberg" by Peter Gradenwitz (*An-*
nual of the Leo Baeck Inst., 1960), pp.241-65; 11. "The
Music of the Kurdistan Jews" by Edith Gerson-Kiwi
(*Yuval*, 1971), pp.266-79. Notes and illustrations for
each article. Modest index. Excellent compilation.

229
WESTRUP, JACK, ed. *Essays Presented to Egon Wellesz.*
London, Eng.:Oxford Univ. Press, 1966; 188pp.,illus.,music.
Tribute volume to musicologist Egon Wellesz (1885-1974).
See "The Genesis of the Liturgical Sanctus" by Eric Wer-
ner, pp.19-32, which presents study in comparative chant
materials, as extension of author's book *The Sacred*
Bridge. No index.

B. Collections of Essays on General Subjects
by Various Authors

230
ALTMANN, ALEXANDER, ed. *Jewish Mediaeval and Renaissance Studies.* (Lown Inst./Brandeis Studies Series,4) Cambridge, Mass.:Harvard Univ. Press, 1967; 384pp.

    See "The Rise of Art Music in the Italian Ghetto; The Influence of Segregation on Jewish Music Praxis" by Israel Adler, pp.321-64. Author stresses the "astonishing chronological coincidence between the rise of art music in Jewish community life and the enforcement of the Ghetto system in Italy." Consideratioan of: musical activities of Salomone Rossi (c.1565-c.1628); cultural interests of Rabbi Leon Modena (1671-1648); attitudes of various music historians towards Jewish musical life of Middle Ages and Renaissance era; Jews and Western art music of those times; art music in Italian Jewish communal life during late 16th and early 17th centuries - Padua, Ferrara, Mantua, Venice and Senigallia (near Ancona). With Hebrew text materials and source notes.

231
BARNETT, R.D., ed. *The Sephardic Heritage; Essays on the History and Cultural Contributions of the Jews of Spain and Portugal.* New York:KTAV, 1971; viii, 640pp., illus., music.
    See "Romances and Songs of the *Sephardim*," by William Samelson, pp.527-51. Sephardic balladry and Ladino folksongs carried into other countries after expulsion of Jews in 1492, in terms of musical and cultural continuity from Iberian life with subsequent adaptations and alterations over centuries in other countries. Music examples and source notes.

232
BARON, SALO W. and ISAAC E. BARZILAY, eds. *The American Academy for Jewish Research Jubilee Volume: 1928-1978.* New York:Columbia Univ. Press,1980;658pp.(2 parts),illus.,music.
    See "Genealogies of Two Wandering Hebrew Melodies" by Eric Werner, pp.573-92. Study of varied origins and comparative melodic representations for *"Eli Tziyon"* - melody in Ashkenazic tradition for lamentation services of *Tisha B'av* (Commemoration of Destruction of Temple) and for motifs related to chant of *"L'Dovid Borukh"* - adaptation of Psalm 144 text as poetic prayer also for Ashkenazic traditions. Source notes and music examples.

233
BEN-AMI, ISSACHAR, ed. *The Sepharadi and Oriental Jewish Heritage: Studies.* Jerusalem,Isr.:Hebrew Univ./Magnes Press, 1982; 630pp., illus., music.
    Collection of scholarly studies and papers presented at First International Congress on Sephardic and Oriental Jewry, held 1982 in Jerusalem, under sponsorship of Faculty of Humanities at Hebrew University. See: "New Perspectives in Judaeo-Spanish Ballad Research" by Samuel G. Armistead, pp.225-36; and, "The Antiquity of Jew-

ish Oriental Musical Tradition" by Amnon Shiloah, pp.405
-12. Other relevant studies in French and Spanish only.
234
BERGER, ABRAHAM, LAWRENCE MARWICK, and ISIDORE MEYER, eds.
*The Joshua Bloch Memorial Volume; Studies in Booklore and
History.* New York: N.Y.P.L., 1960; xix, 219 pp., illus.
   See "*Kinnor, Nebel* — Cithara, Psalterium" by Otto Kinkeldey (1878-1966), pp.40-53, for consideration of some
   bibliographic sources for descriptions of "the 16 words
   in the Hebrew Scriptures which are names of musical instruments." Kinkeldey offers various translations of
   these terms, compares meanings, and surveys archaeological findings. Resource notes and book index. Joshua
   Bloch (1890-1957) was librarian of Jewish Division of
   N.Y.P.L. from 1923 to his death.
235
BRAUNER, RONALD, ed. *Shiv'im; Essays and Studies in Honor
of Ira Eisenstein.* (Publications of Reconstructionist Rabbinical College Series, 1) New York: KTAV, 1977; viii,309pp.
   See "Tensions in the Music of Jewish Worship" by Judith
   Kaplan Eisenstein, pp.231-40. Reflections upon performance practices of liturgical music in the synagogue and
   current diverse developments in styles and trends. Advocacy by author of congregational participation in the
   music of the services, and for better standards of music
   education for children and adults. Reference notes.
236
COHEN, ISRAEL, ed. *The Rebirth of Israel; A Memorial Tribute to Paul Goodman.* London, Eng.: Goldston, 1952; xiv,
338 pp., illus.
   See "Art and Music" by Sadie Wilkinson, pp. 298-310, for
   brief, but interesting, view of interrelated creativity.
237
FRAENKEL, JOSEF, ed. *The Jews of Austria.* London, Eng.:
Vallentine, Mitchell, 1966; xv, 585 pp., illus.
   See "Jews in Austrian Music: Essay on Their Life, History and Destruction" by Peter Gradenwitz, pp.17-24.
   Review of roster of Jewish musicians who flourished in
   Austria, especially Vienna, up to Holocaust era. Author
   fled to Tel Aviv in 1936, and resumed career there as
   musician, music editor and journalist. Also, see "Salomon Sulzer (1804-1890)" by Eric Mandell, pp.221-29,
   which reviews contributions of notable *Hazzan* (cantor)
   who officiated at *Seitenstettengasse Shul*, chief synagogue in Vienna. Source materials cited.
238
FRIEDLANDER, ALBERT H., ed. *Out of the Whirlwind; A Reader
of Holocaust Literature.* New York:Doubleday,1968;viii,536pp
   See "The Art and Music in the *Shoah* (Holocaust)" by
   Paul Veret, pp.259-282. Discussion of creativity by Jews
   who languished in Ghettos and perished in Concentration
   Camps, in terms of materials which have survived and
   "messages" in that legacy of artistry.
239
FRUMKIN, JACOB, GREGOR ARONSON and ALEXIS GOLDENWEISER, eds
Russian Jewry 1860-1917. (trans. from Russian by Mirra

Ginsburg) South Brunswick, N.J.:T. Yoseloff,1966; 492pp.
      Collection of articles on Russian Jewish life before
      revolution. See "Russian Jews in Music" by Gershon Swet,
      pp. 300-21. Some dates and data need correction.
   240
GAER, JOSEPH, ed. *The Best of Recall.* New York: Barnes/
Yoseloff, 1962; 179pp., illus.
      Collection of articles selected from annual publication
      Recall, issued for several years by the Jewish Heri-
      tage Foundation. See two essays: "Ernest Bloch: An Ap-
      preciation" by Albert Goldberg, pp.145-7; and, "Histor-
      ical Sources for the Music of Ancient Israel" by Alfred
      Sendrey (1884-1976), pp.148-52.
   241
GINZBERG, LOUIS and Committee, eds. *Studies in Jewish Bib-*
liography and Related Subjects; In Memory of Abraham Solomon
Freidus (1869-1923). New York:Alexander Kohut (1842-1894)
Memorial Found., 1929; cxxx, 518pp.,illus., music.
      See "A Jewish Dancing Master of the Renaissance (Gugli-
      elmo Ebreo)," by Otto Kinkeldey (1878-1966), pp.329-72.
      Study of cultural figure of late 15th century in North
      Italy. Reference materials, illustrations and sources.
      Article was subsequently published separately under same
      title (Brooklyn, N.Y., 1966).
   242
GOODMAN. PHILIP, ed. *The Hanukkah Anthology.* Phila.: J.P.
S.A., 1976; xxxiii,465pp., illus., music.
      See "Music for *Hanukkah*" by Paul Kavon, pp.412-28 and
      pp.462-465. In context of traditions and customs for
      celebration of this holiday, selection of hymns and
      folksongs for synagogue, community and home. Some re-
      source materials also given.
   243
GOODMAN, PHILIP, ed. *The Passover Anthology.* Phila.: J.P.
S.A., 1961; xxiii,496pp., illus., music.
      See "Music of Passover" by Judith Kaplan Eisenstein,
      pp.272-94. Discussion of music in the observance of this
      holiday in synagogue, community and home. Considered are
      liturgical traditions, music of the *Seder*, or Passover
      feast ritual, and folksongs as well as art music based
      upon history and customs for this celebration. Numerous
      music illustrations.
   244
GOODMAN, PHILIP, ed. *The Purim Anthology.* Phila.:J.P.S.A.
1949; xxxi,525pp., illus., music.
      See "*Purim* in Music" by Abraham Wolf Binder (1895-
      1966), pp.209-21 and pp.442-89. Discussion of musical
      traditions and customs for celebration of this holiday
      in synagogue, community and home. Particular group of
      musical selections — liturgical hymns and folksongs —
      with annotations and translations.
   245
GOODMAN, PHILIP, ed. *The Rosh Hashanah Anthology.* Phila.:
J.P.S.A., 1970; xiv,379pp., illus., music.
      See "The Music of the *Rosh Hashanah* (New Year) Litur-
      gy" by Max Wohlberg, pp.171-84. In context of tradition-

al observances, leading music motifs, chants and hymns
of this holiday for synagogue services, community and
home devotions. Also, see "The *Shofar*," pp.113-18, a
collection of brief commentaries upon historical and
ritual background of this ancient musical instrument and
its centuries-old significant role in worship services
of the High Holy Days - *Rosh Hashanah* (New Year) and
Yom Kippur (Day of Atonement).

246
GOODMAN, PHILIP. ed. *The Shavuot Anthology.* Phila.: J.P.
S.A., 1974; xxv,369pp., illus., music.
   See "Music for *Shavuot*" by Paul Kavon, pp.323-37 and
   pp.363-64. Presentation of suitable music for observance
   of this holiday in synagogue, community and home. Selection of hymns and songs within context of history and
   customs for holiday.

247
GOODMAN, PHILIP., ed. *The Sukkot and Simhat Torah Antholo-*
gy. Phila.:J.P.S.A., 1973; xxxiii,475pp., illus., music.
   See "Music for *Sukkot* and *Simhat Torah*" by Paul
   Kavon, pp.434-442. In context of celebration of these
   holidays in synagogue, community and home, selection
   of suitable traditional hymns and folksongs.

248
GOODMAN, PHILIP, ed. *The Yom Kippur Anthology.* Phila.:
J.P.S.A., 1971; xxix,399pp., illus., music.
   See "The Paradox of *Kol Nidre*" by Herman Kieval,
   pp.84-98, for background study of text and music of
   this significant liturgical portion which over the
   centuries has opened the devotions on the Eve of *Yom
   Kippur* (Day of Atonement). References and notes. Also,
   see "The Music of the *Yom Kippur* Liturgy" by Max
   Wohlberg, pp.99-112 and 397-98, for discussion of liturgical music for this holiday - chants, modes,
   prayer motifs and hymns. Music examples and sources.

249
HERZOG, MARVIN, BARBARA KIRSHENBLATT-GIMBLETT, DAN MIRON,
RUTH WISSE and ALAN HUFFMAN, eds. *The Field of Yiddish;
Studies in Language, Folklore and Literature - Fourth Collection.* Phila.: Inst. for Study of Human Issues, 1980;
vi, 499 pp., illus., music.
   See "The Uses of Printed Versions in Studying the Song
   Repertoire of East European Jews: First Findings" by
   Mark Slobin, pp.329-70. Ethnomusicological explorations
   of published collections of Yiddish folksongs and of
   sheet music, both in East Europe and America, in terms
   of secular musical creativity and popular musical expression of a particular people, during late 19th and
   early 20th centuries. References and music examples.

250
JONAH, DAVID A., ed. *Books at Brown,* vol.22. (Providence,
R.I.: Friends of Library of Brown Univ., 1968; 185pp.,illus.
   See "Yiddish Poets and Playwrights of America; A Preliminary Report on a Recent Addition to the Harris Collection" by Alvin H. Rosenfeld, pp.161-81. Includes information on sheet music of Yiddish theater to be found

in this collection of special materials at the library.
251
KOPPMAN, LIONEL, ed. *Proceedings; National Conference on
Jewish Arts.* New York:J.W.B., 1967; 37 pp., illus.
See "Advancing the Arts in American Jewish Life: The
Conference in Perspective," pp.406, by Irene Heskes. Review in summary of Conference objectives, sessions and
recommendations regarding then current status of Jewish
cultural expression in America: music, literature, arts.
252
LANDMAN, LEO, ed. *Rabbi Joseph Lookstein Memorial Volume.*
New York: KTAV, 1980; xiii, 398 pp., 27 n.p.
See "*Kol 'Isha*: Voice of Woman" by Saul J. Berman,
pp.45-66. Discussion of women's singing voices in terms
of Talmudic writings and other rabbinical sources. Consideration of various traditional positions, pro and
con, concerning this centuries-old religious issue which
has occupied Christian as well as Jewish liturgists:
"Does a woman's voice distract from liturgical concentration and promote illicity?" Cited opinions in this
study tilt towards the affirmative position. Source references documented.
253
LANGNAS, IZAAK and BARTON SHOLOD, eds. *Studies in Honor of
M.J. Benardete (Essays in Hispanic and Sephardic Culture).*
New York:Las Americas, 1965; 501pp., illus., music.
See "Judaeo-Spanish Ballads in a Ms. by Solomon Israel
Cherezli" by Samuel G. Armistead and Joseph L. Silverman, pp.367-88. Study by two professors of Spanish language and literature at U.C.L.A., who specialize in
Sephardic *romanceros*, of collection of several ballads
of Turkish-Balkan Sephardic origin. Materials were collected and printed early in this century in Jerusalem,
where recently acquired by scholar Israel J. Katz during
his own research into Sephardic balladry. Source notes,
facsimiles and glossary of terms. See, also, following
this article, on pp.391-8, music for a Ladino song by
Joachin Rodrigo: "*Triste Estaba El Rey David.*"
254
LIEBERMAN, SAUL, ed. *Salo Wittmayer Baron 80th Birthday
Jubilee Volume.* New York:Academy for Jewish Research/Colum-
bia Univ. Press,1974; 3vols.: vol.1 - viii,554pp.; vol.2 -
pp.556-1095; vol.3 - [540pp. Hebrew text only].
Collection of essays by various scholars. See: "Two
Types of Ritual and Their Music," by Eric Werner,
(vol.2) pp.975-1008. Historical and ethnomusicological
considerations of early aspects of Jewish liturgical
music, in terms of two interacting formative elements -
sacrifice/hierarchy/art forms and sacred word/text/
folklore. Reflections upon ancient antecedents and
Biblical concepts, Qumran literature, and subsequent
influences upon liturgical music developments in Church
and Synagogue over early centuries. Source notes.
255
LOWINGER, SAMUEL and Committee, eds. *Ignaz Goldziher Memorial Volume.* Jerusalem,Isr.: Hebrew Univ. Press, 1948;

475 pp., illus., music.
    See "About Five-Tone Scales and the Early Hebrew Melo-
    dies" by Hungarian scholar Bence Szabolcsi (1899-1973),
    pp.309-13. References and music. Valuable brief study.
    256
MILLGRAM, ABRAHAM E., ed. *Sabbath - The Day of Delight.*
Phila.: J.P.S.A., 1944; xxx,495pp., illus., music.
    See "Sabbath in Music" by Abraham Wolf Binder (1895-
    1966), pp.301-18, pp.395-473, and pp.479-486. Discussion
    with ample musical examples of liturgical chants, hymns,
    table songs (*Z'mirot*) and folksongs for traditional
    observance of Sabbath day in synagogue, community and
    home. With glossary of terms, footnotes and references.
    257
PASSOW, ISADORE and SAMUEL TOBIAS LACHS, eds. *Gratz Col-
lege 75th Anniversary Volume: 1895-1970.* Phila.: Gratz
College, 1971; x, 283pp., 24 n.p., illus., music.
    See "Seventy-five Years in Jewish Music" by Clare Polin
    Schaff, pp.229-42. General survey of developments in the
    field of Jewish music - studies, publications and com-
    positions - over past 75 years in Europe, America and
    Israel. Musical illustrations.
    258
PATAI, RAPHAEL, ABRAHAM LOPES-CARDOZO and DAVID de SOLA-
POOL, eds. *The World of the Sephardim.* (Herzl Institute
Series, 15) New York: Herzl Press, 1960; 71 pp., music.
    See "The Music of the *Sephardim*" by Abraham Lopes-
    Cardozo, pp.37-71, which explains aspects of liturgical
    music heritage of the Spaniolic Jews in traditions of
    Spanish-Portuguese and Mediterranean branches of Jewish
    life. Among topics considered: *Hazzan* (cantor) and
    his role as music leader, various Sabbath, holiday and
    festival musical liturgies, and some special "sacred
    songs" and chant motifs. Additional overview of anthem
    Hatikvah as melodic reflection of age-old Sephardic
    prayer chant for *Tal* (Dew). Music illustrations.
    259
PATAI, RAPHAEL, FRANCIS LEE UTLEY, and DOV NOY, eds. *Studies in Biblical and Jewish Folklore.* (Indiana Univ. Folklore Series, 13; and Amer. Folklore Soc. Memoir Series, 51)
Bloomington, Ind.: Indiana Univ. Press, 1960; vii, 374 pp.,
illus., music.
    Collection of studies by scholars of Jewish folklore and
    traditions, customs and folk creativity, with special
    section devoted to five articles on aspects of Jewish
    folksong, pp. 187-284. 1. "The Musical Vocabulary of
    Ashkenazic *Hazzanim* (cantors)" by Hanoch Avenary, on
    pp. 187-200, which treats such topics as musical terms,
    special repertoire, continuity of heritage and perform-
    ance styles for cantorial musician, in context of role
    as liturgical leader as well as folk artist. 2. "Social
    Background of East European Yiddish Folk Love Songs" by
    Yehoash Dworkin, on pp. 210-24, which investigates some
    particular folksong texts and their melodies, as the re-
    flection of cultural patterns in courtship and marriage.
    3. "Synthesis and Symbiosis of Styles in Jewish-Oriental

Music" by Edith Gerson-Kiwi, on pp. 225-34, which deals
with liturgical music materials that the author has collected and studied among Israelis ingathered from other
Near Eastern areas, in terms of authenticity and folk
continuity. 4. "Some Aspects of Comparative Jewish Folksong" by Ruth Rubin, on pp. 235-54, which draws attention to parallels in European Yiddish folksong with folk
traditions - Jewish and non-Jewish - of Canada and U.S.
in more recent times. 5. "Bridal Songs and Ceremonies
from San'a, Yemen" by Johanna Spector, on pp. 255-84,
which reports upon research collection done 1951-1953 in
Jerusalem among Oriental Yemenite Jewish groups, tracing
in folksong the entire wedding ceremonial, through the
delineation of 12 wedding selections, as sung by the
women. Array of resource information, notes and music
illustrations for articles. Also consult book index.

260
PETUCHOWSKI, JACOB, ed. *Contributions to the Scientific
Study of Jewish Liturgy.* New York: KTAV, 1970; xxviii,
502 pp., illus., music.
See "The Doxology in Synagogue and Church" by Eric
Werner, pp.318-70, which examines aspects of liturgico-
musical interdependence between the two religions in
their worship services. This article originally appeared
in *Hebrew Union College Annual*, vol 19, 1945/46, and
was substantially incorporated into Werner's extensive
publication on this subject area: *The Sacred Bridge*
(Columbia Univ. Press, 1959). Source notes, references
and musical examples.

261
SCHEIBER, ALEXANDER, ed. *Semitic Studies in Memory of Im-
manuel Loew.* Budapest/Jerusalem: Hebrew Univ. Press, 1947;
xii, 555 pp., illus., music.
Multi-lingual collection of articles, including works by
several scholars who perished in the Holocaust. Editor,
as survivor, gathered materials after his liberation and
assembled volume as testament to Hungarian scholarship.
See "A Jewish Musical Document of the Middle Ages; The
Most Ancient Noted Biblical Melody" by musicologist
Bence Szabolcsi (1899-1973), pp. 131-33, in English text
with music illustrations. Introduction of a musical and
iconographic discovery: Barcelona-Cairo Codex c. 1400.

262
SCHWARZ, LEO, ed. *The Menorah Treasury; Harvest of Half a
Century.* Phila.:J.P.S.A.,1964; xvii,963pp., illus., music.
See "Ernest Bloch and Modern Music" by John Hastings,
pp.769-87, a philosophically-directed essay on the composer and his works, with musical examples. Also, see
"Guglielmo Ebreo of Pesaro and the Ballet" by Walter
Sorell, pp.788-802, for discussion of noted dancing
master (fl. 15th cent.) of Jewish lineage who created
and taught dances in Northern Italy at ducal courts of
Urbino and Florence. It is generally believed that he
devised dance patterns which subsequently led to the
ballet form. Articles in this volume previously appeared
in issues of *The Menorah Journal* (New York,1915-1962).

263
SHAKED, S., Y. SHENKMAN and Committee, eds. *Proceedings
of Fourth World Congress of Jewish Studies*, vol.2 (Jerusalem,Isr.:W.U.J.S., 1968; 225pp+490 Heb.p., illus., music.
   Summaries of papers presented at Congress held at Hebrew
   Univ. in Jerusalem, Summer 1968, as given in either Eng.
   or Heb. texts. See following music materials in English:
   "Written Tradition and Contemporary Practice in Biblical
   Cantillation of the Samaritans" by Johanna Spector, pp.
   153-5 (including comparative charts of Samaritan pat-
   terns and qualities of cantillation, and table of 10
   musical examples); "The Religious Works and thought of
   Arnold Schoenberg" by Peter Gradenwitz, pp.147-51; "The
   Scope and Aims of Jewish Music Research (Isolation or
   Integration)" by Eric Werner, pp.157-61. Also, see fol-
   lowing English abstracts of music materials presented in
   Hebrew: "The New Music Fragment of Obadiah the Norman
   Proselyte and Its Importance for Jewish Music Research"
   by Israel Adler, p.208; "Gentile Song as a Source of In-
   spiration for Israel Najara" by Hanoch Avenary, p.209;
   "Four Differentiae in the Samaritan Reading of the Law"
   by Shlomo Hofman, p.208; "Sources of Falaquera's Chapter
   On Music in the *Sefer Hamevaqqesh*" by Amnon Shiloah,
   p.207; "Music in the Mediaeval Biblical Exegesis" by
   Herzl Shmueli, p.209; "Musical Ethos in the theory and
   Practice of the Jews" by Michal Smoira, p.207.
264
SHINAN, AVIGDOR and Committee, eds. *Proceedings of the
Fifth World Congress of Jewish Studies*, vol.4 (Jerusalem,
Isr.:W.U.J.S., 1969; 303pp.+318 Heb.p., illus., music.
   Summaries of papers presented at Congress held at Hebrew
   Univ. in Jerusalem, summer 1969, as given in either Eng.
   or Heb. Texts. See following music materials in English:
   "The 'Myth' of the Sephardic Musical Legacy from Spain"
   by Israel J. Katz, pp.237-43; "Jewish Song from Cochin,
   India (With Special Reference to Cantillation and the
   Shingli Tunes)" by Johanna Spector, pp.245-65 (ex-
   tensive musical examples, pp.252-65); See following Eng-
   lish abstracts of music materials presented in Hebrew:
   "Science of Music and Jews of 13th and 14th Centuries"
   by Hanoch Avenary, p.283; "Jewish Folk Dance Customs as
   Reflected in the Memorial Literature of European Jewish
   Communities" by Zev Friedhaber, p.293; "Cantillation of
   the Bible by the Karaites" by Shlomo Hofman, p.278; "Attempts to Define Style of Hebrew Song With Aid of the
   Computer" by Ruth Katz and Dalia Cohen, p.300; "Chironomy and Head Movement in Reciting Hebrew Scriptures" by
   A. Laufer, p.290; "Two Commentaries on 'Canon of Avi-
   cenna' (Section on Analogy of Pulse Action to Elements
   of Music)" by Amnon Shiloah, p.292; "*Ne'ima* - Attempt
   at Elucidation of Term" by Michal Smoira, p.282.
265
**SOCIETY for HISTORY of CZECHOSLAVAK JEWS, Publication Com-
mittee, eds.** *The Jews of Czechoslavakia; Historical Studies
and Surveys*, vol.1. Phila.:J.P.S.A., 1968; 583pp.
   See "Music" by Paul Nettl (1889-1972), pp. 539-58, a

brief biographical overview of notable Czechoslavakian
Jewish musicians. Includes some valuable information on
musical activities at Terezin (Theresienstadt) Concentration Camp during the Holocaust era. Also see index.

266
SOLIS-COHEN, EMILY, ed. *Hanukkah: The Feast of Lights.*
Phila.:J.P.S.A., 1937; xix,400pp., illus., music.
See *"Hanukkah* in Music" by Abraham Wolf Binder (1895-
1966), pp.59-63, pp.68-81, pp.341-44, and pp.367-70.
Discussion of musical traditions and presentation of
particular liturgical and secular melodies – hymns and
folksongs – associated with celebration of this holiday
in synagogue, community and home.

267
TALMAGE, FRANK and DOV NOY, eds. *Studies in Jewish Folklore.* Cambridge, Mass.: Association for Jewish Studies,
1980; xiii, 408 pp., illus., music.
Proceedings of a regional conference of the Association
for Jewish Studies held at Spertus College of Judaica in
Chicago, May 1977. See three articles relevant to field
of Jewish music: 1. "Recent Developments in Judeo-Spanish Ballad Scholarship" by Samuel G. Armistead, pp.21-
32, which surveys some recent studies by scholars in
this area, noting significance of this work for comparative considerations in Pan-Hispanic balladry due to the
archaic origins of Spaniolic-Jewish folksong; 2. "Stylized Performances of a Judeo-Spanish Traditional Ballad:
La Mujer Enganada by Israel J. Katz, pp.181-200, con-
centrating upon one folksong, citing research and published collections of Manuel Manrique de Lara (1863-
1929), Abraham Zebi Idelsohn (1882-1938) and Alberto
Hemsi (1897-1975), as well as some other compilations of
such materials by Leon Algazi (1890-1971) and Isaac
Levy, comparing all their various versions of this folksong; 3. "The Evolution of a Musical Symbol in Yiddish
Culture" by Mark Slobin, pp.313-30, which considers the
music interval of the augmented second as a Jewish folkloric symbol, and surveys its musical application in
liturgical and secular modes, variously referred to as
Ahava Rabba, Ukrainian Dorian, Phrygian and Arabic
Hidjaz; with some specific examples of this modal use
in Yiddish folksongs and then in early popular songs of
turn of century in East Europe and America, and with
references to music of Yiddish theater and some leading
musical figures of Jewish stage. Resources, notes and
music for each of three articles. Also consult index.

268
WEINREICH, URIEL, ed. *The Field of Yiddish; Studies in
Language, Folklore and literature.* New York: Linguistic
Circle/Columbia Univ. Press, 1954; ix, 317pp., illus, music.
See "America in East European Yiddish Folksong" by
Eleanor Gordon Mlotek, pp.179-95, for discussion of the
influences poetically and musically of mass immigration
movement to America from Eastern Europe around turn of
century. Examples of Yiddish folksongs created and sung
by people who planned to emigrate and then did leave for

America, and the folksongs of those who may have thought
about leaving but never did. Folksongs also of communication between those now in America with families and
friends left behind in the Old World. Important cultural
expression of that era. Notes and music illustrations.
269
WEINREICH, URIEL, ed. *The Field of Yiddish; Studies in
Language, Folklore and Literature - Second Edition.* The
Hague, Neth.: Mouton, 1965; vii, 289 pp., illus., music.
See "Traces of Ballad Motifs in Yiddish Folksong" by
Eleanor Gordon Mlotek, pp.232-52, which is a comparative
study of elements in European ballads and folksongs —
themes, motifs, topical similarities of texts and anal-
ogous music materials — also found among Yiddish folk
music examples. Notes, sources and music illustrations.
270
WEINREICH, URIEL, ed. *For Max Weinreich on His Seventieth
Birthday; Studies in Jewish Languages, Literature and Society.* The Hague, Neth.: Mouton, 1964; x,527pp.,illus., music.
See "International Motifs in the Yiddish Ballad" by
Eleanor Gordon Mlotek, on pp. 209-28. Analysis of motifs
of 11 Yiddish ballads compared to balladic types in collection of European folksongs done 1882-1896 by Francis
James Child (1825-1896). Author introduces parallels in
lyrical themes of texts, and also considers similar folk
materials in several collections of Yiddish folksongs,
citing such sources. Valuable preliminary study of topic
which warrants further in-depth examination. Notes and
music examples.
271
WRIGHT, G. ERNEST and DAVID NOEL FRIEDMAN. *The Biblical
Archeologist Reader.* Garden City, N.Y.: Doubleday Anchor,
1961; xvi, 342 pp., illus.
See "Musical Instruments of Israel" by Ovid R. Sellers,
pp.81-94. General survey of topic, with particular relevance to archeological sources for verification of
biblical materials. No index.

C. On Musical Subjects by One Author

272
AMMER, CHRISTINE. *Unsung: A History of Women in American
Music.* (Contributions on Women's Studies Series, 14) West-
port, Conn.: Greenwood Press, 1980; x, 317 pp.
Includes information on several composers who have writ-
ten works of specific Jewish connection — Miriam Gideon,
Shulamith Ran, Elizabeth Swados and Judith Lang Zaimont.
273
AMRAM. DAVID. *Vibrations: An Autobiography.* New York:
Macmillan, 1968, 469 pp. illus.
Includes details of composer-performer Amram's Jewish
lineage, with references to some compositions of Judaic

inspiration.
274
BAKST, JAMES. *A History of Russian-Soviet Music.* New
York:Dodd, Mead, 1966; vi,406pp., illus.
    Survey treatment, especially of 1800 to Soviet times,
which includes information on musicians of generally
recognized Jewish lineage, though scant mention is made
of Jewish music in Russia. Ironically, Rimsky-Korsakov
(1844-1908) as advocate of Russian nationalism in music,
had encouraged young Jewish musicians in St. Petersburg
and Moscow music conservatories of late 19th century, to
seek out and collect Jewish folksongs and write music of
Jewish inspiration. In 1908, the St. Petersburg Society
for Jewish Folk Music was founded. Subsequently, many of
its members emigrated to Europe, Palestine and America.
After 1917 Revolution, during Stalin era and into more
recent times, specifically Jewish music creativity has
sharply declined and the few studies, collections and
publications of Jewish folksongs appear to sustain a
deliberate political bias.
275
BAUER, MARION. *Twentieth Century Music; How It Developed
and How To Listen to It.* (New York: G. P. Putnam's Sons:
1933; xi, 349 pp., illus., music.
    General background information on several 20th century
composers in Europe and America, of Jewish lineage.
276
BLUNT, WILFRED. *On Wings of Song: A Biography of Felix
Mendelssohn.* New York: Charles Scribner's Sons, 1974;
288 pp., illus.
    Treats early life, family and Judaic lineage of composer
Felix Mendelssohn (1809-1947) in great detail. Emphasis
upon matters of personality, background and life, rather
than music itself. Some inaccuracies concerning Jewish
customs, but interesting biography nonetheless.
277
BONANNI, FILIPPO. *The Showcase of Musical Instruments: All
152 Illustrations from the 1723 "Gabinetto Armonico" Published in Rome.* ed. with intro. and captions by Frank Ll.
Harrison and Joan Rimmer. New York: Dover Press, 1964; xii,
305 pp., illus.
    Original 18th century edition was dedicated by Bonanni
(b. 1658) "to King David." Music iconographic materials,
including reproductions of biblical instruments. New introduction gives background on this early publication.
English annotations for all materials.
278
BOR, JOSEF. *The Terezin Requiem.* trans. from Czech by
Edith Pargeter. New York: Alfred A. Knopf, 1963; 112 pp.
    Holocaust music subject. Author, a survivor of Terezin
(Theresienstadt), Auschwitz, Birkenau and Buchenwald
Concentration Camps offers this tribute to murdered
musicians. Description of 500 singers and instrumen-
talists who rehearsed and performed the Verdi Requiem
before Adolph Eichmann in 1944. All, including their devoted conductor, Raphael Schaechter, were shipped off to

the gas chambers.
279
BRIGGS, JOHN. *Leonard Bernstein: The Man, His Work and His
World.* Cleveland: World Publishing, 1961; 274 pp., illus.
    Simple biographical treatment sketching background of
    Bernstein's career, with information on his Jewish back-
    ground. Attention to some compositions of Judaic inspi-
    ration and to early concerts with Israel Philharmonic.
  280
BUKOFZER, MANFRED F. *Studies in Medieval and Renaissance
Music.* New York: W.W. Norton, 1950; 324 pp., illus., music.
    See Chapter 6, pp.190-216, for references to Jewish
    dancing master of Renaissance, Guglielmo Ebreo of Italy.
  281
CARNER, MOSCO. *Of Men and Music.* London, Eng.: J. Wil-
liams, 1945; 182 pp., illus., music.
    See: chapter 2 "Judaism in Music," for subjective dis-
    cussion on topic, with examples.
  282
CHAMBERS, GEORGE B. *Folksong - Plainsong: A Study in Origins and Musical Relationships.* London, Eng.: Merlin Press,
1956; viii, 120 pp., illus., music.
    See Chapter 7 "The Jewish Musical Traditions," pp.69-75.
    Analysis of qualities, forms and styles of church music,
    particularly in reference to folksong. Judaic origins of
    music for worship cited, noting materials in several
    studies on subject. Preface by Ralph Vaughn Williams.
  283
CHASE, GILBERT. *The Music of Spain: 2nd Revised Edition.*
New York: Dover Press, 1959; 383 pp., illus., music.
    Sweep of Iberian-Spanish music history, includes refer-
    ences to Jewish music and musicians. Consult index. See:
    pp. 223-4 — "Another authority, Medina Azara, gives much
    importance to a fourth factor, the Hebraic, attempting
    to show a strong analogy between Andalusian *cante jondo*
    and the Jewish synagogal chant. There was unquestion-
    ably a considerable Jewish influence in Moslem Spain."
  284
COHN, ARTHUR. *The Collector's Twentieth Century Music in
the Western Hemisphere.* Phila.: J.B. Lippincott, 1961;
256 pp., illus.
    Simple biographical summaries and program notes for ros-
    ter of composers and their works available on records.
    Included are: Ernest Bloch, Aaron Copland and Lukas
    Foss, for whom information is given on Judaic background
    and some Jewish-inspired works.
  285
COLLAER, PAUL. *A History of Modern Music.* trans. from
French by Sally Abeles. Cleveland: World Publishing, 1961;
415 pp., illus., music.
    Includes materials on Schoenberg, Milhaud, Bloch, Cop-
    land, Gershwin, Tansman and Weill, wirh some Judaic per-
    spectives, within sweep of 20th century creativity.
  286
DAVIS, LOUIS S. *Studies in Musical History.* New York:
G.P. Putnam, 1887; iv,164pp.

See section on "Spirit of Jewish Music," pp.10-7,
for discussion of Biblical music expression.

287
DICKINSON, EDWARD. *Music in the History of the Western Church; With an Introduction on Religious Music Among the Primitive and Ancient Peoples.* New York: Scribners, 1902; 426pp., illus., music.
 Survey of development of liturgical music by historian
 Edward Dickinson (1853-1946). See Chapter 1 "Primitive
 and Ancient Religious Music," pp.1-35; and, Chapter 2
 "Ritual and Song in Early Christian Church," pp.36-69.
 Some consideration of biblical music and of early syna-
 gogue chant. Limited data, though references to such
 sources as works of Engel and Stainer, and to Jewish
 hymnal (1893) of Kaiser and Sparger. Also consult index.

288
ENGEL, CARL. *The Music of the Most Ancient Nations, Particularly of the Assyrians, Egyptians and Hebrews; With Special References to Recent Discoveries in Western Asia and in Egypt.* repr.ed. Freeport,N.Y.:Books for Libraries Press, 1970; 379pp., illus.,music. (repr.ed. London,Eng.:M.Reeves, 1911; orig.ed. London,Eng.:J. Murray, 1864)
 Fascinating early work, with notable illustrations, all
 reflecting 19th century growth of musical scholarship,
 and studies of Carl Engel (1818-1882). See Chapter 6
 "Music of the Hebrew," pp.277-365. Engel's survey includes wide variety of Judaic elements (such as music of
 Falashas, or Abbysinian Jews) and he reflects upon Jewish liturgical motifs in mainstream western musics. Engel was born and educated in Germany, emigrated to London in 1844 and there devoted himself to music research,
 teaching and bibliographic collection. He left his personal library to the museum of South Kensington, later
 called "Victoria and Albert." Facsimiles and musical
 examples. Hebrew terms romanized. Also consult index.

289
ENSEL, GUSTAVE S. *Ancient Liturgical Music; A Comprehensive and Historical Essay.* Paducah, Ken.,1880; 230pp.,music
 Origin and development of sacred music from earliest
 times, with comparative illustrations of music used in
 worship rituals of synagogue, church and mosque (Islam).

290
FARMER, HENRY GEORGE. *Historical Facts for the Arabian Musical Influence.* London, Eng.: William Reeves, 1930; ix, 376 pp., illus., music.
 References to Jewish music throughout text. Consult in-
 dex. H. G. Farmer (1882-1965) was notable musicologist.

291
FARMER, HENRY GEORGE. *A History of Arabic Music to the 13th Century.* London, Eng.: Luzac Press, 1929; xv, 264 pp., illus., music.
 References to Hebrew music and to Judeo-Arabic musicians
 by leading music scholar H. G. Farmer (1882-1965). Consult index for relevant information.

292
FARMER, HENRY GEORGE. *The Organ of the Ancients - from
Eastern Sources (Hebrew, Syriac and Arabic).* London, Eng.:
William Reeves, 1931; xxiii, 185 pp., illus., music.
    H. G. Farmer (1882-1965) bases origins of organ as music
    instrument upon biblical sources, considering such He-
    brew words as *'ugab* and *magrepha*, with the other
    terms of hydraulis and organum. References to biblical
    and talmudic literature as well as rabbinic commentaries
    along with early Arabic writings. See: pp. 21-44. Farmer
    has left a legacy of intriguing studies of mid-eastern
    musics of Ancient and Middle Age periods. Foreword by
    Rev. Francis William Galpin (1858-1945).
293
FARMER, HENRY GEORGE. *Studies in Oriental Musical Instruments.* Glascow, Scot.: Civic Press, 1939; 98 pp., illus.
    Considerations of Arabic instrumentations and music, and
    inter-relationships over centuries. References to work
    of Jewish scholar Robert Lachmann (1892-1939), who in
    1929 had been director of Department of Extra-European
    Music at Hebrew University in Jerusalem; and to studies
    of Curt Sachs (1881-1959) who had then been professor of
    musicology at University of Berlin. H. G. Farmer (1882-
    1965) was music scholar of broad range.
294
FENELON, FANIA and MARCELLE RAUTIER. *The Musicians of
Auschwitz.* trans. from French by J. Landry. London, Eng.:
Joseph and Atheneum, 1977; ix, 262 pp.
    Personal account of ordeals inflicted upon musicians in
    Concentration Camps, and of their struggles to survive
    or at least try to retain some self-respect at death.
    Through all, making of music sustained spirits. Memoir
    of Holocaust survivor, Paris-born singer and pianist
    Fania Fenelon (1908-1983).
295
FENLON, IAIN. *Music and Patronage in 16th Century Mantua.*
vols.1 and 2. Cambridge,Eng.:Cambridge Univ. Press, vol.1 -
1980;xi,234pp.,illus.,music; vol.2 - 1982;xiv,174pp.,,music.
    In volume 1, musicologist Iain Fenlon discusses cultural
    life during time of Gonzaga ducal leaders in Mantuan
    area of North Italy, and their patronage of music. Back-
    ground given on Jewish communities and musical involve-
    ment with courts of era. In Volume 2, he considers works
    of specific composers (1581-1606), including music by
    Salomone Rossi Ebreo (c.1565-c.1628).
296
FREEDLAND, MICHAEL. *Irving Berlin.* New York: Stein and
Day, 1974; 224 pp., illus.
    An endorsed biography which reviews Berlin's early life
    and Jewish parentage, with references to such influences
    upon his later years and career. Author notes that in
    1959, Berlin wrote a work entitled "Israel."
297
GARTENBERG, EGON. *Vienna; Its Musical Heritage.* Univ.
Park, Penn.: Penn. State Univ. Press, 1968; 262 pp., illus.
    Brief biographies of musical figures in Vienna before

World War II, along with a narrative history of the city
itself. Included is an essay on the creative Jews of
Vienna, noting several musicians, among them Arnold
Schoenberg (1874-1951). Consult index for subjects.
298

GERSON-KIWI, EDITH. *The Persian Doctrine of Dastga Composition - Phenomenological Study in the Musical Modes.* Tel
Aviv, Isr.: I.M.I., 1963; 48 pp., music.
Analysis in terms of intonations and classifications by
leading Israeli music scholar and educator. Study here
adds to field of comparative modal traditions in Near
Eastern musics.
299

GODDARD, JOSEPH. *The Rise of Music.* New York: Scribners,
1908; xv, 398 pp., illus., music.
See section on "Ancient Jewish Music," pp. 39-63.
300

GOLDBERG, ISAAC. *Tin-Pan-Alley; A Chronicle of the American Popular Music Racket.* New York:John Day, 1938; 341pp.
George Gershwin (1898-1937) wrote brief introduction for
book, which traces out history early in this century of
commercial business of popular music. Details of various
publishers, many of Jewish lineage. Author is both in-
genuous and outrageous: "The history of music publishing
immediately after the Spanish-American War may be summed
up in the phrase 'more of the same.' Jewish names were
becoming more prominent, and with them Jewish commercial
methods. To assume that there had been no hustlers on
Music Row before the Jews arrived would be stupid; perhaps it is a coincidence that with their coming the in-
dustry began to hum. It is reasonable, however, to at-
tribute much of Tin-Pan-Alley's early progress to the
more intense competition introduced by Jewish firms."
301

GOLDRON, ROMAIN. *Ancient and Oriental Music.* trans. from
French by Stella Sturman. London, Eng.: H.S. Stuttman,
1968; 172 pp., illus., music.
General treatment of topic with references to types of
biblical and post-biblical music for worship.
302

GROUT, DONALD J. *A History of Western Music: 3rd Edition*
rev.ed. with Claude V. Palisca. New York:W.W. Norton, 1980;
849pp.,illus.,music. (repr.ed. New York:W.W. Norton, 1973;
xiv,818pp.,illus.,music;orig.ed. New York:W.W. Norton,1960)
Reflections on Hebrew music in first chapter and other
scattered passages (see index). References to several
composers' works of Judaic inspiration, such as Copland
and "Vitebsk," Milhaud and "Sacred Service," Schoenberg
and "Moses and Aaron." Yet, why the skimming over of the
works of Ernest Bloch with designation "Swiss American?"
303

HAMM, CHARLES. *Yesterdays; Popular Song in America.* New
York: W.W. Norton, 1979; xxii, 533pp., illus.
Musicological study of American popular song as "mirror
of society that created it." Included in broad-ranging
historical account are activities in America of Lorenzo

da Ponte (1749-1838), songs of British tenor John Braham (1777-1856) and a roster of others of Judaic lineage
in 19th and 20th centuries. Extensive consideration of
Tin-Pan-Alley, with note of "Jewish American contributions to popular song." Source notes.
  304

HITCHCOCK, H. WILEY. *Music in the United States: A Historical Introduction.* (Prentice-Hall History of Music Series)
Englewood Cliffs, N.Y.: Prentice-Hall, 1969; 270 pp., music.
    Includes roster of composers of Jewish lineage.
  305

HOWARD, JOHN TASKER and GEORGE KENT BELLOWS. *A Short History of Music in America.* New York: Thomas Y. Crowell,
1967; xxvii, 496 pp., illus., music.
    Survey-sweep of American music history from Colonial
    times to 1960's, with considerations of such musicians
    of Judaic lineage as: Damrosch, Mannes, Goldmark, Bloch,
    Blitzstein, Copland, Diamond, Foss, Gershwin, Bernstein,
    Gould, as well as a roster of creators of popular songs.
    Informative on many aspects, except ethnic expressions.
    With discography. Consult index for relevant materials.
  306

HUTCHINSON, ENOCH. *Music of the Bible, or Explanatory Notes
Upon Those Passages in the Sacred Scriptures Which Relate to
Music, Including a Brief View of Hebrew Poetry.* Boston:
Gould and Lincoln, 1864; viii, 513 pp., illus.
    Treatment of music references in Old and New Testaments,
    with citations of passages which mention music, dance or
    musical instruments in New Testament. Reflections upon
    influences of Old Testament music.
  307

JABLONSKI, EDWARD. *Harold Arlen; Happy With the Blues.*
Garden City, N.Y.: Doubleday, 1961; 286 pp., illus.
    Early section of this biography of songwriter Harold
    Arlen treats his background as Hyman Arluck, musically
    gifted son of a Buffalo cantor. "His father's singing
    style, his way with melodic phrases, his ability to im-
    provise hauntingly beautiful melodies, Arlen feels were
    inherited, or at least he lived with it long enough to
    have absorbed it." (p.37) Roster of songs and selected
    discography. Index no help here.
  308

JABLONSKI, EDWARD and LAWRENCE D. STEWART. *The Gershwin
Years.* Garden City, N.Y.: Doubleday, 1958; 313 pp., illus.
    Chronological narrative covering creativity together of
    the brothers — George Gershwin (1898-1937), composer,
    and Ira Gershwin (1896-1983), lyricist. Biographical
    references to aspects of their Jewish lineage and early
    tenement days on the Lower East Side of New York City.
    Listings of their collaborative works. Introduction by
    Carl Van Vechten. Consult index for relevant topics.
  309

JACOB, HEINRICH EDUARD. *Felix Mendelssohn and His Times.*
trans. from German by Richard and Clara Winston. Englewood
Cliffs, N.J.: Prentice-Hall, 1963; 356 pp., illus.
    Popularly styled biography, includes background on Jew-

ish ancestry, family milieu and influences on music for
composer Felix Mendelssohn (1809-1847).

310
JANI, EMILIO. *My Voice Saved Me - Auschwitz 180046.*
trans. from Italian by Timothy Paterson. Milan, It.:
Centauro Editrice, 1961; 152 pp., illus.
    Holocaust music literature. Personal account of Italian
    Jewish operatic tenor, who was in Auschwitz 1943-45 and
    managed to survive. Through it all, he kept singing and
    felt that music sustained his life and spirit.

311
KALLMANN, HELMUT. *A History of Music in Canada 1534-1914.*
Toronto, Can.: Univ. of Toronto Press, 1960; 318 pp.,illus.
    Attention to Jewish musicians of Canada, specifically
    referring to information sources such as Canadian Jew-
    ish Congress Yearbooks.

312
KOWALKE, KIM H. *Kurt Weill in Europe.* (Studies in Musicology, 14) Ann Arbor, Mich.: UMI Research Press, 1979;
vii, 589 pp., illus., music.
    Biographical and analytical study of early life and
    works of composer Kurt Weill (1900-1950), up to 1935,
    when he emigrated to America in flight from the nazis.
    Extensive treatment of music in terms of modes and style
    of expression and European influences.

313
KUNST, JAAP. *Ethnomusicology.* The Hague, Neth.: Martinus
Nijhoff, 1959; 303 pp., music.
    Includes references to Jewish folk music. Jaap Kunst
    (1891-1960) was noted music scholar and dedicated eth-
    nologist, active in international academic activities.

314
KUPFERBERG, HERBERT. *The Mendelssohns; Three Generations
of Genius.* New York:Scribners Sons,1972; ix,272pp., illus.
    Discussion, in popular style, of Jewish philosopher and
    literary figure Moses Mendelssohn (1729-1786), his son
    banker Abraham Mendelssohn-Bartholdy (1776-1835), and
    his son composer (Jacob Ludwig) Felix Mendelssohn (1809-
    1847). Consideration of Jewish cultural achievements in
    18th and early 19th century Germany. Photographs and
    facsimile illustrations. Mendelssohn, along with Mahler
    and Meyerbeer, was attacked as "degenerate Jewish in-
    fluence upon German music" by Wagner, and ultimately by
    nazis who persecuted descendants of Mendelssohn family
    (though long converted to Christianity), hounding them
    into deportation or concentration camp.

315
LANG, PAUL HENRY. *Music in Western Civilization.* New
York: W.W. Norton, 1941; xvi, 1107 pp., illus., music.
    For materials related to Jewish liturgical and secular
    music, consult index listings. In description of rise of
    early Church worship, see pp. 51: "The leaders of wor-
    ship were recruited at first from the ranks of educated
    laymen. They did not occupy an official position in the
    Church and were not ordained; they were respected people
    whose position would be called an honorary one today.

With the office of the cantor, the Christian Church took
over an old synagogue institution, and also in many
cases probably employed musicians who had received their
education in Jewish musical practice and who introduced
their art into the new Christian liturgy. Idelsohn, in
his various publications of the songs of the Oriental
Jews, has given us examples of the astounding vertuosity
of those Jewish cantors."

316
LEICHTENTRITT, HUGO. *Music, History and Ideas.* Cambridge,
Mass.: Harvard Univ. Press, 1938; xxv, 292 pp., illus.
For references to Hebrew music topics and information as
to Jewish in music, consult index listing. Leichtentritt
(1874-1951) perceives the derivation of Church music as
from Jewish-Oriental and Greco-Roman sources, and cites
works of Idelsohn as verification that origins of Gregorian Chant formulas were closely akin to early Jewish
liturgical motifs. (pp. 26) "...a considerable portion
of what is now called Gregorian Chant represents remnants of ancient Hebrew Temple music, inherited by the
Catholic Church." Leichtentritt also discusses Jewish
biblical cantillation traditions in comparison to other
Christian chants. Other materials in book carry forward
into 20th century, including innovations of Schoenberg.

317
LEICHTENTRITT, HUGO. *Music of the Western Nations.* enl.
and ed. by Nicholas Slonimsky. Cambridge, Mass.:Harvard
Univ. Press, 1956; 318pp.,illus.
Posthumous volume of final studies by notable scholar
Hugo Leichtentritt (1874-1951). Considerations of varied
regional and national musical traits, different folk and
art music expressions in relationship to development of
world-wide creativity, and significance of nationalistic
composers' works as universal art. See esp. Chapter 2
"The Hebrews," pp. 23-45. Quirky, but fascinating work.
Foreword by Nicholas Slonimsky. Consult index.

318
MACDONALD, MALCOLM. *Schoenberg.* London, Eng.: J.M. Dent,
1976; xiv, 289 pp., illus., music.
Subjective study of the life of Arnold Schoenberg (1874-
1951), reflecting upon the struggles - economic, social,
political, personal and professional - the composer en-
dured throughout his life. Biographer links up Schoenberg's musical creativity with those varied and often
tragic circumstances. Schoenberg had to manage during
his final years on a pension of thirty dollars a month,
having been rejected in his requests for funds by the
Guggenheim and other foundation grants. Consult index.

319
MAGIDOFF, ROBERT. *Yehudi Menuhin; The Story of the Man and
the Musician.* New York: Doubleday, 1955; 319 pp., illus.
Some biographical details on Menuhin's Judaic lineage.

320
MALM, WILLIAM P. *Music Cultures of the Pacific, Near East,
and Asia.* (Prentice-Hall History of Music Series) Englewood
Cliffs., N.J.: Prentice-Hall, 1967; 169 pp., illus., music.

See: "An Historical Interlude — the Ancient World of the
Near East," pp. 57-59; and, "Jewish Music in the Near
East," pp. 59-62. Also consult index.
321
MELLERS, WILFRED. *Music in a New Found Land; Themes and
Developments in the History of American Music.* New York:
Hillstone/Stonehill, 1975; xv, 545 pp., illus., music.
Dedicated to Aaron Copland and Marc Blitzstein (1905-
1964). Concentration upon particular composers and their
works, including some of Jewish relevance. See index.
322
MENUHIN, YEHUDI. *Unfinished Journey; An Autobiography.*
New York: Alfred A. Knopf, 1977; xvii, 393 pp., illus.
Violinist, conductor and teacher Yehudi Menuhin reviews
his life, family, lineage and career.
323
MILHAUD, DARIUS. *Notes Without Music; An Autobiography.*
trans. from French by Donald Evans. (ed. by Rollo H. Meyers)
Chapters 34 and 35 trans. by Arthur Ogden (ed. by Herbert
Weinstock) New York: Alfred A. Knopf, 1953; 355 pp., illus.
Narrative review of life and work of Darius Milhaud
(1892-1974) with insights by the composer into his
French-Provencal Jewish background, his education and
life experiences, his works and their varied sources of
inspiration. Chronological listing of compositions, with
annotations. Consult index for particular subjects.
324
NATHAN, ISAAC. *An Essay on the History and Theory of Music
and, on the Qualities, Capabilities and Management of the
Human Voice.* London. Eng.: W.B. Whittaker, 1823; 229 pp.,
illus., music.
Discussion of Jewish music in terms of biblical cantillation and liturgical chant included in this work by
English musician and writer Isaac Nathan (1791-1864) who
set to music poetry of Lord Byron ("Hebrew Melodies").
Born in Canterbury, Nathan wrote stage musicals, sacred
and secular choral works and British patriotic songs. He
migrated to Sidney, Australia, where he died.
325
NETTL, BRUNO. *Folk and Traditional Music of the Western
Continents.* (Prentice-Hall History of Music Series) Englewood Cliffs, N.J.: Prentice-Hall, 1965; 213pp.,illus.,music.
References to Jewish folk music in Europe. See index.
326
NETTL, PAUL. *Forgotten Musicians.* New York: Philosophical
Library, 1957; vi, 352 pp., illus.
See: "The Unknown Jewish Minstrel," pp. 28-46, in which
Paul Nettl (1889-1972) describes the music and lifestyle
of the itinerant Jewish fiddler, as village musician of
18th century German-Slavic areas, and other anonymous
Jewish musicians of earlier periods in Europe. He also
considers some known musicians: Suesskind von Trimberg
(Trimpberg, Jewish?) German minnesinger of 13th century,
and Woelffle von Locham (Locheim), German-Jewish song
collector (c.1450). Nettl cites iconographic sources of
17th and 18th centuries, traces Jewish music activities

in Bohemia and notes leading 19th century European musicians of Jewish lineage. Informative and intriguing.
327
NEWLIN, DIKA. *Bruckner, Mahler, Schoenberg.* rev. ed., New
York: W.W. Norton, 1978; xi, 308 pp., illus., music.
Information included on Judaic backgrounds of Gustave
Mahler (1864-1911) and Arnold Schoenberg (1874-1951) and
their relationship, conversions, as well as the social
atmosphere in Vienna and the struggles for positions by
two gifted musicians of Jewish parentage. See index.
328
PAYNE, ROBERT. *Gershwin.* New York: Pyramid Books, 1960;
157 pp., illus.
Light-style biography of George Gershwin (1898-1937),
with references to some traditional Jewish musical
elements in terms of influences upon his creativity.
329
PEYSER, JOAN. *The New Music; The Sense Behind the Sound.*
New York: Delacorte Press, 1971; xiii, 204 pp., illus.
Perspectives on more recent creativity, with information
on works of such composers of Judaic lineage as: Bernstein, Copland, Foss, Gershwin, Milhaud, Schoenberg and
Weill. Introduction by Jacques Barzun. Consult index.
330
PIATIGORSKY, GREGOR. *Cellist; An Autobiography.* New York:
Doubleday, 1965; 273 pp., illus.
Popular-style narrative, which includes much information
about life and career of virtuoso Gregor Piatigorsky
(1903-1976), along with vignettes of his musical colleagues, many of whom also of Judaic background.
331
POLIN, CLAIRE. *Music of the Near East.* New York: Vantage
Press, 1954; xxi, 138 pp., illus., music.
Includes comparative tables, with musical examples, for
cantillations, chants and modal scales of various Near
Eastern musical traditions, in addition to Judaic. Excellent illustrations. Consult index.
332
REESE, GUSTAVE. *Music in the Middle Ages; With an Introduction on the Music of Ancient Times.* New York: W.W. Norton, 1940; xvii, 502 pp., illus., music.
See esp. Chapters 1, 2, 3, 5, 6 and 7 for information
relevant to Jewish music history and influences. Gustave
Reese (1899-1977) was notable musicologist and educator
whose broad range of knowledge and active scholarly in-
quiry strengthened this area of music study in terms of
many diverse elements, including the Judaic. Now, over
four decades later, this work retains its strength and
value for the field. Here, Reese cites such sources as:
Salomon Rosowsky (1878-1962) on biblical cantillation;
Curt Sachs (1981-1959) on antiquity; John Stainer (1840-
1901) on biblical references to music; A. Z. Idelsohn
(1882-1938) on the sweep of Jewish liturgical music expression; H. G. Farmer (1882-1965) on comparative Near
Eastern musics; Robert Lachmann (1892-1939) on North
African ethnomusicology; and Joseph Yasser (1893-1981)

on modal music concepts. Consult index.

333
REESE, GUSTAVE. *Music in the Renaissance.* New York: W.W.
Norton, 1954; xvii, 1022 pp., illus., music.
    Music era treated — c.1300 to 1650. Companion work to
    Music in the Middle Ages, by scholar and educator
    Gustave Reese (1899-1977). Excellent bibliographical
    supplement, pp. 884-946. Consult index for relevant
    materials and topics.

334
REICH, WILLI. *Schoenberg; A Critical Biography.* trans.
from German by Leo Black. London, Eng.: Longman, 1971; xi,
268 pp., illus., music.
    Overview of life and works of Arnold Schoenberg (1874-
    1951), with some attention to his compositions of Judaic
    inspiration, such as "Jacob's Ladder" and "Moses and
    Aaron." Best coverage is of Vienna period. Discussion of
    composer's literary as well as musical creativity. Reich
    notes Schoenberg's growing interest, after 1933, in the
    Zionist movement. Consult index for relevant topics.

335
RIMMER, JOAN. *Ancient Musical Instruments of Western Asia,
in the Department of Western Asiatic Antiquities of the
British Museum.* London, Eng.: British Museum/Probsthain,
1969; xxv, 51 pp., illus.
    Introductory essay for a fine collection of materials at
    the museum, including those from biblical areas in Near
    East. Excellent photographic illustrations.

336
ROSEN, CHARLES. *Arnold Schoenberg.* (Modern Masters Series) New York: Viking Press, 1975; xiv, 113 pp., music.
    General discussion of works by Arnold Schoenberg (1874-
    1951), including references to compositions of Judaic
    inspiration. Consult index.

337
RUFER, JOSEF, ed. *The Works of Arnold Schoenberg; A Catalogue of His Compositions, Writings and Paintings.* trans.
from German by Dika Newlin. London, Eng.: Faber and Faber,
1962; 214 pp., illus., music.
    Included in this collected and annotated roster of the
    varied creativity of Arnold Schoenberg (1874-1951) are
    works of Judaic inspiration, and writings on subjects of
    Jewish interest and concerns, as for example his ad-
    vocacy of a national Jewish homeland and support of the
    establishment of the State of Israel. Consult the table
    of contents for many relevant materials.

338
SACHS, CURT. *The Commonwealth of Art.* New York: W.W. Norton, 1946; xiv, 404 pp., illus., music.
    Curt Sachs (1881-1959) applies the concept of historical
    inter-relationship between art and music in specific
    terms, and thereby offers some intriguing theories. See
    esp. materials on pp. 31-48. Sachs may have tried to
    cover too wide a field area in this book, and several of
    his ideas on nature and style do not appear to have held
    up too well. Among the range of music examples are some

citations from the work of A. Z. Idelsohn (1882-1938).
Consult index for relevant topics.
  339
SACHS, CURT. *The History of Musical Instruments.* New
York: W.W. Norton, 1940; 505 pp., illus.
       Vast compendium of information, since enlarged upon by
       other scholars but nonetheless remaining singularly im-
       portant in its subject area. Curt Sachs (1881-1959) sup-
       plies section on terminology, along with an index of in-
       struments and numerous excellent illustrations. See esp.
       Part ii and notably Chapter 5 "Israel," pp. 105-27, in-
       cluding exposition on the *Shofar*, pp. 110-12. Consult
       index for many relevant items, particularly relating to
       instruments noted in biblical passages. Sachs had been
       a noted scholar in Germany and France before seeking re-
       fuge in this country in 1938. His subsequent roster of
       scholarly publications constitute a valuable legacy.
  340
SACHS, CURT. *Our Musical Heritage; A Short History of
Music.* 2nd ed. Englewood Cliffs, N.J.: Prentice-Hall, 1955;
351 pp., illus., music.
       Curt Sachs (1881-1959) was an outstanding teacher as
       well as scholar, and this work was intended as a peda-
       gogical resource. Consult index for relevant topics.
  341
SACHS, CURT. *Rhythm and Tempo; A Study in Music History.*
New York: W.W. Norton, 1953; 391 pp., illus., music.
       Basic enthnomusicological study resource by scholar
       and educator Curt Sachs (1881-1959). Consult index for
       relevant topics.
  342
SACHS, CURT. *The Rise of Music in the Ancient World: East
and West.* New York:W.W. Norton, 1943; 324 pp.,illus.,music.
       Still a "classic" in its topical area. See esp. Section
       Two "Western Orient," pp 57-102. Consult index for other
       relevant materials. Curt Sachs (1881-1959) was a seminal
       figure in musicology.
  343
SACHS, CURT. *The Wellsprings of Music.* (Jaap Kunst, ed.)
The Hague, Neth.:Martinus Nijoff,1962;xi,228pp.,illus.,music
       Collection of essays by Curt Sachs (1881-1959) as his
       final studies in ethnomusicology — origins and descrip-
       tions, cultural patterns, instrumental and vocal music,
       folk musicians and composers of art-music. Constitutes a
       "summing-up" of many ideas as well as Sachs' scholarly
       invitation to further examinations of these areas by
       others ahead. Among range of considerations are works of
       Avenary, Gerson-Kiwi, Idelsohn, Lachmann, Spector and
       Werner. References also to *Kol Nidre* and Babylonian
       Jewish liturgy. Consult index. This posthumous volume
       was edited by ethnomusicologist Jaap Kunst (1891-1960)
       who did not live to see it in print.
  344
SAMINSKY, LAZARE. *Music of Our Day: Essentials and Proph-
ecies.* repr. ed. Freeport, N.Y.: Books for Libraries Press,
1970; xxvi, 390 pp., illus. (enl. ed. New York: Thomas Y.

Crowell, 1939; xxvi, 390 pp. illus.; orig. ed. New York:
Thomas Y. Crowell, 1932; 313 pp.)
    Four sections of subjective essays on musical topics by
    Lazare Saminsky (1882-1959), who was music director of
    Temple Emanu-El in New York City, and earlier had been
    active figure among Jewish musicians in Moscow before
    coming to this country in 1920. In Russia, Saminsky had
    collected, arranged and published Jewish folksongs. Here
    he was a composer, arranger, choral director, educator,
    writer, and active member of the Jewish Music Forum.
    345
SANDERS, RONALD. *The Days Grow Short; Life and Music of*
*Kurt Weill.*New York: Holt, Rinehart, 1980; 469 pp., illus.
    Biographical account, without special musical analysis,
    of life and career of Kurt Weill (1900-1950), in Europe
    and after 1935 in America. Discussion of various social,
    cultural and political influences upon his work. Though
    Weill's Jewish lineage appeared to have little relevance
    to his general creativity, soon after arrival here he
    composed some liturgical selections upon commission. One
    of those works, a lovely setting of the Friday evening
    Kiddush (sanctification of wine), remains a favorite
    among young cantors, especially for pulpit auditions.
    346
SCHWARTZ, CHARLES. *Gershwin; His Life and Music.* New
York: Bobbs-Merrill, 1973; 428 pp., illus., music.
    Serious biographical study of George Gershwin (1898-
    1937), including references to some Jewish qualities in
    his music. Discography. See appended materials and the
    index for relevant topics.
    347
SCHWARZ, BORIS. *Music and Musical Life in Soviet Russia -*
1917-1970. New York: W.W. Norton, 1972; ix, 550 pp., illus.
    Survey by violinist and educator Boris Schwarz (1906-
    1983) of general musical milieu as it evolved, with
    political and social strictures, over decades following
    revolution of 1917. Information included on several com-
    posers, performers and educators of Jewish lineage, as
    active in musical life in Soviet Union. Consult index.
    348
SEAY, ALBERT. *Music in the Medieval World.* (The Prentice-
Hall History of Music Series) Englewood Cliffs, N.J.: Pren-
tice-Hall, 1965; 182 pp., illus., music.
    See esp.: "Jewish music practices." pp. 7-12. Discussion
    of influences upon early church music developments. "Of
    greater moment was the Jewish assumption, accepted com-
    pletely, that music was an integral part of liturgy, of
    such importance it could not be dispensed with." (p. 16)
    References to works of A.Z. Idelsohn, Curt Sachs, Alfred
    Sendrey and Eric Werner. Consult index.
    349
SEEGER, CHARLES LOUIS. *Studies in Musicology 1935-1975.*
Berkeley, Cal.: Univ. of Cal. Press, 1977; vii, 357 pp.
    Collection of articles and musicological studies by
    Charles L. Seeger (1886-1979). Relevant materials on
    ethnic creativity in parts of Chapters 10 (pp. 195-210),

11 (pp. 211-21), 12 (pp. 222-36), 16 (pp. 321-29), 17
(pp. 330-34), and 18 (pp. 335-43). With roster of his
writings and music. Also consult index.
350
SHILOAH, AMNON. *The Epistle on Music of the Ikhwan Al-Safa*
(Bagdad, 10th cent.). (Documentation and Studies Series, 3)
Tel Aviv, Isr.: Tel Aviv Univ. Press, 1978; 73 pp.
   Translation, with commentary-discussion, of significant
   treatise on Arabo-semitic music of early period around
   time of decline of Babylonian Diaspora cultural epoch.
351
SOROKER, IAKOV L'VOVICH. *David Oistrakh.* trans. from Yiddish and Russian by J. Vinner. Jerusalem,Isr.:Lexicon House,
1983; viii,183pp., illus.
   Tribute volume for Russian Jewish violinist, conductor
   and music educator David Oistrakh (1908-1974). With
   biographical information, bibliographic references and
   roster of recordings. Hebrew and English texts.
352
STEIN, ERWIN, ed. *Arnold Schoenberg Letters.* trans. from
German by Eithne Wilkins and Ernst Kaiser. New York: St.
Martins Press, 1965; 309 pp., illus.
   Materials selected for publication by Erwin Stein (1885-
   1958) and arranged in five chronological sections, with
   biographical notes and an index of correspondents. The
   letters of Arnold Schoenberg (1874-1951) reflect his
   ideas and experiences, reactions to social and political
   issues of the day, opinions on music and musicians, and
   the background contexts for his compositions, among them
   works of Judaic expression. Stein's collection was posthumously prepared in this English translation. Consult
   general index for relevant topics.
353
STEIN, LEONARD, ed. *Style and Idea; Selected Writings of*
Arnold Schoenberg. trans. from German by Leo Black and Dika
Newlin. New York:St. Martins Press,1975; 559pp.,illus.,music
   Publication prepared for Schoenberg centennial. Total of
   104 pieces of varying lengths, written by Arnold Schoenberg (1874-1951), some 25 of which the composer wrote in
   English. Selection of materials affords perspective on
   personality and opinions of the man, as evolved over the
   years. Note his gracious acknowledgement letter of 1949
   in response to designation of "honorary citizenship" by
   Vienna, a city from which in 1925 he had departed under
   humiliating and discouraging circumstances and which had
   banned his music during the nazi era. Consult the table
   of contents and index for relevant subjects.
354
STEVENSON, ROBERT. *Patterns of Protestant Church Music.*
Durham, N.C.: Duke Univ. Press, 1953; 219 pp.
   See section in Appendices on "The Jewish *Union Hymnal*"
   pp. 177-86, which affords a critical analysis of the
   Hymnal and its use in Jewish liturgical services, with
   consideration of various editions: 1897; 1914; and 1932.

355
STOLL, DENNIS GRAY. *Music Festivals of the World; A Guide to Leading Festivals of Music, Opera and Ballet.* New York: Macmillan, 1963; 310 pp., illus.
　　See in Chapter 18, "The Israel Festival," pp. 259-62. Festivals index. Foreword by Malcolm Sargent.
356
STRASSBURG, ROBERT. *Ernest Bloch: Voice in the Wilderness.* Los Angeles, Cal.: Strassburg/Trident Shop, 1977; vii, 192 pp., illus., music.
　　Biographical study of Ernest Bloch (1880-1959), with an extended section of annotated resource listings on the composer's music, his archival papers and correspondence sources, and some other publications on the man and his music. Consult index.
357
STRUNK, OLIVER, ed. *Source Readings in Music History - From Classical Antiquity to the Modern Era.* London, Eng.: Faber and Faber, 1952; xxi, 919 pp., illus.
　　Selected and annotated by Oliver Strunk (1901-1980), this collection of writings on music ranges in authors from Plato to Richard Wagner, and covers a great assortment of materials. Consult index for relevant topics.
358
STUCKENSCHMIDT, H.H. *Arnold Schoenberg.* trans. from German by Edith Temple Roberts and Roy E. Carter. London, Eng.: John Calder, 1959; 169 pp., illus., music.
　　Biographical study of Arnold Schoenberg (1874-1951) in context of his era and associates - relatives, students and colleagues - especially in Vienna and Berlin. Consult index for relevant topics.
359
STUCKENSCHMIDT, H.H. *Arnold Schoenberg; His Life, World and Work.* trans. from German by Humphrey Searle. New York: Schirmer Books, 1978; xiv, 581 pp., illus., music.
　　Combination of biography, background review and study of works, book generally surveys life and achievements of Arnold Schoenberg (1874-1951) within context of his time and other musicians of that period. Greatly expanded version of Stuckenschmidt's earlier biographical studies on Schoenberg. Consult index for relevant topics.
360
TAWA, NICHOLAS. *The Sound of Strangers, Music Culture, Acculturation and the Post Civil War Ethnic American.* Metuchen, N. J.: Scarecrow Press, 1982; xii, 304 pp.,illus., music
　　Discussion of distinctive ethnomusical traditions among several immigrant groups who came here at the turn of the century. Nicholas Tawa has utilized oral interviews, documentations and other modes of research to examine the legacy of that immigrant musical expression in the Greater New England area. Among groups considered are East European Jews and their Yiddish folksongs, theater popular tunes, and the melodies of Jewish liturgy. Attention is drawn to such topics as: the folk minstrel or *Badkhen*, theatrical performers, music publishers, cantorial artistry (such as that of Yossele Rosenblatt),

synagogue and holiday music and several particular melodies, including *Kol Nidre* and *Eili, Eili*. Consult
index for many relevant subjects.

361
WELLESZ, EGON. *Arnold Schoenberg; The Formative Years.*
enl. ed. London, Eng.: Galliard, 1971; iv, 156 pp., illus.
(repr. ed. New York: Da Capo Press, 1960; 156 pp., illus.;
orig. ed. Oxford, Eng.: Clarendon, 1925 pp., 156 pp.,illus.)
     Egon Wellesz (1885-1974), music scholar and composer,
     was a pupil and then colleague-friend of Arnold Schoen-
     berg (1874-1951). This brief biographical study was ori-
     ginally published in Vienna in 1921 (in German), and re-
     tains interest for its early evaluations of Schoenberg
     as man, teacher and composer, during the years of his
     creativity up to 1920. Wellesz added a new preface for
     enlargement of last edition. Consult index for topics.

362
WELLESZ, EGON. *Eastern Elements in Western Chant; Studies
in the Early History of Ecclesiastical Music.* (Monumenta
Musicae Byzantinae Series, 2) Oxford, Eng. : Oxford Univ.
Press, 1947; 212 pp., illus., music.
     Examination of origins and early development of Liturgi-
     cal chant by musicologist Egon Wellesz (1885-1974). He
     cites Philo's description of liturgical music practices
     among the *Therapeutae* — a dissident Judaic sect living
     near Alexandria — (pp. 52-54), in seeking out sources of
     antiphony and hymn chants of earliest Christians. Usages
     of music in services of early synagogues are explored,
     with reference to the studies of A.Z. Idelsohn (1882-
     1938) as to comparative Near Eastern musics. In seeking
     common sources for plainchant and solo psalmody for syn-
     agogue and church, Wellesz establishes linkages, leading
     to both Roman and Byzantine chants. He notes: "Parallels
     between Gregorian recitation of psalms and Jewish can-
     tillation have already been discovered...It remains an
     important task for comparative musicology to show par-
     allels between Gregorian and Jewish psalmody on the one
     hand, and Byzantine and Jewish psalmody on the other, in
     order to achieve solid foundations for studies in early
     Christian and early Medieval music." (p. 140) Consult
     table of contents and index for relevant topics.

363
WELLESZ, EGON. *A History of Byzantine Music and Hymnogra-
phy.* 2nd ed., rev. and enl. Oxford, Eng.: Oxford Univ.
Press, 1961; xiv, 461 pp., illus., music. (orig. ed. Oxford,
Eng. : Clarendon Press, 1949; xiv, 358 pp., illus., music)
     Scholarly study of origins and development of Byzantine
     liturgical music, viewing early synagogue and church
     services of hymns and psalmody as derived from Temple
     music patterns. Egon Wellesz (1885-1974), musicologist,
     educator and composer, was pupil and then colleague of
     of Guido Adler (1855-1941) and Arnold Schoenberg (1874-
     1951). In this book, Wellesz examines such areas as "The
     Legacy of the Synagogue," (pp. 27-37), and considers
     Judaic liturgical usages by Apostles and other shapers
     of Christian services. He refers to the works of Eric

Werner and of A.Z. Idelsohn (1882-1938). Second enlarged
edition of this volume incorporates newer studies of the
author after 1949, wherein Wellesz further strengthened
his legacy of research into Byzantine church music. Consult table of contents and index for relevant topics.
364

WERNER, ERIC. *Mendelssohn; A New Image of the Composer and
His Age.* trans. from German by Dika Newlin. New York: Free
Press of Glencoe/Macmillan/ Crowell-Collier, 1963; xiii,
545 pp., illus., music.

Scholar Eric Werner places composer and performer Felix
Mendelssohn (1809-1847) within context of his Judaic
lineage and family influences, and treats his personal
life as well as musical career. Biographical study also
affords view of Jewish cultural history of that early
19th century period, and draws attention to significance
of German-Jewish salon milieu of the time. No listings
or detailed analysis of Mendelssohn's music itself. Consult table of contents and index for relevant topics.
365

WERNER, JACK. *Mendelssohn's "Elijah;" An Historical and
Analytical Guide to the Oratorio.* London, Eng.: Chappell,
1965; 109 pp., illus., music.

Discussion of background to composition of the oratorio,
its special text and music setting. Consideration of
some Jewish musical and liturgical influences upon work.
Foreword by Malcolm Sargent. Discography.
366

WESCHLER, LAWRENCE. *Ernst Toch (1887-1964); A Biographical
Essays Ten Years After His Passing.* Los Angeles, Cal.: Toch
Archive/U.C.L.A., 1974; 16 pp., illus.

Brief biography of composer who fled nazi Germany in
1933, came to America and with aid of George Gershwin
(1898-1937) settled in California and wrote music scores
for films from 1936 to his death. Toch also composed
concert works, some of which were of Judaic inspiration.
367

WIORA, WALTER. *The Four Ages of Music.* trans. from German
by M.D. Herter Norton. New York: W.W. Norton, 1965; 233 pp.,
illus., music.

See Section ii, Part 3 "Jewish and Christian Antiquity,"
(pp. 87-97) for discussion of rise of liturgical music
expression and development of musical services for the
Temple rituals, and then for early synagogue and church
devotions - cantillation, chant, psalmody and hymnology.
"Christianity began as a movement within Judaism; hence
the Christian service and its singing grew out of Hebraic models..." (p. 93) Consult appended music tables
and index for relevant materials.
368

WOERNER, KARL H. *Schoenberg's "Moses and Aaron."* trans.
from German by Paul Hamburger. London, Eng.: Faber and
Faber, 1965; 208 pp., illus.

Background of this "unfinished" three-act music drama by
Arnold Schoenberg (1874-1951). Complete libretto in German and in English, with information on performances and

roster of various studies on work itself. Consult index.
369
WRIGHT. O. *The Modal System of Arab and Persian Music A.D.*
1250-1300. London, Eng.: Oxford Univ. Press, 1978; 302 pp.
   Citations from and references to studies by Avenary,
   Gerson-Kiwi, Idelsohn, Lachmann, Shiloah and Spector —
   all prominent Jewish musicologists — but no mention of
   any of them in index listing for this book. Fascinating
   work for what it attempts to present and how its author
   slides around the issues of various Judaic influences.
370
YASSER, JOSEPH. *Medieval Quartal`Harmony; A Plea for Re-*
storation. American Library of Musicology, 1938; 108 pp.
   Materials originally appeared as an extended article in
   3 parts for *The Musical Quarterly*, vol. 33, Apr. 1937,
   pp. 170-200/vol. 33, July 1937, pp. 333-66/vol. 34, July
   1938, pp. 351-85. Musicologist Joseph Yasser (1893-1981)
   added a prefatory note and table of contents for this
   publication. References in text to Jewish cantillations,
   chants and other types of liturgical music in discussion
   of backgrounds of Roman church melodies, and Hebrew and
   Greek sources for Gregorian chant. Yasser's studies of
   modes and chants formulated in terms of his proposal for
   a new theoretic approach to the subject of harmony and
   Medieval music history. No index.
371
YASSER, JOSEPH. *A Theory of Evolving Tonality.* repr. New
York: Da Capo Press, 1975; x, 381 pp., illus., music. (orig.
ed. New York: American Library of Musicology, 1932; x,
381 pp., illus., music)
   Theoretical study by scholar, musician and educator
   Joseph Yasser (1893-1981) which includes references to
   Hebrew cantillations, chants and modes. Glossary of
   technical terms. Consult index for relevant topics.

D. On General Subjects by One Author

372
ABRAHAMS, ISRAEL. *Jewish Life in the Middle Ages.* repr.ed
Phila.:J.P.S.A.,1958; xxvi,452pp. (orig.ed. Cambridge, Eng.:
Goldston, 1896)
   Well respected English publication, reprinted in America
   in honor of 100th anniversary of cultural historian,
   writer and educator Israel Abrahams (1858-1925). Includes information on Jewish musical creativity and
   music customs and practices, in context of author's
   survey of particular epoch in Europe. Consult general
   index for range of musically-related topics discussed.
373
AUSUBEL, NATHAN, comp. and ed. *Treasury of Jewish Folk-*
lore; Stories, Traditions, Legends, Humor, Wisdom and Folk-
songs of the Jewish People. New York: Crown, 1948; xxiv,

741 pp., illus., music.
    See: Part 3 - section on "Cantors," pp.388-92; and,
    Part 6 - "Songs and Dances," pp.650-727, which includes
    melody lines for 65 folksongs, liturgical hymns and
    Hassidic (Pietist) tunes. Hebrew and Yiddish romanized.
    Special attention to history of *Kol Nidre* chant for
    Eve of Day of Atonement. Includes music of Sabbath,
    High Holy Days and Festivals. Materials in context of
    Judaic folklore expressions.
374
COHEN, BOAZ. *Law and Tradition in Judaism.* New York: J.T.
S.A. Press, 1959; xii, 243pp.
    Collection of previously published articles by scholar,
    rabbi and educational leader Boaz Cohen (1899-1968). See
    Chapter 8 - "The Responsum of Maimonides Concerning
    Music," pp.167-81. Originally in *Jewish Music Journal*,
    vol.2,no.2 (New York, 1935).
375
EISENBERG, AZRIEL, ed. *The Synagogue Through the Ages.*
New York: Bloch, 1974; xi, 206 pp., illus.
    See Chapter 12: "The Officiants of the Synagogue,"
    pp. 139-42, treating *Hazzan* (Cantor) and his duties.
376
GASTER, THEODOR H., ed. *The Dead Sea Scrolls (in English
translation).* Garden City, N.Y.: Doubleday, 1956; 350 pp.
    See section on "The Praise of God: Hymns and Psalms,"
    pp.111-225. With introductory essay and source notes.
377
GAY, PETER. *Freud, Jews and Other Germans.* New York: Oxford Univ. Press, 1978; xviii, 289 pp.
    Includes consideration of musicians of Jewish lineage
    such as Arno Nadel (1878-1943), Arnold Schoenberg (1874-
    1951) and Artur Schnabel (1882-1951), within context of
    Judaic cultural expression and mainstream participation
    in Europe, during early decades of this century.
378
GOLDIN, JUDAH. *The Song at the Sea; Being a Commentary in
Two Parts.* New Haven,Conn.:Yale Univ. Press,1971;xxii,290pp
    Background study, interpretations and source materials
    for consideration of the "Song of Moses" - prayer of
    thanksgiving in Book of Exodus, 15th chapter - chanted
    by Moses and Israelites after crossing of Red (Reed) Sea
    and escape from Egyptian slavery. Passage referred to as
    "*Shirta*", an Aramaic word. Significance outlined here
    in terms of religious, ethical, spiritual and cultural
    issues. Some consideration of nature of original intona-
    tion of this liturgical poem. This particular section of
    Biblical text - "*Az Yashir Moshe*" - is chanted in
    morning prayers of all Jewish traditions. Source notes.
379
GOODMAN, PHILIP and HANNA GOODMAN, eds. *The Jewish Marriage Anthology.* Phila.:J.P.S.A.,1965; 360pp.,illus.,music.
    See: Chapter 19 - "Traditional and Folksongs," pp.326-
    36, which includes 9 songs - melody lines with Hebrew
    and Yiddish romanized. English translations. Suitable
    music for Jewish wedding ceremonies and celebrations.

380
HAPGOOD, HUTCHINS. *Spirit of the Ghetto: Studies of the Jewish Quarter of New York.* repr.ed. with intro. by Irving Howe. New York:Schocken Books, 1976; 316pp., illus. (orig. ed. New York:Funk and Wagnalls, 1902; 298pp., illus.)
    See sections on: "A Wedding Bard," pp. 91-98, which discusses the work of *Badkhen* (folk composer-performer) Eliakum Zunser (1840-1913), then an immigrant living on the Lower East Side of New York City; and "The Stage," pp. 113-76, which treats the fascinating early American Yiddish theater of the downtown New York area as it was developing at the turn of the century. Hutchins Hapgood (1869-1944) was a journalist whose keen observations and warm interest provided a lasting memoir of that era and of some of its leading figures.

381
IDELSOHN, ABRAHAM ZEBI. *Jewish liturgy and Its Development.* repr. pbk. ed. New York: Schocken Press, 1966, xix, 404 pp. (repr. ed. New York: Sacred Music Press of H.U.C.-J.I.R., 1956; xix, 404 pp.; orig. ed. New York: Rinehart and Winston, 1932; xix, 404 pp.)
    Scholarly examination of Jewish prayers and orders of services for calendar year. Arranged in two sections: historical development of Jewish worship from ancient times to modern era; and, description of actual liturgy for daily services, Sabbath, holidays, festivals, special observances, home devotions, *Seder* and Sabbath meals hymns. A.Z. Idelsohn (1882-1938) taught liturgy and liturgical music at Hebrew Union College in Cincinnati from 1924 to 1934. Volume comprised of his lecture notes and instruction materials and remains an excellent reference resource. Jewish liturgical music expression traditionally has been shaped by and allied with prayer text and ritual service. Appended are studies of Karaite liturgy and of Judaic connections to early Christian prayers. Consult extensive footnotes, roster of Hebrew titles and fine general index.

382
KARPELES, GUSTAV. *Jewish Literature and Other Essays.* Phila.:J.P.S.A., 1895; 404pp., illus.
    Collection of essays and addresses by German Jewish scholar Gustav Karpeles (1848-1909). See following of his chapter/essays: "Jewish Troubadours and Minnesingers," pp.169-90, which includes reflections on some Jewish poet-singers of 12th to 15th centuries; "The Jewish Stage," pp.229-48, an evaluative commentary; "The Music of the Synagogue," pp.369-80, a consideration of the historical development of Jewish liturgical music from Biblical era to "present time" (late 19th century).

383
KIEVAL, HERMAN. *The High Holydays: A Commentary on the Prayerbook of Rosh Hashanah.* New York: Burning Bush Press, 1959; 234 pp.
    Scholarly consideration of liturgy for services of two days of traditional observances for Jewish New Year (*Rosh Hashanah*). Attention to special prayer motifs,

hymns and cantillations (biblical chants), as well as
soundings of *Shofar* (ram's horn). References to works
of A. Z. Idelsohn (1882-1938) and to various entries on
musical topics in *Jewish Encyclopedia*. Glossary of
Hebrew terms and prayer index.

384

LAZAR, MOSHE. *The Sephardic Tradition: Ladino and Spanish-
Jewish Literature.* trans. from Hebrew and Spanish/Ladino by
David Herman. New York:W.W. Norton, 1972; 222pp.
   Consideration of poetic texts for folksong ballads of
   Spanish-Jewish traditions in vernacular language of Ladino (Spaniolic Jewish dialect), in terms of Spanish
   folksong models of earlier era (pre-expulsion), and the
   variants developed by Jews living in other countries
   over the following centuries. No music.

385

LEDERER, ZDENEK, *Ghetto Theresienstadt.* London, Eng.: Edward Goldston, 1953; viii, 275 pp.
   See Chapter 6: "Life and Art in the Ghetto," pp. 122-44,
   for discussion of music activities at that Concentration
   Camp (also known as Terezin) in Czechoslavakia.

386

MARCUS, JACOB RADER. *The Jew in the Medieval World; A
Source Book, 315-1791.* repr.ed. New York:Harper and Row,
1965; xix,504pp. (orig.ed. Phila.:J.P.S.A., 1938)
   Contains information regarding Jewish music creativity
   and activities of that period. Consult general index for
   numerous topical references.

387

MYERSON, A. and I. GOLDBERG. *The German Jews.* New York:
Alfred A. Knopf, 1933; 161 pp.
   Information on music and musicians, pp. 98-114.

388

NEWMAN, LOUIS I., comp. and ed. *The Hasidic Anthology.*
New York: Bloch, 1944; xc, 720 pp.
   Substantial collection of materials on Hasidic culture,
   which includes background information on Jewish musical
   expression as inherent to that pietist movement's unique
   religious expression.

389

OESTERLEY, WILLIAM OLIVER EMIL. *The Psalms in the Jewish
Church.* London, Eng.:Skeffington, 1910; x,266pp., illus.
   Scholarly study by liturgist W.O.E. Oesterley (1866-
   1950) of Book of Psalms. References to music in texts
   themselves. Consideration of musical services of ancient
   Temple, and chanting of Psalms as traditional hymnody
   of synagogue and church. Consult index for topics.

390

RISCHIN, MOSES. *The Promised City; New York's Jews, 1870-
1914.* Cambridge,Mass.:Harvard Univ. Press,1962;342pp.,illus
   Survey of period includes discussion of Yiddish theater,
   its musical presentations and musicians. Source notes.

391

ROSENFELD, LULLA. *Bright Star of Exile; Jacob Adler and
the Yiddish Theater.*New York:Crowell,1977;xvi,368pp.,illus.
   Origins and background in development of Yiddish theater

as Jewish art. Biography of notable Yiddish actor Jacob
Adler, along with his family and theatrical colleagues.
References to musicians and role of music for Yiddish
stage presentations. Sources and photographs.
392

ROTH, CECIL. *The Jews in the Renaissance.* Phila.:J.P.S.A.
1959; xii,378pp., illus.
See Chapter 11: "The Jews and Renaissance Theater,"
pp.247-70; and, Chapter 12: "Music and the Dance,"
pp.271-304. Broad range of information on creativity
and cultural activities of Jewish musicians during Renaissance Era in Northern Italy. Cecil Roth (1899-1970)
was leading English scholar, writer and educator who
specialized in Jewish cultural history, notably of England and Italy.
393

SANDERS, RONALD. *The Downtown Jews; Portraits of an Immigrant Generation.* New York:Signet/New American,1969;395pp.
Includes details on music and musicians of Yiddish stage
on Lower East Side of New York City during last years of
19th century and into decades of 20th century. Brief
biographies of notable figures of time. Source notes.
394

SANDROW, NAHMA. *Vagabond Stars; A World History of Yiddish
Theater.* New York:Harper and Row, 1977; xii,435pp., illus.
Survey of background and rise of art of Yiddish theater
in Europe and then America during late 19th and 20th
centuries. Information on music and musicians of many
theatrical presentations. Sources and glossary of terms.
395

SCHAUSS, HAYYIM. *The Jewish Festivals; From the Beginnings
to Our Own Day.* trans. from Hebrew by Samuel Jaffe. Cincin-
nati:U.A.H.C., 1938; xiv,320pp., illus.
Includes information on musical customs relating to observances in synagogue services and home celebrations of
Jewish calendar year: Sabbath; Three Festivals (*Pesach,
Shavuot, Sukkot/Simhat Torah*); High Holy Days (*Rosh
Hashanah, Yom Kippur*); *Hanukkah; Purim*; and other
commemorative or special occasions.
396

SCHORSKE, CARL E. *Fin-de-Siecle Vienna - Politics and Culture.* New York: Alfred A. Knopf, 1980; xxx, 378 pp., illus.
Includes considerations of composers Arnold Schoenberg
(1874-1951) and Gustave Mahler (1864-1911) in context of
their Jewish lineage and their activities in mainstream
Viennese musical life of turn-of-century era.
397

SCHWARZBAUM, HAIM. *Studies in Jewish and World Folklore.*
W.Berlin: de Gruyter, 1968; viii,603pp., illus., music.
See section on "Jewish Folksong, Folkmusic and Folk-
dance" pp.409-417, for brief general discussion.
398

SIMONSOHN, SHLOMO. *History of the Jews of the Duchy of
Mantua.* (Diaspora Research Inst. Series, 17) Jerusalem,
Isr.: Kiryath Sepher, 1977; 902 pp. illus.
See Chapter 7: "Literature, Science and the Arts,"

pp. 600-94, which includes information on Jewish music
and musicians in Mantua, especially during late Renaissance period. Details on Salomone Rossi.
399
WEINREICH, MAX. *History of the Yiddish Language.* trans.
from Yiddish by Shlomo Noble and Joshua Fichman. New York:
YIVO and H.U.C.-J.I.R., 1980; x,833pp. (orig. ed. in Yiddish
New York:YIVO, 1973; 830pp.)
Information on folksongs - Yiddish and Sephardic (ladino
Spaniolic Jewish) - and on folk musicians and liturgical
melodies. All materials within context of this survey of
historical development of Yiddish as language and mode
of cultural expression for East European Jewry. Work of
broad scholarship by outstanding specialist in Jewish
linguistics and social history Max Weinreich(1894-1969).
400
WIENER, LEO. *The History of Yiddish Literature in the
Nineteenth Century.* New York: Charles Scribners and Sons,
1899; 402 pp.
See Chapter 4 "The Folksong," pp.53-71; and, Chapter 15
"The Jewish Theater," pp.231-43. Information on Jewish
music and progress of then newly created Yiddish theater
at turn of century. Leo Wiener (1862-1939) was notable
scholar, educator and writer.
401
WIENER, LEO. *Popular Poetry of the Russian Jews.* Phila.:
J.P.S.A., 1898; 58pp.
Treatment of folk poetry genre of Yiddish minstrel-bard
(*Badkhen*) in Eastern Europe, whose texts set to folk
melodies enlightened as well as entertained people. Leo
Wiener (1862-1939) scholar of Jewish literature and history, considers the popular creativity of poet-singers
such as Velvel Ehrenkranz (c.1826-1883), Berl Broder
(c. mid-19th cent.), Abraham Goldfaden (1840-1908), and
Eliakum Zunser (1840-1913), with particular reference to
their literary expressions as well as musical legacy.
402
ZANGWILL, ISRAEL. *Children of the Ghetto.* New York: J.P.
S.A. and Macmillan, 1892/1895; 553pp., illus.
Musical customs for religious observances discussed in
various stories related by author concerning Jewish life
in old Ghetto area of London of late 19th century. See
especially, perceptions of journalist Israel Zangwill
(1864-1926) on early Yiddish theater, in chapter xxi
"The Jargon Players," and his delineation of Naphtali
Herz Imber (1856-1909), poet-creator of *Hatikvah*, here
fictionalized as wanderer-poet Pinchas Melchitzedek.
403
ZANGWILL, ISRAEL. *The Voice of Jerusalem.* New York: Macmillan, 1920/21; 368 pp.
Jewish topical reflections by English writer Israel
Zangwill (1864-1926), including section on "Songs of the
Synagogue," pp. 152-65, devoted to author's translations
into English for congregational uses, of liturgical
hymns of daily services, Sabbath, High Holy Days and
Festivals, as well as other celebrations.

404
ZUNSER, ELIAKUM. *A Jewish Bard; Autobiography.* trans.
from Yiddish by S. Hirdansky and ed. by A.H. Fromenson. New
York:Zunser Jubilee Com.,1905; 61pp.+44n.p., illus.

Informal autobiographical narrative by Yiddish writer,
poet-balladist (*Badkhen*) Eliakum Zunser (1840-1913),
who emigrated to America from Eastern Europe and settled
on Lower East Side of New York City. Yiddish romanized.

405
ZUNSER, MIRIAM SHOMER. *Yesterday: A Memoir of a Russian
Jewish Family.* ed. by Emily Wortis Leider. New York:Harper
and Row, 1978; 270 pp. illus.

Originally written (c.1939) by author as legacy piece
for her family, this posthumous publication, as edited
by a granddaughter, includes background information on
author's father-in-law, the noted *Badkhen* (Yiddish
minstrel-bard) Eliakum Zunser (1840-1913). Miriam Shomer
Zunser (1882-1951) was a founder and active member of
Jewish music organization *Mailamm* (American-Palestine
Music Organization), which flourished in New York City
1932-1942 and aided in establishment of music department
at Hebrew University in Jerusalem.

4.
Articles on Jewish Music Topics

A. In Music Periodicals

406
ALLINGER, HELEN. "The *Shofar* is Sounded." ***Music:A.G.O.***
vol.8,no.9.(New York:American Guild of Organists, 1974),
p.43, illus., music.
   Brief practical exposition for information of organists
   participating in High Holy Days services.
407
ARMISTEAD, SAMUEL, JOSEPH SILVERMAN and ISRAEL KATZ. "Judaeo-Spanish Folk Poetry from Morocco (the Boas Nahon Collection)." ***Yearbook of I.F.M.C.***, vol.2. (Cambridge, Eng.:
I.F.M.C., 1979/80), pp.59-75, music.
   Detailed study of some Sephardic Ladino (Spaniolic-
   Jewish) poetry of folksongs and ballads, extant in
   North African communities. Texts and music lines traced
   back to Spanish origins, noting consistencies as well
   as alterations made through time and geography. Music
   examples, text comparisons and source references.
408
AVENARY, HANOCH. "Abu Salt's Treatise on Music." ***Musica
Disciplina***, vol.6, nos.1/3. (Rome, It.:Inst. of Musicology,
1952), pp.27-32.
   Writings of early Mediaeval scholar Abu L'Salt (1068-
   1134), reflecting ideas among Arabo-Jewish philosophers
   of that time. Source notes.
409
AVENARY, HANOCH. "The Cantorial Fantasia of the 18th and
19th Centuries: A Late Manifestation of the Musical Trope."
YUVAL:Studies of J.M.R.C., vol.1. (Jerusalem, Isr.: Hebrew
Univ./Magnes Press, 1968), pp.65-85, music.
   Study of aspects of synagogue chant in terms of improvisational composition based on traditional melodies and

significant motifs. Particular attention to Ashkenazic
Jews of western Rhineland as to: details of notation;
scope of creativity; traditional old prayer chant of
Alenu L'shabbeah; some other cantorial "fantasias;"
stylistic features; spiritual factors; and, historical
considerations. References to notable cantorial artists
and their creativity in synagogue music. Source notes.
Musical examples on pp.26-34 of supplementary booklet.
    410
AVENARY, HANOCH. "Concept of Mode in European Synagogue
Chant." *YUVAL:Studies of J.M.R.C.*, vol.2. (Jerusalem,Isr.:
Hebrew Univ./Magnes Press, 1971), pp.11-21, music.
    Analysis of the *Adoshem Malakh* modal pattern for Jew-
    ish traditional liturgical music, in terms of: tonal
    range (scale); standard motives; structural connection
    of motives; "ethos" or associations of intellectual and
    emotional nature; and, some concepts for further study
    of this subject. Source notes and musical examples.
    411
AVENARY, HANOCH. "Flutes for a Bride or a Dead Man: The
Symbolism of the Flutes According to Hebrew Sources." *Orbis
Musicae*, vol.1. (Ramat Aviv, Isr.:Tel Aviv Univ. Press,
1971), pp.11-24, illus., music.
    Research study into Biblical and Talmudic sources, as
    well as traditions of other Semitic peoples, in terms of
    flute as musical instrument of ritual and mystical sig-
    nificance for "life and revival." Particular continuity
    of popular symbolism in Judaism until century following
    great Dispersion of 70 C.E. with Roman destruction of
    Second Temple and Jewish Commonwealth, when flute as
    mystic and mythic symbol gradually was excluded from all
    religious rites and customs, though some vestiges re-
    mained in Near East. Facsimiles and source notes.
    412
AVENARY, HANOCH. "Formal Structure of Psalms and Canticles
in Early Jewish and Christian Chant." *Musica Disciplina*,
vol.7. (Rome, It.:Inst. of Musicology, 1953), pp.1-13.
    Comparative study of formative qualities in early syna-
    gogue and early church liturgical music. Israeli music
    educator and scholar Hanoch Avenary considers Judaic
    root sources of church chant, psalmody and hymnology.
    Resource texts and notes.
    413
AVENARY, HANOCH. "The Hassidic *Nigun*: Ethos and Melos of
a Folk Liturgy." *Journal of I.F.M.C.*, vol.16. (Cambridge,
Eng.: I.F.M.C., 1964), pp.60-3, music.
    Brief view of folk music of Hassidic (Pietist) movement
    in terms of origin, creative development and folkloric
    performance, especially of wordless melody (*Nigun*) for
    religious expression. Musical illustrations. Abridged
    version of paper here. Full text, with extended roster
    of music examples, published in a collection of studies
    by Avenary — *Encounters of East and West in Music*
    (Tel Aviv, 1979).

414
AVENARY, HANOCH. "Hebrew Hymn Tunes; The Rise and Develop-
ment of Musical Tradition." *Journal of I.F.M.C.*, vol.4.
(Cambridge, Eng.: I.F.M.C., 1972), pp.161-2.
    Summary of paper treating various forms of Jewish re-
    ligious folksong and hymnology.
415
AVENARY, HANOCH. "Hebrew Version of Abu L'Salt's Treatise
on Music." *YUVAL:Studies of J.M.R.C.*, vol.3. (Jerusalem,
Isr.:Hebrew Univ./Magnes Press,1974), pp.7-82, illus.,music.
    Detailed study covering: Abu L'Salt (1067-1134 - Spain)
    and his work itself; general characterization of this
    music treatise; editorial principles - Hebrew text with
    English translation; and, analytical commentary. With
    diagrams, tables, appendices of Arabic and Hebrew music
    terms, source notes and musical examples.
416
AVENARY, HANOCH. "Northern and Southern Idioms of Early
European Music; A New Approach to an Old Problem." *Acta
Musicologica*, vol.49, no.1. (Kassel, W.Ger.: I.M.S., 1977),
pp. 27-49, illus., music.
    Early developments, notably as to modes and modal pat-
    terns, among various early European and Near Eastern
    groups. Special attention to liturgical usages - Gre-
    gorian, Byzantine, Syrian and Jewish groups from Near
    Eastern areas. Analysis of modal structures, melodic
    shapes and pitch arrangements. References to post-Gre-
    gorian tropes and sequences, and to musical influences
    upon minnesingers and their folksongs of that early era.
    Music examples, comparative tables and source notes.
417
AVENARY, HANOCH. "Paradigms of Arabic Modes in the Genizah
Fragment Cambridge T.S. N.S. 90,4." *YUVAL:Studies of J.M.R.
C.*, vol.4. (Jerusalem,Isr.:Hebrew Univ./Magnes Press,1982),
pp.11-28, illus., music.
    Five fragments concerning music had been discovered in
    Cairo Genizah collection: Ikhwan al-Safa (fl.10th cent.)
    epistle; 3 obscure fragments of unknown or unverified
    sources; and, writings by Ibn al-Akfani (d.1348). Other
    "sixth" fragment is presented here, as a second music
    item ascribed to Obadiah the Proselyte (c.1070-c.1141).
    Hebrew text given, with English translation. Avenary
    analyzes its contents and considers problems of musical
    interpretation. Facsimile illustrations, comparative
    tables, source notes and musical examples.
418
AVENARY, HANOCH. "Reflections on the Origins of the
Alleluia - Jubilus." *Orbis Musicae*, vol.6. (*Asaph* :
Section A). (Tel Aviv, Isr.Tel Aviv Univ. Press, 1978),
pp.34-42, illus., music.
    Comparative study of some early liturgical chant motifs
    and subsequent influences. Source notes and examples.
419
BAHAT, AVNER. "Musical Traditions of the Oriental Jews;
Orient and Occident." *The World of Music*, vol.22,no.2.
(W. Berlin: UNESCO, 1980), pp.46-58, illus.

Various musical patterns and melodic styles of folksongs
and liturgical chants among Jews of Near Eastern traditions. Musical examples and source notes.
420

BAR-AM, BENJAMIN, ed. *Aspects of Music in Israel.* Tel
Aviv, Isr.: I.M.I., 1980; 110pp., illus., music.
See two articles in English texts: "Creation and Tra-
dition in Israeli Folksong; Some Specimen Cases" by
Bathja Bayer, pp.52-60; and, "Diversity Within Unity;
On Musical Traditions of Jewish Communities in Israel"
by Uri Sharvit, pp.31-51. Both articles are studies of
Israeli folkmusic, considering different qualities and
and also similarities. Source notes and music examples.
421

BARASCH, MOSHE. "Traces of Jewish Musicians in Writings of
Lomazzo." *YUVAL:Studies of J.M.R.C.*, vol.1. (Jerusalem,
Isr.:Hebrew Univ./Magnes Press, 1968), pp.86-88.
Milanese humanist Giovanni Paolo Lomazzo (fl. 16th cen-
tury) wrote a major work on theory of art, in which he
included references to iconography based upon Biblical
music, and also referred to several Jewish musicians in
North Italy of his era. He discussed music of Solomon's
Temple, chanting of Psalms and various Temple instru-
ments. Note parallels to other 16th century writer --
Giovanni Pico della Mirandola. Source notes.
422

BAYER, BATHJA. "The Biblical *Nebel*." *YUVAL:Studies of
J.M.R.C.*, vol.1. (Jerusalem,Isr.:Hebrew Univ./Magnes Press,
1968), pp.89-131, illus.
Study of *Nebel* -- Biblical instrument generally considered as a form of harp. Scholar Bathja Bayer examines
that theory in terms of: Bible texts themselves, along
with rabbinical and other scholarly commentaries; Greek
sources, 5th to 3rd centuries B.C.E.; Septuagent, 3rd to
2nd centuries B.C.E.; Aprocrypha, 2nd to 1st centuries
B.C.E.; writings of Qumran community (Dead Sea Scrolls);
Josephus, 1st century C.E.; writers of Roman Empire, 1st
century B.C.E. to 1st century C.E.; *Mishnah* (ca.200 C.
E.). Bayer proposes that *Nebel* may have actually been
"sack or bag" lyre, type of instrument with "skin con-
tainer." However, she concludes that issue remains open.
Facsimile illustrations and source notes.
423

BAYER, BATHJA. "Titles of the Psalms. A Renewed Investigation of an Old Problem." *YUVAL:Studies of J.M.R.C.*, vol.
4. (Jerusalem,Isr.:Hebrew Univ./Magnes Press,1982),pp.29-123.
Extensive and detailed study covering: range of titles
with sources and accessory information (Biblical and
post-Biblical writings); sequences of interpretations
and analyses of titles -- terms used and text references;
and, consideration of "titling" process itself. Comparative tables, source notes and list of cited references.
424

BERLINSKI, HERMAN. "The Organ in the Synagogue." *Music:
A.G.O.*, vol.2,nos.4,7,11 and 12. (New York:American Guild
of Organists, 1968), pp. as indicated below, illus., music.

Article published in four parts: 1. vol.2,no.4; pp.28-
29,43-47. Biblical background, *Magrepha*, rejection of
instrumental music, rise of synagogue liturgy. 2. vol.2,
no.7; pp.28-29,45. Development of various Jewish styles
for liturgical services, folk music influences, East
European traditions and mid-European German synagogues.
3. vol.2,no.11; pp.34-37,46-47. Traditionalists vs. Reformers, organ acceptance in 1841 by liberal Reformers,
symbols of change. 4. vol.2,no.12; pp.22-23, 60. Organ
placement, tonal qualities and utilization in services
of modern Reform congregations.

425
BINDER, ABRAHAM WOLF. "Ernest Bloch's *Avodat Hakodesh*
(Sacred Service)." *American Guild of Organists Quarterly*,
vol.2,no.1.(New York:A.G.O., 1957), pp.7-9, 34-5, music.
Discussion by Jewish musician and educator A.W.Binder
(1895-1966) of major liturgical work for Sabbath morning
service by Ernest Bloch (1880-1959). Attention drawn to
composer's use of traditional elements of liturgical
chant and hymnology. Musical illustrations.

426
BLOCH, ERNEST. "Man and Music." *The Musical Quarterly*,
vol.19,no.3. (New York, 1933), pp.374-81.
Introspective essay by composer Ernest Bloch (1880-1959)
offering his views on human life, musical creativity and
world affairs - as formative influences upon his works.

427
BLOCH, MAX. "Viktor Ullmann; Brief Biography and Appreciation." *Journal of the Schoenberg Institute*, vol.3, no.2.
(Los Angeles, Cal.:Arnold Schoenberg Inst.,1979), pp.150-77.
Composer Viktor Ullmann (1898-1943 Auschwitz/Birkenau)
was pupil and then associate in Europe of Arnold Schoenberg (1874-1951). When nazis first imprisoned Ullmann at
Theresienstadt (Terezin) Concentration Camp, he composed
and conducted music there for the other prisoners. He
especially taught children and led their choral groups,
for which he wrote songs with Hebrew and Yiddish texts.
Ullmann also wrote a children's opera "The Emperor of
Atlantis," which was performed in Ghettos and Camps, and
has since been presented at memorial concerts.

428
BRODY, ELAINE. "Romain Rolland and Ernest Bloch." *The
Musical Quarterly*, vol.68,no.1.(New York,1982), pp.60-79.
English translation of some apparently significant and
mutually influential correspondence between composer
Ernest Bloch (1880-1959) and writer Romain Rolland
(1866-1936). Their contact, which began in 1911 and
lasted until death of Rolland, was enriched by lively
exchanges of ideas and progress reports on creative
works. Rolland encouraged Bloch and at times aided him
in advancing his career.

429
BURSTYN, SHAI. "Early 15th Century Polyphonic Settings of
Song of Songs Antiphons." *Acta Musicologica*, vol.49,no.2.
(Kassel, W.Ger.: I.M.S., 1977), pp.200-7, music.
Study to enlarge understanding of Renaissance settings

of biblical poetry for devotional services. Discussion
of patterns of Judaic and Christian liturgy, texts for
chants and hymnology from 9th century onward. Contro-
versial nature of Song of Songs, with its acceptance into canon of Bible as holy allegory by rabbinical leaders
and such subsequent influence upon attitudes of Church
leaders adapting that allegory to their religious traditions. English and French musical settings. Sources.
430
COHEN, DALIA. "An Investigation into Tonal Structure of
the *Maqamot*." *Journal of I.F.M.C.*, vol.16. (Cambridge,
Eng.: I.F.M.C., 1964), pp.102-6, music.
    Modal patterns in Near East folk and liturgical music.
431
COHEN, DALIA. "The Meaning of the Modal Framework in the
Singing of Religious Hymns by Christian Arabs in Israel."
YUVAL:Studies of J.M.R.C., vol.2. (Jerusalem, Isr.: Hebrew
Univ./Magnes Press, 1971), pp.23-57, illus., music.
    Four areas of consideration in study of examples of this
    modal framework: elements of musical structure - scale,
    range, rhythm, tempo, motifs and other qualities; medi-
    um of performance - vocal and instrumental; role of text
    materials and their qualities; and, "extra-musical" fac-
    tors. Comparisons of Oriental liturgy of Orthodox Church
    and of other Christian, Moslem and Jewish groups in that
    area. Examination of recently gathered materials and
    performance styles. Graphs of modes, comparative tables,
    musical examples and source notes.
432
COHEN, DALIA and RUTH KATZ. "Explorations in the Music of
the Samaritans; An Illustration of the Utility of Graphic
Notation." *Ethnomusicology*, vol.4. (Middletown, Conn.:
Ethnomusicological Soc., 1960), pp. 67-74, illus., music.
    Methodology for study of music among Samaritans (dissi-
    dent Judaic sect) in Israel, whose liturgical traditions
    date back to pre-rabbinical Second Temple Commonwealth
    Era, and whose liturgical music as practiced to present
    times is structured with psalm-singing, antiphony and
    monophonic chant. Technical illustrations and notes.
433
COHEN, DALIA and RUTH KATZ. "Remarks Concerning the Use of
the Melograph in Ethnomusicological Studies." *YUVAL:Studies
of J.M.R.C.*, vol.1. (Jerusalem, Isr.:Hebrew Univ./ Magnes
Press, 1968), pp.155-68, illus.
    Based on their studies done at the ethnomusicological
    section of the Centre for Electronic Music at Hebrew
    University, authors view melograph, used at the Centre
    since 1958, as to: perspective of accurate musical no-
    tation; applicability and limitations; appropriate
    measuring for pitch analysis and tonal qualities; role
    of melograph in research. Graphs and source notes.
434
COHEN, FRANCIS LYON. "Ancient Musical Traditions of the
Synagogue." *Proceedings Annual of Royal Music Association*,
vol.19.(London,Eng.:R.M.A., 1893), pp.135-58, illus., music.
    Text of paper delivered by scholar Francis Lyon Cohen

(1862-1934) at panel session chaired by Sir John Stainer
(1840-1901), whose summary remarks on topic are appended
to this article. Presentation of history and background
of Jewish liturgical cantillations, modal chants and
hymnology. Details of *Shofar*, development of role and
music of *Hazzan* (cantor), special melodies of various
services and different Jewish traditions. Illustrated
with melody lines of music actually presented at time
of lecture in performance by daughter of London cantor.
Cohen cites as precedent for this use of woman's voice:
"In the year 1275 the congregation in the city of Worms
set a monument over the grave of the sweet-voiced and
learned lady Urania, who was the daughter of the chief
Precentor of their synagogue, and who used to chant the
service in the chapel of the Worms synagogue reserved
for women. And in Polish synagogues even now you will
not fail to come across the aged person who acts as a
Saegerin (readeress) for a select circle of associates
less profoundly versed in the Hebrew tongue." Stainer's
appended remarks draw analogies to Ambrosian and Gregorian chants and to possible meanings for biblical term
Selah. Valuable and intriguing materials here.

435
COHEN, JUDITH. "Jubal in the Middle Ages." *YUVAL:Studies
of J.M.R.C.*, vol.3. (Jerusalem,Isr.:Hebrew Univ./Magnes
Press, 1974), pp.83-99.
  Historiographic investigation of two figures mentioned
  in Mediaeval writings on music as "inventors of music" -
  Pythagoras and Jubal. Judith Cohen considers the issues
  of symbolic qualities ascribed to each; commentaries
  written as studies of mythology, Greek history or of
  Biblical analysis; shaping of image of Jubal over centuries of Middle Ages as primary figure; and, literary
  and folkloristic elaborations. Source notes. *229540*

436
COHEN, JUDITH R. "Judaeo-Spanish Traditional Songs in
Montreal and Toronto." *Canadian Folk Music Journal*, vol.10
(Toronto:Canadian Folk Music Society,1982), pp.40-60, music.
  Investigation of extant elements of Ladino, or Judaeo-
  Spanish, folksongs among Sephardic communities in two
  Canadian cities. With backgrounds on ethnic groups and
  consideration of qualities of this folk repertoire.
  Musical examples and source notes.

437
COHON, BARUCH JOSEPH. "Structure of the Synagogue Prayer
Chant." *Journal of A.M.S.*, vol.3, no.1. (Boston: A.M.S.,
1950), pp.17-32, illus., music.
  Exposition of structures and patterns of music content
  and performance in Jewish liturgical services of three
  basic Ashkenazic traditional chant modes: *Mogen Ovos,
  Adonoy Moloch, Ahavo Rabbo*. Comparative charts for the
  modal forms and usages in services. Musical origins,
  history in customs, differences in component musical
  qualities and specific applications in the prayer chants
  and hymnology. Details of *Hazzanuth* (cantorial art).
  Solid study. Music illustrations and source notes.

438
COOPER, MARTIN. "Giacomo Meyerbeer (1791-1864)." *Annual of Royal Musical Association*, vol.90. (London, Eng.: Royal Musical Assoc., 1964), pp.97-129, illus., music.
    Life and work of composer Giacomo Meyerbeer, with consideration of his Jewish ancestry as factor in his creativity as well as personal life. Music examples.

439
EISENSTEIN, JUDITH K. "Mediaeval Elements in the Liturgical Music of the Jews of Southern France and Northern Spain." *Musica Judaica*, vol.1 (New York: A.S.J.M., 1975/76), pp.33-53, music.
    Citing research work and theories of a number of other scholars, discussion of musical interactions and influences of that time between Synagogue and Church – liturgical as well as religious folksongs – as dynamic cultural force in musical continuity and creativity. Consideration of Jewish musical life then, with references to chronological and topically sorted rosters of significant data, studies and music collections. Particular attention to elements of Sephardic music of Iberia and France. Music tables and examples illustrate similarities and salient differences between Christian and Jewish folk music in those areas. Source notes.

440
FARMER, HENRY GEORGE. "Mediaeval Jewish Writers on Music." *Music Review*, vol.3,no.3.(Cambridge, Eng.,1942), pp.183-9.
    Scholar Henry George Farmer (1882-1965) reviews a roster of writers: 9th century – Hunain ibn Ishaq; 10th century – Sa'adya Gaon, Ishaq ibn Suleiman (Isaac Israeli); 12th century – Yehuda Alharizi, Moshe ibn Ezra, Maimonides, Abraham bar Hiyyah; 13th century – Yusif ibn 'Aqnin, Yehuda ben Shmuel 'Abbas, Shem Tob ben Yusif ben Palaqera; 14th century – Immanuel ben Shelomo, Abraham ben Yizhaq and Shem Tob ben Yizhaq Shaprut. Also, Levi ben Gershon (Magister Leo Hebraeus Gersonides) who wrote *"Tractatus Armonicus"* in 1345 for Philip of Vitry, helping launch *Ars Nova* movement. References to Cairo *Geniza* fragments and also to relationships of those writers to Arabic writings of same centuries. Source notes.

441
FENTON, PAUL. "A Jewish Sufi on the Influence of Music." *YUVAL:Studies of J.M.R.C.*, vol.4. (Jerusalem,Isr.:Hebrew Univ./Magnes Press, 1982), pp.124-30.
    Article based upon materials preserved at Bodleian Library. Analysis of Judaeo-Arabic treatise of c.14th century by anonymous (possibly David ben Joshua Maimonides, d. c.1410). Paul Fenton considers elements reflected here of Egyptian Jewish Pietist movement of 13th-14th centuries, which incorporated Sufi musical ideas and practices, such as dance and music at devotions. With Hebrew text and English translation. Source notes.

442
GATTI, G.M. "Ernest Bloch." *The Musical Quarterly*, vol.7. (New York, 1921), pp.20-38, illus., music.
    Biographical study with reflections upon works of com-

poser Ernest Bloch (1880-1959), noting trends and ideas
of his compositions (to 1920) many of which are Judaic
in inspiration, and also his opera "Macbeth." Examples.

443
GERSON-KIWI, EDITH. "The Bards of the Bible." *Studia Musicologica*, vol.7,nos.1/4. (Budapest, Hung.:Hung. Soc. for
Academic Studies,1965), pp.61-70, illus., music.
   Comparative overview of various cantillation patterns
   of traditional biblical recitations for same passages
   of texts by Near Eastern Jews, European Jews, Moslems,
   Druze, Samaritans and Christian groups. Melodic forms
   presented in contexts of bardic folksong and liturgical
   expression, reflecting similarities, parallels and differences. Based on author's research studies among many
   ritual reciters of Bible, as still practiced. Examples.

444
GERSON-KIWI, EDITH. "The Bourdon of the East; Its Regional
and Universal Trends." *Journal of I.F.M.C.*, vol.16. (Cambridge, Eng.:I.F.M.C., 1964), pp.49-55, illus., music.
   Aspects of a particular folk music style found among
   Near Eastern Jewish and Arabic groups, with exploration
   of influences and adaptations. Music examples and notes.

445
GERSON-KIWI, EDITH. "Migrating Patterns of Melody Among
Berbers and Jews of the Atlas Mountains." *Journal of I.F.M.
C.*, vol.19.(Cambridge,Eng.:I.F.M.C.,1967),pp.16-22, music.
   Northwest African folksong traditions among groups of
   Berbers and Jews who have populated area since time of
   destruction of First Temple (586 B.C.E.). Parallels in
   hymnology and other religious folksongs, as well as in
   folk ballads - styles and motival elements. Musical examples of Atlas Jews and Berber tribes as collected by
   author, a notable scholar and educator. Source notes.

446
GERSON-KIWI, EDITH. "The Music of Kurdistan Jews; A Synopsis of Their Musical Styles." *YUVAL:Studies of J.M.R.C.*,
vol.2. (Jerusalem,Isr.:Hebrew Univ./Magnes Press, 1971),
pp.59-72, music.
   Study of cultural-geographical conditions, notably language idioms and influences of: Hebrew for liturgy, Aramaic for liturgy and folk culture, Arabic for secular
   expression and Kurdish for geographical life-style ac-
   commodations - all reflected in music of people. Religious musical variants and secular music of life and
   customs. Also dance songs. Comparative tables and music
   examples. Roster of references.

447
GERSON-KIWI, EDITH "Musicology in Israel." *Acta Musicologica*, vol.30,nos.1/2.(Basel, Switz.:I.M.S.,1958),pp.17-25.
   Report on musicological studies of Israeli scholars,
   highlighting areas of current (to 1958) interests.

448
GERSON-KIWI, EDITH. "On the Musical Sources of the Judaeo-
Hispanic *Romance*." *The Musical Quarterly*, vol.50, no.1.
(New York, 1964), pp.31-43, illus., music.
   Sephardic folksong expression - *Romancero* - in origins

and historical background, and its transmission over
centuries since Spanish expulsion of Jews in 1492. Consideration of Ladino (Spaniolic-Jewish) ballad texts and
their formative influences: French *Chanson*, Judaic old
hymnology and folksong, other varied Near Eastern folk
epic traditions and special folk idioms of Iberian area.
Comparative examinations: melodic patterns - modal and
motival; styles of performance - improvisation, ornamentation and adaptation. Essentially oral folk art tradition among Sephardic Jews. Music examples and sources.
449

GERSON-KIWI, EDITH. "Robert Lachmann; His Achievements and
His Legacy." *YUVAL:Studies of J.M.R.C.*, vol.3.(Jerusalem,
Isr.:Hebrew Univ./Magnes Press, 1974), pp.100-8.
Biographical tribute to scholar and pioneer Jewish eth-
nomusicologist Robert Lachmann (1892-1939), whose career
was tragically short. From 1927 to 1933, he served as a
librarian at music department of Berlin State Library.
In 1930, he was instrumental, with such colleagues as
Curt Sachs (1882-1959), in establishing a Society for
Research of Oriental Music. Dismissed in 1935, he was
able to emigrate and join faculty of Hebrew University,
where he taught, did further research and founded an
Archive of Oriental Music. In this article, Edith Gerson
-Kiwi supplies a summary inventory of Lachmann Archive
at the University, the cataloguing of which became one
of first projects of J.M.R.C. Roster also given of his
books and articles - all in German texts only.
450

GERSON-KIWI, EDITH. "Vocal Folk-Polyphonies of the Western
Orient in Jewish Tradition."*YUVAL:Studies of J.M.R.C.*,vol.
1.(Jerusalem,Isr.:Hebrew Univ./Magnes Press,1968),pp.169-93.
Study of some Hebrew liturgies of East Mediterranean
areas in terms of folk and art polyphonies and stratifi-
cation of polyphony. Analysis of three regional styles:
Yemen Jews, Samaritans and Corfu (Greek Sephardic) Jews.
Attention to prayer chants in solo cantorial and choral
congregational liturgical music, hymnology, psalmody and
harmonized part-singing of religious services. Source
notes. Music examples on pp.16-25 of supplementary book.
451

GERSON-KIWI, EDITH. "Wedding Dances and Songs of the Jews
of Bokhara." *Journal of I.F.M.C.*, vol.2. (Cambridge,Eng.:
I.F.M.C., 1950), pp.17-18.
Summary of study by Israeli musicologist and educator
Edith Gerson-Kiwi of indigenous folk music expression
among Bokharan Jewish women from Southwest Asia, newly
resettled in State of Israel.
452

GOTTLIEB, JACK. "Symbols of Faith in the Music of Leonard
Bernstein." *The Musical Quarterly*, vol.66,no.2. (New York,
1980), pp.287-95, illus., music.
Uses by Leonard Bernstein of Hebrew tunes and Psalm
styles, as well as adaptations of Judaic prayers and
liturgical motifs. Essential influence of the composer's
Jewish faith upon his creativity underscored. Examples.

453
GRADENWITZ, PETER. "Current Chronicle: Israel." *The Musical Quarterly*, vol.40. (New York, 1954), pp.575-80.
Report on musical activities in Israel (as of 1954) —
composers, performers, educators and organizations.

454
GRADENWITZ, PETER. "Felicien David (1810-1876) and French Romantic Orientalism." *The Musical Quarterly*, vol.62,no.4. (New York, 1976), pp.471-506, illus., music.
Study of some particular Palestinian-Near Eastern music influences upon works of French composer Felicien David, as result of his extensive travels in that area, and notably time spent at Jaffa, Ramla and Jerusalem. Biographical information on David and discussion of his social milieu and philosophical ideas. Facsimiles, music examples and source notes.

455
GRADENWITZ, PETER. "Music Publishing in Israel." *M.L.A. Notes*, vol.10,no.3. ([n.p.]: M.L.A., 1953), pp.391-3.
Roster of Israeli publishers and publication activities presented by Peter Gradenwitz, founder and director of Israeli Music Publishing Company of Tel Aviv, Israel.

456
HARRAN, DON. "Musical Research in Israel; Its History, Resources and Institutions." *Current Musicology*, vol.7. (New York: Columbia Univ., 1968), pp.120-7.
Survey report of musicological work, past to present (1968), noting scholars, projects and publications.

457
HELLER, CHARLES. "Traditional Jewish Material in Schoenberg's 'A Survivor from Warsaw' opus 46." *Journal of the Arnold Schoenberg Institute*, vol.3,no.1.(Los Angeles, Cal.: Arnold Schoenberg Inst., 1979), pp.68-74, illus., music.
Discussion of Judaic elements in work by Arnold Schoenberg (1874-1951) for which he created both text and music in 1947, as memorial tribute to victims of the Holocaust. Composition builds to final climax with stark male choir chanting the essential Jewish proclamation of faith: *Sh'ma Yisroel*. Musical illustrations.

458
HERSHBERG, JEHOASH. "Heinrich Schalit and Paul Ben-Haim in Munich." *YUVAL:Studies of J.M.R.C.*, vol.4.(Jerusalem,Isr.: Hebrew Univ./Magnes Press, 1982), pp.131-49, music.
Historical essay detailing aspects of musical life of Munich Jewry in 1920's, at time when both Heinrich Schalit (1886-1976) and Israeli composer Paul Ben-Haim (1897 -1984) began their musical careers there. Influential in that community was Emanuel Kirschner (1857-1938), cantor and scholarly musician, who knew A.Z. Idelsohn (1882-1938) and his work, as well as other notable collectors of synagogue music materials. Composer/liturgist Schalit was born in Vienna but settled in Munich in 1908, where musical relationship with Ben-Haim developed. Schalit convinced Ben-Haim (Paul Frankenburger) to emigrate to Palestine Mandate in 1933. Not long afterwards, Schalit came to United States and remained here to his death.

459
HERZOG, AVIGDOR. "Transcription and Transnotation in Eth-
nomusicology." *Journal of I.F.M.C.*, vol.16. (Cambridge,
Eng.: I.F.M.C., 1964), pp.100-1.
> Summary of presentation on methodology in collection and
> notation of Near Eastern folk music materials. Problems
> and accommodations in seeking for fidelity of versions.

460
HESKES, IRENE. "The Cantor as a Practical Music Leader for
the Community." *Journal of Jewish Music and Liturgy*, vol.4
(New York:C.C.A./Yeshiva Univ., 1981/82), pp.18-19.
> Challenge for broadening of cantorial music activities
> and services beyond specific congregation and into the
> general community — for inspiration and outreach.

461
HESKES, IRENE. "The Cultural Leadership Role of the Can-
tor." *Journal of Synagogue Music*, vol.3, no.3. (New York:
C.A.A./J.T.S.A., 1971), pp.13-16.
> Discussion of various Jewish music communal activities
> as responsibility of cantorial office, beyond service to
> particular congregation as prayer leader, music educator
> and choral director. Importance stressed for special
> programs, music projects and inter-denominational out-
> reach with all types of Jewish music.

462
HESKES, IRENE. "A Duty of Preservation and Continuity:
Collectors and Collections of Jewish Music." *M.L.A.Notes*,
vol.40,no.2. (Canton,Mass.: Music Library Association,
1983), pp. 163-70.
> Discussion of Jewish music collectors: Eric Mandell,
> Arno Nadel (1878-1943) and Eduard Birnbaum (1855-1920),
> and their collections as presently available for examin-
> ation and study at the music library facilities of Gratz
> College for Jewish Studies in Philadelphia, and at the
> libraries of H.U.C.-J.I.R. in New York City and Cincin-
> nati. Details on other library resources for Jewish
> music materials in Israel and America. Consideration of
> bibliographic range in Jewish music publications, as
> well as some notable figures in Jewish musicology.

463
HESKES, IRENE. "The Hebrew Publishing Company Collection;
An Introductory Report." *Sonneck Society Newsletter*, vol.7
no.3. (Boulder, Colo.:Sonneck Soc., 1981), pp.13-14.
> Report on author's project during Summer 1980, in which
> approximately 500 boxes of old Yiddish theater sheet
> music — originally published 1885-1920 — were unpacked,
> sorted and classified. Catalogue collection was prepared
> for further study.

464
HESKES, IRENE. "Tenement Songs: The Popular Music of the
Jewish Immigrants, by Mark Slobin." *Popular Music*, vol.3.
(London/New York:Cambridge Univ. Press, 1984), pp.289-92.
> Detailed book review treating Yiddish theatricals and
> popular music on the Lower East Side of New York City,
> during early decades of this century. Background on ori-
> gins and development of this song genre and its texts.

465
HOFMAN, SHLOMO. "The Destiny of a Yemenite Folk Tune."
Journal of I.F.M.C., vol.20. (Cambridge, Eng.: I.F.M.C.,
1968), pp.25-29, illus., music.
    Consideration of different versions of a sacred poem, or
    Piyyut, traditionally sung by Yemenite Jews during
    domestic ceremonials marking conclusion of Sabbath -
    Havdalah ritual. Reflections on alteration of folksong
    for current performance purposes. Musical examples.
466
HOHENEMSER, JACOB. "The Jew In German Musical Thought Before the 19th Century." *Musica Judaica*, vol.3 (New York:
A.S.J.M., 1980l/81), pp.63-73.
    Posthumous reprint of excerpts from dissertation by Can-
    tor Jacob Hohenemser (1911-1964). Historiographic essay
    covering ideas of such scholars as Charles Burney (1726-
    1814) and Johann Nicholaus Forkel (1749-1818) on subject
    of ancient Biblical/Judaic music. Consideration of in-
    fluence of such writers on subsequent Romantic musical
    thought and Jewish writers on music of 18th and 19th
    centuries. Comparative tables and source notes.
467
IDEL, MOSHE. "Music and Prophetic *Kabbalah*." *YUVAL:
Studies of J.M.R.C.*, vol.4. (Jerusalem,Isr.:Hebrew Univ./
Magnes Press, 1982), pp.150-69.
    Highly theoretical study. Author considers: music as an
    analogy for prophecy-making techniques; as an analogy
    for prophecy itself; and, music as component of tech-
    nique of mystic visionary Abulafia (fl.13th century) and
    his followers. Hebrew texts and English translations.
468
IDELSOHN, ABRAHAM ZEBI. "The Distinctive Elements of Jew-
ish Folksong." *Proceedings Annual of M.T.N.A.*, vol.46.
(Hartford, Conn.: M.T.N.A., 1924), pp.1-16, illus., music.
    Summary of extended lecture on Jewish music - liturgical
    and secular folksong - presented to meeting by Abraham
    Zebi Idelsohn (1882-1938). Outline of historic develop-
    ments and salient qualities of cantillations, chants,
    hymnology and special melodies for Sabbath and holidays
    in various Judaic traditions. Musical illustrations.
469
IDELSOHN, ABRAHAM ZEBI. "The Features of Jewish Sacred
Folksong in Eastern Europe." *Acta Musicologica*, vol.4.
(Leipzig, Ger.:I.M.S., 1932), pp.17-23, illus., music.
    Summary presentation of salient qualities noted in his
    analysis of East European Jewish liturgical music, by
    scholar Abraham Zebi Idelsohn (1882-1938). Attention to
    publication of final volumes of his notable 10-volume
    Thesaurus of Hebrew Oriental Melodies (Leipzig and
    Jerusalem, 1922-32), as well as contents of monumental
    collection amassed by Eduard Birnbaum (1855-1920) and
    housed at H.U.C. in Cincinnati. Musical illustrations.
470
IDELSOHN, ABRAHAM ZEBI. "Musical Characteristics of East
European Jewish Folksong." *The Musical Quarterly*, vol.18,
no.4. (New York, 1932), pp.634-45, illus., music.

In 1932, final volumes of the 10-volume *Thesaurus of Hebrew Oriental Melodies* by Abraham Zebi Idelsohn (1882 -1938) were published in Leipzig, Germany. Article outlines origins, historical development, special musical qualities and various traditions of liturgical and secular musical expression among East European Jews. Intended as musicological introduction for subject matter and author's publications. Music examples and sources.
471
IDELSOHN, ABRAHAM ZEBI. "Parallels Between the Old-French and the Jewish Song." (published in two parts) *Acta Musicologica*, vol.5, no.4 and vol.6, no.1. (Leipzig, Ger.:I.M.S., 1933/34), pp.162-8 and pp.15-22, illus., music.
    Prior to his final debilitating illness, Abraham Zebi Idelsohn (1882-1938) began to study this area of European Jewish music history. Article - in two parts - outlines Idelsohn's research, as progressing, on some old French folksongs in terms of melodic patterns and motifs found in Jewish traditional folksongs and in particular liturgical modes. Comparative tables and music examples.
472
IMBER, NAPHTALI HERZ. "Music of the Ghetto: Melodies of the Mystics or *Hassidim*." *Music*, vol.13.(Chicago, 1897), pp. 697-708.
    Subjective discussion by Naphtali Herz Imber (1856-1897) of the wordless melodies (*Nigunim*) of the Hassidic or Pietistic Jews, who believe that music elevates the spirit, ennobles prayer and opens the Gates of Heaven.
473
IMBER, NAPHTALI HERZ. "The Music of the Psalms: A Culture-Historical Study in Musical Evolution." *Music*, vol. 6. (Chicago, 1894), pp.568-88.
    Naphtali Herz Imber (1856-1897), who wrote the poetry of *Hatikvah* - Jewish anthem of nationhood, spent his last years in New York City, eking out an existence as writer and surviving with support of Jewish philanthropists. In this article, Imber discusses music of Bible, Temple, Psalms, and rise of syagogue sacred song. "Music runs like a thread through all the ages and the dispersions, and as a connecting link between God and man. A religion without music has ever been no religion...Indeed only the wordless, the unspeakable but rich-in-expression, tongue of music is able to answer the riddles of life in such a consoling and satisfactory manner. For only music is able to speak to the inner spirit in its own language whose words are expressions, and whose arguments are feelings. Only on the wings of music can we but make the flight to unseen space: and music is the only medium through which our astral body goes out from its day prison and walks among the celestials, in the realm of the ethereal universe. Music is the language spoken by the angels." Valuable more for writer than information.
474
JACOBSON, SAM L. "Music of the Jews." *Music*, vol.14. (Chicago, 1898), pp.412-16.
    Delineation of unique and historic qualities of Jewish

music. General information on Liturgical modes, hymns
and contemporary (1898) synagogue services in America.
Optimistic outlook for future of modern Jewish music.
475
KANTER, MAXINE. "Traditional High Holiday Melodies of the
Portuguese Synagogue of Amsterdam." *Journal of Musicological Research*, vol.3,no.2.(New York, 1981), pp.223-57, music.
Study of liturgical music - chant hymnology and prayer
songs - traditional to Sephardic Jews who resettled in
Netherlands area of Europe following inquisition and
expulsion from Spain and Portugal in late 15th century.
Influences of Iberian Catholic liturgical materials in
those Sephardic rites, due to crypto-Jewish observances
by forced converts - Marranos, who returned to overt
Judaism when they found safe haven. Comparisons of different melodic patterns. Music examples and sources.
476
KATZ, ISRAEL J. "The Enigma of the Antonio Bustelo Judaeo-
Spanish Ballad Tunes in Manuel L. Ortega's *Los Hebreos en
Marruecos* (1919)." *Musica Judaica*, vol.4 (New York: A.S.
J.M., 1981/82), pp.32-67, illus., music.
Background to a re-examination pf some particular Sephardic folksong elements (tunes collected by Bustelo),
in terms of comparative qualities and melodic characteristics. Consideration of notational variants and geographical musical "reinterpretations" of similar folksong materials, *qua* Jewish folk music traditions.
Ladino (Spaniolic Jewish) texts of songs. Inventory of
"Bustelo Collection." Facsimiles, musical examples and
source notes.
477
KATZ, ISRAEL J. "A Judaeo-Spanish *Romancero*." *Ethnomusicology*, vol.12. (Ann Arbor, Mich.: Soc. for Ethnomusicology, 1968), pp.72-85, illus., music.
Analysis of particular Sephardic ballad - text and
music - by scholar-collector in field.
478
KATZ, RUTH. "On 'Nonsense' Syllables as Oral Group Notation." *The Musical Quarterly*, vol.60, no.2. (New York,
1974), pp.187-94, illus., music.
Investigation of aspects of an oral musical tradition
containing textual interpolations, with particular attention to elements of Samaritan (dissident pre-rabbinic
Judaic sect) liturgical music customs. References to
certain "meaningless" text materials, and also to such
generally used terms of obscure meaning as *Selah* and
Amen. Music examples, tables and source notes.
479
KATZ, RUTH. "Reliability of Oral Transmission: The Case of
Samaritan Music." *YUVAL:Studies of J.M.R.C.*, vol.3.(Jerusalem,Isr.:Hebrew Univ./Magnes press,1974), pp.109-35,music.
Study of phenomenon of cultural transmission within a
particular society: Samaritans (dissident pre-rabbinic
Judaic sect). Consideration of: social structure and
musical continuity; methological aspects; Samaritan community itself; social settings for musical transmission;

and, music analysis (troping, vibrato, tonal structure, glissando). Graphs, source notes and music examples.
480

KATZ, RUTH. "The Singing of *Baqqashot* by Aleppo Jews: A Study in Musical Acculturation." *Acta Musicologica*, vol.40 no.1. (Kassel, W.Ger.:I.M.S., 1968), pp.65-85, illus., music
   Use of melograph as aid in study of performance styles of certain liturgical chant elements. Determination of changes in performances among the generations of Aleppo Jews from northeast area of Syria, close to Turkey and between Euphrates valley and coastline Latakia. Varied influences of contiguous cultures. Illustrations, notes.
481

KAUFMAN, NIKOLAY. "Jewish and Gentile Folksong in the Balkans and Its Relation to liturgical Music of Sephardic Jews in Bulgaria." *Journal of I.F.M.C.*, vol.16. (Cambridge, Eng.:I.F.M.C., 1964), pp.63-64.
   Summary of paper treating elements of Sephardic music in that area of Europe, as collected and studied.
482

KEBEDE, ASHENAFI. "Sacred Chant of Ethiopian Monotheistic Churches: Music in Black Jewish and Christian Communities." *Black Perspectives in Music*, vol.8,no.1.(Cambria Heights, N.Y.: Found. for Research on Afro-American Arts, 1980), pp.21-34, illus., music.
   Includes consideration of liturgical musical traditions among Black Jews of Ethiopia - Falashas (dissident pre-rabbinical Judaic sect). Comparative tables, photographs and music examples.
483

KWALWASSER, JACOB. "Jewish Folksongs." *The Musical Quarterly*, vol.2,no.1.(New York,1925),pp.55-62, illus., music.
   Presentation of melodic styles and rhythmic forms of Yiddish folksongs, with reflections on qualities of Jewish musical expression. Music examples and notes.
484

LEVI, LEO. "Traditions of Biblical Cantillation and Ekphonetics." *Journal of I.F.M.C.*, vol.16. (Cambridge, Eng.: I.F.M.C., 1964), pp.64-65.
   Summary of paper on formalized patterns of biblical recitation and notation for that cantillation - in terms of folk music traditions.
485

LEVINE, JOSEPH. "Toward Defining the Jewish Prayer Modes with Particular Emphasis on the *Adonay Malakh* Mode." *Musica Judaica*, vol.3(New York:A.S.J.M.,1980/81),pp.13-41.
   Comparative study of this mode of Jewish liturgical traditions, in terms of: origins, historical influences and development. Consideration of scholarly work on this subject by: Idelsohn, Werner, Avenary and others. Tracing out of patterns of usage and variants of modal line, with investigation of parallel motifs. Examples of applications in liturgical chants, elaborative arrangements and improvisations, and in compositions. Music tables and illustrations, and source notes.

486
LOEB, LAWRENCE. "The Jewish Musician and the Music of Fars (City of Shiraz)." *Asian Music*, vol.4. (New York: Soc. for Asian Music, 1972), pp.3-14, illus., music.

   Folksongs and folksingers among Persian-Irani Jews, in terms of their distinctively Judaic musical expression and cultural creativity in a particular communal area — southweatern Iran by Persian Gulf, near Mesopotamia and opposite Arabia. Those territorial influences reflected in melodic and folkloric materials as collected and examined by author. Music examples and source notes.

487
McKINNON, JAMES W. "Jubal or Pythagoras; Who is the Creator of Music?" *The Musical Quarterly*, vol.64, no.1. (New York, 1978), pp.1-28.

   Study of attitudes towards music and musical instruments in classical Antiquity, ancient Judaism and early Christianity — epitomized in Judaeo-Christian biblical figure of Jubal and Greco-Roman pagan philosopher Pythagoras. Two opposing attitudes viewed as culturally influential during Middle Ages, Renaissance, into Reformation Era and beyond to 17th and 18th centuries. Essay blends religious philosophy with cultural history and musicology.

488
MLOTEK, ELEANOR GORDON. "Soviet-Yiddish Folklore Scholarship." *Musica Judaica*, vol.2,no.1 (New York: A.S.J.M., 1977/78), pp.73-90, illus.

   Evaluative discussion of various collectors, collections and scholarly studies, as summary of topical field and for assessment of work done. Notice is taken of gradual closing-down of such research into Russian Jewish folksong, with later Stalin years in U.S.S.R. Special attention to contributions of Soviet collector Moshe Bereyovski (d.1961) and Yiddish collectors Yehuda Leib Cahan (1881-1937), A.Z. Idelsohn (1882-1938) as well as most recent work of Ruth Rubin in America. Facsimile illustrations and source notes.

489
MUSSULMAN, JOSEPH. "Mendelssohnism in America." *The Musical Quarterly*, vol.53,no.3. (New York,1967),pp.335-46,illus.

   Performance popularity in 19th century America of music of Felix Mendelssohn (1809-1847), notably his biblical oratorio "Elijah," and strong interest in composer himself, as reflected in writings about him at his death and as idealized musical figure for decades afterwards. Decline of interest by turn of century.

490
NETTL, PAUL. "Jewish Connections of Some Classical Composers." *Music and Letters*, vol.45, no.4. (Oxford, Eng., 1964), pp.337-44.

   Intriguing information collected by scholar Paul Nettl (1889-1972) on some Jewish connections of Bach's sons, the Mozarts — father and son — and Beethoven. For the Bachs, there were Jewish patrons and performers. Leopold Mozart had Jewish performer-colleagues. Wolfgang Mozart is reputed to have had an affair with a Jewess and was

commissioned by several Jewish patrons. He collaborated
with librettist Lorenzo da Ponte who was of Jewish lineage. Ludwig von Beethoven had contacts with Jews in
Vienna and appears to have integrated thematic material
from *Kol Nidre* into his C# minor quartet, opus 131.
491

NETTL, PAUL. "Some Early Jewish Musicians." *The Musical
Quarterly*, vol.17,no1. (New York, 1931), pp.40-46.
   Written while author Paul Nettl (1889-1972) still resided in Prague, Czechoslavakia. Translated from German
for this publication by Theodore Baker. Remarkable little piece for its time, place, circumstance and content.
References to Italian Salomone Rossi (c.1565-c.1628) and
Jewish musicians of 16th, 17th and 18th centuries, especially of Prague area. Treatment of broad scope of
Jewish musical creativity appears to have been shaped as
strong "rebuttal" to what was probably already rising
tide of overt anti-semitism in Europe, spurred by nazis
rising to power. Nettl subsequently fled to America.
492

NEWLIN, DIKA. "The Later Works of Ernest Bloch." *Musical
Quarterly*, vol.33,no.4.(New York,1947), pp.443-59, music.
   Consideration of the Judaic qualities in works of Ernest
Bloch (1880-1959), and comparison with certain elements
in compositions by Gustave Mahler (1864-1911) and works
by Arnold Schoenberg (1874-1951). Discussion of particular Jewish musical motifs and expressions, focussing
upon music of Bloch created from 1922-1938: Poems of the
Sea, Piano Quintet, Studies in Sepia, Sacred Service,
Voice in the Wilderness, Schelomo Rhapsody, Evocations
and Violin Concerto. Musical illustrations.
493

NEWLIN, DIKA. "Self-Revelation and the Law: Arnold Schoenberg in His Religious Works." *YUVAL:Studies of J.M.R.C.*,
vol.1. (Jerusalem,Isr.:Hebrew Univ./Magnes Press, 1968.),
pp.204-20, music.
   Arnold Schoenberg (1874-1951) composed several works
which reflect his Judaic background and religious ideas:
"*Jakobsleiter*," "Moses and Aaron," "*Kol Nidre*" and
settings of some Psalms. In his numerous letters to colleagues over the years, Schoenberg expression many of
those concepts which inspired his creation of the music
as well as the texts for those works. Newlin explores
direction connections between what composer expressed in
his letters and what he set down in compositions. Music
illustrations on pp.35-37 of supplementary booklet.
494

POWERS, HAROLD S. "Mode and Raga." *The Musical Quarterly*
vol.44,no.4. (New York, 1958), pp.448-60.
   Comparative study, referring to works of such scholars
as A.Z. Idelsohn (1882-1938) in Judaic modes, Egon Wellesz (1885-1974) in Oriental and Byzantine liturgical
chants, and Gustave Reese (1899-1977) in Jewish and
Christian ecclesiastical music, as well as to various
Indian sources on *raga*. Author treats issues of improvisation and ornamentation of particularly designated

melodic formulas and motival patterns in liturgical
music and secular folksongs. Investigation as to whether
and what similarities exist between synagogue-church
modes and Indian-Near Eastern chants. Source notes.
495

PRIOR, ROGER. "Jewish Musicians at the Tudor Court." *The
Musical Quarterly*, vol.69,no.2.(New York, 1983), pp.253-65.
Musicians of Jewish lineage in England at the court of
Henry VIII and Queen Elizabeth. Composers, singers and
instrumentalist, dancing masters and music teachers —
of Spanish-Portuguese and Italian Judaic origins. Author
speculates on family groupings of musicians, and varied
changes in names as well as permutations of relationships among those who traveled to and from England at
time, many residing there for extended periods. Some
consideration of musical creativity. Source notes.
496

REIK, THEODORE. "The Shofar." *Music Forum and Digest*,
vol.1,no.3. (New York, 1949), pp.13-16, illus.
Psychoanalyist Theodore Reik (1888-1969) discusses the
nature and purposes of this ancient ritual music instrument of Judaism — its structure, historical use in Jewish traditions, and circumstances in which it has been
sounded. Consideration of reasons for blowing of *Shofar*
(ram's horn) at most holy season in Jewish calendar:
Rosh Hashanah (New Year) services and at conclusion of
Yom Kippur (Day of Atonement) service. Illustrations.
497

RINGER, ALEXANDER L. "Arnold Schoenberg and the Politics
of Jewish Survival." *Journal of Arnold Schoenberg Institute*, vol.3,no.1.(Los Angeles,Cal.:A.S.I.,1979), pp.11-48.
Chronicle of particular activities and writings by composer Arnold Schoenberg (1874-1951) in response to anti-
semitism and rise of nazis to power. Soon after arrival
in America in 1934, Schoenberg addressed a meeting of
the *Mailamm* Society (Jewish music group) in New York
City and advocated establishment of Jewish national
homeland in area of British Mandate of Palestine.
498

RINGER, ALEXANDER L. "Arnold Schoenberg and the Prophetic
Image in Music," *Journal of the Arnold Schoenberg Institute*
vol.1,no.1.(Los Angeles, Cal.:A.S.I., 1976), pp.26-38.
Religious searchings of composer Arnold Schoenberg (1874
-1951) as reflected in various works — texts and music.
499

RINGER, ALEXANDER L. "Faith and Symbol: On Arnold Schoenberg's Last Musical Utterance." *Journal of the Arnold
Schoenberg Institute*, vol.6,no.1. (Los Angeles, Cal.: A.S.
I., 1982), pp.80-95.
Study of last works of Arnold Schoenberg (1874-1951) —
three psalms: "Psalm 130," "*Dreimal Tausend Jahre*,"
and "Modern Psalm." Last remained incomplete at composer's death, ending with his final text words "and
yet I pray." Ringer traces origins of those last works
of spiritual expression back to such early compositions
as "Jacob's Ladder" and "Moses and Aaron," in terms of

subjective nature of texts written by composer as well
as musical inspiration reflecting Schoenberg's mystic
and religious searchings throughout his life. Issue of
incompletion as factor in Schoenberg's spiritual works.
500

RINGER, ALEXANDER L. "Friedrich Gernsheim (1839-1916) and
the lost Generation." *Musica Judaica*, vol.3 (New York:
A.S.J.M., 1980/81), pp.1-12.
　　Relationship of that composer and music educator to his
　　many colleagues in Europe, notably his associations at
　　Stern Conservatory with Hermann Levi (1839-1900), Ignaz
　　Moscheles (1794-1870) and Ferdinand Hiller (1811-1885),
　　among others. Discussion of Gernsheim's talents, work
　　and his relative lack of fulfillment. Source notes.
501

RINGER, ALEXANDER L. "Handel and the Jews." *Music and
Letters*, vol.42,no.1. (London, Eng., 1981), pp.17-29.
　　Examination of inspiration in subject and music for ora-
　　torios of George Frederick Handel (1685-1759). Factors
　　considered: composer's Pietist religious background;
　　deep personal appreciation of Bible texts; friendships
　　with Jews in Germany and Italy, with visits to Venetian
　　Ghetto at Jewish holiday times; substantial support of
　　his oratorio works - especially "Esther and Mordecai"
　　and "Judas Maccabaeus" - by Jewish people in England at
　　public performances and in patronage. Source notes.
502

RINGER, ALEXANDER L. "Musical Composition in Modern
Israel." *The Musical Quarterly*, vol.51, no.1. (New
York, 1965), pp.282-97.
　　Report on several recent (1965) works and on general
　　trends of composition among younger Israelis.
503

RINGER, ALEXANDER L. "Salomon Sulzer, Joseph Mainzer, and
the Romantic *a Capella* Movement." *Studia Musicologica*,
vol.2. (Budapest,Hung., 1969), pp.355-71.
　　For issue honoring 70th anniversary of Hungarian scholar
　　Bence Szabolcsi (1897-1973), article by Ringer on music
　　relationship of composer Joseph Mainzer (1801-1851) and
　　Salomon Sulzer (1804-1890) chief cantor of largest syna-
　　gogue in Vienna - Seitenstettengasse Shul. Sulzer was
　　widely respected and appreciated as cantorial artist,
　　composer-arranger, collector and publisher, musician and
　　educator - a significant figure in 19th century Jewish
　　liturgical traditions, in which vocal renditions not ac-
　　companied by any instrumentation. Source notes.
504

RINGER, ALEXANDER L. "Schoenberg, Weill and Epic Theater."
Journal of the Arnold Schoenberg Institute, vol.4, no.1.
(los Angeles, Cal.:A.S.I., 1980), pp.77-98.
　　Artistic connection (in 1920's and 1930's) between two
　　"products of Central Europe's emancipated Jewry that
　　contributed so mightily to socio-political as well as
　　artistic change." Discussion of how both used dramatic
　　musical forms for reflection of their different ideals:
　　Arnold Schoenberg (1874-1951) - expression of his cul-

tural ideas and spiritual roots; Kurt Weill (1900-1950)
- means of social and political commentary. Each brought
innovations to music drama. Weill's writings cited.

505
RINGER, ALEXANDER L. "Schoenbergiana in Jerusalem." *The
Musical Quarterly*, vol.59,no.1.(New York,1973), pp.1-14.
    Arnold Schoenberg (1874-1951) had told colleagues of his
    wish that materials about his works be included at the
    National library in Jerusalem, Israel. Author reports on
    donation of some materials on Schoenberg by one of his
    students Georg Alter, on occasion of 100th birthday of
    Schoenberg. Also included in archival matter given by
    Alter are music memorabilia of Prague community — scores
    and manuscripts, photographs and varied writings — all
    related to music and musicians of pre-World War II era.

506
ROSS, ISRAEL J. "Cross-Cultural Dynamics in Musical Traditions; the Music of the Jews of Cochin." *Musica Judaica*,
vol.2,no.1(New York:A.S.J.M.,1977/78),pp.50-72, illus.,music
    Historical background of Cochin (Southwestern Coast of
    India) Jewish community, and its particular musical ex-
    pression — liturgical and secular—folk. Comparative
    analysis of cantillation motifs, chant styles and spe-
    cial prayer tunes. Issues of ornamentation and of unique
    prayer melodies which Cochin Jews identify as "Shingli
    Tunes." Discussion of semi-religious songs and some of
    the folksongs. Source notes and substantial presentation
    of musical examples.

507
ROTHSTEIN, ROBERT. "On the Melody of David Edelstadt's
Vakht Oyf." *Musica Judaica*, vol.4 (New York: A.S.J.M.,
1981/82), pp.68-79, illus., music.
    Study of a song whose Yiddish text was written by labor
    poet David Edelstadt (1866-1892), the poetry and musical
    settings of which became enormously popular among Jewish
    workers around turn of century. Yiddish, Russian and
    Polish versions of texts given, along with several me-
    lodic variants, as published and sung in Europe and in
    America. Facsimiles, music examples and source notes.

508
RUBIN, RUTH. "A Comparative Approach to a Yiddish Song of
Protest." *Studies in Ethnomusicology*, vol.2. (New York:
Soc. for Ethnomusicology, 1965), pp.54-75, illus., music.
    Issues reflected in Yiddish folksongs of Eastern Europe
    and American Jewish life. Music as social, economic and
    political expression. Analysis of particular song *"Un
    Du Akerst"* ("And You Plow"). English translations of
    texts, music illustrations and source notes.

509
RUBIN, RUTH. "19th Century Yiddish Love Songs of East
Europe." *Journal of I.F.M.C.*, vol.7. (Cambridge, Eng.:
I.F.M.C., 1955), pp.44-47.
    Summary of paper discussing texts as well as melodies.

510
RUBIN, RUTH. "Shalom Aleichem and Yiddish Folksongs."
Sing Out, vol.9,no.3.(New York,1959/60),pp.21-26, music.

Yiddish writer Shalom Aleichem (1859-1916) not only contributed poetic texts to some poignant folk-like songs
in Yiddish genre, he also supported and disseminated in
Eastern Europe and then America the songs created by
Badkhen (Jewish folk-minstrel) Mark Warshawsky (1845-
1907). Cited is great favorite lyric text *"Shluf Mein
Kind"* ("Sleep My Child") by Shalom Aleichem, which was
set to several melodies. English translation of texts.
511
RUBIN, RUTH. "Yiddish Folksongs Current in French Canada."
Journal of I.F.M.C., vol.12. (Cambridge, Eng.: I.F.M.C.,
1960), pp.76-78.
Summary of paper on materials collected by author.
512
SABANEYEV, LEONIDE. "The Jewish National School in Music."
(trans. from Russian by S.W. Pring) *The Musical Quarterly*,
vol.15,no.3. (New York, 1929), pp.448-68.
Leonide Sabaneyev (1881-1968) wrote from Moscow. His article is polemical, but an effort to survey background
and early rise, at beginning of this century in Russia,
of self-awareness among Russian musicians - scholars,
critics, composers, performers - a movement in which
also Russian-Jewish musicians were swept along. Jews began to shape art music expression out of their folksongs
and liturgical traditions. Sabaneyev concludes that the
Jewish people "must speak to the world in a musical
language of its own."
513
SACHS, CURT. "Primitive and Mediaeval Music: A Parallel."
Journal of A.M.S., vol.13, nos.1/3. (Phila.: A.M.S., 1960)
pp.43-49.
Journal edition was dedicated to Otto Kinkeldey (1878-
1966) on occasion of his 80th birthday. Contribution by
Curt Sachs (1881-1959) is overview with commentary on
interrelationships of musical expressions during early
and later Antiquity, especially in terms of music of religious observances and rise of formalized patterns of
liturgy in Judaeo-Christian contexts. This article appeared in print after Sachs had passed away, and may be
his last piece of professional writing.
514
SCHOENBERG, ARNOLD. "A Four-Point Program for Jewry."
Journal of the Arnold Schoenberg Institute, vol.3, no.1.
(los Angeles, Cal.:A.S.I., 1979), pp.49-67.
Posthumous publication of article originally issued by
composer Arnold Schoenberg (1874-1951) in German text in
1933 as elaboration of his 1924 piece on "Zionismus."
Revised English version was presented at a meeting in
New York City of Mailamm Society (Jewish music group) in
1934 and then presented in California in 1938. Schoenberg sets out his proposal for "an independent Jewish
State," a political answer in Jewish nationhood.
515
SHARVIT, URI. "Musical Realizatioan of Biblical Cantillation Symbols (*Te'amim*) in the Jewish Yemenite Tradition."
YUVAL:Studies of J.M.R.C., vol.4. (Jerusalem,Isr.: Hebrew

Univ./Magnes Press, 1982), pp.179-210, illus., music.
    Based upon field work collection and study, treatment of
    Yemenite *Pentateuch* (Five Books of Moses) recitation
    as performed in following: various synagogue services;
    Bible study sessions; and, educational practices in the
    Heder (religious school). Considered are: Pentateuch
    recitation in Yemenite communities; Yemenite concept of
    their cantillation system; formal principles of the six
    special Pentateuch tunes; the music; and, some conclu-
    sions regarding various forms of recitation patterns and
    their elaborations. Comparative tables, graphs, source
    notes, cited references and musical examples.
516
SHELEMAY, KAY KAUFMAN. "Historical Ethnomusicology? Re-
constructing Falasha Liturgical History." *Ethnomusicology*,
vol.24,no.2. (Ann Arbor, Mich.: Soc. for Ethnomusicology,
1980), pp.233-58, illus., music.
    Scholarly inquiry into formative influences upon li-
    turgical music of Falashas - Black Jews of Ethiopia -
    as observed, collected and studied at present time.
    Consideration of Judaic and Christian elements, folk
    music patterns and problems of continuity in oral
    transmission. Music examples and source notes.
517
SHELEMAY, KAY KAUFMAN. "A Quarter-Century in the Life of a
Falasha Prayer." *Yearbook of I.F.M.C.*, vol.10. Cambridge,
Eng.: I.F.M.C., 1978), pp.83-108, illus., music.
    Study of liturgical music among Black Jews - Falashas -
    dissident pre-rabbinic Judaic sect residing in areas of
    Ethiopia probably since before destruction of Temple in
    586 B.C.E. Consideration of alterations brought about by
    social changes and difficulties of continuity, as ob-
    served by author-collector, an ethnomusicologist. Music
    examples and source notes.
518
SHELEMAY, KAY KAUFMAN. "*Seged*: A Falasha Pilgrimage
Festival." *Musica Judaica*, vol.3. (New York: A.S.J.M.,
1980/81), pp.42-62, illus., music.
    Study based upon research among Falashas, considering:
    Seged holiday, its significance and its customs of
    observance; liturgy and melodic chants of holiday; an
    analysis of musical elements in comparative tables. Ap-
    pendices of liturgical order of services for *Seged* and
    translations of texts for music examples. References,
    source notes and musical illustrations.
519
SHILOAH, AMNON. "The Arabic Concept of Mode." *Journal of
A.M.S.*, vol.34,no.1.(Phila.:A.M.S.,1981), pp.19-42, illus.
    Re-evaluative study of concepts concerning Near Eastern
    modes by Israeli scholar of Islamic music history. Re-
    ferences to work of Henry George Farmer (1882-1965) and
    of various earlier (13th to 18th century) Arabic sources
    and writings on music of Islam. Terminologies as carried
    over into more recent studies. Tables and source notes.

520
SHILOAH, AMNON. "Musical Passage in Ibn Ezra's 'Book of
the Garden'." *YUVAL:Studies of J.M.R.C.*, vol.4.(Jerusalem,
Isr.:Hebrew Univ./Magnes Press, 1982), pp.211-24.
    Study of writings of Moses ibn Ezra (1055-1135 - Spain),
which mention music, and in particular one philosophical
and philological work. Hebrew text and English translation. Comparative tables and source notes.
521
SHILOAH, AMNON. "The Symbolism of Music in the Kabbalistic
Tradition." *The World of Music*, vol.20, no.3. (W.Berlin:
UNESCO, 1978), pp.56-65, illus.
    Aspects of musical reflections in *Kabbalah* - Jewish
mystical religious expression - especially associated
in Judaic traditions with interpretation of Sabbath and
assigning of particular powers to music in itself. Out
of *Kabbalah* arose much religious folklore and musical
expression, notably spiritual folksongs or *Zemirot*.
522
SHILOAH, AMNON and EDITH GERSON-KIWI. "Musicology in Israel, 1960-1980." *Acta Musicologica*, vol.53, no.2. (Kassel,
W.Ger.: I.M.S., 1981), pp.200-16.
    Survey of field, with background information and current
activities on: Ethnomusicological Institute for Jewish
Music; Sound Archives and Laboratories for Musical Research at Hebrew University in Jerusalem; various de-
partments of musicology at Israeli universities; Israel
Musicological Society; exhibitions and publications -
periodicals, monographs and books; recordings. Also,
summary of areas of current study projects in Israel.
523
SHILOAH, AMNON, RUTH TENE and LEA SHALEM, comps. *Music
Subjects in the Zohar: Texts and Indices (Inventory of Jewish Musical Sources, Series B,1).* (YUVAL Monograph Series,
5) Jerusalem,Isr.:Hebrew Univ./Magnes Press,1977;xiii,166pp.
    Prepared in association with the Jewish Music Resource
Center at Hebrew University. Source listings with an
English text introduction for the materials. *Zohar* is
13th century collection of Biblical commentaries according to *Kabbalah*, or mystical interpretations.
524
SHMUELI, HERZL. "Oriental Elements in Israeli Song."
Journal of I.F.M.C., vol.16. (Cambridge, Eng.: I.F.M.C.,
1964), pp.29-38, illus., music.
    Examination of some popular Israeli folksongs, in terms
of Near Eastern motival elements. Music illustrations.
525
SINGER, JACOB. "The Music of the Synagogue." *Annual Proceedings of M.T.N.A.*, vol.37. (Hartford, Conn.: M.T.N.A.,
1915), pp.205-13.
    Presentation by rabbi and scholar Jacob Singer (1883-
1964) of Jewish liturgical music from biblical times,
rise of synagogue and its various musical traditions
and forms, development of cantorial artistry, growth of
music over centuries throughout world, innovative ideas
of 19th century European liturgists, and more recent

Articles on Jewish Music Topics   117

musical creativity in America. Source notes.

526
SLIM, H. COLIN. "Gian and Gian Maria, Some Fifteenth and
Sixteenth Century Namesakes." *The Musical Quarterly*, vol.
57, no.4. (New York, 1971), pp.562-74, illus.
> Investigation of backgrounds and activities of several
> lutenists of Judaic lineage, who served as composers and
> performers at Papal service in Rome and at Renaissance
> courts in Venice, Florence, Urbino, Mantua and other
> communities in northern Italy. Variations of names are
> traced, in addition to documentation of families, tra-
> vels, creativity and employers. Source notes.

527
SLOBIN, MARK "Notes on Bukharan Music in Israel." *YUVAL:*
Studies of J.M.R.C., vol.4. (Jerusalem,Isr.:Hebrew Univ./
Magnes Press, 1982), pp.225-39, music.
> Based upon research done in 1971 among Bukharan Jews (of
> Central Asian origin) resettled in Israel. Mark Slobin
> considers musical backgrounds - liturgical and secular
> music; performers and performance styles - in terms of
> cultural backgrounds, retention and transmission of a
> special heritage. Actual studies made with particular
> family of musicians (in Israel since 1936) who seem to
> have maintained their distinctive Bokharan repertoire.
> Some song texts with translation into English, source
> notes, references cited and musical examples.

528
SMITH, CARLETON SPRAGUE. "Curt Sachs and the Library Mu-
seum of the Performing Arts." *Musica Judaica*, vol.4 (New
York: A.S.J.M., 1981/82), pp.8-19.
> Tribute article to life and work of Curt Sachs (1881-
> 1959) from colleague and friend, who first met him in
> Berlin in 1932, and was instrumental in assisting Sachs
> to emigrate to this country. Influences noted which
> shaped Sachs' scholarly career here. Their early mutual
> ideas for establishment of a Music Library and Museum in
> New York is described, affording interesting facts about
> those plans as ultimately developed. Carleton Sprague
> Smith was Chief of Music Division of New York Public
> Library and worked for eventual creation of Lincoln
> Center Music Research Library.

529
SPECTOR, JOHANNA. "Classical *'Ud* Music in Egypt With
Special Reference to *Maqamot*." *Ethnomusicology*, vol.14,
no.2.(Ann Arbor, Mich.: Soc. for Ethnomusicology, 1970),
pp.243-57, illus., music.
> Study of instrumental folk music, qualities and styles
> of performance improvisations, based upon traditional
> modal patterns of Near East. Music examples and notes.

530
SPECTOR, JOHANNA. "Musical Styles in Near Eastern Jewish
Liturgy." *Journal of Music Academy*, vol.26.(Madras, India,
1956), pp.122-30, illus., music.
> Report on author's collected materials from among Near
> Eastern groups - liturgical cantillation and chant, re-
> ligious ceremonial folksongs and instrumental customs.

531
SPECTOR, JOHANNA. "The Role of Ethnomusicology in the
Study of Jewish Music." *Musica Judaica*, vol.4 (New York:
A.S.J.M., 1981/82), pp.20-31, music.
    Scholar and educator Johanna Spector outlines method-
    ology by which Jewish music studies may deal with: an-
    thropology, archaeology, linguistics, cultural history
    and musicology itself. Elaboration of ethnology as form
    of "cultural anthropology" and various aspects of col-
    lection and interpretation of oral traditions. Compara-
    tive tables of Jewish modes in their origins, develop-
    ments and variant influences. Consideration of diversity
    of Jewish styles. Music examples and source notes.
532
SPECTOR, JOHANNA. "Samaritan chant." *Journal of I.F.M.C.,*
vol.16. (Cambridge,Eng.: I.F.M.C., 1964), pp.66-9.
    Summary of paper which reports on author's collection
    of liturgical folksong materials among Samaritan (pre-
    rabbinic dissident Judaic sect) groups living in Israel.
533
SPECTOR, JOHANNA. "Samaritan Chant." *Journal of Music
Academy*, vol.38.(Madras,India,1967), pp.104-12, music.
    Report on author's collection and study of liturgical
    musical materials among Samaritans (pre-rabbinic dissi-
    dent Judaic sect) residing in Israel. Music examples.
    Johanna Spector, scholar and educator in America and
    Israel, has specialized in ethnomusicological studies
    of various Oriental-Asiatic Jewish groups.
534
SPECTOR, JOHANNA. "Shingli Tunes of the Cochin Jews."
Asian Music, vol.3,no.2. (New York: Soc. for Asian Music,
1972), pp.23-28, music.
    Study of some melodic patterns and tune examples as col-
    lected by author from among Cochin Jews of southern part
    of India, along Malabar Coast area at the Arabian Sea.
    Musical illustrations.
535
SPECTOR, JOHANNA. "The Significance of Samaritan Neumes
and Contemporary Practice." *Studia Musicologica*, vol.7,
nos.1/4. (Budapest, Hung.:Soc. for Arts and Sciences, 1965),
pp. 141-53, illus., music.
    Examination of notation traditions of Samaritans (dis-
    sident pre-rabbinic Judaic sect) for cantillation of
    Scriptures and liturgical prayer chanting motifs. Col-
    lected materials by author among groups resident in
    Israel. Music examples and source notes.
536
STEIN, LEON. "Schoenberg's Jewish Identity (A Chronology
of Source Material)." *Journal of the Arnold Schoenberg Institute*, vol.3,no.1.(Los Angeles,Cal.:A.S.I.,1979),pp.3-10.
    Collection of materials relating to particular aspects
    of life and work of composer Arnold Schoenberg (1874-
    1951) which underscore his Judaic lineage and sense of
    Jewish connection. Facsimiles and source notes.

537
STRUNK, OLIVER. "Byzantine Psalmody and Its Possible Connection with Hebraic Cantillation." *Bulletin of American Musicology Society*, nos.11/13. ([?]:A.M.S.,1948), pp.19-21.
　　Abstract of paper presented by scholar and educator Oliver Strunk (1901-1980) at symposium on "Ancient Hebrew and Early Christian Melody," held at Temple Emanu-El in New York City on occasion (1946) of 10th anniversary of "Three Choir Festivals" organized by composer and conductor Lazare Saminsky (1882-1959).

538
SZABOLCSI, BENCE. "Hebrew Recitative-Types in Hungary." *Journal of I.F.M.C.*, vol.16. (Cambridge, Eng.: I.F.M.C., 1964), pp.65-66.
　　Summary of paper treating some elements of Jewish liturgical folksong encountered by author.

539
SZABOLCSI, BENCE. "The 'Proclamation Style' in Hebrew Music." *YUVAL:Studies of J.M.R.C.*, vol.1. (Jerusalem, Isr.: Hebrew Univ./Magnes Press, 1968), pp.249-50, music.
　　Brief study of elements of Biblical cantillation as collected by Hungarian scholar Bence Szabolcsi (1899-1973) among East European Ashkenazic synagogue traditions of Hungarian-Polish-Balkan areas. Musical illustrations on pp.38-39 of supplementary booklet.

540
THOMSON, JOAN. "Giacomo Meyerbeer: The Jew and His Relationship with Richard Wagner." *Musica Judaica*, vol.1 (New York: A.S.J.M., 1975/76), pp.54-486, illus.
　　Study of Jacob Meyer Beer (1791-1864), who achieved fame as opera composer Giacomo Meyerbeer. Discussion of his family background, life as Jew in Europe's musical society, and issues of cultural assimilation and accommodation at that time. Early relationship between Meyerbeer and Richard Wagner (1813-1882) explored, with attention to mounting hostility of Wagner, culminating in his writing (but at first not signing) *Das Judenthum in Der Musik* in 1850, a vicious anti-semitic piece particularly attacking Meyerbeer. Influence of Meyerbeer's operas upon Wagner's creativity are viewed in this context, along with legacy of influences of both upon subsequent musical developments. Source notes.

541
VELIMIROVIC, MILOS. "Egon Wellesz and the Study of Byzantine Chant." *The Musical Quarterly*, vol.62,no.2. (New York, 1976), pp.265-77, illus.
　　Author, as former student and then colleague of scholar and educator Egon Wellesz (1885-1974), pays tribute to his valuable work in Ancient Greek, Near Eastern, early Christian and Byzantine musical developments. References to comparative studies of A.Z. Idelsohn (1882-1938) and others in early liturgical music. Source notes.

542
WAESBERGHE, JOSEPH SMITS van. "The Treatise on Music Translated into Hebrew by Juda ben Isaac (Paris B.N. Heb. 1037,22v-27v)." *YUVAL:Studies of J.M.R.C.*, vol.2.(Jerusa-

lem,Isr.:Hebrew Univ./Magnes Press, 1971), pp.129-61, illus.
     Study as invited response to article in *YUVAL*, vol.1
     (1968) by Israel Adler providing Hebrew text of this
     treatise, with his detailed commentary (in French only).
     J.S. van Waesberghe presents a summary of data as to
     earlier origins, and historical significance, of the
     materials contained in the various chapters of this im-
     portant work by Juda ben Isaac (fl.late 15th century,
     in Southern France). Extensive research documentation
     assembled, with reflections on *Ars Nova* and other
     cultural developments. Tables and source notes.
   543
WEISSER, ALBERT, ed. "Lazare Saminsky's Years in Russia
and Palestine: Excerpts from an Unpublished Autobiography."
Musica Judaica, vol.2.(New York:A.S.J.M.,1977/78),pp.1-20.
     Informative piece concerning early life and work of com-
     poser, conductor and music director Lazare Saminsky
     (1882-1959), before he came to U.S. in 1920. Includes
     Saminsky's personal reflections on several notable
     Russian composers of that time, as well as his travels
     in Caucasus area collecting Jewish folksongs and his
     brief sojourn in Palestine Mandate. Annotations in form
     of "footnotes" added by Albert Weisser (1918-1982).
   544
WEISSER, ALBERT. "The Music Division of the Jewish Ethnographic Expedition in the Name of Baron Horace Guinzbourg
(1911-1914)." ***Musica Judaica***, vol.4. (New York: A.S.J.M.,
1981/82), pp.1-8.
     Posthumous publication of a last study by scholar and
     educator Albert Weisser (1918-1982), reflecting gradual
     decline of collection and publication of Jewish folk
     music expression in Russian communities following rise
     of Stalin in U.S.S.R. Overview of early collectors and
     collections, with some consideration of work of Soviet
     Jewish ethnomusicologist Moshe Beregovski (1892-1961).
   545
WERNER, ERIC. "Felix Mendelssohn - Gustave Mahler: Two
Borderline Cases of German-Jewish Assimilation." ***YUVAL:***
Studies of J.M.R.C., vol.4. (Jerusalem,Isr.:Hebrew Univ./
Magnes Press, 1982), pp.240-64.
     Discussion of parallels, and differences, in assimilated
     patterns of life and work of Felix Mendelssohn (1809-
     1847) and Gustave Mahler (1864-1911). Comparative con-
     siderations of backgrounds, families, education, careers
     and creative works. Reflections on attitudes of each to-
     wards Judaism and Jewish musicians, and their individual
     experiences with anti-semitism of their time and place.
   546
WERNER, ERIC. "If I Speak in the Tongues of Man: St.
Paul's Attitude Toward Music." ***Journal of A.M.S.***, vol.13,
nos.1/3. (Phila.:A.M.S., 1960), pp.18-23.
     Edition of journal was dedicated to Otto Kinkeldey
     (1878-1966) on occasion of his 80th birthday. Eric Wer-
     ner discusses attitude toward music of Paul of Tarsus,
     in terms of his origins as Diaspora Jew, with linkages
     to worldly Hellenism and to strict observances of Phar-

isaic Judaism. Paul's admonitions against instrumental
music to early Christians and his objections to singing
voices of women in services, as well as his advocacy of
psalmody and simplicity of chant, appear to reflect influences particularly of his Pharisee background. Notes.
547
WERNER, ERIC. "The Influence of Jewish Music on the Gregorian Chant." *Annual Proceedings of M.T.N.A.*, vol.66.
(Pittsburgh: M.T.N.A., 1944), pp.241-7, music.
    Early study bu scholar and educator Eric Werner of com-
    monality in origins of church and synagogue chant pat-
    terns and motifs. Musical examples.
548
WERNER, ERIC. "Musical Aspects of the Dead Sea Scrolls."
The Musical Quarterly, vol.43,no.1.(New York,1957),pp.21-37
    In view of early Hebraic nature of these scrolls of the
    Qumran Essenes (monastic pre-rabbinical Judaic sect),
    attention is drawn to musical aspects of those materials
    in terms of vocal forms, styles of musical expression
    as well as references to music instruments and uses of
    musical terms themselves. Consideration of marginal
    signs in scrolls as possible "neumes" or ecphonetic
    markings for use in chanting of thanksgiving hymns and
    other passages. Possible forerunners of later Masoretic
    notations for scriptural cantillations in Jewish tra-
    ditional services, and comparison with subsequent uses
    of neumes as found in Byzantine manuscripts. References
    to descriptive writings of Philo of Alexandria concern-
    ing Therapeutae sect. Werner advances intriguing ideas
    and investigates some possible interrelationships with
    respect to these scrolls. Article dedicated to his col-
    league Curt Sachs (1881-1959) on occasion of his 75th
    birthday. Illustrations of some neumes and source notes.
549
WERNER, ERIC. "Musical Tradition and Its Transmitters Between Synagogue and Church." *YUVAL:Studies of J.M.R.C.*,
vol.2.(Jerusalem,Isr.:Hebrew Univ./Magnes, 1971), pp.163-80.
    Examination of concept of "national folksong" and its
    applicability in musical traditions of synagogue, and
    attitudes of Western music historians to issue of extent
    of Jewish influences upon origin and shaping of early
    Christian liturgical music. Elaborations of some ideas
    explored by author in his book *The Sacred Bridge* (New
    York, 1959) and in his other writings on comparative
    early synagogue and church music. Consideration of the
    Octoechos (eight modes of music) and survey of works
    by numerous scholars over past 300 years in terms of
    their different opinions as to roots of church chants,
    psalmody and hymnology. References also to studies by
    Jewish music scholars of 19th and 20th century in
    Europe, America and Israel.
550
WERNER, ERIC. "The Oldest Sources of Octave and Octoechos"
Acta Musicologica,vol.20.(Basel.Switz.:I.M.S.,1948),pp.1-9
    Origins in Near Eastern and Greek cultures of musical
    concepts of "octave" and "Octoechos" during Ancient and

Mediaeval eras. Biblical text headings of Psalms appear
to suggest octaval modal instructions for chanters, or
at least references to "eight" as melodic term. Considerations of numerological significances of "seven" and
"eight" in liturgical calendar of observances for Judaic
and Christian religions. "Eight" church modes, and other
influences in ritual music as developed. Source notes.

551
WERNER, ERIC. "The Psalmodic Formula *'Neannoe'* and Its
Origin." *The Musical Quarterly*, vol.28. (New York, 1942),
pp.93-99, illus., music.
     Study of meanings and applications of group of syllables
as verbal formulas in Byzantine chant, tracing to some
possible Talmudic and other Hebraic origins. Comparisons
in performance patterns with Hebrew melismatic chant
word "*Alleluia*." Reference to cultural interchanges
in early Mediaeval times between Judaic and European
Byzantine groups. Speculations on term *"Neannoe"* as
related to some Hebrew words. Music examples.

552
WERNER, ERIC. "Report of the First International Congress
of Jewish Music (Held in Paris, Nov. 1957)." *The Musical
Quarterly*, vol.44,no.2. (New York, 1958), pp.242-4.
     Summary of topics covered and roster of participants.
Included at Congress was first European performance of
work *"Kol Nidre"* by Arnold Schoenberg (1874-1951).

553
WHITE, PAMELA C. "The Genesis of 'Moses and Aaron.'"
Journal of the Arnold Schoenberg Institute, vol.6,no.1.
(Los Angeles, Cal.: A.S.I., 1982), pp.8-55.
     Discussion of this work — text and music — as "one of
the most profoundly personal creative statements" by
Arnold Schoenberg (1874-1951). Author documents sources
of ideas and progress of work. "The opera is the first
large-scale musical work for which Schoenberg wrote a
text with specifically Jewish subject matter, and, al-
though the opera remains unfinished, it nevertheless em-
bodies all of the major philosophical components of the
maturely developed Jewish faith at which Schoenberg arrived by the middle 1920's." He worked on "Moses and
Aaron" from 1927 to 1932. Schoenberg did reconvert to
the Jewish faith in Paris, October 1933. Author traces
out correspondence by composer regarding his reflections
on Judaism itself and on his other works of Jewish inspiration or relevance. Source notes.

554
WOERNER, KARL H. "Arnold Schoenberg and the Theater."
(trans. from German by Willis Wager) *The Musical Quarterly*
vol.48.(New York, 1962), pp.444-60, illus., music.
     Discussion of works by Arnold Schoenberg (1874-1951):
"Die Jacobsleiter" ("The Jacob's Ladder") and "Moses
and Aaron." Compositions viewed in terms of dramatic
qualities and textual significance, as well as music.

555
WOHLBERG, MAX. "The Music of the Synagogue as a Source of
the Yiddish Folksong." *Musica Judaica*, vol. 2. (New York:

A.S.J.M., 1977/78), pp.21-49, music.
Cantor, scholar and educator Max Wohlberg considers
issue of dynamic crossover of melodies from religious
musical expression into secular Jewish folksong. Analysis of music materials as found in a number of collections of Jewish music and in works of other scholars.
Extensive selection of music examples. Source notes.

556
WOLFF, HELLMUTH C. "Mendelssohn and Handel." (Trans. from
German by Ernest Sanders and Luise Eitel) *The Musical Quarterly*, vol.45,no.2.(New York,1959),pp.175-90, illus., music
Influences of works of G.F. Handel (1685-1759), notably
his oratorios on biblical subjects, upon musical career
of Felix Mendelssohn ((1809-1847), who edited and conducted performances of those Handel works, especially
"Israel in Egypt." Mendelssohn wrote organ parts for the
oratorios "Joshua" and "Solomon." Music illustrations.

557
YASSER, JOSEPH. "The Cantillation of the Bible; Salomon
Rosowsky." *The Musical Quarterly*, vol.44,no.3. (New York,
1958), pp.393-401, illus., music.
More than a review of *The Cantillation of the Bible:
The Five Books of Moses*, (New York, 1957) by Salomon
Rosowsky (1878-1962), this is an in-depth essay by educator, scholar and musician Joseph Yasser (1893-1981) on
the topic itself - the traditional cantillation patterns
for chanting of the *Torah* (Five Books of Moses) according to Ashkenazic East European Jewish liturgy. Tribute is also paid to scholarly dedication and achievements of Rosowsky. Source notes and music examples.

558
YASSER, JOSEPH. "The *Magrepha* of the Herodian Temple; A
Five-Fold Hypothesis." *Journal of A.M.S.*, vol.13, nos.1/3.
(Phila.: A.M.S., 1960), pp.14-42, illus.
Extensive and comprehensive study of the nature and use
of the *Magrepha*, an instrument noted as employed in
the services at the Second Temple. Scholar Joseph Yasser
(1893-1981) investigates different descriptions and explanations for this instrument, or perhaps implement,
and advances some theories based upon his research into
Talmudic and other old rabbinic writings, as well as
early Christian materials, and various pictorial repre-
sentations. Yasser considers whether the *Magrepha* is a
type of wind-fed organ or else a ritual fire shovel. Illustrated with diagrams and facsimiles. Source notes.
This edition of the *Journal of A.M.S.* was dedicated to
Otto Kinkeldey (1878-1966) on his 80th anniversary.

B. In General Periodicals

559
ADLER, ISRAEL. "Synagogue Chants of the 12th Century: The
Music Notations of Obadiah, the Proselyte." *Ariel*, vol.15.
(Jerusalem, Isr.:Arts and Letters, 1966), pp.27-41, illus.
     Examination of earliest identified written examples of
     Jewish liturgical music, as attributed to Obadiah the
     Norman Proselyte (c.1070-c.1141). Facsimile illustra-
     tions and source notes.
560
ALGAZI, LEON. "Jewish Religious Music." *The Jews and Our-
selves*, vol. 2, no.3. (London, Eng.: Judaism and Christian-
ity in the World of Today, 1964), pp.92-98.
     General survey of various styles of Jewish hymnology,
     with examples.
561
ARMISTEAD, SAMUEL and JOSEPH SILVERMAN. "Hispanic Balladry
Among the Sephardic Jews of the West Coast." *Western Folklore*, vol. 19, no. 4. (Berkeley, Cal.: Western Folklore
Soc., 1960), pp.229-44.
     Background of Judaeo-Spanish communities, cultural ex-
     pression and particular consideration of some collected
     materials in Los Angeles, San Francisco and Seattle.
     Analysis of origins and versions of several Sephardic
     ballads - texts and melodic patterns. Source notes.
562
ARMISTEAD, SAMUEL and JOSEPH SILVERMAN. "A Judaeo-Spanish
Derivative of the Ballad of 'The Bridge of Arta'." *Journal
of American Folklore*, vol.76. (Austin, Tex.:Amer. Folklore
Soc., 1963), pp.16-20.
     Background and various versions of a Sephardic ballad
     popular among Jews of Salonika and Larissa, and trans-
     ported with migrations to America. Ladino (Spaniolic-
     Jewish) texts with English translations. Ballad as no-
     tated in studies among Sephardic Jews of Los Angeles and
     New York City. Source notes.
563
ARMISTEAD, SAMUEL and JOSEPH SILVERMAN, "A New Collection
of Judaeo-Spanish Ballads." *Journal of Folklore*, vol. 3.
(Bloomington, Ind.: Folklore Inst., 1966), pp.133-53.
     Study of collected materials - texts and styles.
564
ARMISTEAD, SAMUEL and JOSEPH SILVERMAN. "Rare Judaeo-Spanish Ballads from Monastir (Yugoslavia) Collected by Max A.
Luria." *American Sephardi*, vol. 7/8. (New York: Yeshiva
Univ., 1975), pp.50-61.
     Consideration of some Sephardic folksong sources, texts
     and styles. Reference notes.
565
AVENARY, HANOCH. "The Earliest Notation of Ashkenazic Bi-
ble Chant (Amman - MSS, ab, 1511)." *Journal of Jewish Studies,* vol.26, no.1/2. (Oxford, Eng.:Inst. of Jewish Studies/
W.J.C., 1975), pp.132-50, illus., music.

Two manuscripts of the Christian Hebraist Caspar Amman
(1460-1524) appear to antedate 1518 publication of other
Christian Hebraist Johann Reuchlin (1455-1522) and help
to fix earliest origins of some melodic motifs to 10th
century, and codification of Hebrew biblical chant accents according to Tiberian system of Aharon ben Asher
(fl. 7th century). Facsimile illustrations, source
notes and musical examples.

566
AVENARY, HANOCH. "A *Geniza* Find of Sa'adya's Psalm -
Preface and Its Musical Aspects." *H.U.C. Annual*, vol. 39.
(Cincinnati: H.U.C., 1968), pp.145-62, illus., music.
Analytical study, with transcription of Hebrew texts,
facsimiles of original manuscripts, tables of trans-
lations and interpretations of musical terms.

567
AVENARY, HANOCH. "*Geniza* Fragments of Hebrew Hymns and
Prayers Set to Music (Early 12th Century)." *Journal of Jewish Studies*, vol.16, nos.3/4. (London, Eng.:Inst. of Jewish
Studies/W.J.C., 1965), pp.87-104, illus., music.
Description of documents affording evidence of centuries
old Jewish liturgical usages, in study of the Norman
Proselyte Obadyah (c.1070-c.1141) and his music notation
material, in terms of transcription and interpretation
of those neumes signs. Consideration of problems in the
scholarly analysis of characteristics of music and text,
especially in light of more recently discovered items in
Cairo Geniza collection. Facsimiles, musical examples,
area map and source notes.

568
AVENARY, HANOCH. "Pseudo-Jerome Writings and Qumran Tradition." *Revue de Qumran*,vol.13.(Paris,Fr.,1963),pp.15-21.
Examination of archeological materials in terms of early
comparative liturgical poetics and practices.

569
BAYER, JEROME. "The Future of Jewish Music." *Menorah
Journal*, vol.5, no.2. (New York, 1919), pp.109-14.
Plea for new compositions based upon Jewish melodic
motifs and traditional chants.

570
BECKER, HEINZ. "Giacomo Meyerbeer: On the Centenary of His
Death." *Leo Baeck Institute Yearbook*, vol.9. (London,Eng.:
East and West Library, 1964), pp.178-201, illus.
Evaluative study of life and works of opera composer
Giacomo Meyerbeer (1791-1864), with reflections on his
Jewish lineage and social circumstances, as well as pro-
fessional activities. Including correspondence between
Meyerbeer and Richard Wagner (1813-1882). Source notes,
facsimiles and photographs.

571
BENARDETE, MAIR JOSE. "A Sheaf of Sephardic Songs." *Le
Judaisme Sephardi*, vol.26. (Paris, Fr.:World Sephardi Org.,
1963), pp.1101-10.
Study of the poetic language and style of performance,
with full texts, of 15 ballads in Ladino (Spaniolic-
Jewish) and with English translations.

572
BINDER, ABRAHAM WOLF. "Isaac Offenbach." *Leo Baeck Institute Yearbook*, vol.14. (London, Eng.:East and West Inst.,
1969), pp.215-23, illus.
    Brief biographical study, with annotated listing of
    manuscripts presently in Klau Library of H.U.C.-J.I.R.
    in New York City from estate of Cantor Isaac Juda Eberst
    von Offenbach (1779-1850). He was notable liturgist of
    his time and father of operetta composer Jacques Offen-
    bach (Jacob Levy Eberst von Offenbach 1819-1880). With
    facsimiles and source notes.
573
BINDER, ABRAHAM WOLF. "New Trends in Synagogue Music." *C.
C.A.R. Journal*,no.8.(New York:C.C.A.R.,1955), pp.12-15.
    Critique by synagogue musician - composer, educator and
    music director - A.W.Binder (1895-1966) of newer ideas
    and developments in composition and musical performance
    in Reform congregational services.
574
BOKSER, BEN ZION. "The Organ and Jewish Worship; A Statement by the Committee on Jewish Law and Standards." *Conservative Judaism*, vol.17, nos.3/4. (New York: J.T.S.A.,
1963), pp.113.
    Follow-up statement in same issue of journal, which
    features discussion regarding role of the organ as
    musical instrument for Conservative worship services.
    (Philip Sigal - "pro;" Samuel Rosenblatt - "anti.")
    Bokser's commentary straddles issue, but tilts toward
    "no organ." Interesting polemic.
575
BROD, MAX. "Modern Music in Israel." *Jewish Quarterly*,
vol.2. (London,Eng.:W.J.C., 1954/1955), pp.35-9.
    Review of composers, organizations and general musical
    life in State of Israel (1948-1954).
576
BROD, MAX. "Some Comments on the Relationship Between
Wagner and Meyerbeer." *Leo Baeck Institute Yearbook*, vol.
9. (London,Eng.:East and West Library, 1964), pp.202-5.
    Brief analytical commentary on the musical and personal
    relationship between Giacomo Meyerbeer (1791-1864) and
    Richard Wagner (1813-1882). Consideration of Meyerbeer's
    influences (direct and indirect) upon Wagner's career
    and musical works, especially early ones.
577
BUSZIN, WALTER E. "Religious Music Among the Jews." *Con-
cordia Theological Monthly*, vol.39, no.7. (St. Louis, Mo.:
Concordia Theol. Sem., 1968), pp.422-31.
    General survey of Jewish hymnology, for information of
    Lutheran denomination readership.
578
CHARLESWORTH, JAMES H. "A Prolegomenon to a New Study of
the Jewish Background of the Hymns and Prayers in the New
Testament." *Journal of Jewish Studies*, vol.33, nos.1/2.
Oxford, Eng.:Centre for Hebrew Studies/W.J.C.,1982)pp.265-86
    Overview of numerous scholarly studies of relationship
    between early Judaic and Christian psalmody and hymn-

ology, in terms of particular texts, styles of chants
and usage in services. Influences of early synagogue
liturgy upon formative Christian liturgy. Comprehensive
roundup of source materials and scholarship on this significant topic. Journal edition was issued in honor of
65th birthday of Israeli scholar Yigal Yadin.

579
COHEN, DALIA and RUTH KATZ. "The Melograph in Ethnomusicological Studies." *Ariel*, vol.21. (Jerusalem, Isr.: Arts
and Letters, 1967/68), pp.60-64, illus.
    Report on accoustical technical research work, in terms
    of folk music collection and analysis, by two members of
    Hebrew University faculty.

580
COHEN, FRANCIS LYON. "Rise and Development of Synagogue
Music." *The Jewish Chronicle*, vol.47. (London, Eng.,1888),
pp.80-135, illus., music.
    Materials prepared by scholar and journalist Francis
    Lyon Cohen (1862-1934) for the Anglo-Jewish Historical
    Exhibition, held in 1887 at the Royal Albert Hall in
    London. Historical survey of Jewish liturgical music
    from biblical times, Temple Era, rise of synagogue music
    traditions and forms - cantillation, chant, hymnology -
    and cantorial office. Music examples and sources.

581
COHEN, FRANCIS LYON. "Some Anglo-Jewish Song Writers: John
Braham and Isaac Nathan - Hebrew Melody in Concert Room."
J.H.S.Journal, vol.2.(London,Eng.:Jewish Historical Society
of England, 1895), pp.7-13, illus.
    Brief biographical study of two interesting figures -
    John Braham (1777-1856) and Isaac Nathan (1791-1864), by
    Anglo-Jewish musician F.L. Cohen (1862-1934).

582
COHEN, IRVING. "Synagogue Music in the Early American Re-
public." *Annual of Jewish Studies*, vol.5. (Phila.: Gratz
College, 1976), pp.17-23, illus.
    For American bicentennial celebration issue, a survey of
    the rise of synagogue music and development of Jewish
    hymnology in 18th and early 19th century American life.

583
COHON, SAMUEL. "Abraham Zebi Idelsohn." *C.C.A.R. Annual*,
vol.49. (En.p.]: C.C.A.R., 1939), pp.287-91.
    Memorial tribute to "father" of modern Jewish musicology
    Abraham Zebi Idelsohn (1882-1938), which is a lovely and
    informative eulogy contributed by one of his colleagues
    at H.U.C., rabbi and educator Samuel Cohon (1888-1959).
    Eulogist notes that Idelsohn demonstrated the existence
    of Jewish music, defined its essential characteristics,
    and presented its historical development. References are
    made to Idelsohn's monumental 10-volume *Thesaurus of
    Hebrew-Oriental Melodies*, and to his two textbooks on
    Jewish music and Jewish liturgy, as well as numerous
    important research articles in leading journals.

584
DALVEN, RACHEL and ISRAEL J. KATZ. "Three Traditional
Judaeo-Greek Hymns and Their Tunes." *The Sephardic Scholar,*

vol.4. (New York:American Society of Sephardic Studies at
Yeshiva Univ., 1982), pp.84-101, music.
 Elements of Jewish Greek musical traditions — Sephardic,
 Romaniote and Italian. Study by two scholars — musicologist Israel J. Katz and ethnologist Rachel Dalven. Based
 upon collected folksong materials. Particular consideration of three hymns: *Purim* song and two hymns for
 celebration of circumcision rite. Melody lines with comparative and analytical musical tables, affording varied
 renditions of same songs. English translations of texts.
 Source notes and references.
 585

DAVIDSON, ISRAEL. "*Kol Nidre.*" *American Jewish Yearbook,*
vol.25. (New York:A.J. Com., 1923), pp.180-94.
 Consideration of various materials related to important
 liturgical hymn which opens service of *Yom Kippur* Eve
 (onset of Day of Atonement) in Jewish observances. The
 generally-known melody is chanted in Ashkenazic traditions, but Sephardic and Oriental Jews intone the prayer
 in simple devotional chant motifs, while Southern French
 and Northern Italian Jews were accustomed to recitation
 of that text silently. Source notes.
 586

EINSTEIN, ALFRED. "Salomone Rossi as Composer of Madri-
gals." *H.U.C. Annual*, vol.23, no.2. (Cincinnati: H.U.C.,
1950/51), pp.383-96, illus., music.
 75th anniversary publication of annual. See Section 7 —
 "Music and Arts" — which includes article by Alfred Einstein (1880-1952), who passed away shortly after writing
 piece and thus did not see it into print. Good introduction to study of music of Salomone Rossi Ebreo de
 Mantua (c.1565-c.1628). Facsimiles and music examples.
 587

FARMER, HENRY GEORGE. "Maimonides on Listening to Music."
Journal of Royal Asiatic Society, vol.45. (London, Eng.:
Royal Asiatic Soc., 1933), pp.867-84.
 Study of tracts by Maimonides (Moses ben Maimon, 1135-
 1204), which state his views on nature and role of music
 in spiritual expression. Henry George Farmer (1882-1965)
 did several studies on musical ideas and perspectives of
 this formative figure in rabbinical history.
 588

FINESINGER, SOL BARUCH. "Musical Instruments in the Old
Testament." *H.U.C. Annual*, vol.3. (Cincinnati: H.U.C.,
1926), pp.21-76, illus., music.
 Solid discussion, which includes valuable treatment of
 the *Shofar*, along with consideration of other biblical
 instruments. Notes; illustrations; roster of references.
 589

FINESINGER, SOL BARUCH. "The *Shofar*." *H.U.C. Annual*,
vols.8/9. (Cincinnati: H.U.C., 1931/32), pp.193-228.
 Excellent resource piece, with ample references, on the
 historically significant ritual instrument of Jewish
 traditions, the *Shofar*.

590
FRANZBLAU, ABRAHAM N. "The Reform Cantor — Educator; Something New Under the Sun." *C.C.A.R. Journal*, no.8. (New York:C.C.A.R., 1955), pp.20-3.
Broadening role of cantor in Reform congregations as music educator for children, choir director for adults, as well as musical leader for liturgical services. Educator and rabbinical scholar Abraham Franzblau (1901-1983) founded a school for training of religious school teachers in 1923 as part of J.I.R. in New York City, and continued as its director after 1947 and the merging of of H.U.C.-J.I.R. He was instrumental in founding and shaping of School for Sacred Music of H.U.C.-J.I.R.

591
FREEDEN, HERBERT. "Jewish Theater Under the Swastika." *Leo Baeck Institute Yearbook*, vol. 1. (London,Eng.:East and West Library, 1956), pp.142-62.
Cultural activities of Jewish *Kulturbund* (Cultural Association) in Berlin and its theatrical and musical programs from 1933 to 1938. Of those involved, some few managed to escape the continent, but most were shipped to Concentration Camps and perished in the Holocaust.

592
GERSON-KIWI, EDITH. "The Legacy of Jewish Music Through the Ages." *In the Dispersion*, vol.3. (Jerusalem, Isr.: W.Z.O., 1963/1964), pp.149-72, music..
Consideration of sweep of Jewish musical developments from Biblical era to 20th century, by Israeli musicologist and educator Edith Gerson-Kiwi. Includes following topics: Biblical music and subsequent influences upon liturgical traditions; song in Asiatic Jewish communities (Yemen, Iraqi, Babylonian and Kurdish Jews; Persian and neighboring countries); music of Spanish-Sephardic Jews (Morocco, Algeria, Tunisia, Egypt, Greece, Cochin); musical expression of special Jewish tribes and sects (Falashas and Karaites); and, music of Ashkenazic Jews (Western and Eastern Europe). With 23 musical examples — melody lines and texts. Hebrew and Yiddish romanized.

593
GIDEON, HENRY. "Music and the Folk." *The Menorah Journal* vol.8,no.6. (New York, 1922), pp.353-62, illus., music.
Study of melody line of Jewish origin used by Modeste Musorgsky (1839-1881) in his biblical cantata "Joshua," and later quoted in part on the composer's tombstone. Author also considers some other folksong melody lines utilized by composers of that era, and notes significant work in Russia of the St. Petersburg Society for Jewish Folk Music, established in 1908. Reference to collection of East European Jewish folksong materials by Yiddishist J.L. Cahan (1881-1937), and then recent (c.1920) uses of Jewish folk motifs by composer Ernest Bloch (1880-1959).

594
GOITEIN, SHELOMO DOV. "Obadyah, a Norman Proselyte." *Journal of Jewish Studies*, vol.4, no.2. (London, Eng.: Inst. of Jewish Studies/W.J.C., 1953), pp.74-84.
Scholarly study in light of then recent discovery of a

new fragment of "Scroll" of Obadyah/Obadiah (c.1070-
c.1141). Examination of two items from Cairo Geniza -
"letters" referring to conquest of Jerusalem by the
Crusaders, with consideration of background of Obadyah
as figure in Jewish cultural history of that era. Author
is historian and faculty member of Hebrew University.
This article further elaborates upon his prior article
for this journal (vol.3,no.4; 1952; pp.162-77) treating
Crusaders and their capture of Jerusalem. Source notes.
595

GOLB, NORMAN. "The Music of Obadiah the Proselyte, and His
Conversion." *Journal of Jewish Studies*, vol.18, nos.1-4.
(London,Eng.:Inst. of Jewish Studies/W.J.C.,1967), 43-63.
    Author examines works of other scholars on this topic -
    Israel Adler, Hanoch Avenary, Alexander Scheiber and
    Eric Werner - regarding nature of music left by Obadyah
    (c.1070-c.1141), early figure in Jewish and general mu-
    sic history. Differing interpretations in study of same
    materials serve to sharpen focus upon this interesting
    topical area. Source notes.
596

GOLB, NORMAN. "Obadiah the Proselyte; Scribe of a Unique
12th Century Hebrew Manuscript Containing Lombardic Neumes."
Journal of Religion, vol.45.(Chicago, 1965), pp.153-6.
    Author takes strong position on the Lombardic musical
    nature of music manuscript of Obadiah (c.1070-c.1141),
    Norman minstrel, who converted to Judaism c.1102.
597

GOLDFADEN, ABRAHAM. "How I Founded the Yiddish Stage."
trans. from Yiddish and ed. by Bernard G. Richards. *Jewish
Heritage*, vol.7,no.1. (Washington,D.C.:B'nai B'rith, 1964),
pp.32-35, illus.
    Reflections by "father" of Yiddish musical theater and
    composer of numerous Yiddish operettas Abraham Goldfaden
    (1840-1908). Prepared for publication by journalist and
    communal leader Bernard G. Richards (1877-1971).
598

GOODING, DAVID. "There is a Time to Sing and a Time to Re-
frain from Singing." *C.C.A.R. Journal*, vol.52. (New York:
C.C.A.R., 1966), pp.41-45.
    Polemical issues of quality and substance for congre-
    gational participation at Reform congregation services.
599

GORALI, MOSHE. "The Bible in Music." *Ariel*, vol.42.
(Jerusalem, Isr.: Arts and Letters, 1976), pp.34-45, illus.
    Information on collection, preparation and presentation
    of a major exhibition of instruments, artifacts, music
    materials and replications, developed and sponsored by
    the Haifa Music Museum and AMLI Library.
600

GORALI, MOSHE. "Musical Instruments in Ancient Times."
Ariel, vol.29. (Jerusalem, Isr.: Arts and Letters, 1971),
pp.68-73, illus.
    Details of collection, preparation and presentation of
    an exhibition by Haifa Music Museum and AMLI Library.

601

GORIN, BERNARD. "The Yiddish Theater in New York." *The Theater*, vol.2,no.2.(New York,1902), pp.16-17, illus.
     Included in this article by journalist and critic of that time are references to "operetta" theatricals by Abraham Goldfaden (1840-1908), and to popular songs performed on Jewish stage at turn of century. Photographs.

602

GOTTLIEB, JACK. "Prayer and Music: A Joyless Noise." *Conservative Judaism*, vol.22, no.2. (New York:J.T.S.A., 1968), pp.55-72, illus., music.
     Presentation illustrating contributions which composers might make on behalf of meaningful prayer music. Author proposes school program of study in liturgical music. Followed in same issue by "response" from Max Wohlberg.

603

GRADENWITZ, PETER. "Gustave Mahler and Arnold Schoenberg." *Leo Baeck Institute Yearbook*, vol.5. (London,Eng.:East and West Library,1960), pp.262-84, illus., music.
     Consideration of Jewish elements in their backgrounds, influences upon musical creativity, and divergent outlooks toward Jewish faith of two pivotal music figures – Gustave Mahler (1860-1911) and Arnold Schoenberg (1874-1951). Analysis of texts written by Schoenberg for his works of Judaic content. "Arnold Schoenberg seems to have found the answer to many a question which Gustave Mahler had asked and was unable to solve."

604

GRADENWITZ, PETER. "Israel's Music: A Colorful Panorama of Trends and Styles." *Ariel*, vol.22. (Jerusalem, Isr.: Arts and Letters, 1968), pp.68-75, illus., music.
     Survey of notable Israeli composers and their more recent works in larger forms.

605

GUTTMACHER, ADOLF. "Reverend (Cantor) Alois Kaiser: In Memoriam." *C.C.A.R. Yearbook*, vol. ([n.p.]: C.C.A.R., 1908/09), pp.175-8.
     Biographical tribute by rabbi and writer Adolf Guttmacher (1861-1915) to Alois Kaiser (1840-1908), the Hungarian-born Baltimore cantor, composer and compiler-arranger of Jewish hymnology. Kaiser, with New York cantor and music director William Sparger (1860-1904), prepared first *Union Hymnal* for Reform congregations in 1897. Alois Kaiser had trained in the boy-choir of the great cantor of Vienna Salomon Sulzer (1804-1890) and instituted celebration in America in 1904 of the 100th anniversary tribute for Sulzer. Kaiser also served as president of the early Society of American Cantors.

606

GUTTMAN, ADOLPH. "The Life of Salomon Sulzer." *C.C.A.R. Yearbook*, vol.14. ([?]: C.C.A.R., 1904), pp.227-36.
     Text of an address delivered at the annual conference of C.C.A.R. by rabbi and scholar Adolph Guttman (1854- ?), as part of special commemorative service held to honor 100th anniversary of Salomon Sulzer (1804-1890), notable cantorial artist who served at largest congregation in

Vienna — Seitenstettengasse Shul — and was significant
liturgical composer, arranger, collector and teacher of
Jewish music for worship.
607
HARRAN, DON. "Musicology in Israel: Its Resources and In-
stitutions." *Ariel*, vol.27. (Jerusalem, Isr.: Arts and
Letters, 1970), pp.59-66, illus.
    Survey of studies done and currently underway in musi-
    cology, and some related research projects, by various
    scholars in Israel.
608
HAYWOOD, CHARLES. "The Gentile Note in Jewish Music."
Chicago Jewish Forum, vol.4,no.3.(Chicago,1946), pp.167-73.
    Discussion of some non-Jewish musicians who have com-
    posed selections for synagogue services, particularly
    Reform congregations, during the 19th century.
609
HERSHBERG, JEHOASH. "Bracha Zefira: Tradition and Change
in Yemenite Music." *Ariel*, vol.49. (Jerusalem, Isr.: Arts
and Letters, 1979), pp.90-114, illus., music.
    Biographical review of folk musician, collector and per-
    former Bracha Zefira. Native born Israeli of Yemenite
    ancestry, she has been strong influence upon shaping of
    modern folk music collection and expression in Israel.
610
HERSHBERG, JEHOASH. "Josef Tal's Musical Hommage to Else
Lasker-Schueler (1869-1945)." *Ariel*, vol.41. (Jerusalem,
Isr.:Arts and Letters, 1976), pp.83-93, illus., music.
    Discussion of a musical work by Israeli composer Josef
    Tal, whose style involves uses of extended tonality and
    the electronic media.
611
HERSHBERG, JEHOASH. "Paul Ben-Haim and Bracha Zefira: The
Early Years in Israel." *Ariel*, vols.45/46. (Jerusalem,
Isr.: Arts and Letters, 1978), pp.5-27, illus., music.
    Information on early years of musical collaboration be-
    tween European born and classically trained composer
    Paul Ben-Haim (Frankenburger) and Yemenite Israeli born
    folk music collector and performer Bracha Zefira. Both
    have substantially influenced shaping of modern Israeli
    musical forms — folk and art.
612
HESCHEL, ABRAHAM JOSHUA. "The Task of *Hazzan* (Cantor)."
Conservative Judaism, vol.12, no.2. (New York: J.T.S.A.,
1958), pp.1-8.
    Sensitive philosophical view by theologian and scholar
    Abraham Joshua Heschel (1907-1972) of role of cantor in
    Conservative traditional worship services, as prayer
    leader and setter of suitable atmosphere for congre-
    gational devotions. Beautiful and inspirational piece of
    writing on this subject. "Song is the most intimate ex-
    pression of man."
613
HESKES, IRENE. "Arnold Schoenberg: A Biographical Study."
Jewish Frontier, vol.27, no.9.(New York, 1960), pp.38-42.
    Consideration of Judaic aspects in life and works of

composer Arnold Schoenberg (1874-1951).
614
HESKES, IRENE. "Imber and *Hatikvah*." ***Congress Weekly***,
vol.23, no.19. (New York: A.J. Cong.,1956), pp.10-11.
    Discussion of life and activities of poet and journalist
    Naphtali Herz Imber (1856-1897) whose poem *Tikvatenu*
    ("Our Hope") forms text of Jewish anthem of nationhood.
615
HESKES, IRENE. "Leonard Bernstein: Musician and Jew." ***The
Reconstructionist***, vol.27. no.14. (New York: Jewish Reconstructionist Found., 1961), pp.26-30.
    Study of Judaic influences upon the creativity of com-
    poser and conductor Leonard Bernstein.
616
HESKES, IRENE. "The Man Who Wrote *Hatikvah*." ***Jewish Affairs***, vol.2, no.8.(Johannesburg, S.Afr., 1956), pp.19-21.
    Study of life and activities of poet and journalist
    Naphtali Herz Imber (1856-1897), whose poem *Tikvatenu*
    ("Our Hope"), first published in 1886 in Jerusalem, was
    set to a traditional Jewish folk melody and became the
    anthem of Zionist movement in 1897 and then nationhood.
617
HESKES, IRENE. "Music Festivities in Israel." ***Congress
Bi-Weekly***, vol.30,no.15.(New York:A.J.Cong.,1963),pp.21-22.
    Survey of musical activities in State of Israel.
618
HESKES, IRENE. "Music of the Holocaust Era." ***U.P.T.A.
Beacon***, vol.2., no.6. (New York:J.E.C./B.J.E., 1963),
pp.3, 7-8.
    Overview of musical legacy of Holocaust Era, in terms of
    folksongs collected from among survivors, and the music
    created subsequently in memorial tribute to martyrs.
619
HESKES, IRENE. "Music of the Holocaust Period." ***Recall***,
vol.3, no.1. (Beverly Hills, Cal.: Jewish Heritage Found.,
1963), pp.34-38.
    Discussion of significance of Jewish musical expression
    during Holocaust Era in the Ghettos and Concentration
    Camps. Overview of some collections of that music as a
    form of living legacy from the martyrs.
620
HESKES, IRENE. "The National Jewish Music Council Cele-
brates its 25th Anniversary." ***J.W.B. Yearbook***, vol.18.
(New York: J.W.B., 1969), pp.40-43.
    Summary of history of Jewish music organization from its
    formation in 1945 to anniversary year of 1969, citing
    contributions made to advancement of the art in America
    by means of program activities, annual music festival
    themes and projects, publications and nation-side com-
    munal cultural services.
621
HESKES, IRENE. "Songs of the Martyrs." ***Jewish Frontier***,
vol.28, no.9. (New York, 1961), pp.45-46.
    Discussion of legacy of song materials from Holocaust.

622
IDELSOHN, ABRAHAM ZEBI. "The Ceremonies of Judaism." *The Jewish Layman*, vol.3,nos.1-9 (Cincinnati:N.F.T.B.,1928/29), pp.i-xxxviii, illus., music.

> Article published in 9 sections, as supplementary pages for each edition of monthly journal of National Federation of Temple Brotherhoods — Reform synagogues organization. Outline of customary liturgical music for all observances of Jewish calendar year, presented by music educator and scholar A.Z. Idelsohn (1882-1938). *High Holy Days, Shofar.* vol.3,no.1 (Sept.1928); pp.i-vi. *Sukkot.* vol.3,no.2 (Oct.1928); pp.vii-x. *Sabbath.* vol.3,no.3 (Nov.1928); pp.xi-xiv. *Hanukkah.* vol.3,no.4 (Dec.1928); pp.xv-xviii. *Daily Ceremonies in Home and Synagogue.* vol.3,no.5 (Jan.1929); pp.xix-xxii. *Ceremonies for Special Occasions in Life of Individual.* vol.3,no.6 (Feb.1929); pp.xxiii-xxvi. *Purim - Feast of Lots.* vol.3,no.7 (Mar.1929); pp.xxvii-xxx. *Pesach - Passover.* vol.3,no.8 (Apr.1929); pp.xxxi-xxxiv. *Feast of Weeks -Shavuot.* vol.3,no.9 (May 1929); pp.xxxv-xxxviii. Photographs, facsimiles and musical examples. Hebrew terms romanized.

623
IDELSOHN, ABRAHAM ZEBI. "Hebrew Music...in the Recital of the Pentateuch (*Torah*)." *Journal of Palestine-Oriental Society*, vol.1. (Jerusalem, Brit. Mandate: Pal.-Oriental Soc., 1921), pp.80-94, illus., music.

> Abraham Zebi Idelsohn (1882-1938) studied, taught music in a children's school and collected Jewish folk and liturgical materials in Jerusalem during the years 1906 to 1922. This article considers the musical intonations in the chanting of the Five Books of Moses (*Torah*), according to various different Judaic traditions. Details for this study based upon Idelsohn's extensive collections and doumentations. Ample music examples.

624
IDELSOHN, ABRAHAM ZEBI. "The *Kol Nidre* Tune." *H.U.C. Annual*, vols.8/9. (Cincinnati: H.U.C., 1931/32), pp. 493-509, illus., music.

> Excellent resource study on this topic, debunking some "myths" concerning origins of *Kol Nidre* hymn, and placing this *Yom Kippur* (Day of Atonement) liturgical prayer text and distinctive melody into an historical perspective as form of old Jewish sacred minnesong from South German area. With thematic music versions and comparative tables.

625
IDELSOHN, ABRAHAM ZEBI. "The *Mogen Ovos* Mode; A Study in Folklore." *H.U.C. Annual*, vol. 14. Cincinnati: H.U.C., 1939), pp.559-74, illus., music.

> Posthumously published study by scholar Abraham Zebi Idelsohn (1882-1938), which traces origins of that mode pattern to 3rd century and ties its special motifs to Jewish hymn melody of *Yigdal*. "The *Mogen Ovos* mode constitutes an important element in Jewish song. It is the deepest expression of the Jewish soul and will live

as long as the Jewish people live." That mode is a form
of the aeolian minor.

626

IDELSOHN, ABRAHAM ZEBI. "Song and Singers of the Synagogue
in the 18th Century (With Special Reference to the Birnbaum
Collection of the H.U.C. Library)." *H.U.C. Annual*, vol.2.
(Cincinnati: H.U.C., 1925), pp. 397-424, illus., music.

> For "Jubilee Issue" of the *H.U.C. Annual*, significant
> contribution by scholar Abraham Zebi Idelsohn (1882-
> 1938), introducing the monumental music collection of
> European cantor and scholar Eduard Birnbaum (1855-1920),
> which was acquired by H.U.C. library in 1923 and then
> installed in its rare book archives in 1924. Idelsohn
> was engaged by H.U.C. in 1925 to teach liturgical music
> and to serve library as special archivist for Birnbaum
> materials. That collection contains many notable and
> rare items from 17th, 18th and 19th century synagogue
> and cantorial literature. Subsequent to his appointment
> at H.U.C., Idelsohn was to base contents of volumes 6,
> 7 and 8 of his 10-volume *Thesaurus of Hebrew-Oriental
> Melodies* upon his studies of the Birnbaum Collection.
> Excellent article. Facsimiles and music examples.

627

IDELSOHN, ABRAHAM ZEBI. "Synagogue Music - Past and Present." *C.C.A.R. Yearbook*, vol.33. ([?]: C.C.A.R., 1923),
pp.344-55, illus., music.

> Text of excellent paper - surveying rise of synagogue
> service officiants, cantillation of Bible, liturgical
> chants, and hymnology - delivered by Abraham Zebi Idel-
> sohn (1882-1938), which made strong impression upon C.C.
> A R. constituency and led to Idelsohn's appointment in
> 1925 to faculty of H.U.C. in Cincinnati. In tracing the
> historical development of synagogue music, Idelsohn
> raises some issues and draws attention to special music
> qualities. "The *Piyyut* and its melody brought a de-
> cided change not only in the characteristics of the syn-
> agogue chant but also in its execution, for the popular
> leader of the prayer, the volunteer precentor, was done
> away with, and in his stead came the permanent and pro-
> fessional precentor who lives by his art. Thus the
> *Piyyut* gave birth to the institution of *Hazzanuth*,
> changing the fundamental meaning of the word *Hazzan* -
> superintendent, officer, beadle - to singer, cantor and
> precentor." Fine musical illustrations.

628

IDELSOHN, ABRAHAM ZEBI. "Traditional Songs of the German
(*Tedesco*) Jews in Italy." *H.U.C. Annual*, vol.11. (Cincinnati: H.U.C., 1936), pp.569-91, illus., music.

> Discussion by scholar Abraham Zebi Idelsohn (1882-1938)
> of some particular liturgical materials, based upon his
> studies of music in collection of Cantor Eduard Birn-
> baum (1855-1920) acquired in 1923 by library of H.U.C.
> Reference notes and excellent music examples.

629

IDELSOHN, ABRAHAM ZEBI. "The Value of Music in the Present
Day Jewish Renascence." *Avukah Annual*, Fifth Anniversary

Edition 1925/3Ø.(New York:Avukah Zionist Fed.,193Ø),pp.79-84
    Advocacy by scholar and educator Abraham Zebi Idelsohn
    (1882-1938) of collection, preservation, performance
    and new creativity in Jewish music on part of rising
    generation of Jewish youth.
    63Ø
KARAS, JOZA. "The Use of Music as a Means of Education in
Terezin." *Shoah*, vol.1, no.2. (New York: Holocaust Studies
Inst./N.J.R.C., 1978), pp.8-9.
    Discussion of music activities - performances and com-
    positions - by prisoners at Terezin (Theresienstadt)
    Concentration Camp during Holocaust Era. Author has col-
    lected music materials salvaged from Terezin, and has
    encouraged publication and performance of these works.
    631
KATZ, ISRAEL J. "Published Sources Containing Melodies of
Judaeo-Spanish Romances Listed in Ramon Menendez Pidal's
Catalogo." *Journal of Sephardic Studies*, vol.1. (New
York: Yeshiva Univ., 1968/69), pp.12-16.
    Annotated roster of Sephardic ballad studies, as brief
    bibliography of Sephardic *romancero*. Compiled in tri-
    bute to scholar Ramon Mendez Pidal (1869-1929) who had
    collected and published Sephardic ballads and thematic
    material early in century and was pioneer in this field.
    632
KATZ, ISRAEL J. "Toward a Musical Study of the Judaeo-
Spanish *Romancero*." *Western Folklore*, vol.21, no.1.
(Berkeley,Cal.:Western Folklore Soc., 1962),pp.83-91, music.
    Study of Sephardic balladry - origins , developments and
    adaptations - over centuries of geographical transpor-
    tation and musical influences.
    633
KEREN, ZVI. "The Influence of the Hebrew Language on Con-
temporary Israeli Art Music." *Bulletin of Studies*, vol.25.
(London, Eng.:School of Oriental and African Studies, 1962),
pp.2Ø9-24, illus.
    Intriguing study of shaping effect of texts upon musical
    works of contemporary Israeli composers.
    634
KIEVAL, HERMAN. "The Curious Case of *Kol Nidre*." *Com-
mentary*, vol.45. (New York: A.J. Com., 1968), pp. 53-58.
    Background study by rabbinical scholar on texts, as well
    as traditional Ashkenazic chant motifs, of this prayer
    which for centuries has opened services of *Yom Kippur*
    Eve (onset of Day of Atonement). Meaning of hymn poem
    placed in context of its particular musical intonation.
    635
KLEIN, JOSEPH. "Congregational Participation in Synagogue
Music."*C.C.A.R. Journal*,no.8. (N.Y.:C.C.A.R.,1955),pp.16-19
    Advocacy of congregational singing in Reform services,
    with recommendations for proper musical participation.
    636
KOHLER, KAUFMANN, ed. "C.C.A.R. Committee on Synagogue
Music: Report on Hymnal Developments." *C.C.A.R. Yearbook*,
vol.3. ([?]: C.C.A.R., 1892/1893), pp.23-3Ø.
    Report on developments leading to preparation and publi-

cation of first *Union Hymnal* in 1897, edited by two
notable figures in synagogue music of that time — Alois
Kaiser (1840-1908) and William Sparger (1860-1904). On-
going progress reports of this committee of C.C.A.R. appear in all issues of *C.C.A.R. Yearbook* as that first
edition was planned and shaped, and then as subsequent
discussion and work was done for a second fully revised
edition of *Union Hymnal* issued in 1914. The Committee
on Synagogue Music functioned in cooperation with the
early Cantors Association of America (predecessor to
current American Conference of Cantors — Reform Judaism)
in terms of matters of cantorial standards and choir
music practices, and liturgical music itself.

637
LANDIS, JOSEPH. "Yiddish Theater: The Troubled Muse."
Jewish Book Annual, vol.34(New York:J.B.C.,1976/77),pp.32-41
Historical overview of Yiddish theater developments from
first formalized presentations in 1876 by Abraham Goldfaden (1840-1908). Tracing of traditional patterns of
Jewish secular and religious cultural expression over
centuries, and influences of 19th century European arts.
Progression of Yiddish dramatic and musical theater in
decades of its growth, flowering and then decline in
more recent years in America. Source notes.

638
LENTSCHNER, SOPHIE. "Field Work in Jewish Music." *The Re-
constructionist*, vol.5. (New York: Jewish Reconstructionist
Found., 1939), pp.10-16.
Overview of field of Jewish music research, examining
reasons for "neglect" of scholarly studies in earlier
periods and new "beginnings" of modern scholarship at
time (1939). Tributes to valuable work by Abraham Zebi
Idelsohn (1882-1938), and Robert Lachmann (1892-1939).
Shortly before his death, Lachmann had established an
institute of Jewish musicology at Hebrew University in
Jerusalem, which was to collect and study music of the
Oriental Jews, and to train musicologists for systematic
research and publication in Jewish music.

639
LEVIN, SAUL. "Traditional Chironomy of the Hebrew Scrip-
tures." *Journal of Biblical Literature*, vol.87. (Phila.:
Soc. of Biblical Literature, 1968), pp.59-70, illus.
Hand and finger motions stylized to signal modulations
of voice in chanting of Judaic Bible Scriptures.
Linkage of these signs to printed tropes, or neumes,
which are interpreted musically by reciter of passages
(*Ba'al Kore*) at traditional Jewish services. Sources.

640
LIST, KURT. "Renaissance of Jewish Music: A Report on Progress." *Commentary*, vol.4. (New York:A.J.Com.,1947)pp.527-34
Survey of developments in Jewish music collection, composition and performance, through World War II.

641
MacCURDY, RAYMOND and DANIEL STANLEY. "Judaeo-Spanish Bal-
lads from Atlanta, Georgia." *Southern Folklore*, vol.15.
(Gainesville, Fla.:Southern Folklore Soc.,1957), pp.221-38.

Group of Sephardic ballad materials collected among Jews
in an American community.

642

MARCUSON, ISAAC, ed. "C.C.A.R. Committee on Synagogue
Music: Report on Hymnal Developments." *C.C.A.R. Yearbook*,
vol.40. ([?]: C.C.A.R., 1930), pp.89-96.
Report includes detailed description of third edition —
completely revised and enlarged — of *Union Hymnal*, as
edited by Abraham Wolf Binder (1895-1966). First edition
had appeared in 1897 and an altered version as second
edition in 1914. This totally new third edition was issued publicly in 1932, though completed at time of this
Committee report, as presented to full convention of
C.C.A.R. in 1930 for its approval. This *Union Hymnal*
contained 266 hymns, including new compositions and arrangements and more traditional chant materials. The
report includes presentation by Binder and commentaries
by notable roster of rabbis. Note: The name of this C.C.
A.R. Committee was changed in 1965/66 to "Committee on
Liturgy and Music," and then in 1976 again changed to
"Committee on Music."

643

MARCUSON, ISAAC, ed. "C.C.A.R. Committee on Synagogue
Music: Report on Liturgical Music Developments." *C.C.A.R.
Yearbook*, vol.38. ([?]):C.C.A.R., 1928), pp.68-71.
From volume 3 of *C.C.A.R. Yearbook* onward, annual reports of Committee on Synagogue Music afford chronology
of various projects and achievements in behalf of Jewish
liturgical music in America. For example, vol.32/33 of
1923/24 notes acquisition of Birnbaum Collection of Jewish liturgical music for holdings of H.U.C. library in
Cincinnati, and subsequent vol.33/34 of 1924/25 details
appointment of Abraham Zebi Idelsohn (1882-1938) to
faculty of H.U.C. and as library curator for Birnbaum
Collection. In vol.38, here cited, plans of Committee
are outlined for preparation of a completely new *Union
Hymnal*, to be edited by Abraham W. Binder (1895-1966).

644

MILLER, EVELYN. "The Learned *Hazzan* of Montreal : Reverend Abraham de Sola (1825-1882)." *The American Sephardi*,
vols.7/8. (New York:Yeshiva Univ., 1975), pp.22-43.
Biographical study of Sephardic cantorial musician of
Spanish-Portuguese Jewish traditions, who settled and
served congregations in Canada in 19th century.

645

MILLER, JOSEPH. "The Religious Functions of the *Shofar*
in Talmudic Times." *Jewish Forum*, vol.12, nos.9-12 and
vol.13, nos.1-8. (New York, 1929/30), pp. as noted below.
Valuable study published in eight parts and presented in
clear informative style. Work available only in these
separate editions of journal: "Religious Functions of
the *Shofar* in Talmudic Times," (vol.12,no.9; 1929, pp.
373-9, 398); "Religious Functions (New Year and Day of
Atonement)," (vol.12,no.10; 1929, pp.449-56); "On the
Eve of Sabbath and Festivals," (vol.12, no.11; 1929, pp.
510-3); "On Fast Days," (vol.12,no.12; 1929, pp.552-4);

"For Repentance of Individuals and Communities," (vol.13
no.1; 1930, pp.28-30); "At Ceremony of Excommunication,"
(vol.13,no.2; 1930, pp.82-5); "At Funerals," (vol.13,
no.5; 1930, pp.208-10); "And Proclamation of Law," (vol.
13, no.8; 1930, pp.308-12). During 500-years formation
of *Talmud*, in Babylonian Era, *Shofar* developed into
unique instrumental expression for religious ceremonials
and functions. It took firm position in minds and hearts
of people for endurance, hope, repentance and Messianic
redemption. Footnotes conclude 8-part article.
646
MISHORI, NATHAN. "Chamber Music at the Tel Aviv Museum."
Ariel,vol.29.(Jerusalem,Isr.:Arts and Letters,1971)pp.35-37
    Background information on concerts at museum 1936-1961.
647
MOSSE, GEORGE. "The Image of the Jew in German (19th Century) Popular Culture." *Leo Baeck Institute Yearbook*, vol.
2. (London,Eng.:East and West Library, 1957), pp.218-27.
    Consideration of 19th century writings reflecting the
    popular image of the Jew in literature, in works of some
    leading literary and cultural figures. Discussion of
    Richard Wagner's tract on "The Jews in Music."
648
NEWLIN, DIKA. "Arnold Schoenberg's Religious Music." *The
Reconstructionist*, vol.19. (New York:Jewish Reconstuction-
ist Found., 1959), pp.16-21.
    General discussion of compositions by Arnold Schoenberg
    (1874-1951), which reflected his Judaic perspectives, as
    to textual materials and manner of musical settings.
649
ORGAD, BEN ZION. "Questions of Art and Faith." *Ariel*,
vol.39.(Jerusalem, Isr.:Arts and Letters, 1975), pp.85-95.
    Reflections on creativity and religious expression by a
    noted Israeli composer.
650
PFEIFFER, AUGUST FRIEDRICH. "On the Music of the Ancient
Hebrew." trans. from Latin and German by G.A. Taylor. *The
Biblical Repository*, vol.6. (Andover, Mass.:Gould and New-
man, 1835), pp.136-72 and pp.357-411, illus., music.
    English translation, in two parts, of "classic treatise"
    by German liturgist August Friedrich Pfeiffer (1640-
    1698). Discussion of Biblical music - text references,
    particular musical instruments, Biblical figures associ-
    ated with music, and musical services of ancient Temple.
    Facsimiles and music examples. Hebrew romanized.
651
POOL, DAVID de SOLA. "Music of the Synagogue." *Menorah
Journal*, vol.3, no.5. (New York, 1917), pp.146-55.
    Sephardic rabbi, communal leader and scholar David de
    Sola Pool (1885-1970) surveys the wide range of Jewish
    liturgical melodies in various traditions, and cites
    some particularly significant hymns of Sephardic as well
    as Ashkenazic rituals. He points up "the haunting beauty
    of the Ashkenazic chant for *Kol Nidre*," and notes that
    such music reflects centuries of Jewish history.

652
REIDER, JOSEPH. "Idelsohn's History and Other Works in
Jewish Music." *Jewish Quarterly Review*, vol.19. (Phila.:
Dropsie College, 1928/29), pp.313-9.
   Discussion of collection work, research studies and
   publications of Abraham Zebi Idelsohn (1882-1938).
653
REIDER, JOSEPH. "Revival of Jewish Music." *Menorah Jour-
nal*, vol.5, nos.6 and 7.(New York,1919),pp.218-25;pp.280-8.
   Issued in two sections, article first concentrates on
   scholarly research work of Abraham Zebi Idelsohn (1882-
   1938) and his collection of Jewish music in Jerusalem.
   Second section discusses some compositions of Judaic inspiration and expression by Ernest Bloch (1880-1959).
654
REVELL, E.J. "Biblical Punctuation and Chant in Second
Temple Period." *Journal for Study of Judaism*, vol.7.
(Leiden, Neth., 1976), pp.181-98, illus.
   Jewish Masoretic punctuation and cantillation signs considered, with references to Samaritan accentuation, in
   search for earliest examples of biblical chant. With
   references and comparative tables.
655
ROSENBLATT, SAMUEL. "The Organ and Jewish Worship; Reply."
Conservative Judaism, vol.17, nos.3/4.(New York: J.T.S.A.,
1963), pp.106-12.
   Statement against playing of organ during Conservative
   traditional worship services, citing sources in rabbini-
   cal writings. Response to proposal in this same issue by
   Philip Sigal for use of organ instrumentation.
656
RUBIN, RUTH. "19th Century History in Yiddish Folksong."
New York Folklore Quarterly, vol.15. (Cooperstown, N.Y.:
Folklore Soc., 1959), pp.220-8.
   Adaptations in Yiddish folksong texts of East European
   Jewish history - political, economic, social, cultural -
   as reflections of struggle for survival. Consideration
   of songs of European migrations and of emigrations to
   America. Fine translations of Yiddish texts, with per-
   ceptive analysis of meanings.
657
RUBIN, RUTH. "19th Century Yiddish Folksongs of Children
in Eastern Europe." *Journal of American Folklore*, vol.65.
(Austin,Tex.:Amer. Folklore Soc., 1952), pp.227-54, music.
   Study of special area of Jewish folksongs - texts and
   melodic styles - with translations of Yiddish lyrics.
   Attention to parallels as well as differences with the
   children's songs of other East European folk groups.
658
RUBIN, RUTH. "Slavic Influence in Yiddish Folksongs."
Folklore and Society, vol.1. (Hatboro, Penn.: Folklore
Assoc., 1966), pp.131-52, music.
   Historical analysis of Slavic melodic influences in
   terms of motifs, modes and scales, as well as particular
   melody patterns. Examples of text and music parallels.
   English translations of texts and source notes.

659
RUBIN, RUTH. "Some Aspects of Comparative Jewish folksong"
New York Folklore Quarterly, vol.12. (Cooperstown, N.Y.:
Folklore Soc., 1956), pp.87-95, music.
    Study of East European folksongs in terms of influences
    of other ethnic groups, and of Jewish history, geography
    and customs, upon shaping of folk texts and melodies.

660
RUBIN, RUTH. "Yiddish Folksongs of Immigration and the
Melting Pot." *New York Folklore Quarterly*, vol.17, no.3.
(Cooperstown, N.Y.:Folklore Soc., 1961), pp.173-82.
    Concentration upon some Yiddish folksongs whose texts
    reflect problems of physical migration, cultural adjust-
    ment, social acculturation and economic survival of East
    European Jews who came here to the "New Golden World."
    "Why did I come to America? What happiness did I find
    here?" Fine sensitive translations of Yiddish texts.

661
RUBIN, RUTH. "Yiddish Folksongs in New York City." *New
York Folklore Quarterly*, vol.2, no.1. (Cooperstown, N.Y.:
Folklore Soc., 1946), pp.15-23.
    Analysis of several Yiddish songs - folk and theatrical
    popular - reflecting life early in this century of tene-
    ment Jewish immigrants on the Lower East Side of New
    York City. Sensitive translations of Yiddish texts.

662
RUBIN, RUTH. "Yiddish Folksongs of World War II." *Jewish
Quarterly*, vol.2,no.2. (London,Eng.:W.J.C.,1963), pp.12-7.
    East European folksong creativity arising out of Holo-
    caust Era and war itself. Yiddish music created and sung
    in Ghettos, Concentration Camps and in Soviet Russia
    territories. Sensitive translations of Yiddish texts.

663
SCHACK, WILLIAM. "Bracha Zefira: Folksinger." *Menorah
Journal*, vol.25. (New York, 1937). pp.111-5, illus.
    Profile of Yemenite Jerusalem-born folksinger and
    folklore collector, Bracha Zefira.

664
SCHEIBER, ALEXANDER. "The Origins of Obadyah, the Norman
Proselyte." *Journal of Jewish Studies*, vol.5, no.1. (Lon-
don, Eng.:Inst. of Jewish Studies/W.J.C., 1954), pp.32-35.
    Consideration by Hungarian scholar Alexander Scheiber of
    newly-discovered item in Kaufmann Geniza Collection,
    with further information on Obadyah/Obadiah (c.1070-
    c.1141) and music notation materials ascribed to him.
    Appended on pp.35-37 is translation of those Geniza
    fragments by J.L.Teichler.

665
SCHINDLER, KURT. "The Russian Jewish Folksong." *Menorah
Journal*, vol.3,no.3.(New York, 1917), pp.146-55, music.
    Informative study by scholar and music conductor Kurt
    Schindler (1882-1935) treating various elements in East
    European Yiddish folk music, citing specific examples.
    Translations of Yiddish texts. Reference notes.

666
SCHIRMANN, JEFIM. "The Function of the Hebrew Poet in Mediaeval Spain." *Jewish Social Studies*, vol.16, no.3. (New
York:Conf. on Jewish Relations, 1954), pp.235-52.
    Study of the poet as creative figure and professional
of that early era in Spain, including role of music in
poetic presentations and formal recitations of poetry --
instrumental accompaniments and singing. Source notes.
667
SCHIRMANN, JOSEPH. "Hebrew Liturgical Poetry and Christian
Hymnology." *Jewish Quarterly Review*, vol.44.(Phila.:Drop-
sie College, 1953), pp.123-61.
    Comparative study of particular prayer texts of Jewish
and Christian hymns -- parallels and influences.
668
SCHWARZSCHILD, STEVEN, "Survey of Current Theological Literature: Theology in Music." *Judaism*, vol.10. (New York:
J.T.S.A./A.J.Cong., 1961), pp.368-73.
    Overview of scholarly studies of hymnology and liturgy.
669
SHILOAH, AMNON. "Musical Traditions: Leaves from the Diary
of a Collector of Folk Music." *Ariel*, vol.31. (Jerusalem,
Isr.:Arts and Letters, 1972), pp.18-29.
    Account of author's personal experiences in his study
and collection of various ethnic musical traditions ingathered to Israel over recent decades.
670
SHILOAH, AMNON. "Status of the Oriental Musical Artist."
Ariel.vol.36.(Jerusalem,Isr.:Arts and Letters,1974)pp.79-83
    Highlighting musical activities of Yemenite and other
Near Eastern style Jewish musicians, in terms of unique
qualities and popularity in Israel.
671
SIGAL, PHILIP. "The Organ and Jewish Worship: A Proposal."
Conservative Judaism, vol.17, nos.3/4. (New York:J.T.S.A.,
1963), pp.93-105.
    Presentation in favor of organ instrumentation at Sab-
bath and holiday Conservative traditional services, with
citation of arguments from biblical, Talmudic and rabbinical sources. Same issue has "reply" against use of
organ by Samuel Rosenblatt, and a statement of the Rabbinical Committee on this matter by Ben Zion Bokser.
672
SINGER, JACOB. "Jewish Music Historically Considered." *C.
C.A.R. Yearbook*, vol.23.([?]:C.C.A.R.,1913/14), pp.232-48.
    Valuable overview for its time by rabbi and educator
Jacob Singer (1883-1964), covering Jewish music from
biblical times, Temple Era and rise of synagogue music --
traditions, forms, hymnology, musicians -- into modern
developments. "Change and modernization must not erase
tradition." References to Salomon Sulzer (1804-1890) and
other leading figures in 19th century Jewish liturgical
music. Author also proposes establishment of formalized
courses of study for training of cantors. "Our rabbinical seminaries would do well to include a study of synagogue music in their curriculum. Such a course might be

pursued with profit in conjunction with the study of our
liturgy...Wherever possible the personnel of the choir
should consist preferably of worshipers."
673
SONNE, ISAIAH and ERIC WERNER. "The Philosophy and Theory
of Music in Judaeo-Arabic Literature." (Presented in Two
Sections) *H.U.C. Annual*, vols. 16 and 17. (Cincinnati: H.
U.C., 1941 and 1942/43), pp.251-319 and pp.511-72.
    Excellent collaborative work. First section outlines
    position of music in Jewish culture of Middle Ages, de-
    fines and classifies that music, describes philosophy of
    music and musical theories of that era. With appended
    materials, including terminology and translation of He-
    brew passages. Second section of study presents, with
    introductory commentary, specific Medieval tracts that
    deal with music by such historic rabbinical figures as
    Maimonides (1135-1204), al-Harizi (d.1250) and Gerson-
    ides (1288-1344). Copious footnotes for each section.
    See other studies of same topical area by such scholars
    Henry George Farmer (1882-1965), Hanoch Avenary and Is-
    rael Adler, as well as the later works of Eric Werner.
674
SPECTOR, JOHANNA. "On Jewish Music." *Conservative Judaism*
vol.21,no.1.(New York:J.T.S.A./R.A.A., 1966), pp.57-72.
    Survey of field of Jewish musicology, noting leading re-
    searchers, types of scholarly studies, methodologies for
    collection, analysis and development of materials. With
    some concluding reflections upon range of topics await-
    ing further investigation.
675
SPECTOR, JOHANNA. "On the Trail of Oriental Jewish Music
Among the Yemenites." (Two-Part Article) *The Reconstructionist*, vol.18, nos.5 and 11. (New York:Jewish Reconstructionist Found., 1952), pp.7-12 and pp.8-14.
    Description of author's field collection activities and
    studies of various types of Yemenite musical materials
    among Jews ingathered to State of Israel. Outline of
    methodology and some thematic analysis. Early work by
    leading scholar of Jewish ethnomusicology.
676
SPECTOR, JOHANNA. "Yemenite Wedding Songs." *The Reconstructionist*, vol.24, no.12. (New York:Jewish Reconstructionist Found., 1958), pp.11-16.
    Introduction to collection and study of Oriental Jewish
    women's folksongs by notable ethnomusicologist. Patterns
    of wedding customs also noted.
677
STEIN, LEON. "The Identity of Jewish Music." *Chicago Jewish Forum*, vol.1, no.3. (Chicago, 1943), pp.12-19.
    Critical overview of qualities attributed to Jewish
    musical expression in creativity and performance.
678
STEIN, LEON. "Three Centuries of Jewish Music in America."
Chicago Jewish Forum,vol.13,no.2.(Chicago,1954),pp.108-13.
    Brief exploration of types of Jewish musical expression
    in America from first arrivals - Sephardic Jews - in

1654 and over centuries since then. Varied styles, traditions of music and changing cultural expressions with
each new group of immigrants to this country.
679
STERN, MALCOLM. "The Function of Music in Our Worship."
C.C.A.R. Journal, no.52. (New York,C.C.A.R.,1966),pp.46-48.
Consideration by rabbi and scholar of role of music in
Jewish ritual devotions.
680
STRAUS, RAPHAEL. "Was Susskint von Trimperg a Jew? An In-
quiry into 13th Century Cultural History." *Jewish Social
Studies*, vol.10, no.1. (New York:Conf. on Jewish Relations,
1948), pp. 19-30.
Examination of background of the minnesinger (fl. 13th
cent.) who has been noted in music history and often
cited as of Jewish lineage. Author outlines various
sources for differences of opinion on the issue of his
ancestry, and tilts toward negative viewpoint. Refer to
other studies on Suesskind von Trimberg for perspective.
681
SWARD, KEITH. "Jewish Musicality in America." *Journal of
Applied Psychology*, vol.17, no.6. (Worcester, Mass., 1933),
pp.675-712.
Study of Jewish musical creativity and performance as
particular form of expression of American acculturation.
682
TOEPLITZ, URI. "Thirty Years of Music." *Ariel*, vol 14.
(Jerusalem, Isr.: Arts and Letters, 1966), pp.5-14, illus.
Overview of musical developments -- composers, performers
and educational as well as professional institutions --
which have developed in land of Israel. Particular interest in leading musicians and evolving musical styles.
683
TUCKMAN, WILLIAM. "Civil War Composers and Musicians."
Journal of American Jewish Historical Society, vol. 53.
(Waltham, Mass.: A.J.H.S., 1963), pp.70-5.
Introduction to topic of American Jewish hymnodists of
mid-19th century, with some special attention to life
and work of Sigmund Schlesinger (1835-1906).
684
WEISGALL, HUGO. "The Case for Modern Jewish Music." *Recall*, vol.2, no.2. (Beverly Hills, Cal.:Jewish Heritage
Found., 1959), pp.39-44.
Statement of position on Jewish musical creativity in
America by noted composer and educator. Specific recom-
mendations made for future activities.
685
WEISGALL, HUGO. "Jewish Music in America." *Judaism*,
vol.3.(New York: J.T.S.A./A.J. Cong., 1954), pp.427-36.
Evaluative survey of field and strong presentation of
recommendations for future creative endeavors.
686
WERNER, ERIC. "Abraham Zebi Idelsohn: In Memoriam." *The
Reconstructionist*, vol.29, no.3. (New York: Jewish Recon-
structionist Found., 1963), pp.14-18.
Respectful evaluation of scholarly work of Abraham Zebi

Idelsohn (1882-1938) upon occasion of 25th anniversay of
his passing. Particular attention given to Idelsohn's
10-volume *Thesaurus of Hebrew-Oriental Melodies*, as
monumental achievement in field of Jewish musicology.
687
WERNER, ERIC. "The Cantillation of the Bible." *Jewish
Quarterly Review*, vol.49.(New York, 1959), pp.287-92.
Critical analysis of research work on this subject -
notably East European Ashkenazic cantillation melodic
and motival patterns - in terms of studies and publication by Jewish musicologist, liturgist and educator
Solomon Rosowsky (1878-1962).
688
WERNER, ERIC. "The Conflict Between Hellenism and Judaism
in the Music of the Early Christian Church." *H.U.C. Annual*
vol.20.(Cincinnati:H.U.C., 1947), pp.407-70, illus., music.
Extensive article outlining author's studies in comparative liturgy, with introductory background to subject,
as well as discussion of Hellenistic Jewish, Christian
and musical sources. Werner presents musical details of
notation, structure, form and melos in early synagogue
and church liturgy, and notes influences of ethnic and
local traditions together with gradual expansion of Hel-
lenized Christianity. Musical examples and reference
notes. Materials were expanded by author for his major
work *The Sacred Bridge* (New York, 1959).
689
WERNER, ERIC. "The Current Trend in Jewish Liturgical Music." *Contemporary Jewish Record*, vol.6, no.6. (New York:
A.J. Com., 1943), pp.607-15.
Overview of newer developments in American Jewish liturgical music, particularly at Reform congregations.
690
WERNER, ERIC. "The Doxology in Synagogue and Church: A
Liturgico-Musical Study." *H.U.C. Annual*, vol.19. (Cincinnati: H.U.C., 1945/46), pp.275-351, illus., music.
Significant study by scholar and educator Eric Werner,
presented in two parts: liturgical (pp.175-328) and musical (pp.329-51). Liturgical section outlines ideas of
doxology (hymns in praise of God), notes outstanding
doxologies of early synagogue and church services, and
considers the *Hallelujah* in the doxology. Musical section offers Masoretic evidence of responsorial renditions, psalmodic forms in Jewish and Christian liturgy,
melismas and ornamentations in varied forms, musical
traditions and parallels in the doxologies. Music examples, glossary of terms and source notes. Material expanded in Werner's subsequent book *The Sacred Bridge*
(New York, 1959).
691
WERNER, ERIC. "The Family Letters of Felix Mendelssohn -
Bartholdy." *Bulletin of N.Y.P.L.*, vol.65, no.1. (New York:
N.Y.P.L., 1961), pp.5-20.
Preliminary study by Werner, in preparation for his subsequent book: *Mendelssohn: A New Image of the Composer
and His Age* (New York, 1963).

692
WERNER, ERIC. "The Hebrew Elements of the *Te Deum.*"*Israel Studies Annual*, vol.16 - Orlinsky Edition. (Jerusalem, Isr.:Isr. Exploration Soc.,1982), pp.227-34, illus., music.
> Comparative study in early synagogue and church elements of liturgy and hymnody, with consideration of origins, similarities and developmental differences for a particular prayer. Examination of "Hebraicisms" in Church thanksgiving hymn *Te Deum*, linking with text matter of *Kedusha* section of Jewish services, with styles of Hebrew poetry and post-biblical prayers, and musically to ancient Judaic melismatic and motival patterns. Comparative texts, music illustrations and source notes.

693
WERNER, ERIC. "Hebrew and Oriental Christian Metrical Hymns; A Comparison." **H.U.C. Annual**, vol.23, no.2 - 75th Anniversary Celebration Issue.(Cincinnati:H.U.C., 1950/51), pp.397-432, illus., music.
> Study of parallels in Judaic and Byzantine Christian liturgical music - prayer texts and hymnody - c.11th century. Consideration of interrelationships of various Near Eastern liturgies during Middle Ages. Descriptions, comparisons and parallelisms for such hymns as *Romanos, Dies Irae* and *Unesane Tokef*. Music examples, comparative tables and source notes. Materials subsequently developed for book *The Sacred Bridge* (New York, 1959).

694
WERNER, ERIC. "*Hosanna* in the Gospels." **Journal of Biblical Literature**, vol.65. (Phila.: Soc. of Biblical Literature, 1946), pp.97-122, illus., music.
> Adaptation and liturgical use of *Hoshana* (*Hosanna*) Judaic psalmody and hymn refrain, whose origins date from pre-Temple era religious rituals. A study in comparative liturgical elements. Tables and source notes.

695
WERNER, ERIC. "Liberalism and Traditionalism in Synagogue Music."**C.C.A.R.Journal**,no.8(New York:C.C.A.R.,1955)pp.9-11
> Observations by scholar and educator Eric Werner concerning various traditional music practices which either were retained or have now been returned to services of Reform congregations, blending with newer music styles.

696
WERNER, ERIC. "Manuscripts of Jewish Music in the Eduard Birnbaum Collection of Hebrew Union College Library." **H.U.C. Annual**, vol.18. (Cininnati: H.U.C., 1943/44), pp. 397-428, illus., music.
> Scholar Eric Werner first joined H.U.C. faculty at its campus in Cincinnati, and soon began to devote much attention to an extensive valuable collection of Jewish liturgical music acquired in purchase (1923/24) by H.U.C. Library from heirs in Germany of cantor, scholar and collector Eduard Birnbaum (1855-1920). This article expands upon an earlier article by Abraham Zebi Idelsohn (1882-1938) which describes contents of Birnbaum Collection (*H.U.C. Annual*, vol.2, 1925). Werner here provides overview of scope and significance of this col-

lection, considers some of its rare manuscripts, and
presents information on Birnbaum's writings on Jewish
music. Facsimiles, music illustrations and source notes.
697

WERNER, ERIC "Melito of Sardis; First Poet of Deicide."
H.U.C. Annual, vol.37.(Cincinnati:H.U.C., 1966), pp.191-210
    Study of an early Christian hymn and hymnodist (fl. mid
    2nd cent.), with relationship to hymnology of early syn-
    agogue - texts, forms and music patterns. Source notes.
698

WERNER, ERIC. "New Light on the Family of Felix Mendelssohn." *H.U.C. Annual*, vol.26. (Cincinnati: H.U.C., 1955),
pp.543-65, illus.
    Study of Mendelssohn family papers which had been made
    available to author for preparation of an extended bio-
    graphical work on Felix Mendelssohn (1809-1847). Letters
    and documents disclose conflicting sentiments among the
    family members relating to conversion to Christianity
    and sustained connection to Judaism with recognition of
    Jewish ancestry. Werner reflects upon nature of composer
    and his particular feelings about his Jewish lineage and
    background, with possible effects upon his musical ideas
    and creativity. Facsimiles and source notes.
699

WERNER, ERIC. "Notes on the Attitude of the Early Church
Fathers Towards Hebrew Psalmody." *Review of Religion*, vol.
7. (New York, 1942/43), pp.339-52, music.
    Early studies by scholar and educator Eric Werner in de-
    velopment of his concepts of comparative Christian and
    Judaic liturgical music, and common roots of Church and
    synagogue psalmody and hymnody. Music examples. Notes.
700

WERNER, ERIC. "The Oldest Sources of Synagogue Chant."
Proceedings Annual, vol.16. (New York: Amer. Acad. for Jewish Research, 1946/47), pp.225-31, illus., music.
    Author seeks to identify a fragment of music manuscript
    as piece of liturgical music chanted by Marranos, or
    Crypto-Jews, in their secret devotions. He supplies fac-
    simile illustrations and musical transcriptions. Note: A
    brief response here (pp.231-2) by Sephardic rabbi and
    communal leader D.A. Jessurun Cardozo (1895-1972) seeks
    to modify Werner's conclusions by stating that this mu-
    sic was likely written down in Northern Italy, rather
    than in Northern Spain as Werner contends. Fascinating.
701

WERNER, ERIC. "The Origin of the Eight Modes of Music; A
Study in Musical Symbolism." *H.U.C. Annual*, vol.21. (Cin-
cinnati:H.U.C., 1948), pp.211-55, illus., music.
    Article dedicated by Eric Werner to his "friend and
    teacher" Curt Sachs (1881-1959). Comparison of Syrian,
    Byzantine, Roman and Judaic modes - origins, shapes, and
    varied usages. Principle of *Octoechos* explored. Music
    examples, comparative tables and source notes.
702

WERNER, ERIC. "The Origin of Psalmody." *H.U.C.Annual*,
vol.25.(Cincinnati:H.U.C.,1954), pp.327-45, illus., music.

Comparative study of psalmody — origin, development and usage — in three monotheistic religions of Judaism, Islam and Catholic "Gregorian" Christianity. Consideration of literary parallelisms and influences upon music of psalmody in solo and choral expression. Music examples, comparative tables and source notes. Among research materials gathered by scholar Eric Werner for his subsequent publication *The Sacred Bridge* (New York, 1959).

703

WERNER, ERIC. "Preliminary Notes for a Comparative Study of Catholic and Jewish Musical Punctuation." *H.U.C. Annual* vol.15.(Cincinnati:H.U.C., 1940), pp.335-66, illus., music.
Article dedicated to memory of Abraham Zebi Idelsohn (1882-1938), whom Eric Werner succeeded on faculty for Jewish liturgical music at H.U.C. in Cincinnati. One of earliest of Werner's studies in comparative liturgical music. Consideration of cantillation and chant signs, and their musical interpretations in recitation of the Scriptures at Catholic and Jewish services. Comparative tables, musical illustrations and source notes.

704

WERNER, ERIC. "The Role of Tradition in the Music of the Synagogue." *Judaism*, vol.13. (New York:J.T.S.A./A.J. Cong. 1964), pp.156-63.
Consideration of tradition as formative, and often restrictive, influence upon historical developments in Jewish liturgical music. Evaluative reflections upon various research studies in this field.

705

WERNER, ERIC. "Traces of Jewish Hagiolatry." *H.U.C. Annual*, vol.51.(Cincinnati:H.U.C.,1981),pp.39-60,illus.,music
Comparative examination of ancient traditions of martyrology — ritual veneration of martyrs in early Christian liturgies and parallels with early Judaic observances. Over centuries, some Jewish martyrology has continued: *Megillat Ta'anit* (Scroll of Fasting) memorializing tragic events in history; festive *Lag B'omer* (between Passover and Pentecost) honoring martyr Rabbi Simeon Bar Yohai; recitation of *Kinot* (dirge-hymns) for martyrs; tributes to heroic Maccabean martyrs at *Hanukkah*; pilgrimages to tomb of biblical Patriarchs at Hebron and to graves of notable rabbinical scholars; mourning period during Jewish month of *Ab* for destruction of Temple and Dispersion; recitations from Crusades time of local books of European community martyrs; special prayers for dead during Jewish religious calendar year; most recent *Yom Hashoa* commemoration of victims of Holocaust Era. Music examples and source notes.

706

WERNER, ERIC. "*Tribus Agathas* (The Good Way)." *Journal of Ecumenical Studies*, vol. 13. (Phila.: Temple Univ., 1976), pp.143-54.
Comparative view of hymnological continuity in Judaism and Orthodox Church. Some similarities in developments. Examples cited and source notes.

707
WERNER, ERIC "*Trop* and *Tropus*: Etymology and History.
H.U.C. Annual, vol.46. (Cincinnati: H.U.C., 1975), pp.289-
96, illus., music.
>   Aspects of Ashkenazic chant of Scriptures – cantillation
>   of biblical texts. Historical investigation of rise of
>   traditions, especially in terms of writings of such a
>   notable rabbinical leader and shaper of Jewish religious
>   customs as Rashi (Rav Solomon ben Isaac, 1040-1105).
>   Some comparisons of Judaic chant with other forms of re-
>   ligious biblical chant. Music examples and source notes.

708
WERNER, ERIC. "The True Source of Jewish Music." *Commentary*, vol.7, no.4.(New York:A.J.Com.,1949), pp.382-7.
>   Viewpoint expressed concerning Jewish music – nature and
>   origins – wwith respect to liturgical expression. Eric
>   Werner had transferred from H.U.C. in Cincinnati to the
>   faculty of newly-formed (1948) School of Sacred Music of
>   H.U.C.-J.I.R. in New York City.

709
WERNER, ERIC. "Two Obscure Sources of Reuchlin's *De Ac-
centibus Linguae Hebraicae.*" *Historica Judaica*, vol.16,
no.1. (New York, 1954), pp.39-54.
>   Study of materials by Johann Reuchlin (1455-1522), the
>   Christian humanist, grammarian and Hebraist, who en-
>   deavored to notate musically the Jewish tropal signs for
>   traditional cantillation of the Bible. References and
>   source notes.

710
WERNER, ERIC. "What Function Has Synagogue Music Today."
C.C.A.R. Journal,vol.8,no.4.(New York:C.C.A.R.,1966)pp35-40
>   Strong statement advocating high musical standards for
>   proper continuity, sensitive creativity and artistic
>   performance of liturgical music in America.

711
WOHLBERG, MAX. *"Beiti-Beit T'fillah."* *Conservative Judaism*, vol.13, no.3. (New York: J.T.S.A., 1959), pp.27-36.
>   Reflections by cantor and music educator on role of the
>   *Hazzan* (cantor) in Conservative traditions of worship,
>   and nature of liturgical music in behalf of prayer.

712
WOHLBERG, MAX. "Prayer and Music: A Rejoinder." *Conservative Judaism*, vol.22,no.2.(New York:J.T.S.A.,1968),pp.73-6.
>   Cantor and educator Max Wohlberg responds to an article
>   in same issue written by Jack Gottlieb, regarding study
>   and practice of Jewish liturgical music for traditional
>   Conservative synagogue services.

713
WOHLBERG, MAX. *"Shiru Lo*: Aspects of Congregational
Song." *Conservative Judaism*, vol.23, no.1. (New York:
J.T.S.A., 1968), pp.58-66, music.
>   Melodies of congregational responses in prayers – past
>   and present – considered as to their melodic sources,
>   qualities of tune elements and liturgical texts.

714
WULSTAN, DAVID. "Sounding of the *Shofar.*" *Galpin Society Journal*, vol.26. (London, Eng.: Galpin Soc., 1973), pp.29-46, illus., music.
>   Sounds and ritual musical roles of *Shofar* and trumpet
>   in biblical antiquity. Various theories of music intona-
>   tion and performance. Glossary of music instruments in
>   Bible. Facsimiles, music illustrations and source notes.

715
YASSER, JOSEPH. "Musical Heritage of the Bible; A Critical Appraisal of Solomon Rosowsky's Research in Cantillation." *Annual of Jewish Social Sciences*, vol.12. (New York: YIVO, 1958/59), pp.157-75, illus., music.
>   Extended analysis by musicologist Joseph Yasser (1893-
>   1981) of studies by liturgist Solomon Rosowsky (1878-
>   1962) in biblical cantillation for the *Torah* (Five
>   Books of Moses), according to Jewish musical chant tra-
>   ditions of East European Ashkenazic groups. References
>   to research of other scholars. Music examples and notes.

716
YASSER, JOSEPH. "New Guide-Posts for Jewish Music." *The Academy Bulletin*, vol.3. (New York: Jewish Acad. of Arts and Sciences, 1937), pp.3-10.
>   Recommendations by musician, scholar and educator Joseph
>   Yasser (1893-1981) for developments in American Jewish
>   music - liturgical, folk and art - especially in terms
>   of encouragement and training of young musicians as com-
>   posers, performers and scholars.

717
YASSER, JOSEPH. "References to Hebrew Music in Russian Mediaeval Ballads." *Jewish Social Studies*, vol.11, no.1. (New York: Conf. on Jewish Relations, 1949), pp.21-48, music.
>   Study which opens up field of inquiry regarding signifi-
>   cant interrelationship of Jewish music and Russian folk-
>   song - melodically, topically and even in terms of some
>   specific Hebraicisms and Slavic qualities. Musician, ed-
>   cator and scholar Joseph Yasser (1893-1981) compares de-
>   tails of *Hazzanuth* (cantorial art) with Russian art of
>   *Demestvo* (Slavic folk epic balladry) in varied forms
>   since Middle Ages. Source notes.

718
YOFFIE, L.R.C. "Songs of the Twelve Numbers and the Hebrew Chant of *Echod Mi Yodea.*" *Journal of American Folklore*, vol.62. (Austin, Tex.: Amer. Folklore Soc., 1949), pp.382-411, illus., music.
>   Analytical study of patterns of songs with verses based
>   upon number sequences, here from one to twelve. Textual
>   "pyramiding," styles of musical settings and customs of
>   folk performances. Focus on special folksong hymn of the
>   numbers - *Echod Mi Yodea* ("One, Who Knows One?") - as
>   sung by groups of celebrants concluding Passover *Seder*
>   (holiday ritual feast) for Jewish traditions. Musical
>   illustrations and source notes.

5.
Jewish Music Periodicals:
Issues and Contents

719
A.C.C. Reports and Newsletter. American Conference of Cantors — Reform Judaism. New York: A.C.C./H.U.C.-J.I.R.; from 1960 —; RAYMOND SMOLOVER, ed.

Informal newletter issued at least twice each year. Organization established as presently structured in 1955. Contents: announcements and brief reports, with details of annual convention meeting. Copies may be examined at A.C.C. office in New York City.

720
AMLI Studies in Musical Bibliographies Series. Haifa Music and Ethnology Museum and AMLI Library. Haifa, Isr.: AMLI Press; from 1970 —; MOSHE GORALI, series ed.

No.1 (1970) — *The Bible in English Music: William Byrd (1543-1623) and Henry Purcell (1659-1695).* CLAUDE ABRAVANEL and BETTY HIRSHOWITZ, comps.; 32pp.,illus., music; English and Hebrew texts.

No.2 (1970) — *Bibliography of Jewish Music Periodicals in Hebrew, Yiddish and Other Languages.* NINA BENZOOR, comp.; 36pp., illus.; English and Hebrew texts.

No.3 (1970) — *Bibliography of Jewish Music Bibliographies.* MARCELLA SEGRE, comp.; 32pp.; English and Hebrew texts.

No.4 (1975) — *Yiddish Folk Plays: Abraham Goldfaden's Work.* EZRA LAHAD, comp.; 34pp.; Yiddish text only.

No.5 (1979) — *The Old Testament in the Works of Johann Sebastian Bach (1685-1758).* MOSHE GORALI, BETTY HIRSHOWITZ and TALI TUREL, comps.; 48pp, illus., music; Hebrew, English and German texts.

No.6 (1982) — *The Old Testament in the Works of George*

Frideric Handel (1685-1759). MOSHE GORALI and RIVKA
WATSON, comps.; 44pp., illus., music; English and He-
brew texts.
        721
Bat Kol ("Echo"). Israel Composers' League. Tel Aviv:Isr.:
I.C.L./I.M.I.; 1955-1965; various editors.
        Hebrew text only. Irregularly issued resume of meetings
        and other activities of members of League.
        722
C.A.A. Annual Conference Report. Cantors Assembly of Amer-
ica - Conservative Judaism. New York: C.A.A./J.T.S.A.; from
1947 --; SAMUEL ROSENBAUM, ed.
        Report of organization activities and proceedings of an-
        nual conference of C.A.A., with summaries of meetings,
        abstracts of speeches and list of concerts as presented.
        C.A.A. was established in 1947. Proceedings of first
        conference that year dealt with "Jewish Music in the
        Synagogue," and was held at J.T.S.A., under auspices of
        then department of music of United Synagogue of America.
        Subsequently, C.A.A. was formalized and motion was made
        to establish a cantorial seminary at J.T.S.A. Copies of
        C.A.A. Annual Report may be examined at office in New
        York City.
        723
Cantor's Voice: C.A.A. Newsletter. Cantors Assembly of A-
merica - Conservative Judaism. New York: C.A.A./J.T.S.A.;
1951-1966; SAMUEL ROSENBAUM and CHARLES DAVIDSON, eds.
        Brief articles, short reviews of new publications - in
        literature, scores and recordings, and information on
        organization and membership activities. Some issues with
        music or facsimile illustrations. Irregularly published,
        but at least twice each year. Reflected outlook and work
        of C.A.A., established in 1947. Contributors among noted
        cantors and Jewish musicians of time. Copies may be ex-
        amined at office in New York City.
        724
C.C.A. Annual Report. Cantorial Council of America - Or-
thodox Judaism. New York:C.C.A./Yeshiva Univ.; 1962-1973;
MACY NULMAN, ed.
        Proceedings report, irregularly issued over 11 years.
        Included organizational and membership activities. Those
        materials now included in *Journal of Jewish Music and
        Liturgy.* C.C.A. was established in 1960 by music de-
        department - cantorial studies at Yeshiva Univ. Copies
        of proceedings available at office in New York City.
        725
Documentation and Studies Series. Department of Musicolo-
gy and School of Jewish Studies at T.A.U. Ramat Aviv, Isr.:
Tel Aviv Univ. Press; 1975 --; HANOCH AVENARY, series ed.
        Vol.1 (1975/78) *Eduard Birnbaum: Jewish Musicians at
        the Court of the Dukes of Mantua (1542-1628).* Original
        text in German; Hebrew edition (1975); English edition
        (somewhat revised and augmented - 1978). JUDITH COHEN,
        ed.; 52pp., illus., music.

        Vol.2 (1976/78) *The Ashkenazic Tradition of Biblical*

*Chant Between 1500 and 1900: Documentation and Musical
Analysis.* Hebrew edition (1976); English edition
(1978). HANOCH AVENARY; 87pp., illus., music.

Vol.3 (1976/78) *The Epistle on the Music of the Ikhwan
Al-Safa (Bagdad 10th Century).* Hebrew edition (1976);
English edition (1978). AMNON SHILOAH; 73pp., illus.
726
G.T.M. Newsletter. Guild of Temple Musicians. Chicago,
Ill.: G.T.M.; from 1977 --; JUDITH KARZEN, ed.
   Irregularly issued, but at least once a year. Informa-
   tion about organization, membership, details of annual
   conference meeting (held in association with A.C.C. -
   Reform Judaism), and brief pieces on aspects of Temple
   music - publications and studies. Copies may be secured
   from office in Chicago.
727
Inventory of Jewish Musical Sources: Series A. (RISM -IAML
/UNESCO; Munich, W.Ger.:Henle) Jewish National and University Library. Jerusalem, Isr.: Hebrew Univ./Magnes Press;
1975 --; ISRAEL ADLER, series ed.
   Vol.1 (1975) *Hebrew Writings Concerning Music in Manuscripts and Printed Books from Geonic Times up to 1800
   (RISM, B, ix2).* ISRAEL ADLER, comp.; lviii, 390pp.

   Vol.2 (in preparation) *Hebrew Notated Sources in Manuscripts and Printed Books up to 1800 (RISM, B, ix4).*
   ISRAEL ADLER, comp.
728
I.S.M. Dukhan (Cantorial Pulpit). Israel Institute for
Sacred Music. Jerusalem, Isr.: I.S.M./Hekhal Shlomo; from
1959 --; YUVAL NE'EMAN, ed.
   Hebrew text only. Articles and reports on cantorial
   music and musicians in Israel. Copies available from
   office in Jerusalem.
729
I.S.M. Renatyah (Musical Soundings). Israel Institute for
Sacred Music. Jerusalem, Isr.: I.S.M./Hekhal Shlomo; from
1968 --; AVIGDOR HERZOG and URI SHARVIT, eds.
   Hebrew text only. Issued at irregular intervals. Pedagogical guides and materials for traditional liturgical
   music education of school children and cantorial students. Copies may be secured from office in Jerusalem.
730
I.S.M. Yedioth (Newsletter). Israel Institute for Sacred
Music. Jerusalem, Isr.:I.S.M./Hekhal Shlomo; 1970-1978;
M.S. GESHURI, ed.
   Hebrew text only. Issued annually for 8 years. News-
   letter presenting information on activities, issues and
   publications related to liturgical music in Israel.
   Copies may be examined at office in Jerusalem.
731
Israel Studies in Musicology. Israel Musicological Society
Jerusalem, Tel Aviv and Ramat Aviv: Isr. Music Depts. of -
Hebrew Univ., Bar Ilan Univ., and Tel Aviv Univ.; 1978 --;
LEA SHALEM, series ed.

Vol.1 (1978) *Israel Studies in Musicology - A Birthday
Offering to Edith Gerson-Kiwi and Hanoch Avenary.*
ELIHU SCHLEIFER and LEA SHALEM, eds.; 193pp., illus.,
music. Contents - ISRAEL ADLER: :Foreword: Two Nestors
of Israeli Musicology." BATHIA CHURGIN: "A New Edition
of Beethoven's Fourth Symphony: Editorial Report." JO-
ACHIM BRAUN: "Beethoven's Fourth Symphony: Comparative
Analysis of Recorded Performances." MEIR WIESEL: "The
Presence and Evaluation of Thematic Relationships and
Thematic Unity." DON HARRAN: "On the Question of Manner-
ism in Early Music." DALIA COHEN: "Meter and Rhythm in
Music and Poetry." BRUNO NETTL and AMNON SHILOAH: "Per-
sian Classical Music in Israel: A Preliminary Report."
JEHOASH HIRSHBERG and DAVID SAGIV: "The 'Israeli' in
Israeli Music: The Audience Responds." JOSEPH TAL: "In
Memoriam: Oedoen Partos." AVNER BAHAT: "Traditional Ele-
ments and Dodecaphonic Technique in the Music of Oedoen
Partos (1907-1977)."

Vol.2 (1980) *Israel Studies in Musicology - Dedicated
to Joseph Tal.* BATHIA CHURGIN and LEA SHALEM, eds.;
210 pp., illus., music. Contents - ISRAEL ADLER: "The
Schoenbergiana at the Jewish National and University Li-
brary." EDITH GERSON-KIWI: "Melodic Patterns in Asiatic
Rituals: The Quest for Sound Alienation." URI SHARVIT:
"The Role of Music in the Yemenite *Heder.*" LEONARD
RATNER: "Texture and Rhetorical Elements in Beethoven's
Quartets." BETH SHAMGAR: "Dramatic Devices in the Re-
transitions of Beethoven's Piano Sonatas." EVA BADURA-
SKODA: "Prolegomena to a History of the Viennese Forte-
piano." ELLEN ROSAND: "*L'Orfeo*: The Metamorphosis of a
Musical Myth." ELIHU SCHLEIFER: "Lamentations and Lamen-
tation Tones in the Mexican Choirbooks at the Newberry
Library, Chicago." JOSEPH DORFMAN: "Tonal Concepts in
the Instrumental Chamber Works of Paul Hindemith." ZVI
KEREN: "Variants of the Blues Progression."

Vol.3 (in preparation) SHAI BURSTYN and LEA SHALEM, eds.
732
J.L.M.S.A. Bulletin. Jewish Liturgical Music Society of
America. New York:J.L.M.S.A.; 1963-1973; PAUL KAVON, ed.
     Issued at least once each year as newsletter of this
     organization. Included brief essays, reviews of scores
     and recordings, reports of meetings - lectures and con-
     certs - held during year. Some issues with music. J.L.M.
     S.A. was founded in 1963 by A.W. Binder (1895-1966) and
     continued to function until superceded by formation of
     American Society for Jewish Music in 1973. Copies may be
     examined at A.S.J.M. office in New York City.
733
J.M.C.A.A. Journal. Jewish Ministers Cantors Association
of America. New York: J.M.C.A.A.; 1904 --; ed. committees.
     Irregularly issued as "souvenir album" for special oc-
     casions. In 1897, organization appears to have assumed
     designated name. Earlier group has been known as the
     "Society of American Cantors." Copies of albums may be

examined at office in New York City.
No.1. (1904) *Celebration of 100th Anniversary of Salomon Sulzer:Album*. Gala program details (March 22, 1904, New York City), with summaries of addresses, messages of greetings from members, photographs of cantors, and some music. Yiddish, Hebrew and English texts.

No.2 (1924) *Celebration of 30th Anniversary of J.M.C.A.A.: Album*. Gala program details (February 3, 1924, New York City), with summaries of addresses, messages of greetings from members, photographs of cantors, and some music. Yiddish, Hebrew and English texts.

No.3 (1937) *Fortieth Anniversary Album*. Details for several program events, summaries of addresses, messages of greeting from members, photographs and biographical sketches of cantors. Yiddish, Hebrew and English texts.

No.4 (1947/48) *Fiftieth Anniversary Album*. Details for several gala events, including cantorial concert held at Old Metropolitan Opera House in New York City, December 9, 1947, as well as greetings from members, photographs and "ads". Yiddish, Hebrew and English texts.

Note: Over subsequent years, J.M.C.A.A. has circulated, at irregular intervals, newsletters to its memberships, and continues to prepare glossy programs for distribution at its gala events. However, "souvenir albums" as above — extensive in length (250-350 pages), with many photographs, greetings from colleagues and biographical sketches of cantors — are no longer published.

734
Jewish Music Forum Bulletin. Jewish Music Forum: Society for the Advancement of Jewish Musical Culture. New York: [n.p.]; 1940-1957; Committee of eds.
     Based in New York City, Jewish Music Forum was active from 1939 to 1960, meeting at various synagogues and private locations. Editions of *Bulletin* were issued at irregular intervals, and contained some abstracts of papers delivered by many notable figures in Jewish music of that time. Also included — outlines of meetings held 3-4 times each year, roster of membership, and sometimes music illustrations for abstracts. This organization was preceded by the *Mailamm*:American-Palestine Music Association (1929/32-1939). In turn, the Forum was superceded with formation by A.W. Binder (1895-1966) of the Jewish Liturgical Music Society of America (1963-1973). All those organizations were based in New York City, but drew membership from across country and included some of most active musicians in Jewish and general music life. Copies of *Jewish Music Forum Bulletin* (as originally printed and circulated) may be found in some Judaica libraries. (Full collection was bound into one volume and presented to several libraries in America and Israel by courtesy of philanthropist Jakob Michael.) Issues as published: 1940; 1941; 1942; 1943; 1944; 1945; 1946/7;

1948; and, 1949/55. English text.
735
Jewish Music Journal. New York: [n.p.]; 1934-1935; JACOB
BEIMEL, founder and ed.
Liturgical musician - cantor, composer and educator -
Jacob Beimel (1880-1944) shaped this briefly-issued
publication, which presented short articles and general
information on Jewish music activities, with some music
illustrations. Yiddish, Hebrew and English texts. There
were five issues, with some notable musicians as contributors of commentaries and other items. Copies may
be examined in Judaica libraries.
Vol.1,no.1.(July 1934); 44pp. Contributors: Binder, Beimel, Davidson, Idelsohn, Jassinowsky, Reider; music by
Beimel, Maslov, Rubenstein, Warshawsky.

Vol.2,no.1.(Mar/.Apr. 1935); 36pp. Contributors: Binder,
Bugatch, Singer; music by Beimel, Binder, Katchko. (In-
cluded information on activities and membership of the
Mailamm Society in New York City.)

Vol.2,no.2.(May/June 1935); 36pp. Contributors: Beimel,
Cohen, Friedlaender, Idelsohn; music by Marcello, Beimel, Nowakowsky.

Vol.2,no.3.(Sept./Oct. 1935); 36pp. Contributors:Adolph,
Beimel, Binder, Huberman; music by Vigoda, Wolfert.

Vol.2,no.4.(Nov./Dec. 1935); 36pp. Contributors: Alman,
Beimel, Dirigent; Music by Beimel. Index of 5 issues.
736
Jewish Music Notes. Jewish Music Council of Jewish Welfare
Board. New York: J.M.C./J.W.B.; 1946-1978; various eds.
Semi-annual bulletin (2-4 sides) prepared as June and
December "insert" for *J.W.B. Circle,* organizational
publication. *Jewish Music Notes* appeared attached to
similar type of bulletin prepared by Jewish Book Council
of J.W.B. Contents included brief articles, reviews of
music scores, recordings and books related to liturgical
and secular Jewish music. Also featured was highlight
information for dates, themes and resource materials in
connection with nation-wide programming for annual "Jewish Music Festival" season, generally from *Purim* holiday to eve of Passover. Program focus on other calendar
days for special Jewish music programs: *Shabbat Shira*
(Sabbath of Song); *Yom Ha-shoa* (Holocaust Commemoration); and *Yom Ha-atzmauth* (Israel Independence Day).
Jewish Music Council was established in 1945 by group of
Jewish musicians and social workers, and sponsored by
J.W.B. which serves Jewish centers and "Y"s throughout
country. Professional directors for J.M.C. were: Leah
Jaffa Rosenbluth (1948-1965) and Irene Heskes (1968-
1980). Contributors to *Jewish Music Notes* included
many notable leaders in Jewish music, all of whom served
on voluntary basis as an Executive Board for Council.
Issue copies may be examined at office of J.W.B. in New

York City.

738

Journal of Jewish Music and Liturgy. Cantorial Council of America and Cantorial Training Institute – Orthodox Judaism. New York: C.C.A./Yeshiva Univ.; 1976 --; MACY NULMAN, ed.

Vol.1.(1976); 50pp. Contents – MICHAEL DUBKOWSKI: "A Bicentennial Assessment of the History, Contributions and Achievements of the American Cantorate." WALTER ORENSTEIN: "Notes on the Liturgy." MACY NULMAN: *"Mah Yafit* – The Intriguing Fate of the Sabbath Table Hymn." PINHAS JASSINOWSKY: (reprint) "Congregational Singing." trans. by Solomon Berl. MACY NULMAN: "Highlights in the History of the Cantorial Council of America." Music section.

Vol.2.(1977/78); 69pp. Contents – JOSEPH REIDER: "Secular Currents in the Synagogue Chant in America." MORRIS SILVERMAN: "Comments on Texts of *Siddur* (Prayerbook)." MACY NULMAN: "Musical Service of Syrian Synagogue: Its Structure and Design." (reprint) "19th Century Contract of a *Hazzan* (cantor) in Berditchev." trans. by Macy Nulman. ERNEST BLOCH: (reprint) "Memorable Experience at an East Side Synagogue Service." Music section.

Vol.3.(1979/80); 34pp. Contents – GERSON APPEL: *"Sheliah Tsibbur* in *Halakha* and Jewish Tradition." ARON FRIEDMANN: (reprint) "Synagogue Song – A Study: Part 1" trans. by Herman Lieber, with additional materials by Macy Nulman and Stephen Powitz. GERSHON EPHROS: "Mainstream of Synagogue Music – Eastern and Western Music." Music section.

Vol.4.(1981/82); 41pp. Contents – STEPHEN POWITZ: "Musical life in the Warsaw Ghetto." AVROM BAKER: "Illustrations of Songs of the Zodiac for *Tal* (dew) and *Geshem* (rain) Prayers." MOSHE DERLOVE: "Music of Obscure *Piyyutim* for *Tal* and *Geshem*." IRENE HESKES: "The Cantor as a Practical Music Leader for the Community." ARON FRIEDMANN (reprint) "Synagogue Song – A Study: Part 2." trans. by Herman Lieber, with additional materials by Macy Nulman and Stephen Powitz. Music section.

Vol.5.(1982/83); 47pp. Conents – PINKHAS MINKOWSKI: (reprint) *"Hazzanuth* (Cantorial Art)." trans. by Solomon Rybak. HERSHEL SCHACHTER: *"Halakha* and *Minhagim* (law and customs) for the *Shatz* (prayer leader) and Congregation." ABRAHAM SCHWADRON: *"Un Cavritico* – The Sephardic Tradition." MOSHE SCHONFELD: "The Vilna Gaon's Interpretations of the *Te'amim* (cantillation signs)." Music section.

738

Journal of Synagogue Music. Cantors Assembly of America – Conservative Judaism. New York: C.A.A./J.T.S.A.; 1967 --; various eds.

Vol.1,no.1(Feb.1967); CHARLES DAVIDSON, ed.; 61pp. Contents – EDITH GERSON-KIWI: "Legacy of Music Through the Ages." SAUL MEISELS: "In Memoriam: A.W. Binder (1895-

1966)." MORRIS LEVINSON: "From the Introduction to *'Kol Israel'*." STUART FORTICHA and MOSES SILVERMAN: "*Rosh Hashana* 1966." PETER GRADENWITZ: "Trends in Contemporary Jewish Music." Reviews and music section.

Vol.1,no.2(Sept.1967); C.D., ed.; 52pp. Contents – SAMUEL ROSENBAUM: "Prayer: A Lost Art." ERIC WERNER: "The Concept of Musical Tradition in the Synagogue." CHARLES DAVIDSON: "A Landmark Case: Role of the Cantor." ERIC MANDELL: "A Collector's Random Notes on the Bibliography of Jewish Music." Reviews, letters and music section.

Vol.1,no.3(Jan.1968); C.D., ed.; 55pp. Contents – LAWRENCE LOEB: "*Hazzanuth* in Iran." CHARLES DAVIDSON: "Cantors – A Second Landmark Case." PAUL KAVON: "Joshua Samuel Weisser (1888-1952)." ALBERT WEISSER: "Lazar Weiner: A Tribute." Reviews, letters and music section.

Vol.1,no.4(Aug.1968); C.D., ed.; 67pp. Contents – ERIC MANDELL: "Salomon Sulzer 1804-1890." AVIGDOR HERZOG: "On Preservation and Renewal of the Music of the Synagogue." DAVID J. PUTTERMAN: "Congregational Singing." MORRIS LEVINSON: "Personal Articles of Faith." SAMUEL ROSENBAUM: "Epitaph for Jewish Music?" Reviews, music section

Vol.2,no.1(Feb.1969); C.D., ed.; 63pp. Contents –CHARLES DAVIDSON: "A Quarter Century of Synagogue Music in America." ABRAHAM MISHCON: "Disputed Phrasing in the *Siddur* (prayerbook)." ISRAEL J. KATZ: "A Judaeo-Spanish *Romancero*." Reviews and music section.

739
Journal of Synagogue Music. (continued)
Vol.2,no.2(Aug.1969); MORTON SHAMES, ed.; 55pp. Contents – ALBERT WEISSER: "Need for a New History of Jewish Music: A Preliminary Study." ALFRED SENDREY: "Adventures of a Bibliography." JOSEPH LEVINE: "Abba Yosef Weisgal at Eighty: An Appreciation." Reviews, letters and music section.

Vol.2,no.3(Nov.1969); M.S., ed.; 47pp. Contents – HERBERT FROMM: "Contemporary Synagogue Music in America." ISSACHAR FATER: "Gershon Serota: An Appreciation." DAVID J. PUTTERMAN: "Rocking the Temple." SAUL MEISELS: A New Sound in the Synagogue: Kingsley." Reviews, letters and music section.

Vol.2,no.4(Apr.1970); M.S., ed.; 76pp. Contents – HERMAN BERLINSKI: "High Holyday Music of Bezalel Brun." MAX WOHLBERG: "Salomon Sulzer and the Seitenstettengasse Temple." ROBERT SWAN: "Design and Use of the Pipe Organ in the Synagogue." JOHN KATZ: "Hassidism in Jazz." Reviews and music section.

Vol.3,no.1(Sept.1970); M.S., ed.; 44pp. Contents – JUDITH K. EISENSTEIN: "A New Look at Music in Jewish Education." ISRAEL ADLER: "Synagogue Chants of the 12th

Century." DANIEL CHAZANOFF: "Salomone Rossi, Ebreo."
A.Z. IDELSOHN: (reprint) "The *Kol Nidre* Tune." Reviews
and music section.

Vol.3,no.2(Feb.1971); M.S., ed.; 70pp. Contents — ABRA-
HAM LUBIN: "Influence of Jewish Music and Thought in
Certain Works of Leonard Bernstein." MAX WOHLBERG:"Notes
on Music: Old and New." DANIEL CHAZANOFF: "Importance of
Rossi in the Musical Life of the Mantuan Court." A.Z.
IDELSOHN: (reprint) "Songs and Singers of the Synagogue
in the 18th Century." Reviews and music section.

Vol.3,no.3(Sept.1971); M.S., ed.; 56pp. Contents — HY-
MAN SKY:"Some Classic Studies in Liturgy." IRENE HESKES:
"The cultural Leadership Role of the Cantor." ABRAHAM
LUBIN: "Certain Works of Leonard Bermstein." Reviews and
music section.

Vol.3,no.4(Dec.1971); M.S., ed.; 64pp. Contents — JACK
GOTTLIEB: "A Jewish Mass or Catholic *Mitzvah*." ALFRED
Sendrey; "Translations in English Bibles of Hebrew Mu-
sical Terms." SAMUEL ADLER: "Music in the American Syna-
gogue." ALBERT WEISSER: "A.M. Bernstein (1866–1932)."
Reviews and music section.

740
Journal of Synagogue Music. (continued)
    Vol.4,nos.1/2(Apr.1972); MORTON SHAMES, ed.; 116pp; "The
    Twenty-fifth Anniversary Issue" — Reprints and New Ma-
    terials. Contents — KURT LIST AND CHEMJO VINAVER: "Syna-
    gogue Music: Traditional and Modern." (1948) ADOLPH
    KATCHKO: "Changing the Concepts of *Hazzanuth*." (1949)
    LEON LEIBREICH: "An Interpretation of the Sabbath Eve
    Liturgy." (1950) LEIB GLANTZ: "The Musical Basis of
    Nusakh Ha-tefillah." (1952) MAX WOHLBERG: "History of
    the Musical Modes of the Ashkenazic Synagogue and Their
    Usage." (1954) ABRAHAM J. HESCHEL: "Task of the *Hazzan*
    (cantor)." (1957) A.W. BINDER/GERSHON EPHROS/HERBERT
    FROMM/SHOLOM SECUNDA: "Creating Synagogue Music for A-
    merica: A Discussion." (1961) HERMAN BERLINSKI/JOSEPH
    FREUDENTHAL/ERWIN JOSPE/OSCAR JULIUS: "A Forum on Syna-
    gogue Music." (1963) MAURICE SAMUEL: "The Wonder of the
    Psalms." (1965) SAMUEL ROSENBAUM: "Epitaph for Jewish
    Music?" (1968) Reviews, letters and music section.

    Vol.4,no.3(Dec.1972); M.S., ed.; 62pp. Contents — SAMUEL
    ADLER: "Music in the American Synagogue." ROGER STAUM:
    "Synagogue Music in 18th Century Amsterdam." IRA GOLD-
    BERG: "Jewish Music as a Bridge of Understanding." DAVID
    CHAZANOFF: "Salomone Rossi and Claudio Monteverdi."
    MICHAEL ISAACSON: "Synagogue Music of Ben Steinberg."
    Reviews and music section.

    Vol.4,no.4(May 1973); M.S., ed.; 54pp. Contents — ABRA-
    HAM LUBIN: "Understanding the Role of the *Hazzan* (can-
    tor)." CLAIRE POLIN-SCHAFF: "Origin and Aspects of Early
    American Psalmody." IRA GOLDBERG: "Using Recordings Cre-

atively in the Classroom." Reviews and music section.

Vol.5,no.1(Oct.1973); M.S., ed.; 72pp. Contents — JACK
KESSLER: "A Serial Approach to *Hazzanuth*." JOZA KARAS:
"Music in Terezin." MORTON SHAMES: "A Landmark Case in
Cantorial Litigation." Reviews and music section.

Vol.5,no.2(June 1974); M.S., ed.; 50pp. Contents — HER-
BERT FROMM: "Salomone Rossi." MILFORD FARGO: "Music for
a Centennial." ARIO HYAMS: "*Kol Nidre*: The Word in Ab-
solute Music." DAVID CHAZANOFF: "Salomone Rossi and His
Company of Musicians." MORTON SHAMES: "Legal Status of
the *Hazzan*." Reviews and music section.

741
Journal of Synagogue Music. (continued)
Vol.5,no.3(Dec.1974); MORTON SHAMES, ed.; 59pp. Con-
tents — MORTON SHANOK: "Motivators and Motivation in
Jewish Music." CLAIRE POLIN: "A Welsh 'Grace'?" MARIO
CASTELNUOVO-TEDESCO:(reprint) "Music for the Synagogue."
MAX WOHLBERG: "Varying Concepts of *Ne'emah* and Their
Place in Liturgy." SAMUEL ROSENBAUM: "Songs of the *Beis
Ha-medresh*." ISRAEL ADLER: "Memorial Life and Tradi-
tions of the Portuguese Jewish Community of Amsterdam in
the 18th Century." Reviews and music section.

Vol.6,no.1(Apr.1975); M.S., ed.; 61pp. Contents — DANI-
EL CHAZANOFF: "An Analysis of Salomone Rossi's Sonata
Detta la Moderna (1613)." MORTON SHAMES and SHOSHANNA
IGRA: "A Cantor Travels Westward: From the Autobiography
of Hirsch Weintraub." PINCHAS JASSINOWSKY: (reprint)
"*Hazzanim* and *Hazzanuth*." MAX WOHLBERG: "Music and
Musicians in the Works of Sholom Aleichem." MICHAEL MI-
NER: "Todros Greenberg." Reviews and music section.

Vol.6,no.2(Oct.1975); M.S., ed.; 64pp. Contents — MICHA-
EL ISAACSON: "Synagogue Music is Dead?" ELLIOT GERTEL:
"Challenge of Synagogue Music." ELEANOR GORDON MLOTEK:
"America in East European Yiddish Folksong." DANIEL
CHAZANOFF: "Articulating Music with Foreign Language
Study." MAX WOHLBERG: "The Subject of Jewish Music."
Reviews, letters and music section.

Vol.6,no.3(Mar.1976); M.S., ed.; 63pp. Contents — PIN-
CHAS SPIRO: "*Haggadah*: A Search for Freedom." PETER
NAGY-FARKAS: "Music in the Synagogue: A Composer's View-
point." DANIEL CHAZANOFF: "Salomone Rossi's *Hashirim*."
GERSHON EPHROS: "Hazzanic Recitative: A Unique Contri-
bution to Our Musical Heritage." MAYNARD GERBER: "An
American *Hazzan* In Sweden." Reviews and music section.

Vol.6,no.4(July 1976); M.S., ed.; 57pp. Contents — HER-
BERT FROMM: "Heinrich Schalit (1886-1976)." ALBERT
WEISSER: "Autobiographical Sketch: J.S. Weisser (1880-
1952)." ROBERT STRASSBURG: "Alfred Sendrey (1884-1976):
In Memoriam." MAX WOHLBERG: "Fading Footprints." Re-
views, letters and music section.

Vol.7,no.1(Nov.1976); M.S., ed.; 62pp. Contents — MAX
WOHLBERG: "A Unique Chapter in the History of the American Cantorate: Part 1." ELLIOT GERTEL: "Theological Reflections on Music in Prayer." IRA GOLDBERG: "Records in
the Jewish School: A Lesson and Approach." ABRAHAM LUBIN
"Phenomenon of Non-Acceptance of the Unfamiliar." HANOCH
AVENARY: "Concept of Mode in European Synagogue Chant:
An Analysis of the *Adoshem Malakh Steiger*." Reviews,
letters and music section.

742
Journal of Synagogue Music. (continued)
Vol.7,no.2(Feb.1977); MORTON SHAMES, ed.; 51pp. Contents — MAX WOHLBERG: "A Unique Chapter in the History
of the American Cantorate: Part 2." JEROME KOPMAR: "Synagogue Youth Choir: An Experience in Education." BELSKIN
GINSBURG: "*Hazzanuth* in America." RICHARD NEUMANN:
"Contributions of Sholom Kalib." JOSHUA JACOBSON: "Jewish Music Versus Jewish Worship." Reviews, music section

Vol.7,no.3(June 1977); M.S., ed.; 63pp. (Issued as 70th
Birthday Tribute to Cantor Max Wohlberg) Contents —
MAX WOHLBERG: "*Hazzanuth* in Transition." MAX WOHLBERG:
"Emerging Image of the Conservative Cantor." JOSEPH
PRICE: "Max Wohlberg: Biographical Sketch and Biblio-
graphy." Brief Tribute Essays by: JEFFREY WOHLBERG,
THEODORE STEINBERG, GERSHON EPHROS, MORTON LEIFMAN,
DAVID KOGEN, HUGO WEISGALL, ALBERT WEISSER, HARRY WOHL-
BERG, SHIMON FROST, SAMUEL CHIEL, GERSON COHEN. Music
section of Max Wohlberg's cantorial works.

Vol.7,no.4(Oct.1977); M.S., ed.; 63pp. Contents — DANIEL
CHAZANOFF: "Influence of Salomone Rossi's Music: Part 1"
SAM PESSAROFF: "Commissioning: The Historic Contribution
of David Putterman." HERBERT FROMM: "Influence of German
Jewish Composers on the American Synagogue." NORMAN H.
WAREMBUD: "Copyright Protection." Reviews, letters and
music section.

Vol.8,no.1(Jan.1978); M.S., ed.; 48pp. Contents — HER-
BERT FROMM: "The Tetragrammaton in Music." PINCHAS SPIRO
"*Havdalah*: A Sabbath Pageant of Farewell." ELLIOT GER-
TEL: "The Organ Controversy Reconsidered." C.S. LEWIS:
"On Church Music." Reviews and music section.

Vol.8,no.2(May 1978); M.S., ed.; 39pp. Contents — MAY-
NARD GERBER: "An American Cantor in Sweden." SAMUEL
ROSENBAUM: "In Memoriam: Norman Warembud (1912-1978)."
NORMAN H. WAREMBUD: "A Brief History of the Jewish Music
Published in America." Reviews and music section.

743
Journal of Synagogue Music. (continued)
Vol.8,no.3(Aug.1978); MORTON SHAMES, ed.; 43pp. Contents — SHALOM KALIB: "An Introduction to Todros Greenberg's *Tefillot*." Index section for *Journal of Synagogue Music*, by Title and Author. Letters.

Vol.8,no.4(Dec.1978); M.S., ed.; 68pp. Contents — HYMAN
SKY: "Development of the Office of the *Hazzan* Through
the Talmudic Period." ABRAHAM LUBIN: *"Minhag Ashkenaz*:
A Millenium in Song." SHALOM KALIB: "Outline for a Project in Synagogue Music." Reviews and music section.

Vol.9,no.1(Mar.1979); M.S., ed.; 51pp. Contents — LOTTIE
HOCHBERG: *"Haftarah* for the Off-Key Singer." MARTIN
LEUBITZ: *"Bar/Bas Mitzvah* Instruction: A New Approach"
ROBERT STRASSBURG: "A *S'lichot* Happening." LINDA HORO-
WITZ: "Jewish Choral Tradition: Antiquity." DANIEL CHA-
ZANOFF: "Influence of Salomone Rossi's Music: Part 2."
MAX WOHLBERG: "Gershon Ephros (1890-1978)." Reviews,
letters and music section.

Vol.9,no.2(June 1979); M.S., ed.; 47pp. Contents — SAM
WEISS: *"Cantus Firmus* of Arnold Schoenberg's *Kol
Nidre*." PINCHAS SPIRO: "The Musical Legacy of Gershon
Ephros (1890-1978)." STEPHEN RICHARDS: "Music and Prayer
in Reform Worship." SAMUEL ROSENBAUM: "Surviving Future
Shock in Liturgical Music." Reviews and music section.
744
Journal of Synagogue Music. (continued)
Vol.9,no.3(Nov.1979); ABRAHAM LUBIN, ed.; 91pp. Con-
tents — DANIEL CHAZANOFF: "Influence of Salomone Rossi's
Music; Part 3." SAMUEL ROSENBAUM: "New Ideas for Litur-
gical Services." MAX WOHLBERG: "Thoughts on the Hazzanic
Recitative." Reviews and music section.

Vol.9,no.4(Mar.1980); A.L., ed.; 44pp. Contents — CHAR-
LES HELLER: "Traditional Jewish Material in Schoenberg's
"A Survivor from Warsaw'." CHARLES DAVIDSON/DAVID TILMAN
/MICHAEL ISAACSON: "Surviving Future Shock: Some Other
Views." ELLIOT GERTEL: "Two Sabbath Eve Prayers: New
Translations and Commentary." Reviews and music section.

Vol.10,no1.1(July 1980); A.L., ed.; 79pp. (with this issue, official shift to semi-annual publication) Contents — MAX WOHLBERG: "Memorial to David Putterman (1901
-1979)." KARL H. WOERNER: (reprint) "Religious Element
in Schoenberg's Work." ELLIOT GERTEL: "Sabbath Eve A-
midah: A New Translation and Commentary." SAMUEL ROSEN-
BAUM: "Gleanings from *Die Hazzonim Velt* (Warsaw Publication, 1933-1935)." MAXINE RIBSTEIN KANTER: "High Holy
Day Hymn Melodies in the Portuguese Synagogue of Amsterdam." MORDECAI YARDEINI: "Sound of Singing in the Cat-
skills." Reviews and music section.

Vol.10,no.2(Dec.1980); A.L., ed.; 93pp. Contents — ARN-
OLD ROTHSTEIN: "A Practical Proposal to Upgrade the
Level of Taste in the Music of the Synagogue." MAXINE
RIBSTEIN KANTER: "High Holy Day Melodies in the Spanish
and Portuguese Synagogue of London." JACK GOTTLIEB:
"Symbols of Faith in the Music of Leonard Bernstein."
DANIEL CHAZANOFF: "Influence of Salomone Rossi's Music:
Part 4." ELLIOT GERTEL: *"L'cho Dodi*: A New Translation

and Commentary." Reviews and music section.

Vol.11,no.1(July 1981); A.L., ed.; 80pp. Contents – JOS-
EPH LEVINE: "*Missinai* Melodies in the Modal Chant of
Abba Yosef Weisgal." PINCHAS SPIRO: "Rejuvenation of the
Weekday Modes." HANS H. STUECKENSCHMIDT: (reprint) "Arn-
old Schoenberg's *Kol Nidre* and the Jewish Elements in
His Music." BARUCH J. COHON: (reprint) "The Structure of
the Synagogue Prayer Chant." Reviews and music section.

Vol.11,no.2(Dec.1981); A.L., ed.; 65pp. Contents – ELLI-
OT GERTEL: "*Kabbalat Shabbat* Psalms: A New Translation
and Commentary." ERIC WERNER: (reprint) "Genealogies of
Two Wandering Hebrew Melodies." AKIVA ZIMMERMAN: "They
Were Four: Machtenberg, Alter, Putterman and Kalenberg."
SAMUEL ROSENBAUM/MOSHE KOUSSEVITZSKY: "The Old *Hazzan*
of Kiev: A Legend from Hazzanic Folklore." Reviews,
letters and music section.

745
Journal of Synagogue Music. (continued)
Vol.12,no.1(June 1982); ABRAHAM LUBIN, ed.; 75pp. Contents – GAIL POSNER KARP: "Evolution of the *Aleynu*:
1171 to Present." BARUCH J. COHON: "A Century of A.Z.
Idelsohn: On the Hundredth Anniversary of His Birth
(1882-1938)." KENNETH COHEN: "A Talk With Lazar Weiner."
SAMUEL ROSENBAUM: "Lazar Weiner (1897-1982): Rebel With
a Cause." Reviews and music section.

Vol.12,no.2(Dec.1982); A.L., ed.; 97pp. Contents – JACK
BLOOM: "Who Become Clergymen?" MAX WOHLBERG: "Samuel Vigoda's 'Legendary Voices'." JOSEPH LEVINE: "Psalmody."
CHARLES DAVIDSON: "The *Torah* Reading Program at Congregation Adath Jeshurun." Reviews and music section.

Vol.13,no.1(June 1983); A.L., ed.; 76pp. Contents –
SAMUEL ROSENBAUM: "A Look Back: Rabbi Israel Goldfarb
and the Cantors Conference, 1924." ROBERT STRASSBURG:
"A Festival of Jewish Music in Los Angeles." PINCHAS
SPIRO: "*Yalkut Zimrotai*: Appraisal and Applause."
JEFFREY ZUCKER: "Edward Stark (1856-1918): American
Cantor-Composer at the Turn of the Century." Reviews
and music section.

746
Musica Hebraica. World Centre for Jewish Music in Pales-
tine. Jerusalem, Pal. Mandate: W.C.J.M.P., 1938; HERMANN
(GERSHON) SWET, ed.
Only one issue appeared – 1938; 84pp., illus., music;
Hebrew, German, French and English texts for articles,
as written. Contributors (each brief piece) – HERMANN
SWET (Jerusalem); ERIC WERNER (Breslau); JOSEPH YASSER
(New York); MARY TIBALDI-CHIESA (Milan); DARIUS MILHAUD
(Paris); MAX BROD (Prague); ERICH WALTER STERNBERG (Tel
Aviv); ARNO NADEL (Berlin); HEINRICH SEMON (Tel Aviv);
KARL SOLOMON (Jerusalem); EDITH GERSON-KIWI (Jerusalem);
ANNALIESE LANDAU (Berlin); OSKAR GUTTMAN (Berlin); MOSCO
CARNER (London); NICOLAI LOPATNIKOFF (London). Also, a

roster of international membership given. Note: Dr.
Salli Levi, with a committee of music colleagues, founded the World Centre for Jewish Music in Palestine, in
Jerusalem in 1937, enlisting membership from America and
Europe. *Musica Hebraica* intended as regular publica-
tion for this organization. Some concerts and lectures
were presented in Jerusalem and Tel Aviv 1937/39, but
all activities ceased with outbreak of World War II in
September 1939. Copy of this singular issue may be examined in Judaica libraries.
747
Musica Judaica. American Society for Jewish Music. New
York: A.S.J.M., 1975 --; ISRAEL J. KATZ, series ed.
American Society for Jewish Music was established in
1973 in New York City, superceding Jewish Liturgical
Music Society of America (1963-1973) as active music
organization sponsoring lectures and concert programs,
and publishing *Musica Judaica* as annual journal devoted to Jewish music - liturgical, folk and art.
Vol.1(1975/76); ISRAEL J. KATZ and ALBERT WEISSER, eds.;
120pp. Contents - ISRAEL J. KATZ: "Abraham Zebi Idelsohn
(1882-1938): A Bibliography of His Collected Writings."
JUDITH K. EISENSTEIN: "Mediaeval Elements in the Liturgical Music of the Jews of Southern France and Northern
Spain." JOAN L. THOMSON: "Giacomo Meyerbeer (1741-1864):
The Jew and His Relationship With Richard Wagner." AL-
BERT WEISSER: "The Music of Europe and the Americas -
19th and 20th Centuries, in the *Encyclopaedia Judaica*"
ISRAEL J. KATZ:"Alfred Sendrey (1884-1976) In Memoriam."
Necrology, roster of membership, reports of meetings and
concert programs, facsimiles and photographs, music il-
lustrations, list of new publications and reviews.

Vol.2,no.1(1977/78); ISRAEL J. KATZ and ALBERT WEISSER,
eds.; 115pp. Contents - ALBERT WEISSER, ed.: "Lazare
Saminsky's Years in Russia and Palestine: Excerpts From
an Unpublished Autobiography." MAX WOHLBERG: "Music of
the Synagogue as a Source of the Yiddish Folksong."
ISRAEL ROSS: "Cross-Cultural Dynamics in Musical Traditions: The Music of the Jews of Cochin." ELEANOR GOR-
DON MLOTEK: "Soviet-Yiddish Folklore Scholarship." JACK
GOTTLIEB: "Arthur Wolfson (1012-1977) In Memoriam." ERIC
WERNER: "Music, Masoretic Accents and *Hazzan* in the
Encyclopaedia Judaica." Necrology, roster of membership, reports of meetings and concert programs, facsimiles and photographs, music illustrations, list of new
publications and reviews.

Vol.2,no.2(1978/79); ISRAEL J. KATZ and ALBERT WEISSER,
eds.; vi,57pp. Contents - MARSHA BRYAN EDELMAN: "An
Index to Gershon Ephros' *Cantorial Anthology*."

Vol.3(1980/81); ISRAEL J. KATZ and ALBERT WEISSER, eds.;
113pp. Contents - ALEXANDER L. RINGER: "Frederick Gernsheim (1839-1916) and the Lost Generation." JOSEPH LEVINE
"Toward Defining the Jewish Prayer Modes; With Parti-

cular Emphasis on the *Adonay Malakh* Mode." KAY KAUFMAN
SHELEMAY: "*Seged*: A Falasha Pilgrimage Festival." JA-
COB HOHENEMSER: "The Jew in German Musical Thought Before the 19th Century." HANOCH AVENARY: "An Encycloped-
ist's Ailments: Reviewing the Reviews of the *Encyclopaedia Judaica* on Jewish Music." ERIC WERNER: "A Reply
to Hanoch Avenary." Necrology, roster of membership, reports of meetings and concert programs, facsimiles and
photographs, music illustrations, list of new publications and reviews.

Vol.4(1982): ISRAEL J. KATZ, ALBERT WEISSER and LAURA
LEON COHEN, eds.; 145pp. (dedicated to memory of Albert
Weisser) Contents — ALBERT WEISSER: "Music Division of
the Jewish Ethnographic Expedition in the Name of Baron
Horace Guinzbourg, 1911–14." CARLETON SPRAGUE SMITH:
"Curt Sachs (1881–1959) and the Library Museum of the
Performing Arts." JOHANNA SPECTOR: "Role of Ethnomusic-
ology in the Study of Jewish Music." ISRAEL J. KATZ:
"Enigma of the Antonio Bustelo Judaeo-Spanish Ballad
Tunes in Manuel L. Ortega's *Los Hebreos en Marruecos*."
ROBERT ROTHSTEIN: "On the Melody of David Edelstadt's
Vacht Oif." ISRAEL J. KATZ: "In Memoriam: Albert
Weisser (1918–1982)." MARSHA BRYAN EDELMAN: "In Memori-
am: Lazar Weiner (1897–1982)." HERMAN BERLINSKI: Joseph
Yasser (1893–1981): A Personal Recollection." Necrology,
roster of membership, reports of meetings and concert
programs, facsimiles and photographs, music illustra-
tions, list of new publications and reviews.

Vol.5 (1983): ISRAEL J. KATZ AND LAURA LEON-COHEN, eds.
137pp. Contents — LAURA LEON-COHEN: "Hugo Weisgall's
"The Golden Peacock" — A Stylistic and Interpretive An-
alysis of Two Songs." JOHN H. BARON: "Frederick Emil
Kitziger of New Orleans: A 19th Century Composer of
Synagogue Music." JOSEPH A. LEVINE: "The Biblical Trope
System in Ashkenazic Prophetic Reading." JUDITH LAKI
FRIGYESI: "Modulation as an Integral Part of the Modal
System." MACY NULMAN: "Development of the *Hallel* Chant
as Reflected in Rabbinic Literature." JAMES H. JOHNSON:
"Antisemitism and Music in 19th Century France." Reviews
and necrology. Roster of membership, reports of meetings
and concert programs. Facsimiles and musical examples.
List of new publications and contents of past issues.

748
Musical Traditions In Israel: Record Album Brochures. National Sound Archives and Jewish Music Research Centre. Jerusalem, Isr.:Hebrew Univ./Magnes Press, 1976 —; AVIGDOR
HERZOG and Research Committee, eds.

  Brochures prepared for each recording album, with historical background, music and text commentaries and with
  other explanatory materials. Hebrew and English texts.
  Fold-over sheets of 8–12 sides, in 3 columns of text.
  Album 1(1976): "Hassidic Tunes for Dancing and for Re-
  joicing."
  Album 2(1979): "Synagogal Art Music of 12th to 13th

Centuries: Religious Poems, Cantatas and Choral Works."
Album 3(1980); "Sephardic Songs from the Balkans."
Album 4(1982); "Jewish Yemenite Songs From the *Diwan*."
749
Orbis Musicae; Studies in Musicology. Dept. of Musicology/
Tel Aviv Univ. Ramat Aviv,Isr.:T.A.U. Press, 1971 --; ed.bd.
Issued at irregular intervals. Articles in English, Ger-
man and French texts, as written. Focus of contents on
music topics related to "Mediterranean subjects and as
an East-West musical forum."
No.1(1971); HANOCH AVENARY, ed.; 104pp., illus., music.
Contents - ERIC WERNER: "In Memoriam: Higinio Angles
(1888-1969); Scholar and Friend." HANOCH AVENARY:
"Flutes for a Bride and a Dead Man; The Symbolism of the
Flute." AMNON SHILOAH: "*Un Probleme Musical de Thabit
ibn Qurra.*" ECKHARD NEUBAUER: "*Drei Makamen des Asik
Divani.*" MOHAMMAD TAGHI MASOUDIEH: "*Die Matnawi Melo-
die in der Persischen Kunstmusik.*" HANS TISCHLER: "On
the Need of New Editions of Early Polyphonic Music."
EGON WELLESZ: "*Errinerungen an Gustav Mahler und Arn-
old Schoenberg.*" PAUL A. PISK: "New Music in Austria
During the 1920's." H.H. STUCKENSCHMIDT: "Opus 19,no.3;
Eine Schoenberg Analyse." DON HARRAN: "The Israel Composers' Workshop, Aug.1970." Reviews and music section.

No.2(1972); EDITH GERSON-KIWI, ed.; 204pp. illus.,music.
Contents - YEHUDI MENUHIN: "Possible Influences of In-
dian Classical Music on Future Western Music." OTHMAR
WESSELY: "*Zur Ars Inveniendi im Zeitalter des Barock.*"
BENCE SZABOLCSI: "*Spuren Weltlicher Gesangs-formen im
Juedischen Gebetbuch des Mittelalters.*" JAN VAN BIEZEN:
"Middle Byzantine *Kontakion*; Notation of Codex Ash-
burnhamensis 64 and the *Akathistos* Hymn." BRUNO NETTL:
"Notes on Persian Classical Music of Today." BRIGITTE
SCHIFFER: "*Neue Griechische Musik.*" ERIC WERNER: "In
Memoriam: Bence Szabolcsi (1899-1973)." Reviews; music.

Nos.3/4(1973/74); EDITH GERSON-KIWI, ed.; 153pp.,illus.,
music. Contents - PAUL COLLAER: "Darius Milhaud; *Pour
Celebrer son 80 Anniversaire.*" EDITH GERSON-KIWI: "Two
Anniversaries of Two Pioneers in Jewish Ethnomusicology:
Abraham Zebi Idelsohn (1882-1938) and Robert Lachmann
(1892-1939)." KARL GUSTAV FELLERER: "*Compone alla
Mente.*" KARL-WERNER GUEMPEL: "*Eine Katalanische Ver-
sion der Mensurallehre des Guillermus de Palio.*" JEHO-
ASH HIRSHBERG: "The Relationship of Text and Music in
Machaut's Ballads." HANS TISCHLER: "Coordination of Se-
parate Elements; Chief Principle of Mediaeval Art." DA-
LIA COHEN and RUTH KATZ: "Quantitative Analysis of Mono-
phonic Music." WALTER KAUFMANN: "Parallel Trends of
Musical Liturgies and Notations in Eastern and Western
Asia." HANOCH AVENARY: "Discrepancy Between Iconographic
and Literary Presentation of Ancient Eastern Musical Instruments." ARIE SACHS: "Forgotten Piano Works of the
19th Century, Retrieved." DON HARRAN: "*Testimonium
No.2,* 1971." Reviews, letters and music section.

750
Orbis Musicae: Studies in Musicology. (continued)
No.5(1975/76); EDITH GERSON-KIWI, ed.; 108pp; illus.,
music. Contents — HANS TISCHLER: "New Approach to
Structural Analysis of 13th Century French Poetry."
BENJAMIN RAJECZKI: *"Zum Problem der Musikalischen
Renaissance in Ungarn."* GHIZELA SULITEANU: "Experi-
mental Method in Ethnomusicology, and Some Experiments
Utilized in Collecting and Study of Lullabies With the
Rumanian People." NOEMI BAHAT-RATZON: *"Le Soff - Pro-
cession Dansee dans les Ceremonies du Mariage Druze."*
JANE MINK ROSSEN: "Ethnomusicological Field Work in
Bellona Island; A Preliminary Report." AVNER BAHAT: "In
Memoriam: Solange Corbin (1903-1973); On the Third Anni-
versary of Her Death." EDITH GERSON-KIWI: "In Memoriam:
Mme. de Chambure (Genevieve Thibault) (1902-1975)."
Reviews and music section.

No.6(1978); also appears as: *Assaph: Studies in Arts -
Section A;* HANOCH AVENARY, ed.; 110pp., illus., music.
Contents — ROSE BRANDEL: "Reflections on the Origins of
the *Alleluia - Jubilus."* JOSHUA DORFMAN: "Thematic
Organization in the String Quartets of Paul Hindemith."
JOHANAN BRAUN: "Sound of Beethoven's Orchestra." Reviews
and music section.

No.7(1979/80); also appears as: *Assaph: Studies in Arts
- Section A;* HANOCH AVENARY, ed.; 128pp., illus.,music.
Contents — MIRA FRIEDMAN: "David/Orpheus in 'The Sources
of Music' by Chagall." ERIC WERNER: "Pseudo-Plutarch's
View on the Theory of Rhythm." JUDITH FRIGYESI and PETER
LAKI: "Free-Form Recitative and Strophic Structure in
the *Hallel* Psalms." WALTER SALMEN: *"Zur Ikonographie
Muzierend-Jubelnder Frauen Alt-Israels."* SUSANNA WIECK-
SHAHAK: "Wedding Songs of Bulgarian-Sephardic Jews."
Reviews and music section.

751
Tatzlil - The Chord. Annual Forum for Music Research and
Bibliography. Haifa, Isr.: Haifa Music and Ethnology Museum
and AMLI Music Library, 1960-1980 (20 issues); illus.,music.
MOSHE GORALI, series ed.
Hebrew texts, with very brief abstracts of some articles
in each issue. Collected studies, music reports and reviews of new publications — scores and literature, as
well as critiques of major concerts in Israel. Contributors include large roster of Israeli musicians — educators, scholars, journalists, publishers, composers, performers. Some materials from musicians in Europe and
America, but presented in Hebrew texts. Each issue of
approximately 150-200 pages, of which 4-6 in English
text. Facsimiles and photographs, musical illustrations,
and resource listings for articles. Copies available
from Haifa Museum/AMLI Library in Haifa, Israel.

752
YUVAL Monograph Series. Jerusalem, Isr.: Jewish Music
Research Centre at Hebrew Univ./ Magnes Press, 1974 --;
ISRAEL ADLER, series ed.
> Vol.1(1974); *Musical Life and Traditions of the Portu-
> guese Jewish Community of Amsterdam in the 18th Century.*
> ISRAEL ADLER; 144pp., illus., music.

> Vol.2(1974); *Robert Lachmann: Posthumous Works, 1.*
> EDITH GERSON-KIWI, ed.; 59pp, illus., music. German
> text only. (1. *Die Musik im Volksleben Nordafricas*;
> 2. *Orientalische Musik und Antike.*)

> Vol.3(in preparation); *A.Z. Idelsohn: Toledot Ha-negina
> Ha-ivrit, vols.2/3.* (from the Idelsohn Archives at the
> Jewish National and University Library, Jerusalem)
> Hebrew text only.

> Vol.4(1976); *A.Z. Idelsohn Archives at the Jewish Na-
> tional and University Library: Catalogue.* ISRAEL ADLER
> and JUDITH COHEN, comps. and eds.; 147pp., illus.
> Hebrew and English texts.

> Vol.5(1977); *Music Subjects in the Zohar: Texts and
> Indices.* (Inventory of Jewish Musical Sources, Series
> B,1) AMNON SHILOAH, RUTH TENE and LEA SHALEM, comps.
> and eds.; xiii,166pp. Hebrew and English texts.

> Vol.6(1977); *An Israeli Folksong: A Methodological Ex-
> ample of Computer Analysis of Monophonic Music.* DALIA
> COHEN and RUTH KATZ; 90pp. illus., music.

> Vol.7(1978); *Robert Lachmann: Posthumous Works, 2.*
> EDITH GERSON-KIWI, ed.; 207pp., illus., music. German
> text only. (*Gesaenge der Juden auf der Insel Djerba.*)
> New edition of original work by Lachmann (1892-1939).

753
YUVAL: Studies of the Jewish Music Research Centre. Jeru-
salem, Isr.: Hebrew Univ./Magnes Press, 1968 --; ISRAEL
ADLER and BATHJA BAYER, series eds.
> Vol.1(1968); ISRAEL ADLER, HANOCH AVENARY and BATHJA
> BAYER, eds.; xiv,252pp.,+60 Heb.p., illus., music.
> French, Hebrew and English texts. Contents - ISRAEL
> ADLER: "*Le Traite Anonyme du Manuscrit Hebreu 1037 de
> la Bibliotheque Nationale de Paris.*" HIGINIO ANGLES:
> "*La Musique Juive dans l'Espagne Medievale.*" HANOCH
> AVENARY: "The Cantorial Fantasia of the 18th and 19th
> Centuries." MOSHE BARASCH: "Traces of Jewish Musicians
> in the Writings of Lomazzo." BATHJA BAYER: "The Biblical
> *Nebel.*" JACQUES CHAILLEY: "*Nicomaque, Aristate et
> Terpandre Devant la Transformation de l'Heptacorde Grec
> en Octocorde.*" DALIA COHEN and RUTH KATZ: "Remarks Con-
> cerning the Use of the Melograph in Ethnomusicological
> Studies." EDITH GERSON-KIWI: "Vocal Folk-Polyphonies of
> the Western Orient in Jewish Tradition." AVIGDOR HERZOG
> and ANDRE HAJDU: "*A la Recherche du Tonus Peregrinus*

dans la Tradition Musicale Juive." DIKA NEWLIN: "Self-
Revelation and the Law; Arnold Schoenberg in His Religious Works." AMNON SHILOAH: "*Deux Textes Arabes In-
edits sur la Musique*." BENCE SZABOLCSI: "The 'Proclamation Style' in Hebrew Music." Brief English summaries
of following Hebrew text section: NEHEMIA ALLONY: "The
Term *Musiqah* in Mediaeval Jewish Literature." SHLOMO
HOFMAN: "The Reading of Marka's Poems by the Samaritans
on the Sabbath." Brief Hebrew summaries of non-Hebrew
section. Facsimile illustrations. Music examples for
articles provided in separately bound booklet, 48pp.
This issue was dedicated to Eric Werner "in appreciation
of his achievements in field of Jewish music studies."

Vol.2(1971); AMNON SHILOAH and BATHJA BAYER, eds.;
x,182pp.+48 Heb.p., illus., music. French, English and
Hebrew texts. Contents — Prefatory remarks in English
and French by editors. ISRAEL ADLER: "*Fragment Hebra-
ique d'un Traite Attribue a Marchetto de Padoue*."
HANOCH AVENARY: "The Concept of Mode in European Syna-
gogue Chant." DALIA COHEN: "The Meaning of the Modal
Framework in the Singing of Religious Hymns by Christian
Arabs in Israel." EDITH GERSON-KIWI: "The Music of
Kurdistan Jews; A Synopsis of Their Musical Styles."
ANDRE HAJDU: "*Le Niggun Meron*." AMNON SHILOAH:
"*Qalonimus ben Qalonimus: Ma'amar Be-mispar La-hokmat:
Chapitre iii, Paragraphe 6 (La Musique)*." JOSEPH SMITS
VAN WAESBERGHE: "The Treatise on Music Translated into
Hebrew by Juda ben Isaac (Paris B.N. Heb. 1037, 22v —
27v)." ERIC WERNER: "Musical Tradition and Its Trans-
mitters Between Synagogue and Church." Brief English
summary of following Hebrew section: NEHEMIA ALLONY:
"*Ne'ima/Nagma* and *Musiqa* in Mediaeval Hebrew Liter-
ature." Brief Hebrew summaries of non-Hebrew section.
Facsimile illustrations and musical examples.
754
YUVAL: Studies of the Jewish Music Research Centre.
(continued)
Vol.3(1974); ISRAEL ADLER and BATHJA BAYER, eds.; 292pp.
+52 Heb.p., illus., music. French, English and Hebrew
texts. Contents — HANOCH AVENARY: "The Hebrew Version of
Abu l'Salt's Treatise on Music." JUDITH COHEN: "Jubal in
the Middle Ages." EDITH GERSON-KIWI: "Robert Lachmann:
His Achievements and His Legacy." RUTH KATZ: "The Reliability of Oral Transmission; The Case of Samaritan
Music." YAACOV MAZOR, ANDRE HAJDU and BATHJA BAYER: "The
Hassidic Dance — *Niggun*; A Study Collection and Its
Classificatory Analysis." AMNON SHILOAH: "*En Kol — Com-
mentaire Hebraique de Sem Tov ibn Saprut sur le Canon
d'Avicenne*." Brief English summaries of following He-
brew section: NEHEMIA ALLONY: "Melody and Poetry in the
Kuzari." EZRA FLEISCHER: "The Influence of Choral Ele-
ments on the Formation and Development of the *Piyyut*
Genres." Brief Hebrew summaries of non-Hebrew section.
Facsimile illustrations and musical examples.

Vol.4(1982): ISRAEL ADLER, BATHJA BAYER and LEA SHALEM,
eds.; 266pp.+68 Heb.p., illus., music. English and He-
brew texts. Contents — HANOCH AVENARY: "Paradigms of
Arabic Modes in the Geniza Fragment Cambridge T.S. N.S.
90,4." BATHJA BAYER: "The titles of the Psalms; A Renewed Investigation of an Old Problem." PAUL FENTON: "A
Jewish Sufi on the Influence of Music." JEHOASH HIRSH-
BERG: "Heinrich Schalit and Paul Ben-Haim in Munich."
MOSHE IDEL: "Music and Prophetic *Kabbalah*." EDWIN
SEROUSSI: "Eduard Birnbaum; A Bibliography." URI SHARVIT
"The Musical Realization of Biblical Cantillation Symbols (*Te'amim*) in the Jewish Yemenite Tradition."
AMNON SHILOAH: "The Musical Passage in Ibn Ezra's 'Book
of the Garden'." MARK SLOBIN: "Notes on Bokharan Music
in Israel." ERIC WERNER: "Felix Mendelssohn — Gustave
Mahler; Two Borderline Cases of German-Jewish Assimilation." Brief English summaries of the following Hebrew
section: ISRAEL ADLER: "Collectanea Concerning Music in
the Hebrew Manuscript, London, British Library, Or.
10878." MOSHE IDEL: "The Magical and Theurgic Interpretation of Music in Jewish Sources from the Renaissance to Hassidism." Brief Hebrew summaries of non-Hebrew section. Facsimiles and musical illustrations.

6.
Instruction and Performance Resources on Jewish Music

A. Educational and Pedagogical Publications

755
ADLER, KARL and MACY NULMAN, PAUL STEINBERG, HUGO WEISGALL.
"Section B — Descriptions of Three Schools of Cantorial
Musical Training." In *The Cantorial Art.* (New York: J.M.C.
1966) pp. 71-88.
> Locations, entrance qualifications and special courses
> in Jewish music and cantorial studies at: Yeshiva Uni-
> versity (Orthodox), Jewish Theological Seminary of Amer-
> ica (Conservative) and Hebrew Union College (Reform).

756
ARIAN, PHILIP. "Structuring Music Program for the School."
Synagogue School Quarterly, vol.25. (New York: U.A.H.C.,
1967), pp.26-9.
> Pedagogical guidelines for Reform Sunday schools.

757
BINDER, ABRAHAM WOLF. *Biblical Chant.* New York: Philosophical Library, 1959; 125pp., music.
> Textbook for study of cantillation of Bible according to
> Ashkenazic East European-American usage. Introductory
> information on prescribed motival chanting of scriptural
> passages. Descriptions and musical interpretations of
> actual tropes, or cantillation signs, with a study pro-
> cedure. Benedictions for readings of different Biblical
> portions on various occasions: Sabbaths, Festivals, High
> Holy Days, weekdays. Chant patterns for *Torah* (Five
> Books of Moses), *Haftarah* (Prophets) and *Ketuvim*
> (Scrolls - Esther, Ruth, Ecclesiastes, Lamentations,
> Song of Songs). A.W. Binder (1895-1966) was an educator,
> music director, composer and organizational leader in
> Jewish music, who also taught Biblical chant to rabbini-
> cal and cantorial students at H.U.C.-J.I.R. in New York.

758
BRIN, RUTH F. *The Sabbath Catalogue.* New York: KTAV,
1978; 128 pp.
    Section 4: "Songs," pp. 75-82, devoted to usages of
    appropriate music materials for young children in early
    grades of religious schools.
759
COOPERSMITH, HARRY. "Jewish Music Education in the Hebrew
Schools of New York." *Jewish Education*, vol.19, no.2.
(New York: N.C.J.E., 1948), pp.23-7.
    Harry Coopersmith (1902-1975) trained, placed in employ-
    ment and guided many young music educators. He enlarged
    scope of music curriculum in all types of Jewish schools
    whether full-day, afternoon, or single-day Sunday. He
    tirelessly advocated the stabilization of Jewish music
    as fundamental part of Jewish studies in all schools.
    Article reflects his ideas and activities.
760
COOPERSMITH, HARRY. *Six Year Song Curriculum for Hebrew
Schools.* New York: J.E.C./B.J.E., 1949; 8pp.
    Pedagogical commentary and guidelines for listing of
    suitable music materials — liturgy and folksong — for
    gradings of afternoon Hebrew schools. Coopersmith (1902-
    1975) was a leading educator, teacher-trainer and col-
    lector-arranger of Jewish music.
761
COOPERSMITH, HARRY. *Teaching Aids in Jewish Music Education: Revised Edition.* New York: B.J.E., 1960; 25pp.
    Enlarged version of informal resource materials prepared
    in 1950. Guidelines for teaching in classroom, assembly
    and children's services. Techniques for development of
    choirs, large choruses, and coaching youth cantorial
    "leaders." Harry Coopersmith (1902-1975) was director of
    music department of J.E.C./B.J.E. from 1939 to 1968.
762
EISENBERG, AZRIEL. *Curriculum for the Small Jewish Reli-
gious School: In English-Speaking Communities.* New York:
United Synagogue of America, 1973; 214pp.
    Teaching guides for Conservative branch of Judaism. See
    section on "Group Activities with Music," pp. 180-98,
    which includes additional information on Jewish music,
    contributed by Irene Heskes.
763
EISENBERG, YEHUDA. *A Curriculum in Tefilah (Prayer) for
Yeshiva Day Schools.* New York: Cantorial Training Inst. of
Yeshiva Univ., 1976; 80 pp.
    Pedagogical guidebook for Orthodox Jewish traditional
    all-day schools. See section devoted to musical chanting
    of prayer texts, pp. 58-74. Additional music information
    given by cantors Macy Nulman and Sherwood Goffin.
764
EISENSTEIN, JUDITH KAPLAN. "A New Look at Music in Jewish
Education." *Pedagogical Reporter*, vol.22. (New York: A.A.
J.E., 1971), pp.7-8.
    Re-evaluation of pedagogical ideas by noted educator and
    collector-arranger of Jewish music, whose earliest work

in field commenced in 1929 as writer, advocating better
methods for teaching Jewish music to children.
765
EPHROS, GERSHON, comp. *Cantorial Curriculum Materials:*
Weekday Services. New York:H.U.C.-J.I.R./School of Sacred
Music, 1952; 40pp., music.
 Guides for liturgical music studies prepared by cantor,
 composer, compiler-collector and educator Gershon Ephros
 (1890-1978). Hebrew liturgy texts romanized.
766
FREED, ISADORE. *Harmonizing the Jewish Modes.* New York:
Sacred Music Press of H.U.C.-J.I.R., 1958; 69 pp., music.
 Textbook for training of composers, arrangers, organists
 and others working in Jewish music as accompanists or
 music directors. Introduction and special explanatory
 chapter provide details on Jewish liturgical modes and
 chant motifs. Balance of book offers guidance and suggestions for harmonization, modulation and musical style
 of presentation. Exercises are included for student use.
 Freed (1900-1960) was music director, organist, composer
 and educator, who taught this subject at School of
 Sacred Music of Hebrew Union College in New York City.
767
FRIEDMAN, DEBBIE. *Musical Curriculum for Hebrew.* New
York: Behrman House, 1982; 41 pp., music.
 Teaching guide, using music materials - songs and dance
 activities - to teach Hebrew language to children.
768
GLANTZ, LEIB and YEHOSHUA ZOHAR. *Rinat Ha-kodesh - Prayer*
Modes. Tel Aviv, Isr.: I.M.I., 1965; 119 pp., music.
 Text for training cantors in traditional prayer modes
 and motifs for leadership of services on weekdays, Sabbaths, Festivals and High Holy Days. Melody lines with
 Hebrew texts romanized. Cantor Leib Glantz (1898-1964)
 founded Jerusalem Inst. of Liturgical Music in 1961.
769
GOLDMAN, ALEX J. *A Handbook for the Jewish Family; Under-*
standing and Enjoying the Sabbath and Holidays. New York:
Bloch, 1958; xix, 420 pp., illus.
 Guide materials, including melody lines of religious
 hymns, holiday tunes and folksongs. Hebrew and Yiddish
 romanized. Music suitable for family-home celebrations.
770
HESKES, IRENE. "Music for Adult Education." *Adult Jewish*
Leadership, vol.2,nos.4/5.(New York:J.E.C.,1955), pp.7-8.
 Guidelines for use of Jewish music materials for adult
 educational and participatory activities. Note: Jewish
 Education Committee (J.E.C.) changed its title in 1960
 to Board of Jewish Education (B.J.E.).
771
HESKES, IRENE. "Suggestions for a Jewish Music Festival."
Jewish Community Center Programming Aids, vol.30, no.4.
(New York:J.W.B., 1969), pp.16-7.
 Ideas for Jewish music festival program planning of con-
 certs and other events at religious schools, communal
 centers, synagogues and for organizations.

772
HESKES, IRENE. "Toward a Different Approach to Music in the One-Day-a-Week School." *The Jewish Teacher*, vol.22, no.1. (New York: U.A.H.C., 1953), pp.12-4.
    Guidelines presented for use of Jewish music materials in religious school education at Reform congregations.
773
HESKES, IRENE. "Unit Outline Covering Topic of Hassidic Music." *The Jewish Teacher*, vol.22, no.3. (New York: U.A.H.C., 1954), pp.10-2.
    Curriculum of Jewish music materials highlighting a particular topical area.
774
IDELSOHN, ABRAHAM ZEBI. *Manual of Musical Illustrations for Hebrew Union College Lectures on Jewish Music and Jewish Liturgy.* Cincinnati: H.U.C. Press, 1926; 88 pp., music.
    With annotations, 127 music examples which demonstrate Idelsohn's class lectures on such topical areas as: all types of biblical chants; special prayer modes and their motival variants; liturgical hymnology for Sabbaths, festivals and High Holydays; religious folksongs of different origins and styles. Traditions of Ashkenazic, Sephardic and Yemenite liturgies included. Comparative melodic table. Attention to motifs of *Hatikvah* and of *Yigdal*, with parallel melodic examples in other cultures. A. Z. Idelsohn (1882-1938) taught liturgy and liturgical music at Hebrew Union College in Cincinnati 1924-1932, while serving as cataloguer-curator for the Birnbaum Collection of Jewish Liturgical Music housed at the college library.
775
JOSPE, ERWIN. "Towards a Music Program in the Jewish Religious School." *The Jewish Teacher*, vol.10, no.2. (Cincinnati:U.A.H.C., 1942), pp.19-26.
    Ideas for integration of Jewish music into regular studies of Reform congregational schools.
776
KATCHKO, ADOLPH, comp. *Cantorial Curriculum Materials: Sabbath Services.* New York:H.U.C.-J.I.R./School of Sacred Music, 1951; 53pp., music.
    Guides for liturgical music studies prepared by cantor, music collector and educator Adolph Katchko (1887-1958). Hebrew liturgy texts romanized.
777
NEUMANN, RICHARD. *Jewish Music Guide.* New York:B.J.E., 1980; 31pp.
    Guide for teachers and advanced students. Resource information included.
778
NEUMANN, RICHARD. *Music for the Jewish School.* New York: B.J.E., 1981; 27pp.
    For early grade levels, pedagogical roster of suitable liturgical and folksong materials. With teaching guide.
779
NEUMANN, RICHARD. *The Roots of Biblical Chant.* New York: B.J.E., 1980; 14pp., music.

For students and music educators, origins of tropal cantillation signs for *Torah* (Five Books of Moses) and
Haftarah (Prophets). Charts and other information.

780
NEUMANN, RICHARD. *Shiron Lahumash - Bible in Song.* New
York: B.J.E., 1981; 28pp., music.
Pedagogical aid for chanting of Bible passages according
to tropal cantillation signs. For training *Bar Mitzvah*
and *Bas Mitzvah* students.

781
NEUMANN, RICHARD. *Song Curriculum and Training Guide: Music for the Jewish School.* New York: B.J.E., 1975; 27pp.
Based upon earlier pedagogical aids prepared by Harry
Coopersmith, updated guide for music in 3rd grade level
and above. Neumann succeeded Coopersmith as music super-
visor at that educational agency.

782
ORENSTEIN, WALTER. *The Cantor's Manual of Halakhah (Traditions).* New York: Cantorial Council of Yeshiva Univ.,
1965; 167 pp.
Background information and ritual patterns of cantorial
office. By history and custom, prescribed religious duties for calendar year of services and congregational
life-cycle events. Study of the professional role of the
Hazzan (cantor) as traditional *Sheliah Tsibbur* (the
Leader in Prayer). Scholarly work.

783
PERLZWEIG, ABRAHAM, comp. *A Manual of Neginoth (the Cantillations).* London,Eng.:P.Valentine, 1912; 60pp., music.
Handbook arranged for synagogue, school and home for instruction of traditional Ashkenazic cantillations of the
Pentateuch (*Torah*), Prophets (*Haftarah*) and Scrolls
of Esther and Lamentations, as well as benedictions for
all recitations. Prepared under sponsorship of London
Association of Precentors. Hebrew texts romanized.

784
PESSIN, DEBORAH and TEMIMA GEZARI. *Jewish Kindergarten: A
Manual for Teachers.* New York: U.A.H.C., 1944; ix,329pp.,
illus., music.
Throughout text, inclusion of suggestions and guidelines
for use of Jewish music materials, especially for cele-
brations of special events and for teaching of Jewish
Festivals, High Holy Days and Sabbath rituals.

785
POLITZER, DAVID. *A Music Guide for the Jewish Schools.*
Chicago:B.J.E., 1980; 33pp.
Curriculum of music for all calendar observances, as
arranged by grade levels and topics.

786
PORTNOY, JOSEPH L. *Music Curriculum for Jewish Religious
Schools.* New York: U.A.H.C., 1967; iv,76pp.
With introductory background, guidelines and suggested
materials for use by educators in Reform congregational
religious schools. Information classified according to
graded levels of primary, intermediate and advanced.
Recommendations for activities. Roster of resources.

787
RESNICK, HYMAN. *Music Guide for Jewish Schools.* Chicago:
B.J.E., 1965; 36pp.
> Describes range of music for use in Jewish religious
> schools and offers listings of suitable liturgical and
> secular selections. Recommendations for activities and
> for listening sessions with recordings.

788
ROSENBAUM, SAMUEL. *Guide to Haftarah Chanting.* New York:
KTAV, 1973; v, 154 pp., music.
> Textbook for teaching of proper cantillation (ritual
> chants) according to tropal signs, melodic motifs and
> music styles, for the *Haftarah* (Prophets) portion of
> the Bible. Music examples, study guides and structured
> lessons. Pedagogical aid in preparation of students for
> *Bar Mitzvah* and *Bas Mitzvah* recitations.

789
ROSENBAUM, SAMUEL. *Guide to Torah Reading: A Manual for
the Torah Reader.* New York KTAV and United Syn. of A.,
1982; 145 pp., music.
> Textbook for learning of proper interpretation of all
> tropal signs and musical motifs for cantillation (ritual
> chant) of the *Torah* (Five Books of Moses) portion of
> the Bible. Structured as a lesson book, with exercises.
> Musical illustrations for study texts.

790
ROSENBAUM, SAMUEL. *Hazzan's Manual.* New York: C.A.A./
Transcontinental/U.A.H.C., 1971; 208pp., music.
> Guide and textbook resource for cantorial leadership in
> performance of religious services. Includes materials on
> prayer modes and motifs, cantillation chants, improvi-
> sations and hymnology. Covers broad range of musical
> knowledge necessary for qualified *Hazzan* (Cantor).

791
SPIRO, PINCHAS. *Haftarah Chanting: A Course for Bar and
Bas Mitzvah.* New York B.J.E./Tara, 1976; 164pp., music.
> Handbook for learning cantillation (traditional chant
> according to tropal signs, musical motifs and styles),
> for training of candidates for *Bar Mitzvah* and *Bas
> Mitzvah*. Student textbook with charts and musical il-
> lustrations. Originally published informally by author
> (cantor and educator) in 1964.

792
STERN, ABRAHAM. *Setting the Scene for a Synagogue and Com-
munity Music Program.* New York: Cantorial Training Inst. of
Yeshiva Univ., 1970; 25 pp.
> Guide for traditional music education of youth and adult
> groups in Orthodox congregations. Includes background,
> suggested approaches, ideas for activities and recommen-
> dations for choosing and training of music leaders.

793
WERNER, ERIC. *In the Choir Loft: A Manual for Organists
and Choir Directors in American Synagogues.* New York: U.A.
H.C., 1957; vi,55pp., music.
> Seven instructive essays giving historical introduction
> to Jewish music, American liturgical developments, de-

scriptions of styles and forms, qualities and structures
for renditions of Jewish liturgical music at Reform
services. Intended for use by general musicians seeking
to enter into the field of Jewish musical performance
as organists, singers, choral leaders, music arrangers,
composers or accompanists. Texts are based upon courses
given at H.U.C.-J.I.R. by scholar/educator Eric Werner.

794
ZEITLIN, SHNEUR ZALMAN and HAIM BAR-DAYAN. *Megillah of*
Esther and Its Cantillation. Jerusalem, Isr.: Kiryath
Sepher, 1974; 192 pp., music.
> Guidebook for the proper cantillation (ritual chant) of
> the *Megillah* (Sacred Scroll) of the Book of Esther,
> which is chanted during the synagogue services for the
> celebration of the Jewish holiday of *Purim*. Extensive
> musical examples, with analysis. Intended as textbook
> for learning of this special material – structure, mode
> and motifs.

B. Program Aids and Guide Manuals

795
BINDER, ABRAHAM WOLF. *Jewish Music Movement in America:*
An Informal Lecture – Enlarged Edition. New York: J.M.C.,
1975; 36 pp. (orig. ed. – New York: J.M.C., 1975; 22 pp.)
> Lecture, with suggestions of suitable music examples for
> text material, prepared in 1963 by A. W. Binder (1895-
> 1966) composer, music director, educator and communal
> leader. Later edition has second introduction and an
> addenda of updated materials contributed by Irene Hes-
> kes. Intended as program aid for informal presentations.

796
EISENSTEIN, JUDITH KAPLAN. *Music for Jewish Groups.* New
York: J.W.B., 1942; 44 pp.
> Program aid for use by group leaders of organizations
> and at community centers. Guidelines for group-singing
> activities, suggestions for music projects, techniques
> of leadership, uses of recorded music, ideas for pro-
> gramming for Jewish holidays and special events.

797
EISENSTEIN, JUDITH KAPLAN. *The Scope of Jewish Music.* New
York: J.M.C., 1948; 15 pp., music.
> Lecture text on backgrounds of Jewish music, with recom-
> mendations for musical illustrations. Intended for pre-
> sentation to informal groups. Includes materials taken
> from various sources of liturgical music.

798
EISENSTEIN, JUDITH KAPLAN and IRENE HESKES. *Israeli Music:*
Program Aid. New York: J.M.C., 1978; 78 pp.
> Lecture text with indications for music illustrations –
> "Song of Exile and Return," by Judith K. Eisenstein; and
> section of annotated resources for use in programs on

Israeli music, prepared by Irene Heskes. Intended for general informal presentations with live or recorded music, and text may be accommodated to needs.
799

HESKES, IRENE. *Highlighting Jerusalem With Music - Guide-lines and Sources.* New York: J.M.C., 1980; 8pp., music.
Compilation of resource materials - program ideas, anno-tated lists of recordings and performance scores, Yid-dish, Hebrew and Ladino song texts. Includes music lines for "Jerusalem of Gold." Hebrew and Yiddish romanized.
800

HESKES, IRENE. *Jewish Music Programs: Concerts, Liturgical Services and Multi-Arts Events: and, How to Commission New Works: Guidelines, Procedures and Examples.* New York: J.M.C., 1978; 142 pp.
Sampling of 99 varied programs presented during music festivals 1974-1977 for communal groups and synagogues throughout the country. Section on development of pro-jects for commissioning of new works of Jewish interest. Brief articles, including: "My Experiences in Jewish Music," pp. 120-24 by Mario Castelnuovo-Tedesco (1895-1968), and other program aid materials.
801

HESKES, IRENE. *Jewish Music Programs: Concerts, Liturgical Services and Special Events.* New York: J.M.C., 1973; 86 pp.
Sampling of 103 varied programs for celebrations of Jew-ish music festivals 1970-1973, as presented by communal groups and synagogues throughout the country. Various special themes highlighted.
802

HESKES, IRENE. *Music of the Sephardic and Oriental Jews: Program Resources.* New York: J.M.C., 1972; 17 pp.
Prepared to promote programming with this special music, utilizing informal group-music and recordings.
803

HESKES, IRENE. Music Program Aids: A Bicentennial Arts Re-source. New York: J.M.C., 1975; 28 pp.
Guidelines for Jewish music programming in celebration of the American Bicentennial year 1976.
804

HESKES, IRENE. *Resource: Cultural Arts Agencies and Varied Funding Data.* New York: J.M.C., 1973; 12 pp.
Compilation of information related to sources of funds for use in development of Jewish music projects.
805

JAFFA, LEAH and Committee. *A Jewish Composer by Choice - Isadore Freed: His Life and Work.* New York: J.M.C., 1961; 95 pp., illus.
Prepared to highlight programming in memory of composer, organist, music director and educator Isadore Freed (1900-1960). Program aid includes biographical essay, listing of works and examples of Freed's own skillful development of many fine Jewish music programs during his career as synagogue music leader. Photographs.

806
JAFFA, LEAH and Committee. *The Music of Abraham Ellstein
(1907-1963) and Max Helfman (1901-1963).* New York: J.M.C.,
1964; 14 pp., illus.
  Tribute publication for two composers of Jewish liturgical music. Biographical information, listings of works
  and programming suggestions.

807
LANDAU, ANNELIESE. *The Contributions of Jewish Composers
to the Music of the Modern World.* enl. rev. ed. New York:
N.F.T.S.,1966;94pp.(orig.ed. Cincinnati:N.F.T.S.,1946;84pp.)
  Roster of 72 musicians of 19th and 20th century Europe,
  America and Israel considered in six topical sections
  for amateur group study sessions: Romanticism, Paris
  Grand Opera; Modern European School; Russia; Israel; and
  America. Guidelines for discussion of each topic, and
  lists of recommended readings and recordings. Materials
  intended for programs of sisterhoods and other adult
  groups, and shaped for presentation by their leaders.

808
MIRON, ISSACHAR. *A Profile of Israeli Music Today.* New
York: J.M.C., 1964; 15 pp., illus.
  Lecture treating wide range of musical creativity and
  activity in the State of Israel (as of 1963/64). Sug-
  gestions for musical programs.

809
MLOTEK, JOSEPH. *Mordecai Gebirtig – Troubadour of Our People.* New York: W.C.O., 1970; 20 pp., music.
  Narration as resource for program performances of ten
  particular songs by Mordecai Gebirtig (1871-c.1942), the
  much beloved folk musician (*Badkhen*) and composer of
  Yiddish songs – melodies and texts. His songs have so
  grown in popularity as to be considered as folksongs of
  the people. Melody lines with Yiddish texts romanized.
  Lecture places Gebirtig (who was murdered in the Cracow
  Ghetto by the nazis) and his musical legacy within context of pre-World War II East European Jewish culture.

810
MLOTEK, JOSEPH and URIEL WEINREICH. *Love in Yiddish Folklore: Program for Groups.* New York:W.C.O.,1968;23pp.,music.
  Narrative to be read along with performances of ten particular Yiddish folksongs. Text places music in cultural
  and social contexts. Melody lines. Yiddish romanized.

811
PERLA, SHOSHANA with SAM E. BLOCH and ABRAHAM P. GANNES.
Israel Independence Day Program Materials. New York: Jewish
Agency – American Section, 1970; 350 pp., music.
  See music section, pp. 293-335, for specific music pro-
  gram planning aids, and melody lines for 44 folksongs.
  Hebrew texts romanized.

812
RUBIN, RUTH. *Warsaw Ghetto Memorial Program.* New York:
W.C.O., 1967; 23 pp., music.
  Simple narration with music examples, arranged for use
  by amateur groups for Holocaust memorial programs. Me-
  lody lines, with Yiddish romanized and English trans-

lations, for seven songs from Ghettos and Concentration
Camps. Lecture sets background for this particular
musical creativity, now considered as precious legacy.
    813
RUBIN, RUTH. *The Yiddish Folksong: An Illustrated Lecture.*
New York: J.M.C., 1974; 34 pp., music.
    Lecture for presentation with twelve particulasr Yiddish
    folksongs. Melody lines, with Yiddish lyrics romanized.
    Additional roster of music scores and recordings for use
    with lecture narration. Survey of 19th and 20th century
    cultural and social milieu of East European Jews.
    814
RUBIN, RUTH. *Yiddish Folksongs of Social Significance: A*
*Program for Groups.*New York: W.C.O., 1968; 24 pp., music.
    Narrative lecture with music examples for group-singing
    activities. Melody lines and Yiddish texts romanized for
    14 folksongs. Background and perspectives on materials.
    815
WOHLBERG, MAX. *The Music of the Synagogue.* New York: J.M.
C., 1947; 20 pp., music.
    Lecture text by cantor-educator treating broad scope of
    synagogue music from post-biblical era to 20th century.
    Musical illustrations given for each topical area: can-
    tillation or biblical chant, liturgical modes and motifs
    of sacred melodies and hymnology. Hebrew romanized. In-
    tended for educational presentation and group activity.

C. Publishers of Jewish Music: Catalogues

    816
ASHBOURNE PUBLICATIONS; Elkins Park, Penn. *Catalogue.*
Charles Davidson, ed., 1983; folder.
    Annotated roster of Jewish liturgical and secular music
    selections — full services, choral works and children's
    cantatas. Flyers also for various individual works.
    817
BOARD OF JEWISH EDUCATION OF GREATER CHICAGO, ILL. *Music*
Resource Publications. David Politzer, ed., 1980; 12pp.
    Annotated roster of materials — liturgical chant aids,
    song books, hymnals and recordings.
    818
BOARD OF JEWISH EDUCATION OF GREATER NEW YORK CITY, N.Y.
Music Notes Catalogue. Richard Neumann, ed., 1980;4pp.; and
Music Materials for Children and Adults. Richard Neumann,
ed., 1981; 16pp., illus.
    Annotated rosters of music education resources — song
    books and hymnals, choral arrangements, recordings.
    819
HAIFA MUSIC MUSEUM and AMLI LIBRARY; Haifa, Israel. *Publi-*
cations Catalogue. Moshe Gorali, ed., 1978; 2pp.
    Annotated listing of several Jewish music publications
    and of brochures prepared and issued in connection with

traveling exhibitions of music, musical instruments and archaeological music materials from Israel.
820

ISRAEL DANCE INSTITUTE (A.Z.Y.F.); New York,N.Y. *Resource Sheet:Publications and Activities.* 1980; 2pp.
    Annotations for 8 dance books, with other information.
821

ISRAEL HISTADRUTH: MERKAZ L'TARBUTH — DEPT. OF CULTURE AND EDUCATION; Tel Aviv, Israel. *Catalogue of Music Publications.* Shlomo Kaplan, ed., 1974; 48pp.; and *Supplement.* Shlomo Kaplan, ed. (posthumous publication), 1980; 17pp.
    Annotated rosters of song collections, choral books, performance scores and music textbooks. With information on Israeli composers. Prepared by educator and choral director Shlomo Kaplan (1909-1979).
822

ISRAEL INSTITUTE FOR SACRED MUSIC — MINISTRY FOR RELIGIOUS AFFAIRS; Jerusalem, Israel. *I.I.S.M. Catalogue.* 1978; 6pp.
    Roster of publications — traditional liturgical music collections, educational materials for cantorial training, and music aids for cantors and choir leaders.
823

ISRAEL MUSIC INSTITUTE; Tel Aviv, Israel. *I.M.I. 20th Anniversary Catalogue: 1961-1981.* William Elias and Juana Guinzberg eds., 1981; 46pp.; and *I.M.I. Eliezer Peri Educational Series: Instrumental Music.* William Elias and Esther Bright, eds., 1982; 38pp.
    First catalogue provides information on 20 years of publication activities of I.M.I., and annotated roster of music scores, literature and recordings. Second catalogue presents rosters of graded music scores (easy, medium and advanced), with annotations and information on various composers. Note: I.M.I. also has prepared individual "catalogue" listings for Israeli composers, with descriptions of their works and biographical data.
824

ISRAEL MUSIC PUBLICATIONS; Jerusalem, Israel. *I.M.P. Catalogue.* Peter Gradenwitz and Robert Kleiman, eds., 1983; 28pp.
    With annotated index of composers, rosters of scores for all types of instrumentation, solo and choral music, and some literature items. I.M.P. was established in 1949 by musicologist Peter Gradenwitz.
825

JEWISH MUSIC RESEARCH CENTRE AT HEBREW UNIVERSITY; Jerusalem, Israel. *J.M.R.C. Publications Catalogue.* Israel Adler ed., 1975; 8pp.
    Annotated listings of literature prepared for three series: *YUVAL — Studies of J.M.R.C.; YUVAL — Monographs;* and, *Inventory of Jewish Music.*
826

LEAGUE OF COMPOSERS IN ISRAEL; Tel Aviv, Israel. *Israel Music Weeks: Catalogue Series (1965-1970).* Menahem Avidom, ed. — 1965/118pp.; 1966/69pp.; 1967/48pp.; 1968/96pp.; 1969/29pp.; 1970/16pp.; and, *Israel Musicians Catalogue.* Ami Maayani and Benjamin Bar-Am, eds., 1972; 37pp.

Listings of Israeli composers, with annotated rosters of
their works and reports on music events and educational
activities in Israel. Note: L.C.I. has current updated
listings for particular musicians and music groups.
827

THEODORE PRESSER PUBLISHERS; Bryn Mawr, Pa. *Selection of*
Music for Use in Jewish Services and Concerts. 1978;folder.
Annotated listing of vocal and instrumental scores.
828

SALABERT EDITIONS; Paris, Fr./New York, N.Y. *Collection of*
Jewish Music: Mizmor. 1978; sheet.
Listing of solo/choral works and instrumental music.
829

SUBAR MUSIC PUBLISHERS; Ramat Hasharon, Israel. *Catalogue.*
1980; 4pp.
Listings of song book collections of popular Israeli
songs and brochures of various entertainers.
830

TARA PUBLICATIONS; Cedarhurst, N.Y. *Music and Recording*
Catalogue. Velvel Pasternak, ed., 1982/83; 47pp., illus.
Annotated and descriptive listings of all types of Jewish music materials: song books, hymnals, music score
collections, liturgical compilations, vocal sheets,
literature and recordings (cassettes and disc albums).
831

TRANSCONTINENTAL MUSIC PUBLICATIONS — UNION OF AMERICAN
HEBREW CONGREGATIONS; New York, N.Y. *Master Catalogue.*
Judith Tischler, ed., 1982; v,61pp.
Comprehensive roster by leading publisher and distribu-
tor of Jewish music materials. Contents: Part 1 — Alphabetical roster of composers and their works. Part 2 —
Annotated music listings for following: synagogue services of Sabbath, High Holy Days, Three Festivals,
Hanukkah, Purim, and other liturgical occasions; Jewish "life cycle" music (birth, marriage and death);
secular vocal and instrumental works of Jewish inspiration; cantatas and other musico-dramatic selections.
Part 3 — Music catalogue listings of other publishers
for which T.M.P. serves as representative agency: The
Gershon Ephros Cantorial Foundation; New Horizons Publications; Hatikvah Publications; Mills Music/Jewish
Catalogue; Sacred Music Press of H.U.C.-J.I.R.; Cantor's
Assembly of America; and, miscellaneous out-of-print
reproductions. T.M.P. was founded in 1938 by musician
and editor Josef Freudenthal (1903-1964).
832

UNITED SYNAGOGUE OF AMERICA; New York, N. Y. *Catalogue of*
Publications. 1980; 30pp., illus.
Among large roster of educational materials, includes
annotated listing of some suitable music, pp.12-13.
833

WORKMEN'S CIRCLE ORGANIZATION; New York, N.Y. *The Yiddish*
Plus Catalogue. Joseph Mlotek, ed., 1983; 22pp.
Annotated roster of educational materials for children
and adults. Includes Jewish music — song books, records
and literature — on pp.4-12.

834
ZAMIR CHORALE; New York, N.Y./Tel Aviv, Israel. *Repertoire Catalogue.* Stanley Sperber and Mati Lazar, eds., 1978; 6pp.
   Annotated listing of Jewish choral arrangements.

7.
Jewish Music Collections

A. Anthologies: Liturgical and Secular

835

ABINUM, ELIEZER and JOSEPH PAPO, comps. and eds. *Liturgie Sephardie.* London,Eng.:World Sephardi Federation, 1959; xiv,113pp., music.

>   Collection of 102 melody lines for liturgical chants of Oriental (Near Eastern) and Mediterranean *Sephardim* (Spaniolic Jews). Biblical cantillations, prayer chants and various hymn-tunes for Sabbath, Three Festivals — *Sukkot* (Tabernacles), Passover and *Shavuot* (Pentecost) — as well as for *Selichot* (Penitential Days), *Rosh Hashanah* (New Year) and *Yom Kippur* (Day of Atonement). Introduction (in French only) by Ovadiah Camhy. Music transcriptions by Franz Reizenstein. Hebrew liturgical texts romanized. Some Ladino (Judaeo-Spanish) texts. Note different chant melody for *Kol Nidre* (as well as for entire opening liturgy of *Yom Kippur* Eve given here for Sephardic traditions) in contrast to more generally known liturgical music of Ashkenazic Jews for that holy service.

836

ADAQUI, YEHIEL and URI SHARVIT, comps. and eds. *A Treasury of Jewish-Yemenite Chants.* Jerusalem, Isr.:Institute for Sacred Music/Hekhal Shlomo, 1982; 237pp., illus., music.

>   Range of over 200 music line examples, with historical background and commentary concerning Yemenite-Oriental Jewish liturgical music and ritual customs. Music here reflects various differences between Yemenite liturgical melodies and chant motifs, and liturgical music of other Judaic traditions. Music for entire calendar year of religious observances — Sabbath, High Holy Days, Festivals and other special days — organized into three sections:

liturgical chants (male); men's religious folksongs; and
women's songs. Yehiel Adaqui (d.1980) was authority on
on Yemenite music and compiled extensive collection of
folk materials. Scholar Uri Sharvit has annotated and
edited this publication. Texts mostly in Hebrew, with
some English translation. Facsimiles and photographs.
    837
ADLER, ISRAEL, ed. *Ceremonie Musicale Pour Inauguration de
la Synagogue a Sienne, en 1786: Volunio Gallichi and Fran-
cesco Drei, comps.* Tel Aviv,Isr.:I.M.I.,1965; 98pp.,,music.
    Special Italo-Jewish traditional liturgical music for
    services of Northern Italian Ashkenazic Jews in Siena
    c.18th cent. Cantorial solos, SATB choir parts, option-
    al accompaniment on strings and continuo. Edition has
    Hebrew and French texts. Hebrew liturgy romanized.
    838
ADLER, ISRAEL, comp. and ed. *Three Synagogue Chants of the
12th Century (Obadiah, the Proselyte).* Tel Aviv, Isr.: I.M.
P., 1969; 35pp., music.
    Melody lines, in original facsimiles and musical tran-
    scriptiion for three significant liturgical fragments:
    Mi Al Har Horev (Eulogy of Moses); *Baruch Ha-gever*;
    and *Wa-eda Ma* — attributed to Obadiah (c.1070-c.1141).
    Notation and arrangement by Andre Hajdu. Prefatory text
    by Israel Adler presented in French, German and English.
    Hebrew liturgy text romanized.
    839
**AGUILAR, EMANUEL ABRAHAM and DAVID AARON DE SOLA, comps.
and eds.** *The Ancient Melodies of the Liturgy of the Spanish
and Portuguese Jews.* London, Eng.: Wessel, 1857; ii,23pp.+
iv,62pp., illus., music.
    Melody lines of 71 liturgical selections for solo voice
    with some (male) choir parts, for traditional services
    of English Sephardic congregations, notably Bevis Marks
    Temple in London. Music rendered, *a cappella*, for en-
    tire calendar year of Sabbath, High Holy Days, Festivals
    and other special days. Prefatory essay by David Aaron
    de Sola (1796-1860) on historical background of poetic
    hymnology and Sephardic liturgical traditions — texts
    and music. Musical arrangements prepared for publication
    by Emanuel Abraham Aguilar (1824-1904). Hebrew liturgy
    texts romanized. Earliest edition of this anthology.
    840
ALGAZI, LEON, comp. and ed. *Chants Sephardis.* London,
Eng.:World Sephardi Federation, 1958; xvi,63pp., music.
    Collection of 81 selections in two parts: 1. Traditional
    Liturgical Chants of Oriental Sephardic Groups — 44
    melody lines for Sabbath, High Holy Days and Festivals;
    2. Ladino (Spaniolic Jewish) Folksongs in Judaeo-Spanish
    Style — 37 melody lines, including different versions of
    secular songs from Mediterranean areas. Introductory
    essays, in French text only, by noted Sephardic musician
    Leon Algazi (1890-1971) and by Ovadiah Camhy, director
    of the World Sephardi Federation. Algazi provides back-
    ground on collection. Hebrew liturgy texts romanized.

841
ALTER, ISRAEL, comp. and ed. *Cantorial Recitatives for
Hallel (Praise), Tal (Dew) and Geshem (Rain).* New York:
H.U.C.-J.I.R./S.M.P., 1962; 27pp., music.
    Collection of 14 traditional Hazzanic chant motifs —
    melody lines only. Hebrew liturgical texts romanized.
842
ALVAR, MANUEL LOPEZ, comp. and ed. *Cantos de Boda Judaeo-
Espagnoles.* (*Publicaciones des Estudios Sefardies*, Series
2,no.1)Madrid,Sp.:Inst. Arias Montano,1971;xxv,400pp.,music.
    Study of large collection of folklore — poetic litera-
    ture — in Ladino (Judaeo-Spanish) vernacular tongue of
    Sephardic Jews of Mediterranean and North African areas.
    Special attention to poetry set into ballad folksongs —
    with consideration of forms and styles, contents, modes
    of transmission, as well as factors of linguistics and
    cultural influences. See musical transcription of melody
    lines for 28 Sephardic folksongs, pp.345-69. Music no-
    tation by Maria Rubisto. Spanish and Ladino texts only.
843
AVENARY, HANOCH, comp. and ed. *Hebrew Hymn Tunes; The Rise
and Development of a Musical Tradition.* Tel Aviv, Isr.: I.
M.I., 1971; 43pp., music.
    Collection of 15 liturgical melody lines of European and
    Oriental origins, with their variants, presented in a
    literary and historical setting. Attention to musical
    styles and poetic forms. Prayer texts of 7th to 16th
    centuries; melodies from 18th and 19th centuries. Back-
    ground information in Hebrew and English texts. Hebrew
    liturgical texts romanized. Facsimiles.
844
AVENARY, HANOCH, comp. and ed. *Il Primo Libro Delle Can-
zonette a Tre Voci: Di Salomone Rossi (Venezia 1589).* Tel
Aviv,Isr.:I.M.I., 1975; 50pp., illus., music.
    Edition prepared by scholar Hanoch Avenary of complete
    set of canzonettas based on original Rossi edition, as
    preserved in Vienna at Austrian National Library. Fac-
    similes of original edition reproduced alongside of the
    modern musical transcription. With commentary and other
    critical details given in English and Hebrew text. Some
    Italian text material. Music of 19 songs for 3 voices,
    a cappella. Hebrew texts romanized. Source notes.
845
AVERY, LAWRENCE, comp. and ed. *Selected Recitatives by
Cantor David Roitman (1884-1943).* New York:H.U.C.-J.I.R./
S.M.P., 1961; 20pp., music.
    Melody lines for six liturgical selections by outstand-
    ing figure in cantorial art. Hebrew texts romanized.
846
BAER, ABRAHAM, comp. and ed. *Ba'al Tefillah, oder Der
Praktische Vorbeter.* repr.ed. New York:H.U.C.-J.I.R./S.M.P.
1953; xl,358pp., music. (4th ed. Nuernberg,1930; 3rd ed.
Frankfurt a.M.,1901; 2nd.ed. Gothenburg, 1883; orig.ed.
Leipzig/Gothenburg, 1871/1877.)
    Reprint edition based upon Gothenburg, 1883 edition.
    Comprehensive anthological source book of traditional

cantorial music for practice of prayer leadership, according to Ashkenazic (German, Polish, East European)
and Sephardic (Spanish, Portuguese) rituals. Abraham
Baer (1834-1894) was Chief Cantor of leading congregation in Gothenburg, Sweden, from 1857 to his death. He
prepared this anthology, incorporating liturgical collections of 18th and 19th century cantorial music, and
shaped a thesaurus of musical settings for every prayer
in the Jewish calendar year of devotions. Baer's compilation early on became important and popular cantorial
resource, reaching a 4th edition in Europe. American
edition was first volume issued in reprint series of liturgical music reference works by School of Sacred Music of H.U.C.-J.I.R. Contents: Four sections offering
approximately 1500 melody lines — in variants for different traditions — for cantorial solo with (male) choir
responses. Part 1 — services of weekdays, hymns, Scroll
of Esther, Lamentations, *Hallel* (praises), new month
(*Rosh Hodesh*), *Hanukkah, Purim, Tisha B'av, Selichot*
(penitential prayers), circumcisions, weddings, funerals
and Grace blessings for meals. Part 2 — Sabbaths: full
roster of liturgy from onset (*Kabbalat Shabbat*) to
conclusion (*Havdalah*). Part 3 — Festivals: *Sukkot,
Simhat Torah* (Tabernacles and celebration of Bible);
Pesach, Seder (Passover and festive meal); *Shevuot*
(Weeks — Pentecost). Part 4 — High Holy Days: *Rosh Hashanah* (New Year) and *Yom Kippur* (Day of Atonement).
Introductory essay, annotations and index prepared by
Abraham Baer, in German text. Brief prefatory remarks in
English for reprint edition. Hebrew liturgy romanized.
847
**BENHAROCHE-BARALIA, M.J. and MOISE ALVAREZ-PEREYRE, comps.
and eds.** *Chants Hebraiques Traditionnels en Usage dans la
Communaute Sephardie de Bayonne.* Biarritz,Fr.:Zadoc Kahn,
1961; xliv,192pp., illus., music.
Compilation of 258 liturgical selections for cantorial
solo and choir/congregational responses, according to
Minhag (tradition) of Sephardic synagogues in Southern
France — Bayonne, Bordeaux, Biarritz, Pyrenees area.
Materials for Sabbath, High Holy Days, Festivals and
other services for calendar year. Published as memorial
dedication for Jewish martyrs of Holocaust Era and for
notable liturgists and rabbinical figures who perished.
Introductory information on history of Sephardic synagogue music in France presented by compilers, Jewish
liturgical musicians. Prefatory pieces by Chief Rabbi
Jacob Kaplan, by communal leader M.A. Salzedo, and by
noted composer-arranger Leon Algazi (1890-1971). French
texts. Index of prayers. Hebrew liturgy romanized.
848
**BEREGOVSKII, MOISEI IACOVLEVICH and ITZIK FEFFER, comps.
and eds.** *Yidisher Folkslider. (Yiddish Folksongs).* Moscow/
Kiev,U.S.S.R.:Meluche/Ukrainishe Natsion, 1938; 531pp.,music
Compilation by two Soviet Yiddishists — folklorist and
scholar Moisei Beregovskii (1894-1941?) and journalist/
poet Itzik Feffer (1900-1951) — of Yiddish folksongs of

Soviet Jewry. Collection of 295 melodies, arranged according to topical categories: work and struggle; army
recruits and prisoners; love ballads; weddings and celebrations; family life; lullabies; children's songs;
humor, including Hassidic satires; religious topics;
Soviet life; dance tunes. Some annotations with Yiddish
song texts. Words under melody lines romanized.
849

**BEREGOVSKII, MOISEI IACOVLEVICH and MEIR I. VINER, comps.
and eds.** *Yidisher Musik-Folklor. (Yiddish Folk Music).*
Moscow,U.S.S.R.:Meluxiser Musik, 1934; 230pp., music.
Compilation prepared under sponsorship of Institute for
Jewish People's Culture of Ukrainian Education Academy/
Ethnographic Section - Cabinet for Music Folklore, by
Soviet Yiddishist and ethnic scholar Moisei Beregovskii
(1894-1941?) with assistance of Jewish musician Meir
Viner ([?]). Melodies of 140 Yiddish popular folksongs,
with some some prefatory remarks in Yiddish and Russian.
Materials reflect influences of Soviet life in various
topics and tunes. Yiddish for music lines romanized.
Note: A second volume issued in 1937 (28pp.) presents
instrumental arrangements of some of these folksongs.
850

BERNSTEIN, ABRAHAM MOSES, comp. and ed. *Musikalishe Pinkas
- A Collection of Zemiroth and Folk Melodies.* repr.ed. New
York:C.A.A./J.T.S.A., 1958; xxviii,96pp., music. (orig. ed.
Vilna and Berlin, 1927).
Liturgical collection compiled by East European cantor
Abraham Moses Bernstein (1865-1932), of melody lines for
Sabbath and Festivals, as *a cappella* vocal selections.
Yiddish preface. Hebrew liturgical texts romanized.
851

BICK, MOSHE, comp. and ed. *Jewish Wedding; Melodies and
Memories.* Haifa,Isr.:Haifa Music Museum and AMLI Library,
1964; 36pp., illus., music.
Research collection of 20 melody lines for traditional
folksongs and folk dance tunes of wedding celebration,
including procession and ceremony. Materials collected
from Bessarabian East European sources - oral history
and folk musicians. Background essay and song texts only
in Hebrew print. Photographs and map of European area.
852

BIRNBAUM, ABRAHAM BER, comp. and ed. *Omanut Ha-hazzanut/
Die Kunst des Judischen Kantorate.* repr.ed. New York:H.U.C.
-J.I.R./S.M.F.,1954;186pp.,music.(orig.ed. Berlin 1908/12).
Melody lines for traditional East European Ashkenazic
liturgical music, collected by Cantor Abraham Ber Birnbaum (1865-1922). Arranged in two sections: 1. Sabbath,
97pp; and, 2. High Holy Days, 95pp. Recitatives - solo
cantorial chants, with responses for choir (male) and
congregation, *a cappella.* Some added arrangements in
"concert style." Hebrew liturgical texts romanized.
853

CAHAN, YEHUDAH LEYB, comp. and ed. *Yidishe Folkslider Mit
Melodien (Yiddish Folksongs with Melodies).* New York:YIVO/
Inst. for Jewish Research, 1957; 560pp., illus., music.

Compilation by Yiddish folklorist Y.L. Cahan (1881-1937)
of 560 items — folksongs and poetry — collected in East
Europe during years 1896-1912. Cahan first prepared his
materials for publication in Vilna 1912/1920, and then
with YIVO shaped an edition 1925/1930, much of which
was saved from Holocaust destruction. Present version
by YIVO was issued here under editorial direction of
Yiddish scholar Max Weinreich (1894-1969). Contents include melodies of 205 selections under topical headings
of: courtship ballads; dances and wedding songs; lullabies and children's tunes; songs of family life and of
work; political and social ballads; religious chants and
holiday songs. Texts, including annotations, footnotes,
sources and index, in Yiddish. Brief prefatory remarks
(8pp.) in English by Max Weinreich. Words for music
lines romanized.

854
COHN, ALBERT, comp. and ed. *Chants Religieux pour le Tem-*
ple Israelite der Bruxelles. Brussels, Belg.:Venderaumera,
1853/63, 135pp., music.

 Collection by French scholar and musician Albert Cohn
(1814-1877) of traditional liturgical music traditions
(Mid European Ashkenazic) for Flemish Jewish community
of Brussels. Melody lines for Sabbath, High Holy Days,
Festivals. French text material. Hebrew texts romanized.

855
CONSOLO, FEDERIGO, comp. and ed. *Libro Dei Canti d'Israele*
Antichi; Canti Liturgici del Rito Degli Ebrei Spagnoli.
Florence, It.: Bratti, 1892; vii,231pp., music.

 Collection of 445 melody lines compiled by liturgical
musician and violinist Federigo Consolo (1841-1906), for
entire calendar year of services — Sabbath, High Holy
Days, Festivals and other special ritual days — in the
tradition of the Italian Jews of Spaniolic-Sephardic
origin, particularly as practiced at the synagogue of
Livorno. Brief preface in Italian by rabbi of community
David Castelli (fl.19th cent.). Music presented for solo
voice, *a cappella*. Hebrew liturgical texts romanized.

856
CREMIEU, JULES SALOMON and MARDOCHEE HANANIEL CREMIEU,
comps. and eds. *Zemirat Israel — Chants Hebraiques Suivant*
le Rite des Communautes Israelites de L'ancien Comtat Ver-
naissin. Marseilles/Paris,Fr.:Delanchie/Durlacher, 1885;
vii,227pp., music.

 Published under auspices of Grand Rabbi of Marseilles,
Consistory of France, 208 selections, melody lines only,
for liturgical tradition of Jewish communities of South
France (the old papal territories of Avignon, Carpentras
Comtadin, Lunel, Aix, Arles, etc.). This tradition of
French Jewry differs from other Sephardic traditions and
contrasts with Ashkenazic liturgical music of France. It
is a special branch of French Judaism in which composer
Darius Milhaud (1892-1974) was born and bred. Milhaud
arranged five liturgical chants of this Comtadin tradition as works for voice and piano in concert style,
with Hebrew and French texts (pub. Paris: Heugel, 1934).

Compilation by liturgical musicians Jules Cremieu (1842–
[?]) and Mardochee Cremieu (fl.19th cent.) includes selections for Sabbath, High Holy Days, Festivals and
other special days, for cantorial solo with some choir
responses, *a cappella*. Introduction, commentary and
annotations in French text. Hebrew liturgy romanized.
857

DAVID, SAMUEL, comp. and ed. *Musique Religieuse, Ancienne
et Moderne.* Paris, Fr.:Consistoire Israelites de Paris/
Durlacher, 1895; xxiv,391pp., music.
    Collection of 137 liturgical melody lines for calendar
    year of services – Sabbath, High Holy Days, Festivals
    and other special days – in the French Ashkenazic tra-
    dition (a distinction of liturgical music which thrived
    in France at that time). Music arranged for cantorial
    solo, with choir (male). Musician Samuel David (1836–
    1895) pays homage in this publication to such important
    contemporary liturgists of that time as Salomon Sulzer
    (1804–1890, Vienna) and Samuel Naumbourg (1815–1880,
    Paris). French text only. Collection concludes with com-
    piler's setting of Psalm 150. Hebrew texts romanized.
858

DOBRUSHKIN, EZEKIEL and ABRAHAM YUDITSKI, comps./eds. *Yiddishe Folks Lieder ("Yiddish Folksongs").* Moscow,U.S.S.R.:
Der Emes, 1940; 486pp.
    Though this anthological collection presents only Yid-
    dish texts without music, it remains a significant re-
    source concerning Yiddish folksongs extant in Soviet
    Union just before onset of World War II. Yiddish and
    Russian (both romanized) texts of 588 Jewish folksongs
    on topics of: love and courtship; marriage and family;
    children's lullabies and play tunes; humor and satire;
    history and culture; work – trades and farming; revolu-
    tion and Soviet life; struggle and conflict; the Red
    Army – recruits and duties. No religious materials. Com-
    piled by two Soviet folklorists and educators: Ezekiel
    Dobrushkin (1883–?) and Abraham Yuditski (1885–?).
859

DUNAJEWSKY, ABRAHAM, comp. and ed. *Israelische Tempel Com-
positionen fuer den Sabbath.* repr.ed. New York: H.U.C.-J.I.
R./S.M.P.,1955;107pp.,music.(orig.eds.Moscow/Odessa,1893/98)
    Collection of 25 selections for cantorial solo with male
    choir, *a cappella*, for Sabbath services, as compiled
    by Cantor Abraham Dunajewsky (1843–1911). Eastern Europe
    Ashkenazic tradition. Hebrew liturgical texts romanized.
860

EPHROS, GERSHON, comp. and ed. *The Cantorial Anthology;
Traditional and Modern Synagogue Music.* New York: Bloch,
1929–1975; 6 vols., music.
    When the first volume of *The Cantorial Anthology* com-
    piled by Gershon Ephros (1890–1978) was published in
    1929, a preface by A.Z. Idelsohn (1882–1938) introduced
    this collection with these remarks: "In both his selec-
    tion and arrangement he (Ephros) shows profound insight
    into traditional Hebrew liturgy." Ephros, in his own
    preface, then wrote: "Last, but not least, my profound

gratitude and sincere appreciation to Professor Abraham
Zebi Idelsohn, my dear friend and teacher, who has had a
lasting influence on me." In the six volumes of his
Cantorial Anthology, Ephros, as his mentor Idelsohn had
done before him, probes the essence of Jewish liturgical
melodies, assembling materials dating from 12th to 20th
centuries. Gershon Ephros was born in Serotzk, near Warsaw, and began his musical life there as choir boy and
then apprentice cantor. In 1909, he went to Jerusalem,
with a letter of introduction to A.Z. Idelsohn, a school
music teacher, cantor and trainer of music educators.
Ephros became his assistant and, until he left for U.S.
two years later, had a unique opportunity to observe at
close range Idelsohn's methods of research and collection. Idelsohn was investigating various types of Jewish
Near Eastern-Oriental and Sephardic liturgical music
among groups settled in Palestine, utilizing recording
cylinders and transcription notebooks. Ephros accompa-
nied him on collection "visits" and helped notate music.
When Ephros came to New York City in 1911, he was appointed music teacher in Hebrew schools and trainer of
other teachers, and used educational materials developed
by Idelsohn as well as skills and ideas acquired as his
assistant musician. Soon Ephros took cantorial pulpits,
and then began his own labor of research and collection
of Jewish liturgical music among many cantors, choir
leaders and composer-arrangers in America. The fruits
of his work resulted in the 6-volume *Anthology*, which
has become a significant resource for Jewish musicians.
When, in 1922, Idelsohn came here to lecture about his
collections, and then in 1924 joined the faculty of H.U.
C. in Cincinnati, the personal and professional relationship between two liturgist-collectors was resumed,
and continued actively until Idelsohn's death in 1938.

061
EPHROS, GERSHON, comp. and ed. *The Cantorial Anthology;
Traditional and Modern Synagogue Music.* (cont.)
   In his 6 volume *Cantorial Anthology*, Gershon Ephros
   (1890-1978) compiled liturgical selections for cantorial
   solo, with choir response, arranged in the order of the
   services themselves. Included are materials from traditional synagogue music of 12th to 20th century, with
   compositions by notable cantorial figures. Some English
   prefatory materials and annotations for each volume.
   Hebrew liturgy texts romanized.

   Volume 1. Rosh Hashanah (New Year). 2nd ed. 1948;
   (orig. pub. 1929). Contents: xiv - preface and index +
   169pp. music - 97 selections for onset of New Year
   services to conclusion of Holy Day.

   Volume 2. Yom Kippur (Day of Atonement). pub. 1940.
   Contents: viii - preface and index + 327pp. music -
   209 selections for services from Holy Day eve of *Kol
   Nidre* through concluding service for the fast day,
   with variant versions for prayer settings.

Volume 3. Sholosh R'golim (Three Festivals: Sukkot. Pesach, Shavuot). 2nd ed. 1975; (orig. pub. 1948). Contents: x - preface and index + 395pp. music - 233 selections for all services of Tabernacles, Passover, Weeks-Pentecost, *Simhat Torah* (Bible holiday) and various special chants of those Festivals. Later edition also includes compositions by 20th century composers, in addition to traditional liturgical arrangements.

Volume 4. Shabbat (Sabbath). 2nd ed. 1976; (orig. pub. 1953). Contents: xi - preface and index (+ xii-xvi, for music insert) + 395pp. music - 238 selections for entire Sabbath from eve (*Kabbalat Shabbat*) to conclusion (*Havdalah*). Later edition includes arrangements and compositions by 20th century composers, in addition to traditional liturgical collection.

Volume 5. Y'mot Hachol (Weekday Services and Special Occasions). pub. 1957. Contents: viii - preface and index + 345pp. music - 249 selections for weekdays services (morning, afternoon and evening), *Rosh Hodesh* (new month), *Hanukkah, Purim, Tisha B'av* and other special calendar days. Includes traditional chants and musical motifs for circumcisions, weddings and memorial services.

Volume 6. The Recitative (for Rosh Hashanah). pub. 1969. Contents: vi - preface and index + 217pp. music - 180 selections, including compositions and arrangements utilizing liturgical motifs. Intended as supplementary book for *Volume 1. Rosh Hashanah.* Collection presents comprehensive exposition of improvisational recitative form as chanted by traditional cantor/prayer leader. Final page of this last volume of Ephros' *Cantorial Anthology* concludes with musical setting of a "triple *Amen*" - as fitting postscript to this dedicated labor and valuable compilation of Jewish liturgical music.

862
FATER, ISACHAR and B. HELLER, comps. and eds. *Yiddishe Muzik in Poylen.* Tel Aviv, Isr.: World Federation of Polish Jews, 1970; lxxviii,424pp., music.
  Collection of 78 pages of Yiddish folksong materials - melody lines only - from Polish Jewish sources, with an extensive commentary in Yiddish text about sources and materials themselves. Yiddish text for music romanized.

863
FRANCK, JULES, comp. and ed. *Le Guide de L'officiant.*
Paris,Fr.:Temple Israelite/Consistoire,[?];viii,206pp.,music
  Recitatives and chants for cantorial solo, according to French Ashkenazic liturgical traditions, as compiled by French composer-arranger and pianist Jules Franck (1858-[?]) who also served as synagogue choir director for a Paris congregation. Some selections with keyboard accompaniment. French text materials. Hebrew romanized.

864
FREED, ISADORE, comp. and ed. *Sacred Service - Liturgical Works:Salamone Rossi.* New York:T.M.P.,1954; 48pp., music.
.   Collection and transcription of music by Rossi (c.1565-c.1628), prepared by composer, educator and synagogue music director Isadore Freed (1900-1960). Cantorial solo with choir (and added arrangements for optional organ accompaniment) for 15 Sabbath selections. Brief background introduction. Hebrew liturgy text romanized.

865
GASTER, MOSES and ELIAS JESSURUN, comps. and eds. *The Book of Prayer and Order of Service, According to the Custom of the Spanish and Portuguese Jews.* London,Eng.:Henry Frowde, 1901-1906; 5 vols., music.
Compilation of traditional liturgy - order of services - with liturgical music, prepared and issued in 5 volumes: 1. Sabbath, daily services and special occasions - 72 melody lines; 2. High Holy Days: New Year - 14 melody lines; 3. High Holy Days: Day of Atonement - 27 melody lines; 4. *Sukkot* (Tabernacles) - 20 melody lines; and, 5. Passover and *Shavuot* (Weeks-Pentecost) - 19 melody lines. Music materials as final section of each volume. Textual compilation by rabbi and scholar Moses Gaster (1856-1939), and musical section prepared by musician and choral director of Bevis Marks Synagogue in London Elias Jessurun (d. 1934). Hebrew liturgy for melody lines romanized.

866
GEROWITSCH, ELIESER, comp. and ed. *Shire Simrah -Synagogen Gesaenge.* repr.ed. New York:H.U.C.-J.I.R./S.M.P.,1953; vi, 203pp., music. (orig.ed. Rostov/Moscow, 1897).
Cantorial recitatives (liturgical solos) and choir responses, *a cappella*, issued here in three parts bound together in single volume. Compilation of liturgical selections for Sabbath, Festivals and other special days. Elieser Gerowitsch (1844-1913) was notable Russian cantor who had received his formal music education at St. Petersburg Conservatory. Hebrew, German and Yiddish text materials. Some English prefatory remarks for reprint edition. Hebrew liturgy texts romanized.

867
GEROWITSCH, ELIESER, comp. and ed. *Shire Tefillah - Synagogen Gesaenge.* repr.ed. New York:H.U.C.-J.I.R./S.M.P., 1953; iii,207pp., music. (orig.ed. Rostov/Moscow, 1897).
Cantorial recitatives (liturgical solos) and choir responses, *a cappella*, issued here in two parts bound together in single volume. Compilation of liturgical selections for High Holy Days. Elieser Gerowitsch (1844-1913) was cantor of Great Synagogue in Rostov on Don. Hebrew, German and Yiddish text materials. Some English prefatory remarks for reprint edition. Hebrew romanized.

868
GESHURI, MEIR SHIMON, comp. and ed. *Music and Hassidism in the House of Kuzmir/Kazimierz and Its Affiliation: Modzitz.* Jerusalem,Isr.:Negen, 1952; 70pp., illus., music.
Collection of 59 melody lines for *Niggunim* (wordless

devotional tunes) gathered from among Hassidic followers
of several dynastic groups which originally flourished
in Poland area. Anthology divided into two sections:
literature and musicology (only Hebrew print text); and,
melodies themselves. Facsimiles.
869

GINSBURG, SAUL M. and PESACH C. MAREK, comps./eds. *Yevrei-*
skaya Narodnyya Pijesni v Russii ("Jewish Folksongs in Rus-
sia"). St.Petersburg,Russia:Voskhod, 1901; xxx,329pp.
This anthological collection has no music, only texts
(Russian, Yiddish and Hebrew romanized) for 376 folksongs selections, with historical and sociological annotations for materials. However, this work remains as a
landmark ethnomusicological achievement on the part of
two Jewish scholars: Saul M. Ginsburg (1866-1940) and
Pesach S. Marek (1862-1920). No English version as yet.
870

GORALI, MOSHE, GIDEON ALMAGOR and MOSHE BICK, comps. and
eds. *Die Goldene Pave: Anthology of Yiddish Folksongs.*
Haifa,Isr.:Haifa Music Museum and AMLI Library, 1970; xiv,
142pp., illus., music.
Compilation of 70 melody lines, with ethnomusicological
commentary and analysis of materials. Jewish secular and
religious folksongs topically arranged, treating: folk
life, love ballads, labor and trade, Sabbath and other
holidays melodies, Jewish minstrelsy music (melodies of
Badkhen - minstrel, and *Klezmer* - instrumentalist),
children's songs, *Niggunim* (Hassidic melodies). Commentaries and annotations in Hebrew. Prefatory remarks
in English and Hebrew. English abstracts for selections.
871

HEMSI, ALBERTO, comp. and ed. *Coplas Sefardies.* Alexan-
dria,Egypt:Hemsi, 1937; xxii,27pp., music.
Compilation of 36 *romanceros* and *cantigas* (songs and
ballads) of the Middle Eastern Mediterranean Sephardic
Jewish groups in Rhodes, Salonica and Izmir (Smyrna).
Judaeo-Spanish folksong materials from 15th to 19th
centuries. Various versions of selections compiled by
French composer, performer and music collector Alberto
Hemsi (1898-1976). Melody lines, with some piano accom-
paniment. Preface and annotations in French and Spanish.
Song texts in Ladino (Judaeo-Spanish).
872

IDELSOHN, ABRAHAM ZEBI, comp./ed. *Hebraeish-Orientalisher*
Melodienschatz - Thesaurus of Oriental Hebrew Melodies.
repr.ed. New York:KTAV, 1973; 4 vols., music. (orig.eds.
Berlin/Leipzig/Vienna/Jerusalem: Breitkopf u. Haertel/
Benjamin Harz, 1922-1933; 10 vols.)
Credited as the "father of Jewish musicology," Abraham
Zebi Idelsohn (1882-1938) was born in Filsberg, Latvia.
There he studied and practiced cantorial art, and by
1903 had begun to collect liturgical music materials.
Settling in Jerusalem in 1906, Idelsohn started to seek
out and gather its many different Jewish liturgical tra-
ditions - notating, recording and transcribing, often
under most difficult personal circumstances. He taught

Jewish music to school children and the techniques of
music pedagogy to other teachers. He also served congregations as cantor. By 1922, his research studies were
becoming known in Europe and America, and he came here
to lecture. Subsequently, in 1924, he was appointed to
faculty of H.U.C. in Cincinnati and also given assign-
ment as curator for the library's newly acquired Eduard
Birnbaum Collection of Jewish Liturgical Music. While at
those posts, Idelsohn completed work on his monumental
Thesaurus and oversaw publication of its volumes.
During a busy lifetime as scholar, cataloguer-curator,
educator, composer-arranger and cantor, Idelsohn composed musical settings for Jewish poetry and liturgical
services, and contributed articles to world-wide professional journals. He wrote a volume on Jewish prayers
and sacred poetry, compiled and arranged an educational
songbook, and completed an outstanding work - *Jewish
Music, In Its Historical Development* (New York, 1929).
By 1934, a severely incapacitating illness had termina-
ted all his activities, and he passed away among relatives in Johannesburg, South Africa, in 1938.

873
IDELSOHN, ABRAHAM ZEBI, comp./ed. *Hebraeish-Orientalisher
Melodienschatz - Thesaurus of Oriental Hebrew Melodies.*
(cont.)

In his *Thesaurus*, A.Z. Idelsohn (1882-1938) compiled
into separate categories a multitude of widely varied
musical examples of Jewish liturgical music and religious folksongs, ingathered by him from among many different Judaic groups. His collection represents a compendium of Diasporic musical expression. For each of the
ten volumes of his *Thesaurus*, he also included prefatory materials affording helpful guidance to the contents, as well as masterful introductory essays, as
topical studies for each volume in the collection. In
this KTAV reprint edition, English texts are given for
prefaces and introductions of volumes 1, 2, 6, 7, 9 and
10. Texts in volumes 3, 4, 5 and 8 are in German. Some
materials also appeared in Hebrew for Jerusalem editions
and it had been Idelsohn's intention to complete a fully
tri-lingual *Thesaurus*, in Hebrew, German and English.
All texts for musical examples, whether in Hebrew, Aramaic, Ladino or Yiddish, are romanized.

KTAV repr.ed. *Volume 1* (3 volumes of *Thesaurus*) -
Volume 1. Songs of the Yemenite Jews. (orig.pub. 1925)
Contents: xii - index and preface (Eng.) + 47pp. introductory materials (Eng.) + 117pp. music - 203 melody
lines for liturgical chants, hymns and folksongs.
Volume 2. Songs of the Babylonian Jews. (orig.pub.
1923). Contents: ix - index and preface (Eng.) + 32pp.
introductory materials (Eng.) + pp.33-140 music - 194
melody lines for liturgical chants, hymns and folksongs.
*Volume 3. Songs of the Jews of Persia, Bukhara and
Daghestan.* (orig.pub. 1922). Contents: viii - index and
preface (Ger.) + 51pp. introductory materials (Ger.) +

68pp. music — 176 melody lines for Persian liturgical
and folk music, Bukharan hymnology and folksong, and,
Daghestan hymns.

KTAV repr.ed. *Volume 2* (2 volumes of *Thesaurus*) —
Volume 4. Songs of the Oriental Sephardim. (orig.pub.
1922/23). Contents: xv — index and preface (Ger.) +
120pp. introductory materials (Ger.) + pp.121–280 music
— 500 melody lines for Near Eastern/Oriental Sephardic
liturgical chants, religious folksongs, hymns and Ladino
(Spaniolic Jewish) folksongs. Also, liturgical music of
Jews of Aleppo and other Judaeo-Arabic folk music.
Volume 5. Songs of the Moroccan Jews. (orig.pub. 1928/
29). Contents: 16pp. introductory materials and index
(Ger.) + pp.17–119 music — 302 melody lines for liturgical music and religious folksongs.

KTAV repr.ed. *Volume 3* (2 volumes of *Thesaurus*) —
*Volume 6. Synagogue Songs of German Jews in the 18th
Century – According to Manuscripts.* (orig.pub. 1932).
Contents: xxvi — index and introductory materials (Eng.)
+ 234pp. music — 517 melody lines for: 1. manuscripts of
Ahron Beer (1738–1821) of Bavaria (446 synagogue chants
for entire calendar year of devotions); 2. selection of
manuscripts from period 1765 to 1814, by 14 known cantors and anonymous sources (70 liturgicals); and, 3.
several works by non-Jews, including Benedetto Marcello
(1686–1739) and Elhanon Henle Kirchhain (Fl.18th cent.),
and items by Jewish musician Abraham Sagri (fl.16th–17th
cent.) (total: 19 selections).
Volume 7. Traditional Songs of the South German Jews.
(orig.pub. 1933). Contents: lix — preface, introductory
materials and index (Eng.) + 181pp. music — 216 melody
lines for: 1. liturgical services of year; 2. hymns and
religious folksongs; 3. liturgical manuscripts of some
cantors, including Loew Saenger (1781–1843).

KTAV repr.ed. *Volume 4.* (3 volumes of *Thesaurus*) —
Volume 8. Synagogue Song of the East European Jews.
(orig.pub. 1932). Contents: xxxiv — introductory materials and index (Ger.) + 143pp. music — 280 melody lines
for: 1. liturgical services and hymnology for entire
year; 2. liturgical works in manuscript of 13 cantorial
musicians of 19th century Eastern Europe.
Volume 9. Folksong of the East European Jews. (orig.
pub. 1932). Contents: xlii — introductory materials and
index (Eng.) + 211pp. music — 758 melody lines for Jewish folksongs — in Hebrew and Yiddish — classified according to musical qualities and topical nature, and of
late 16th to early 20th century origins; works of known
and unknown folk composers; examples of comparative
folk music; attention to melodic characteristics of
Hatikvah, national anthem, and other popular songs.
Volume 10. Songs of the Hassidim. (orig.pub. 1932).
Contents: xxix — introductory materials and index (Eng.)
+ 72pp. music — 250 melody lines for selections with

texts in Hebrew or Yiddish, and wordless devotional
tunes (*Niggunim*); characteristic musical examples from
various Hassidic rabbinical "courts" and special group
meetings (*Farbrengen*); some satirical tunes of op-
ponents of Hassidism, as music of parody in same style.

874
IDELSOHN, ABRAHAM ZEBI, comp. and ed. *Songs of the Yemenite Jews.* Berlin,Ger./Jerusalem,Brit.Mand.:Benjamin Harz,
1925; xii,117pp., music.
Collection of 226 melody lines compiled by musicologist
A.Z. Idelsohn (1882-1938), based upon his research work
in Jerusalem among Yemenite Jews there early in this
century. Prefatory materials and detailed introductory
commentary in English (translated from German for this
edition). Hebrew texts of selections romanized.

875
JAPHET, ISRAEL MEYER, comp. and ed. *Shire Jeshurun.*
Frankfurt,Ger.:Kauffmann, 1922; xci,160pp., music.
Compilation of German Ashkenazic liturgical music for
cantorial solo and choir responses, for Sabbath, High
Holy Days and Festivals. Posthumous publication of col-
lected materials of cantor and choir conductor Israel
Meyer Japhet (1818-1902). Hebrew liturgy text romanized.

876
**JESSURUN, ELIAS R., EMANUEL A. AGUILAR and DAVID A. DE SOLA
comps. and eds.** *Sephardi Melodies of the Liturgy.* London,
Eng.:Bevis Marks/Oxford Univ. Press, 1931; 150pp., music.
Collection of traditional liturgical chants of services
at Bevis Marks Synagogue of London, according to European Sephardic liturgy. Materials in two sections: 1.
Reproduction of materials of orig. ed. (London, 1857) as
then compiled by E.A. Aguilar (1824-1904) and D.A. de
Sola (1796-1860); and, 2. Additional chants prepared by
Elias R. Jessurun (d.1934), choirmaster of Bevis Marks,
who edited this "revised and enlarged edition." Melody
lines for solo with choir (male), *a cappella*. Some introductory materials. Hebrew liturgy texts romanized.

877
JONAS, EMILE ELIHU, comp. and ed. *Shirat Israel; Recueil
des Chants Hebraiques Anciens et Modernes Executes au Temple
du Rite Portugals de Paris.* Paris,Fr.:Temple Israelite/
A. Durlacher, 1854/1886; viii,156pp., music.
Collection of 39 selections compiled by composer and
music professor at Paris Conservatoire – Emile Elihu
Jonas (1827-1905). Traditional liturgical melodies for
Spanish and Portuguese Sephardic synagogue – Temple
Israelite – in Paris, as well as for other congregations
elsewhere in France. Music for services of Sabbath, High
Holy Days and Festivals, as rendered by cantor soloist
with male choir, *a cappella*. Some organ parts added
for non-devotional occasions. Brief introductory remarks
in French only. Hebrew liturgical texts romanized.

878
KACZERGINSKI, SHMERKE (SHEMARIAH), comp. and ed. *Lider Fun
di Getos un Lagern (Songs of the Ghettos and Concentration
Camps).* New York:World Congress for Jewish Culture/CYCO,

1948; xxxix,436pp., illus., music.
    Compilation of materials — 240 melodies and Yiddish
    poetic texts — collected by Holocaust survivor from
    Vilna, Shmerke Kaczerginski (1908-1954). Published as
    cultural legacy reflecting life and times, struggles
    for existence and resistance of Jews in Ghettos and Con-
    centration Camps of Eastern Europe. Introductory essays
    and annotational commentary given in Yiddish text by
    collector Sh. Kaczerginski and writer/editor H. Leivick
    (Leivick Halper, 1882-1962), provide background details
    on collection, its various sources — musicians, poets,
    performers — and process of compilation. Melodies for
    100 selections edited for publication by choral director
    and music educator Michl Gelbart (1889-1962). Contents
    topically arranged as songs of:Concentration Camps;
    Ghettos; Treblinka Camp; Resistance and Survival. Yid-
    dish texts under melody lines romanized.
    879
KAISER, ALOIS and WILLIAM SPARGER, comps. and eds. *A Collection of the Principal Melodies of the Synagogue From the
Earliest Time to the Present.* Chicago,Ill.:T. Rubovits,
1893; xvii,197pp., music.
    Published as "souvenir" of Jewish Women's Congress held
    under auspices of World's Parliament of Religions. Com-
    pilation by two notable cantorial musicians Alois Kaiser
    (1840-1908) of Baltimore and William Sparger (1860-1904)
    of New York City. Selection of 66 liturgical works. In-
    troductory essay on *Hazzanuth* (cantorial chant) with
    musical illustrations, treating Jewish liturgical modes
    and their historic background, as well as differences
    between traditions of Ashkenazic and Sephardic synagogue
    music. Liturgicals for Sabbath, High Holy Days, Festi-
    vals, *Hanukkah* and other calendar religious days. Some
    "modern" materials included by three leading figures of
    19th century European synagogue music — Sulzer, Lewan-
    dowski and Naumbourg, as well as Psalm settings. Preface
    by Cyrus Adler (1863-1940) who was curator of Oriental
    Antiquities at U.S. National Museum in Washington D.C.,
    placing anthology in perspective of Jewish musical his-
    tory. Hebrew liturgy romanized.
    880
KATCHKO, ADOLPH, comp. and ed. *A Thesaurus of Cantorial
Liturgy.* New York:H.U.C.-J.I.R./S.M.P.,1952; 165pp., music.
    Melody lines for traditional chants of Sabbath and Three
    Festivals — *Sukkot*, Passover and *Shavuot* — according
    to East European Ashkenazic liturgical music patterns,
    compiled by cantor and educator Adolph Katchko (1887-
    1958). Hebrew liturgy texts romanized.
    881
KORNITZER, LEON, comp. and ed. *Juedische Gottesdienstliche
Gesaenge.* 2nd ed. Hamburg,Ger.:Lessmann,1933;96pp.,music.
(orig.ed. Frankfurt,Ger.:Kauffmann,1928;111pp.,music).
    Anthology of liturgical music and religious folksongs,
    melody lines only, compiled by Leon Kornitzer (1875-
    1947) who was cantor and music educator in Hamburg. He-
    brew and German text material. Hebrew liturgy romanized.

882
KRAMER, LEON and OSKAR GUTTMANN, comps. and eds. *Kol She-arith Israel - Synagogue Melodies of Congregation Shearith Israel.* New York:T.M.P.,1942; 72pp., music.
Compilation of 27 liturgical melody lines for Sabbath Eve services throughout year as chanted by solo cantor with male choir responses at Sephardic congregation - Spanish and Portuguese Synagogue of New York City. Both Leon Kramer and Oskar Guttmann (1885-1945) served as music directors at congregation. Hebrew texts romanized.

883
KRIEG, HANS MOSHE, comp. and ed. *Spanish Liturgical Melodies of the Portuguese Israelitish Community of Amsterdam.* Amsterdam,Neth.:Kadimah, 1952/4; 32pp., music.
Collection of 20 melody lines for cantorial solo at Sabbath and Festival services of Amsterdam Spanish and Portuguese synagogue. Based upon earlier 19th century notations of traditional chants as performed in congregations. Hebrew liturgical texts romanized.

884
LEVIN, NEIL and VELVEL PASTERNAK comps. and eds. *Z'mirot Anthology; Traditional Sabbath Songs for the Home.* Cedarhurst,N.Y.:Tara, 1981; xxi,139pp., illus., music.
Compilation of 150 selections - melody lines and choral/chord markings, with annotational remarks - for music associated with four traditional Sabbath meals: 1. Friday evening; 2. Sabbath day; 3. Sabbath late afternoon; and, 4. *Melave Malka* (post-Sabbath, after *Havdalah*-concluding ceremonial). Additional materials for Grace blessings at meals. Several comparative musical settings given for poetic texts. Introductory materials provide background on music collection - traditions, origins, musical developments, styles and forms - as representative of East European Ashkenazic expressions now found in Israel and America. Source notes, glossary of terms, indexes, and English summaries of song texts. Hebrew liturgy and Yiddish lyrics romanized.

885
LEVY, ISAAC, comp. and ed. *Antologia de Liturgia Judaeo-Espagnoles.* Jerusalem,Isr.:Ministry of Education and Culture, 1974; xiv,419pp., music.
Extensive compilation of materials, sections of which were previously issued in some form 1959-1970, by collector and scholar Isaac Levy. Sephardic liturgical music - traditions of Turkey, Salonica, North Africa, and Sephardic groups of Europe (Spanish and Portuguese) and in Israel. Religious music for Sabbaths, High Holy Days, Festivals and other special calendar ritual days. Hebrew and Ladino-Spanish texts. Liturgy romanized.

886
LEVY, ISAAC, comp. and ed. *Chants Judaeo-Espagnoles.* London,Eng.:World Sephardi Federation,1960; viii,87pp., music.
Collection of 97 melody lines of Sephardic folksongs in Ladino (Judaeo-Spanish), including North African as well as European music. Source materials for comparative studies. French text only: introduction by Ovadiah

Camhy (director of World Sephardi Federation); commentary and annotations by compiler, scholar Isaac Levy.
887

LEWANDOWSKI, LOUIS, comp. and ed. *Kol Rinnah U'tefillah.*
repr.ed. New York:H.U.C.-J.I.R./S.M.P., 1954; vi,153pp.,
music. (orig.ed. Berlin, 1871).

Collection of melody lines for cantorial solo with two-
part male choir responses, *a cappella*, for Ashkenazic
mid-European traditions. Music of Sabbath, High Holy
Days and Festivals. Louis Lewandowski (1821-1894) was
leading figure in Jewish liturgical music of 19th century, who served Berlin congregation as music director.
This compilation includes more "old style" traditional
elements than appeared in publications at same time by
his colleague in Vienna Salomon Sulzer (1804-1890). German text materials. Brief English prefatory remarks for
reprint edition. Hebrew liturgy text romanized.
888

LEWANDOWSKI, LOUIS, comp. and ed. *Todah V'zimrah.* repr.
ed. New York:H.U.C.-J.I.R./S.M.P., 1954; ix,338pp., music.
(orig.ed. Berlin, 1876/82).

Compilation of melody lines for cantorial solo with
choir responses (and some optional organ accompaniments)
for Sabbath, High Holy Days and Festivals. Arrangements
appear more "modern" than in his earlier compilation.
[Three notable liturgical musicians shaped mid-European
Ashkenazic synagogue music of 19th century: Salomon
Sulzer (1804-1890) of Vienna; Samuel Naumbourg (1815-
1880) of Paris; and, Louis Lewandowski (1821-1894) of
Berlin. All published compilations of liturgical music.]
German text materials. English prefatory remarks for reprint edition. Hebrew liturgy romanized.
889

LOEB, DAVID, comp. and ed. *Rinat Hakodesh:Liturgical Works
of Leib Glantz.* Tel Aviv,Isr.:I.M.I., 1965-1970, music.
vol.1:*Selichot (Penitential) Services*, 1965; 128pp. vol.2:
Sabbath Services, 1968; 182pp. vol.3: *High Holy Day Services*, 1970; 172pp.

Compilation of liturgical collections, compositions and
arrangements by cantor and educator Leib Glantz (1898-
1964) for cantorial solo and choir responses. Edition
prepared in association with Tel Aviv Institute of Jewish Liturgical Music. Some optional organ accompaniments
for non-ritual performance. Hebrew liturgy romanized.
890

LOVY, ISRAEL, comp. and ed. *Chants Religieux Composes pour
les Prieres Hebraiques.* Paris,Fr.:Temple Israelite/Paris
Consistoire, 1862; 157pp., music.

Posthumous publication of liturgical works compiled for
Sabbath, High Holy Days, Festivals and other special
days by Cantor Israel Lovy (1773-1832) who served pulpit
of Great Synagogue in Paris. Collection and arrangement
of music for Central European Ashkenazic traditions of
of German and French Jewry. Cantorial solos and choir
responses, *a cappella*. Lovy was uniquely innovative
in his musical ideas and influential on those who fol-

lowed him in the 19th century. French, German and Hebrew
text materials. Hebrew liturgy romanized.

891
NAUMBOURG, SAMUEL, comp. and ed. *Chants Liturgiques des
Israelites:Zemirot Yisrael.* repr.ed. New York:H.U.C.-J.I.R.
/S.M.P., 1954; xvii,350pp., music.(orig.ed. Paris, 1847/57).
   Anthology of cantorial chants and choir responses (with
   some organ or piano accompaniments) for Sabbath, High
   Holy Days and Festivals, according to Ashkenazic tra-
   ditions of France and Southern Germany. Compilation by
   Samuel Naumbourg (1815-1880) who was Chief Cantor of the
   Great Synagogue of Paris. This collection includes the
   cantorial materials of Loew Saenger (1781-1843) who had
   served Jewish congregation of Munich. Introductory text
   in French by Naumbourg. English prefatory remarks for
   reprint edition. Hebrew liturgy romanized.

892
NAUMBOURG, SAMUEL, comp. and ed. *Chants Religieux des Is-
raelites:Agudat Shirim.* repr.ed. New York:H.U.C.-J.I.R./S.
M.P.,1954; xlvi,114pp., music. (orig.ed. Paris, 1864/74).
   Compilation of Jewish religious folksongs, including
   hymns, marriage service, psalms and other special liturgical music materials, and with supplement of cantillations according to Ashkenazic traditions of France and
   Southern Germany. Music arranged for cantorial solo with
   choir responses and some optional organ or piano accompaniment, by Samuel Naumbourg (1815-1880) cantor at the
   Great Synagogue of Paris. Introduction in French text by
   Naumbourg. English prefatory remarks for reprint edition. Hebrew liturgy romanized.

893
NAUMBOURG, SAMUEL and VINCENT D'INDY, comps. and eds. *Hashirim Asher Li'Shlomo:Salomone Rossi.* repr.ed. New York:
H.U.C.-J.I.R./S.M.P.,1954;252pp.,music.(orig.ed. Paris,1877)
   Edited republication prepared by Cantor Samuel Naumbourg
   (1815-1880) of Paris with French composer Vincent d'Indy
   (1851-1932). Liturgical music for cantorial solo and
   choir, *a cappella*, by Salomone Rossi Ebreo da Mantua
   (c.1565-c.1628) notable Jewish musician of Northern
   Italy. Based upon original edition published by Rossi
   himself (Venice, c.1623), and with facsimiles as well as
   musical transcriptions. Reproduction of 1877 edition,
   with French text introductory essay. English prefatory
   remarks for reprint edition. Hebrew liturgy romanized.

894
NE'EMAN, YEHOSHUA, comp. and ed. *Nusah La-hazzan: Traditional Chant of the Synagogue (According to Lithuanian -
Jerusalem Musical Tradition).* Jerusalem,Isr.:Inst. for
Sacred Music/Hekhal Shlomo,1972; xii,276pp., music.
   Collection of 392 liturgical melody lines for services
   of High Holy Days, representing East European Ashkenazic
   traditions as practiced in modern Israel. Includes some
   materials published privately by compiler in 1963.
   Melodies presented with essential qualities of "free
   liturgical recitative" in improvisational style. Introductory essay and other annotations in Hebrew text.

Some brief English remarks. Hebrew liturgy romanized.
895
NE'EMAN, YEHOSHUA, comp. and ed. *Tseliley Ha-mikra (Bibli-cal Cantillation).* Jerusalem,Isr.:Inst. for Sacred Music/
Hekhal Shlomo, 1955/1971; 2vols., music.
    Analytical guide, in two volumes, for music foundations
    of cantillations — musical accentuations for recitations
    of Scriptures at services. Vol.1 — (4 parts: chaps. 1 to
    26) covering topics of: structures and features; musical
    analysis according to communities of Lithuania and Po-
    land; Pentateuch (*Torah*) melodic forms; Prophets
    (*Haftarah*) melodic forms. Vol.2 — (4 parts: chaps. 27
    to 49) covering topics of: Scrolls (*Ketuvim*), melodic
    forms of *Ruth, Song of Songs, Ecclesiastes*; Scroll of
    Lamentations; Book of *Esther*; readings for High Holy
    Days. Annotations in Hebrew. Comprehensive anthology of
    cantillation chant elements for East European Ashkenazic
    traditions as practiced in Israel. Liturgy romanized.
896
NEWMAN, JOEL and FRITZ RIKKO, comps. and eds. *Salamone
Rossi: Hashirim Asher Li'Shlomo (The Songs of Solomon).*
New York:Mercury Music/C.A.A./J.T.S.A., 1967; vol.1 — xvi,
261pp., illus., music; vol.2 — x,239pp., illus., music.
    Edited compilation, in 2 volumes, of Jewish liturgical
    works by Salamone Rossi Ebreo da Mantua (c.1565-c.1628).
    Music originally published by Rossi himself in Venice,
    1623. Edition here consists of 33 works — vol.1: 24; and
    vol.2: 9. Musical transcriptions as well as facsimiles
    of early Venetian publication. English annotations and
    translations of texts. Hebrew liturgy romanized. Preface
    by composer Hugo Weisgall. Compilers Joel Newman and
    Fritz Rikko also prepared a thematic index with analysis
    of materials, as "volume 3" (New York, 1973). Consult
    entry under section of "Bibliographies and Catalogues"
    for descriptive details.
897
NOWAKOWSKY, DAVID, comp. and ed. *Gebete und Gesaenge Zum
Eingang des Sabbath; Kabbalat Shabbat.* repr.ed. New York:
H.U.C.-J.I.R./S.M.P., 1955; vii,83pp., music. (orig. ed.
Odessa, 1900).
    Collection of prayer melodies for the Sabbath Eve ser-
    vice — East European Ashkenazic tradition — collected
    by David Nowakowsky (1848-1921) who was cantor for the
    great "liberal synagogue" — the Odessa Broder Shul —
    from 1870 onward, succeeding his mentor, the notable
    Cantor Nissan Blumenthal (1805-1902) upon his retirement
    from that pulpit. Publication consists of melodic chants
    of Blumenthal, as well as Nowakowsky. Hebrew liturgical
    texts romanized.
898
NULMAN, MOSHE, comp. and ed. *Ma'ariv Chants for the Entire
Year: Jacob Wasilkowsky.* New York: C.T.I./Yeshiva Univ.
Press, 1965; 79pp., music.
    Compilation of liturgical chants — cantorial solos and
    choir or congregation responses — for evening services
    of: weekdays, Sabbath, High Holy Days, Festivals and

other special calendar ritual occasions. Melody lines
only. Music collected by East European cantor and choir
leader Jacob Wasilkowsky (1882-1942), who emigrated to
America in 1920 and served Orthodox congregations here.
Some English annotations. Hebrew liturgy romanized.
899
ORTEGA, MANUEL L. *Los Hebreos en Marruecos.* Madrid, Sp.:
Instituto Israelitos, 1934; ix,369pp., illus., music.
In this study of Jews in Morocco, see collection of
melodies (Sephardic Jewish Moroccan traditions) given
on pp.210-36, as well as other relevant materials on
pp.311-69. Spanish and Ladino texts only.
900
PALACIN, ARCADIO de LARREA, comp./ed. *Cancionero Judio del
Norte de Marruecos ("Songs of North Morocco Jews").* Madrid,
Sp.:Instituto de Estudios Africanos,1952-54; 3vols., music.
Vol.1 - *Romances de Tetuan.* 1952; 345pp., music. Collection of musical variants and poetic text materials -
150 melody lines, with incipit tables for 270 different
items. Spanish annotations. Ladino and romanized Hebrew
song texts. Index. Vol.2 - *Romances de Tetuan.* 1952;
377pp., music. Collection of musical variants and poetic
text materials - 131 melody lines, with ballad poems.
Morphological analysis of materials, in Spanish only.
Ladino and romanized Hebrew song texts. Index. Vol.3 -
Canciones Rituales Hispano-Judias. 1954; 288pp.,music.
Liturgical chants, hymns and folksongs from Salonica
(Turkish/Greek tradition) as well as Tetuan. Collection
of musical variants and liturgy texts - 145 melody lines
with Ladino (Judaeo-Spanish) and romanized Hebrew song
texts. Selections for calendar year of religious observances and for "life-cycle" celebrations. Annotations
in Spanish only. Incipit and song title indexes.
901
PASTERNAK, VELVEL, comp. and ed. *Songs of the Hassidim,
vols. 1 and 2.* Cedarhurst,N.Y.:Tara, 1968/71; vol.1:158pp.,
music; vol.2:vii,201pp., music.
Anthology in 2 volumes of Hassidic religious folksongs
(*Niggunim*). Melody lines, with some part-song arrangements and chord symbols, sorted into topical categories
by collector and music publisher Velvel Pasternak. Selections - 170 in vol.1 and 210 in vol.2 - for: Sabbath,
High Holy Days, Festivals, Passover *Seder* (ritual
meal), weddings, religious dances, Psalm chanting and
other special occasions. Music gathered among various
Hassidic groups in Israel and America. Introductory
material and annotations for each volume, treating Hassidic movement and its musical expression. English
translations for some Hebrew texts. Hebrew liturgy romanized. Song indexes.
902
PIATELLI, ELIO, comp. and ed. *Canti Liturgici Ebraici di
Rito Italiano (Hebrew Liturgical Chants of the Italian Rite)*
Rome,It.:Edizione de Santis,1968; xviii,202pp.,illus.,music
Compilation of 154 selections of Jewish Italian musical
liturgy, as transcribed and annotated by Elio Piatelli,

choirmaster of Tempio Maggiore, Great Synagogue of Rome.
Music according to traditional chants of Roman Jewry,
one of oldest settlements in Europe dating back to Roman
Era, and gathered here as special legacy of Jewish community decimated by Nazis. Liturgicals for Sabbath, High
Holy Days, Festivals, Passover *Seder* feast, *Hanukkah,
Purim* and other special calendar days. With several
spiritual texts and Hazzanic works by Italian poets and
musicians. Introductory essay in Italian and English.
Indexes, information tables and illustrations, with some
translations of music texts into Italian and English.
Hebrew liturgy romanized.
903

PRYLUCKI, NOJACH, comp. and ed. *Yiddishe Folkslider (Yiddish Folksongs).* Warsaw,Pol.:Bikher-far-ale, 1911/13;
2 vols., [n.p.], music.
Compilation by Yiddish folklorist Nojach Prylucki/Noah
Prilusky (1882-1944) of various East European Jewish
folksongs and liturgical chants for celebration of holidays and communal religious occasions. Melody lines,
with Hebrew and Yiddish song texts romanized.
904

PRYZAMENT, SHLOMO, comp. and ed. *Broder Zinger - Los Can-
tares di Brody (The Brody Singers).* *The Polish Jews, Series
151.* Buenos Aires,Arg.:Union Central Israelita Polacca en
la Argentina, 1960; 240pp., music.
Compilation of poetic texts, monologue scripts and 50
song selections — melody lines only — of materials performed in repertoire of troupe of East European Yiddish
entertainers of late 19th and early 20th centuries, who
were known as "The Brody Singers." Music topically arranged for: Sabbath and other religious occasions, weddings, community celebrations, *Purim* plays, and other
public presentations. Yiddish and some Spanish texts for
materials, but words for melody lines romanized.
905

PUTTERMAN, DAVID, comp./ed. *Mizmor L'David; An Anthology
of Synagogue Music.* New York:C.A.A.,1979; xii,409pp.,music.
Collection of 125 selections — cantorial solos with SATB
choir and organ (or piano) accompaniments. Liturgical
music by various composers, adapters and arrangers, for
order of services of Friday eve, Sabbath morning, High
Holy Days (*Rosh Hashanah, Yom Kippur*), Three Festivals
(*Sukkot, Pesach, Shevuot*), and other religious observances. Compiled by cantor and educator David Putterman
(1901-1979), who served pulpit of Park Avenue Synagogue
in New York City for over 40 years. During his long
career, Putterman commissioned numerous American composers to write music for synagogue. Some of those works
included here. English annotations. Hebrew romanized.
906

PUTTERMAN, DAVID, comp. and ed. *Synagogue Music by Contemporary Composers; An Anthology of Compositions for Sabbath
Eve Service.* New York:G.Schirmer, 1951; xii,354pp., music.
Compilation of 38 works, composed or arranged for Friday evening services at Park Avenue Synagogue in New

York City. Music created at invitation or commission of
cantor and educator David Putterman (1901-1979). Col-
lection placed in order of prayers for ritual service,
by 30 composers: Berger, Bernstein, Binder, Brant,
Castelnuovo-Tedesco, Chajes, Dessau, Diamond, Foss,
Freed, Fromm, Gould, Grechaninoff, Harris, Helfman,
Jacobi, Levy, de Menasce, Milhaud, Pisk, Rogers,
Rosowsky, Schalit, Smit, Sowerby, Still, Tansman, Weill,
Weinberg, Zilberts. Selections for cantorial solo, with
SATB choir and optional organ accompaniment. English
annotations. Hebrew liturgy romanized.

907
SCHALL, NOAH, comp. and ed. *Hazzanic Thesaurus for Sabbath*
New York:C.C.A./Yeshiva Univ., 1979, 128pp., music.
Collection of 2-part choir selections of traditional
Ashkenazic liturgical music, *a cappella*. Compilation
of several 19th and 20th century liturgists from Eastern
Europe and America. Hebrew liturgy romanized.

908
SCHAPOSCHNIK, GERSHON, comp. and ed. *An Anthology of Haz-*
zanic Recitatives. repr.ed. New York:C.A.A./J.T.S.A., 1963;
120pp., music. (orig.ed. Istanbul, 1934).
Collection of 71 liturgical selections for cantorial
solo (high voice), *a cappella*, for Sabbath, High Holy
Days and Festivals, in the Ashkenazic tradition. Compilation by cantor who served congregation at geographical crossroads between Ashkenazic and Mediterranean
Sephardic traditions, and materials reflect that inter-
action of liturgic musical influences. Hebrew romanized.

909
SCHLEIFER, ELIHU, comp. and ed. *Anthology of Hassidic Mu-*
sic: Chemjo Vinaver. Jerusalem, Isr.:Hebrew Univ./Magnes
Press, 1983; 450pp., illus., music.
Compilation based upon materials in the Chemjo Vinaver
(1900-1973) Archives presently housed at Jewish National
and University Library. In this edition, 104 musical
pieces are arranged into four sections: 1. Sacred Songs;
2. *Zemirot* (holiday hymns) and *Niggunim* (wordless
melodies); 3. Hassidic cantorial art; and, 4. Works for
choir. Vinaver devoted much of his musical energies, in
Europe, America and Israel to building his collection.
Introduction by Elihu Schleifer affords some background
information on music, texts, Hassidic musical customs,
as well as data on some individual selections. Hebrew
liturgy and Yiddish song texts romanized. Source notes.

910
SCHORR, ISRAEL, comp. and ed. *Neginot Baruch Schorr.*repr.
ed. New York:Bloch,1952;250pp.,music.(orig.ed.New York,1928)
Collection of liturgical chants — melody lines only —
for High Holy Days, as compiled, performed and taught by
Chief Cantor of Great Synagogue in Lemberg, Galicia,
Baruch Schorr (1823-1904). Ashkenazic East European
traditional liturgical music. Compilation was prepared
by his son Israel Schorr (1886-1935) who served as cantor for congregations in Galicia and then America. Reissued posthumously. Hebrew liturgy romanized.

911
SLOBIN, MARK, trans./ed. *Old Jewish Folk Music; The Collections and Writings of Moshe Beregovski.* Phila.:Pennsyl-
vania Univ. Press, 1982; xvi,577pp., illus., music.
   Edited translation of ethnological works - collections
   and writings on Jewish folk music - by Soviet Jewish
   folklorist Moisevich (Moshe) Beregovskii (1892-1961).
   Materials contain background information on culture, as
   well as annotations for anthological compilation of over
   400 Yiddish folksongs - melody lines only - and folk
   poetry. English edition prepared by ethnomusicologist
   Mark Slobin. Yiddish song texts romanized.
912
STUTCHEWSKY, JOACHIM, comp. and ed. *Hassidic Tunes for
Sabbath.* Tel Aviv,Isr.:I.M.I., 1970; 27pp., music.
   Compilation of 38 melody lines, as collected from among
   several Hassidic groups of East European origins now
   residing in Israel, by folklorist and musician Joachim
   Stutchewsky (1891-1983). Materials presented as folk
   expressions of spiritual devotion (*Niggunim*): 14 wordless tunes and 24 songs with Hebrew liturgical texts.
913
STUTCHEWSKY, JOACHIM, comp. and ed. *Niggunei Hassidim
(Hassidic Tunes).* Tel Aviv,Isr.:Parnassus,1945; 24pp.,music
   Compilation of melody lines and musical motifs, as collected from among Hassidic groups in Jerusalem area, by
   folklorist and musician Joachim Stutchewsky (1891-1983).
   Materials for devotional expression at Sabbath meals and
   for Passover *Seder* feast. Hebrew texts only.
914
STUTCHEWSKY, JOACHIM comp. and ed. *Niggunim Ha-hassidim.
(Hassidic Melodies.)* Tel Aviv,Isr.: Histadruth Ha-ivrith
1950; 120pp., music.
   Compilation of melody lines for 120 *Niggunim* - devotional tunes and religious folksongs of various Hassidic
   groups, collected in Israel by musician and folklorist
   Joachim Stutchewsky (1891-1983). Hebrew texts only.
915
SULZER, SALOMON, comp. and ed. *Schir Zion - Gottesdienstliche Gesaenge.* repr.ed. New York:H.U.C.-J.I.R./S.M.P.,
1954; xii,540pp., music. (2nd ed. Vienna, 1905; orig. eds.
issued in 3 parts - Vienna, 1839/1865/1889.)
   Compilation of liturgical materials by Cantor Salomon
   Sulzer (1804-1890) in reprint edition based upon 2nd
   edition prepared by his son, cantor and music director
   Joseph Sulzer (1850-1926). Outstanding figure in 19th
   century Jewish music, cantorial artist and liturgical
   music innovator, Salomon Sulzer served pulpit at Great
   Synagogue of Vienna - Seitenstettengasse Shul - where he
   shaped and presented "modernized" liturgical music for
   traditional Orthodox services. Anthology contents: Part
   1 (vii, 226pp.) - Sabbath and Three Festivals (*Sukkot,
   Pesah, Shavuot*); Part 2 (pp.229-347) - High Holy Days;
   Part 3 (pp.351-540) - special Sabbath services, weddings
   and weekdays liturgies, hymns and music for celebrations
   of *Purim, Hanukkah, Tisha B'av.* Melody lines for can-

torial solo with choir responses. Some organ accompaniments for non-devotional use. Included also are several
compositions, setting Jewish liturgical texts, by Franz
Schubert (1797-1828), Joseph Fischhof (1804-1857) and
Ignaz Seyfried (1776-1841). German commentaries, and
Yiddish and Hebrew texts. English prefatory remarks for
reprint edition. Hebrew liturgy romanized.

916
VINAVER, CHEMJO, comp. and ed. *Anthology of Jewish Music:*
Sacred Chant and Religious Folksong of the East European
Jews. New York:Edward B. Marks,1955;xii,292pp.,illus.,music
Compilation of 103 selections – melody lines and some
choral materials, *a cappella* – collected by liturgist
Chemjo Vinaver (1900-1973). Anthology contents: Part 1 –
"Sacred Chant" – Biblical cantillations; prayer chants
for Sabbath, High Holy Days, Festivals (*Sukkot, Pesah,
Shavuot*); Psalm settings, including choral work for
Psalm 150 by Arnold Schoenberg (1874-1951). Part 2 –
"Religious Folksongs" – hymns for Sabbath meals cele-
brations, and Hassidic melodies (*Niggunim*). Introductory commentary and informative annotations for selections. Glossary of Hebrew and Yiddish terms. Hebrew
liturgy romanized.

917
WEINTRAUB, HIRSCH ALTER, comp. and ed. *Schire Beth Adonai*
– Tempelgesaenge in der Gottesdienst der Israeliten. repr.
ed. New York:H.U.C.-J.I.R./S.M.P., 1955; 254pp., music.
(orig.ed. Koenigsberg, 1859; 2nd ed. Leipzig, 1901).
Three sections in one volume of cantorial solos, choir
responses *a cappella* for Sabbath, High Holy Days and
Festivals, with additional music for other special religious occasions in calendar year. Hirsch Alter Weintraub (1811-1882) was trained for cantorial profession
by his father, notable cantorial leader Salomon Kashtan
Weintraub (1781-1829), who served congregation in Alt-
konstantin, Russia. The younger Weintraub held posts in
Dubnow, Russia and then in Koenigsberg, Germany, where
he trained other cantors and named his successor from
among those pupils, Eduard Birnbaum (1855-1920). Scholar
and music collector Birnbaum guided the posthumous 2nd
edition of Weintraub's collected materials. German, Yiddish and Hebrew texts. Some prefatory remarks in English
for reprint edition. Hebrew liturgy romanized.

918
WEISSER (PILDERWASSER), SAMUEL JOSHUA, comp. and ed. *Ba'al*
Tefilloh: Recitatives for Cantor. New York: Metro Music,
1939; 143pp., music.
Collection of melody lines by cantor and choir leader
Samuel Weisser (1888-1952) for traditional East European
Ashkenazic services of Sabbath, High Holy Days and
Festivals. Hebrew liturgy romanized.

919
ZALMANOFF, SAMUEL and SEYMOUR SILBERMINTZ, comps. and eds.
Sefer Ha-niggunim. (Melodies of the Habad Hassidic Sect.)
Brooklyn,N.Y.:Nichoach/Lubavitcher,1957;60n.p.+196pp.,music.
Compilation of melody lines for devotional folksongs

(*Niggunim*) of East European *Habad* sect/Lubavitcher
Hassidim, as collected among groups resident in Brooklyn and Jerusalem. Published in two parts: 1. Collection
of 175 melodies, with Yiddish introductory essay; 2. A
group of 40 melodies, with Yiddish annotations, and concluding with song index for both parts. Materials for
Sabbath, High Holy Days, Festivals, table hymns, general
celebrations and gatherings (*Farbrengen*), weddings,
study and dance motifs. Hebrew and Yiddish texts only.
920
ZEFIRA, BRACHA, comp. and ed. *Kolot Rabim (Many Voices);*
Anthology of Oriental Jewish Hymns and Songs. Ramat Gan,
Isr.:Massada, 1978; v,279pp., illus., music.
Compilation by noted Yemenite-Israeli folksong collector
and performer Bracha Zefira. Annotations provided in Hebrew and some English text for Jewish melodies of Yemenite, Sephardic, Persian, Bokharan and North African
groups, now residing in State of Israel. Some special
arrangements as Zefira herself has performed them over
years of her career. Broad variety of materials in Hebrew, Ladino, Aramaic and Arabic. Song lines romanized.

B. Hymnals and Songsters

921
ADLER, SAMUEL, comp./arr. *Shirey Yeladim - Songs for Chil-*
dren. New York:U.A.H.C., 1970; 48pp., illus., music.
Collection of 40 melodies - prayers, holiday and Bible
songs - for young children of kindergarten through 5th
grade. Musical settings of texts from prayerbook, Bible,
and some materials by poet-educators. Melodies adapted
from Judaic motifs. Simple piano parts. English texts.
922
ALGAZI, LEON, comp./arr. *Six Chansons Populaires.* Paris,
Fr.:Salabert Editions, 1934; 18pp., music.
Collection of six Jewish folksongs, arranged for voice
with piano accompaniment by composer, liturgist and conductor Leon Algazi (1890-1971). French translations and
annotations. Hebrew and Yiddish romanized.
923
ALTMAN, SHALOM, comp./arr. *The Judean Songster.* New York:
Young Judea, 1934; 130pp., music.
Collection of 215 songs, melody lines only, for Sabbath,
holidays, festive occasions, and folksongs of Hassidic
traditions and Zionism. Prepared by music educator and
choral leader Shalom Altman. Yiddish/Hebrew romanized.
924
AMERICAN CONFERENCE OF CANTORS - Committee, comps./eds.
Songster for Congregational and Solo Singing. New York:
A.C.C./H.U.C.-J.I.R., 1953; 20pp., music.
Collection of hymns - melody lines only. Prepared for
first Institute on Sacred Music of American Conference

of Cantors, held in New York City, June 1953. English
texts. Hebrew romanized.

925
AMIRAN, EMANUEL and Committee, comps./eds. *Divrey Shir V'-*
zimrah - Collections of Poetry and Melodies. (Series of 12)
Tel Aviv, Isr.:Dept. of Culture and Education, 1953-1957;
32pp. each, music.
> Series of 12 songsters, with about 40 selections in each
> - melody lines only. Liturgical chants, hymns and folk-
> songs for Sabbath, holidays and festivals during entire
> calendar year of Jewish observances. Prepared by music
> arranger and composer Emanuel Amiran, with advisory com-
> mittee of educators, for Israeli elementary schools and
> Hebrew language classes abroad. Hebrew romanized.

926
AMIRAN, EMANUEL and Committee, comps./eds. *Shiron:Educa-*
tional Songbooks. (Graded Series of 6) Tel Aviv, Isr.: Dept.
of Culture and Education,1952/53; 60pp. each, music.
> Six songsters, graded from 1 to 6 for Israeli elementary
> school levels - melody lines only. Music for Sabbath,
> holidays, celebrations, and also Hassidic tunes and some
> general folksongs. Prepared by composer and advisory
> committee of educators. Hebrew for songs romanized.

927
AMIRAN, EMANUEL and Committee, comps./eds. *Zemer Chen -*
Lovely Tunes. Tel Aviv, Isr.:Tarbut, 1960; 181pp., music.
> Collection of 123 songs for kindergarten and primary
> grade levels of Israeli schools - melody lines only -
> with other educational materials. Prepared by composer
> and music educator Emanuel Amiran, with advisory commit-
> tee. No English texts. Hebrew for songs romanized.

928
BANNISTER, MAURICE, comp. and ARTHUR SOMERVELL, arr.
Hebrew Songs of Palestine. London, Eng.: Boosey, 1931;
iv,31pp., music.
> Collection of 12 songs of early Zionist movement, with
> simple piano accompaniment. English translations;
> Hebrew texts romanized.

929
BAR-ILAN, OPHIRA and MICHA ALMAN, comps./eds. *Hashirim*
Shelanu; Ha-tsad Pizmoni Yisrael - Our Songs; Israeli Hit
Parade. Tel Aviv, Isr.:Subar, 1969; 114pp., illus., music.
> Collection of 52 selections - melody lines with guitar
> symbols. Popular Israeli songs by various current song-
> writers and lyricists (c.1960/69). Photographs of per-
> formers. Hebrew texts only.

930
BAR-ILAN, OPHIRA and AVNER KATZ, comps./eds. *Daber Elay*
B'shirim - Speak to Me With Songs; More Songs of Effi
Netzer. Tel Aviv, Isr.:Subar, 1970; 114pp., illus., music.
> Collection of 44 selections - melody lines with guitar
> symbols. Popular songs by Israeli entertainer and song-
> writer Effi Netzer. Photographs. Hebrew texts only.

931
BAR-ILAN, OPHIRA and AVNER KATZ, comps./eds. *Hava Nashira*
- Let Us Sing; Effi Netzer's Songs. Tel Aviv, Isr.: Subar,

1970; 114pp., illus., music.
    Collection of 44 selections - melody lines with guitar
    symbols. Popular songs by Israeli entertainer and song-
    writer Effi Netzer. Photographs. Hebrew texts only.
    932
BAR-ILAN, OPHIRA and AVNER KATZ, comps./eds. *Pizmonim B'-*
tsimrat - Song Hits At the Top. Tel Aviv,Isr.:Subar, 1971;
114pp., illus., music.
    Collection of 44 selections - melody lines with guitar
    symbols. Popular songs by current Israeli musicians
    (c.1968/71). Photographs. Hebrew texts only.
    933
BASTOMSKY, SOLOMON, comp./ed. and ABRAHAM SLEP, arr. *Unter*
di Grininke Beimelekh - Sammlung fun Lider Mit Noten. ("Col-
lection of Songs With Music.") Vilna,Lith.:Yiddish Folks
Shul, 1931; 96pp., music.
    Collection of 60 selections - melody lines with some
    voice parts for choir. Children's songs for use in Vilna
    Jewish schools. Topics of seasons, holidays, play and
    lessons, lullabies. Prepared by educator Solomon Bastom-
    sky (1891-1941) with music arranger and choral director
    Abraham Slep (?-1943). Yiddish and Hebrew texts only.
    934
BECK, RUDOLPH, comp./arr. *Community Songs with Piano Ac-*
companiment. Chicago:B.J.E., 1958; 77pp., music.
    Collection of 56 popular Jewish folksongs, with simple
    piano accompaniments. Yiddish and Hebrew romanized.
    935
BELARSKY, SIDOR, comp./ed. *Songbook.* New York: Ethnic
Publications, 1970; 256pp., music.
    Collection of 77 Yiddish and Hebrew folksongs and art
    song compositions, with piano accompaniments. Materials
    based upon performance repertoire of Jewish folksinger
    baritone Sidor Belarsky (1900-1975), including music
    from 19th-20th century Eastern Europe and America.
    Yiddish and Hebrew romanized.
    936
BEN-HAIM, PAUL comp./arr. *Shirim L'yeladim - Songs for*
Children. Tel Aviv,Isr.:Tarbut/I.M.P.,1946; 24 pp., music.
    Hebrew tunes arranged by Israeli composer Paul Ben-Haim,
    setting poems of educator Miriam Shliklis. Simple piano
    accompaniments. Hebrew texts romanized.
    937
BIKEL, THEODORE, comp. *Folksongs and Footnotes; An Inter-*
national Songbook. New York:Meridian, 1960; 254pp., music.
    Collection of 84 songs topically organized with intro-
    duction and annotations by Jewish singer/actor Theodore
    Bikel. Includes 28 Jewish folksongs - 19 Yiddish, 1
    Ladino, 8 Hebrew. Simple piano accompaniment; song in-
    dex. Yiddish and Hebrew texts romanized.
    938
BINDER, ABRAHAM WOLF, comp./arr. *Hanukkah Songster.* New
York: Bloch, 1922; 16pp., music.
    Collection of tunes for children's voices, with simple
    piano accompaniments, for celebration of Feast of Lights
    (*Hanukkah*) holiday. Includes complete musical service

for children's observance, as well as 5 English hymns,
all liturgical blessings and 3 Hebrew folksongs — as arranged by American Jewish music director, composer and
educator A.W. Binder (1895-1966). Hebrew romanized.

939
BINDER, ABRAHAM WOLF, comp./arr. *Jewish Folk Songs in Hassidic Style.* New York: Mills Music, 1963; 32pp., music.
    Collection of 10 Hassidic folksongs, with simple piano
    accompaniments, arranged by Jewish music educator and
    liturgical composer A.W. Binder (1895-1966). Prefatory
    materials present background on Hassidic movement and
    its musical traditions. Annotations and English trans-
    lations for songs. Yiddish and Hebrew romanized.

940
BINDER, ABRAHAM WOLF, comp./arr. *The Jewish Year In Song.*
New York: G.Schirmer, 1928; 25pp., music.
    Collection of songs, hymns, prayer tunes and folk melo-
    dies "for synagogue, school and home," selected and ar-
    ranged by Jewish music leader A.W. Binder (1895-1966),
    for 1 or 2 voices, with simple piano accompaniments.
    Some English texts. Hebrew and Yiddish romanized.

941
BINDER, ABRAHAM WOLF, comp./arr. *New Palestinian Folksongs*
New York: Bloch, 1926; 28pp., music.
    Collection of 22 songs from among early 20th century
    settlers on land of Israel, as notated and arranged by
    Jewish music educator and choral leader A.W. Binder
    (1895-1966). Includes liturgical chants, religious hymns
    and folktunes of Yemenite Jews as well as those from
    Eastern Europe, Hassidic melodies, Zionist songs and
    dances. Simple piano accompaniments. English transla-
    tions. Hebrew and Yiddish romanized.

942
BINDER, ABRAHAM WOLF, comp./arr. *Pioneer Songs of Palestine - Shire Halutzim.* New York: Edward B. Marks, 1942;
44pp., music.
    Collection of 20 early Zionist folksongs, with simple
    piano accompaniment, as selected and arranged by Jewish
    music educator A.W. Binder (1895-1966). English trans-
    lations (for singing) by Olga Paul. Hebrew romanized.

943
BINDER, ABRAHAM WOLF, comp./arr. *Purim Songster.* New
York: Bloch, 1922; 16pp., music.
    Collection of tunes for children's voices, with simple
    piano accompaniments, for celebration of Feast of Lots
    (*Purim*) holiday. Prepared by Jewish music educator A.
    W. Binder (1895-1966). English texts; Hebrew romanized.

944
BINDER, ABRAHAM WOLF, comp./arr. *Songs Israel Sings; Yisrael B'shir.* New York: Metro Music, 1951; 39pp., music.
    Collection of 19 Hebrew folksongs, with simple piano ac-
    companiments, in arrangements by music educator A.W.
    Binder (1895-1966). Includes *Hanukkah* songs, as well
    as Yemenite and Hassidic melodies, and musical settings
    of special Hebrew poetry. English annotations for songs.
    Hebrew texts romanized.

945
BINDER, ABRAHAM WOLF and JACOB BEIMEL, comps./arrs. *Pass-over Seder Melodies.* repr.ed. New York:Bloch, 1925; 32pp., music. (orig.ed. New York:Jewish Center, 1919)
     Collection of traditional chants, hymns and folksongs
     for Passover *Seder* (festive meal), including music for
     ceremonials before and after meal. Melodies compiled and
     arranged by two leading figures in Jewish liturgical
     and folk music: A.W. Binder (1895-1966) and Jacob Beimel
     (1880-1944). Some English texts. Hebrew romanized.
946
BINDER, ABRAHAM WOLF and CENTRAL CONFERENCE OF AMERICAN
RABBIS - Synagogue Music Committee, comps./eds. *Musical
Services for Sabbath, Festivals and Special Occasions -
Supplement for Union Hymnal: Third Official Edition.* New
York:C.C.A.R., 1932; pp.315-429 (114pp.), music.
     Collection of 74 selections (hymns 267-341) - melodies
     with SATB choir parts, or with organ (or piano) accom-
     paniments. Separately issued - Part 2. Musical Services
     (pp.315-429) of *Third Union Hymnal* (New York, 1932).
     Prepared for congregational participation in services of
     Sabbath and other religious observances in Jewish calen-
     dar year. This supplementary hymnal was reprinted in
     1942, 1944, 1946, 1948/9 and 1957. English texts and
     translations. Song index. Hebrew romanized.
947
BINDER, ABRAHAM WOLF and CENTRAL CONFERENCE OF AMERICAN
RABBIS - Synagogue Music Committee, comps./eds. *The Union
Hymnal; Songs and Prayers for Jewish Worship - Third (New)
Official Edition.* New York:C.C.A.R.,1932; viii,588pp.,music
     Collection of hymns, responses and liturgical chants -
     melodies, with SATB choir parts, or with simple organ
     (or piano) accompaniments. Completely revised and en-
     larged *Union Hymnal*, prepared by C.C.A.R. with music
     editor A.W. Binder (1895-1966), an educator, composer
     and choral director. Binder re-arranged materials from
     the two earlier *Union Hymnal* editions (1897 and 1914),
     contributed new settings for liturgical texts, invited
     Jewish composers to write hymns based upon traditional
     synagogue chants, and added some responses by leading
     European cantorial musicians. Widely appreciated, this
     Third Union Hymnal was reprinted in 1942, 1944, 1946
     and 1948/9. In 1957, it was reissued with minor modifi-
     cations, and remains as standard hymnal for Reform con-
     gregations. Contents divided into three distinctive
     sections: 1. Hymns (266 selections); 2. Musical Services
     (pp.315-429) - issued separately as supplementary hymnal
     volume: *Musical Services for Sabbath, Festivals and
     Special Occasions* (New York, 1932); and, 3. Services
     for the Religious School - prayers with music responses
     (114 congregational chants), for Sabbath and the other
     religious services of Jewish calendar year. English
     liturgical texts, annotations and translations. Incipit
     and song title indexes. All Hebrew romanized.

948
BONIN, MARY comp./ed. *Hebrew and Yiddish Folksongs.* Lon-
don,Eng.:Elkin (New York:Galaxy), 1961; 21pp., music.
    Collection of Jewish folksongs, with piano accompaniment
    and English translations. Hebrew and Yiddish romanized.
949
BRAHAM, JOHN, comp. and ISAAC NATHAN, arr. *A Selection of*
Hebrew Melodies, Ancient and Modern, Parts 1 and 2. London,
Eng.:Nathan, 1815/1820; 125pp., music.
    Collection of settings of poetic texts by Lord Byron
    (1788-1824), to melodies selected and adapted by two
    English Jewish musicians — singer John Braham (1774-
    1856) and liturgist Isaac Nathan (1792-1864). Issued
    in two separate parts, and then in one volume. Part 1.
    12 solos and 3 SATB selections. Part 2. 12 solos and 4
    SAT/SA selections. English annotations and piano accom-
    paniments. Hebrew texts romanized.
950
BROUNOFF, PLATON, comp./arr. *Jewish Folk Songs.* New York:
Charles K. Harris, 1911; 82pp.+4n.p., music.
    Collection of 50 Yiddish folksongs, topically placed
    according to categories of: courtship, marriage and
    children, religion, work and other political and social
    themes. Yiddish introduction treating language and its
    heritage of literature and music. Platon Brounoff (1863-
    1924) trained at St. Petersburg Conservatory of Music
    and was composer/arranger and choral leader in New York
    City. Some English texts for songs. Simple piano accom-
    paniments. Yiddish romanized.
951
BUGATCH, SAMUEL, comp./ed. *Doros Zingen - B'shiras Hadoros*
- Songs of Our People. New York:Farband,1961; 310pp.,music.
    Collection of 264 Hebrew and Yiddish folksongs — melody
    lines only — in topical roster of: Zionist and Israeli
    songs; Yiddish melodies; Hassidic and liturgical chants;
    hymns; children's school tunes; Sabbath, holidays and
    festivals music; songs of Ghettos and Holocaust era. In-
    troduction in Yiddish and English by compiler Samuel
    Bugatch, Jewish music educator and choral leader. Folk
    composers and poets indicated for many songs. Yiddish
    and Hebrew texts romanized. Expanded edition of earlier
    (1951) informally prepared collection of 245 songs.
952
CARP, BERNARD, comp./ed. *The Jewish Center Songster; Fa-*
vorite Hebrew, Yiddish and English Songs for All Occasions.
New York: J.W.B., 1949; 96pp., music.
    Collection of 105 folksongs — melody lines only — for
    Sabbath, holidays, festivals, general occasions, chil-
    dren's tunes, Hassidic melodies, Hebrew and Yiddish
    songs. Compiled by group leader Bernard Carp for use in
    centers, camps, schools and military services. Some Eng-
    lish annotations. Hebrew and Yiddish romanized.
953
CASTEL, NICO, comp. and RICHARD NEUMANN, arr. *The Ladino*
Songbook. New York:Tara, 1981; 88pp., music.
    Collection of 35 Judaeo-Spaniolic (Ladino) folksongs —

"favorites" of operatic tenor and Sephardic cantorial
artist Nico Castel. Melodies set with guitar symbols and
piano accompaniments, arranged by music educator Richard
Neumann. Annotations and background information on Ladino folksongs by scholar Israel J. Katz. Some English
translations. Ladino and Hebrew texts romanized.
954

CENTRAL COMMITTEE OF JEWS IN POLAND, comps. *Undzer Gezang*
(Our Song). Warsaw,Pol.:Office of Culture and Propaganda
(New York:Jewish Music Alliance), 1947; 218pp., music.
Fascinating songbook for its contents, time and place
of publication. Collection of 91 selections - melody
lines only - topically sorted according to: hymns and
work songs (including *Hatikvah* anthem, and other
Hebrew Zionist songs); partisan-ghetto fighters and
other Holocaust music; Yiddish folksongs; children's
tunes. Hebrew and Yiddish texts only. Lyrics romanized.
955

CENTRAL CONFERENCE OF AMERICAN RABBIS - Liturgy and Music
Committees, comps./eds. *Union Haggadah: Home Seder Service.*
rev.enl.ed. Cincinnati/New York:C.C.A.R./Bloch,1923; xvi,
162pp., music.(orig.ed. Cincinnati/New York:C.C.A.R./Bloch,
1904; ix,108pp., music.)
English text version, with annotations, of *Haggadah*
(order of service) for *Seder* (Passover home ritual
meal), according to Reform congregational practices.
Hymns and folksongs - melody lines with SATB choir parts
or simple piano accompaniments. Editing of music for
1923 edition was prepared by rabbi and educator Samuel
S. Cohon (1888-1959). Original edition (1904) utilized
notations made by cantor and composer Alois Kaiser (1840
-1908). Hebrew song texts romanized. *Note*: Numerous
(probably hundreds) of Passover *Haggadah* editions have
been published by Reform, Conservative and Orthodox
groups. All copies present essentially same modest compilation of melodies with romanized Hebrew texts.
956

CENTRAL CONFERENCE OF AMERICAN RABBIS - Music Committee,
comps./eds. *Union Hymnal for Jewish Worship - Second Offi-*
cial Edition. New York:C.C.A.R./Bloch,1914;xiv,335pp.,music
Revised and enlarged version of first edition of *Union*
Hymnal (New York, 1897). Collection of 226 hymns and
anthems - melody lines, with choir parts and some simple
organ (or piano) accompaniments. Materials from hymnal
of Temple Emanu-El (New York, 1894). Including about 140
melodies of non-Jewish origins, some direct adaptations
from church hymnody. Innovation was addition of section
of responses for children's services. Almost all English
texts. Hebrew romanized. By 1917, C.C.A.R. had formed a
committee to consider preparation of a third completely
altered "more Judaic" *Hymnal* for Reform congregations.
957

CHAJES, JULIUS, comp./arr. *Ten Palestinian Folk Songs.*
New York:Transcontinental, 1944; 11pp., music.
Collection of melodies, with piano accompaniment, ar-
ranged by composer and music educator Julius Chajes for

children's performances. Hebrew texts romanized.
958
CHAPLAINS BOARD, comps. *The U.S.A. Armed Forces Hymnal.*
Washington,D.C.:Supt. of Documents, [1960?]; 512pp., music.
    See Jewish section, pp.77-118, for melody lines - with
    some part-voice arrangements - of 37 liturgical hymns.
    English annotations. Hebrew texts romanized.
959
COHEN, FRANCIS LYON and DAVID MONTAGUE DAVIS, comps./eds.
Kol Rinah V'todah - The Voice of Prayer and Praise. repr.ed
London,Eng.:J. Curwin, 1914; xxiv,248pp., music. (orig.ed.
London,Eng.: Greenberg, 1899)
    "A handbook of synagogue music for congregational sing-
    ing." Prepared under sponsorship of Choir Committee of
    Council of the United Synagogue of Great Britain by
    Francis Lyon Cohen (1862-1934) and musician/educator
    David Montague Davis. F.L. Cohen pursued various careers
    as educator, lecturer, journalist, contributor of arti-
    cles on Jewish music to encyclopedias and journals, and
    for a time served as rabbi to a congregation in Sydney,
    Australia. This edition constitutes a re-working of an
    earlier publication (1889) prepared by Cohen with B.L.
    Mosely (fl.19th cent.). Presented here are 310 hymns -
    melody lines, with some SATB arrangements and sol-fa
    notations - for services of weekday, Sabbath, High Holy
    Days, Festivals and other special liturgical occasions
    or communal celebrations according to Ashkenazic tra-
    ditions. English preface gives background on liturgy
    and music. Hebrew texts romanized.
960
COHEN, FRANCIS LYON and B.L. MOSELY, comps./eds. *Shire
Keneset Yisrael - The Handbook of Synagogue Music for Congregational Singing.*   London,Eng.: Spottiswoode, 1889;
xii,245pp., music.
    Hymnal for entire calendar year of Ashkenazic tradition-
    al services as practiced in Great Britain. Prepared by
    music educator, rabbi and journalist F.L. Cohen (1862-
    1934) and liturgist B.L. Mosely (fl.19th cent.), for use
    of particular London congregation in services and for
    religious school. Collection of 313 selections, with
    SATB choir, *a cappella*. English prefatory materials.
    Hebrew texts romanized.
961
COHEN, GUSTAVE M., comp./arr. *The Orpheus.* Cleveland: S.
Brainard, 1878; 90pp., music.
    Collection of 49 hymns - melody lines, with SATB choir
    and simple piano accompaniment (or organ) - for use at
    American Reform congregations on Sabbath, New Year,
    Hanukkah, Passover, and for Psalm chants. G.M. Cohen
    (fl.19th cent.) was cantor, choir leader and educator.
    Hymn texts in German, English and Hebrew (romanized).
962
COHEN, GUSTAVE M., comp./arr. *The Sacred Harp of Judah; A
Choice Collection of Music for the Use of Synagogue, School
and Home.* Cleveland:S. Brainard, 1864; 50pp, music.
    Collection of 40 selections - with simple piano accom-

paniments (or organ) — for Sabbath services of American
Reform congregations. G.M. Cohen (fl.19th cent.) was
cantor and choir leader at Temple Emanu-El in New York
City (1845-1855). Hymn texts in German and English.
963

COOK, RAY, comp./arr. *Sing for Fun, Books 1 and 2.* New
York:U.A.H.C., 1955/1957; 39pp./63pp., music.
> *Book 1* — Collection of 26 original songs, with simple
> piano accompaniments, for primary grades of the Jewish
> religious school. Topical materials: holidays, Bible and
> general music — in English texts. *Book 2* — Collection
> of 31 original songs, with moderately graded piano ac-
> companiment, for upper grades of the Jewish religious
> school. Topical materials: services hymns, holiday folk-
> songs and general tunes — in English texts with some
> Hebrew romanized.
964

COOPERSMITH, HARRY, comp./arr. *Favorite Songs of the Jewish People.* New York:Transcontinental, 1939; 72pp., music.
> Collection of 35 selections: hymns for Sabbath and holi-
> days, and some folksongs — with simple piano accompani-
> ments. Prepared by music educator Harry Coopersmith
> (1902-1975) while he was music director at Anshe Emet
> Synagogue in Chicago. English texts; Hebrew romanized.
965

COOPERSMITH, HARRY, comp./arr. *Ha-gan Li, Shir Li - Holidays in Song.* New York:J.E.C./B.J.E., 1956; 51pp., music.
> Collection of 24 selections, in two part (SA) music
> lines with simple piano accompaniments, arranged by
> music educator Harry Coopersmith (1902-1975) for use
> with young children's choirs and teaching of Hebrew
> language. Settings of Hebrew poetry of Israeli writer
> Elhanan Indelman, with traditional Jewish folk and
> liturgical motifs and melodies. Hebrew romanized.
966

COOPERSMITH, HARRY, comp./arr. *Hanukkah Songster for
Children's Choral Groups.* New York: J.E.C./B.J.E.,
1940; 25pp., music.
> Collection of 13 *Hanukkah* songs — melody lines set
> for two-part (SA) youth choir, *a cappella*. Prepared
> by music educator Harry Coopersmith (1902-1975) early
> in his career as music director for the Jewish Education
> Committee (later known as Board of Jewish Education)
> of New York City. English translations of song texts.
> Hebrew and Yiddish romanized.
967

COOPERSMITH, HARRY, comp./arr. *Hebrew Songster for Kindergarten and Primary Grades.* New York: J.E.C./B.J.E., 1948;
iv,88pp., illus., music.
> Collection of 86 selections — melody lines only — for
> use in language teaching at Hebrew schools in classes of
> children 5-8 years old. Topically sorted for: home and
> family; school days; prayers of Sabbath, holidays and
> festivals; "people, places and things" in general life.
> Melodies developed by music educator Harry Coopersmith
> (1902-1975) utilizing traditional liturgical and folk

motifs and tunes. Hebrew text romanized.
968
COOPERSMITH, HARRY, comp./arr. *Jewish Choral Book.* New
York:J.E.C./B.J.E., 1941; 28pp., music.
    Collection of 15 selections - Hebrew liturgicals, Has-
    sidic tunes and Yiddish folksongs - arranged in two-part
    (SA) for children's choir, *a cappella.* Prepared by
    music educator Harry Coopersmith (1902-1975). English
    song texts. Hebrew and Yiddish romanized.
969
COOPERSMITH, HARRY, comp./arr. *Jewish Choral Collection.*
New York: B.J.E., 1960/1970; 60pp., music.
    Collection of 50 selections - arranged for SATB with
    simple piano accompaniment. Hymns for Sabbath and other
    liturgical services; various Jewish folksongs. Compi-
    lation by music educator Harry Coopersmith (1902-1975)
    was issued twice by B.J.E. Materials for use by older
    children and adult choruses. Hebrew/Yiddish romanized.
970
COOPERSMITH, HARRY, comp./ed. *Jewish Community Songster.*
Chicago: B.J.E., 1930; 95pp., music.
    Combined one volume edition, prepared by music educator
    Harry Coopersmith (1902-1975), of 6 separately issued
    Little Books of Jewish Songs for Jewish Sunday Schools.
    Melody lines only, for: Sabbath, *Hanukkah, Tu B'shvat,
    Purim, Pesach,* and *Shavuot.* Some English texts;
    Hebrew romanized.
971
COOPERSMITH, HARRY, comp./ed. *Little Books of Jewish Songs
for Jewish Sunday Schools.* Chicago: B.J.E., c.1928; Six
booklets - each 18pp., music.
    Songster collections - melody lines, for: *Hanukkah;
    Tu B'shvat; Purim; Pesach; Shavuot;* and Sabbath. Pre-
    pared as little hymnals for children's use, by music
    educator Harry Coopersmith (1902-1975) early in his
    active and prolific career in Jewish religious schools.
    Materials from pioneer "Goldfarb Songsters" included.
    Some English texts. Hebrew romanized.
972
COOPERSMITH, HARRY, comp./ed. *More of the Songs We Sing.*
New York:United Synagogue of America, 1971; 266pp., music.
    Prepared as "companion supplementary volume" to earlier
    publication *The Songs We Sing* (New York, 1950) also by
    music educator Harry Coopersmith (1902-1975). Collection
    of 194 selections, placed in graded order for Jewish
    school use - melody lines only, with chord symbols and
    some part (SA) and "round" arrangements. Intended for
    camps as well as classrooms. Includes roster of favorite
    hymns for Sabbath and other religious occasions, folk-
    songs in Yiddish, Hebrew and English, and Bible text
    settings. English translations and annotations. Song
    index. Hebrew and Yiddish romanized.
973
COOPERSMITH, HARRY, comp./ed. *The New Jewish Song Book.*
New York:Behrman House, 1965; 192pp., illus., music.
    Collection of 104 selections - melody lines with chord

symbols – for Sabbath and other liturgical services,
Hebrew and Yiddish folksongs, Bible text settings, and
general topics. Compiled for Jewish religious schools
by music educator Harry Coopersmith (1902–1975) in a
graded order from "simple" to "difficult." Some English
songs. Annotations and index. Hebrew/Yiddish romanized.
974

COOPERSMITH, HARRY, comp./ed. *Selected Jewish Songs: For
the Members of the Armed Forces.* New York: J.W.B./A.A.J.E.,
1943; 96pp., music.
Collection of 86 selections – melody lines only – for
Sabbath, High Holy Days, Festivals, other liturgical
and communal services, and some Jewish folksongs. Prepared by music educator Harry Coopersmith (1902–1975),
under sponsorship of Jewish Chaplains Committee/J.W.B.,
for use as hymnal by servicemen during World War II.
English annotations. Hebrew and Yiddish romanized.
975

COOPERSMITH, HARRY, comp./ed. *Songs of My People.* Chica-
go:Anshe Emet Synagogue, 1937; 249pp., illus., music.
Collection of 229 selections – melody lines only – for
wide range of Jewish music for: Sabbath, High Holy Days,
Festivals, Jewish celebrations, hymns and blessings,
Yiddish and Hebrew folksongs, and American patriotic
songs. Harry Coopersmith (1902–1975) began his career as
Jewish music educator in Chicago area. This volume ac-
companies a book of *Prayers and Blessings* (288pp.),
also issued by that congregation. Some English annotations; Hebrew and Yiddish texts romanized.
976

COOPERSMITH, HARRY, comp./arr. *Songs Sacred and Serious.*
New York: J.E.C./B.J.E., 1957; 67pp., music.
Collection of 31 selections – two part (SA) and three
part (SSA) arrangements, *a cappella*, for children's
choirs – prepared by music educator Harry Coopersmith
(1902–1975) for use at Jewish religious schools. Includes: hymns for liturgical services, Sabbath "table
songs" (*Zemirot*), Hassidic melodies, Israeli folksongs
and musical settings of Biblical texts. Some English
annotations and translations. Hebrew romanized.
977

COOPERSMITH, HARRY, comp./ed. *The Songs We Sing – U'lesho-
nenu Rinah.* New York: United Synagogue of America (Phila.:
J.P.S.A.), 1950; xx,453pp., illus., music.
Collection of 265 selections, artistically arranged for
voice and piano by roster of musicians, including such
notable composers as: Bernstein, Binder, Ephros, Freed,
Fromm, Jacobi, Milhaud, Schalit and Weill. Compilation
of Hebrew and Yiddish folksongs, liturgical hymns and
religious chants – melodies for Sabbath, High Holy Days,
Festivals and other ritual occasions, Zionist and Israel
folksongs and folk dance tunes. Outstanding quality publication prepared by music educator Harry Coopersmith
(1902–1975). English annotations and translations for
all materials. Indexes. Hebrew and Yiddish romanized.

978
COOPERSMITH, HARRY, comp./ed. *Songs of Zion.* New York:
Behrman House, 1942; 241pp., illus., music.
Collection of 209 selections - melody lines only - com-
prised of: 126 Zionist and Hebrew folksongs; 83 holiday
and festival hymns. Prepared by music educator Harry
Coopersmith (1902-1975), when he first assumed position
as music director of J.E.C./B.J.E., for training and
supervisory guidance of music teachers in the Jewish
all-day, afternoon, and Sunday schools of greater New
York City area. This songster publication was highly
popular and had 4 printing run-offs from 1942 to 1947.
English annotations for all songs. Some translations
for singing. Hebrew and Yiddish romanized.

979
COOPERSMITH, HARRY, comp./arr. *Supplementary Songs to
Festival Songsters.* New York:J.E.C./B.J.E.,1947;54pp.,music
Collection of 44 selections - melody lines, two (SA) and
three part (SSA) choir arrangements, and several simple
piano accompaniments - prepared by music educator Harry
Coopersmith (1902-1975) for use in training choral lead-
ers for Jewish schools. Includes hymns and folksongs for
calendar year religious services and celebrations. Some
English texts. Hebrew and Yiddish romanized.

980
**COOPERSMITH, HARRY, GERSHON EPHROS and JACOB BEIMEL, comps.
/eds.** *Sabbath Services in Song: Friday Evening and Sabbath
Morning.* New York:Behrman/J.E.C.(B.J.E.),1948;128pp.,music.
Basic Sabbath hymnal for youngsters, prepared by music
educator Harry Coopersmith (1902-1975), in association
with two notable liturgical musicians - Gershon Ephros
(1890-1978) and Jacob Beimel (1880-1944). Intended for
use in classrooms and at children's congregational services. Includes 187 selections - melody lines only - for
traditional liturgical chants, hymns and some composed
music: 56 for Friday evening; 114 for Sabbath morning;
and, 17 *Hallel* (Praises) hymns. Hebrew romanized.

981
COOPERSMITH, HARRY and MEYER LEVIN, comps./eds. *Haggadah.*
New York:Behrman House, 1968; 96pp., illus., music.
The *Haggadah* is the handbook for the order and text of
the ritual service at the *Seder*, or festive meal of
the Passover holiday. This edition contains special annotations by author Meyer Levin, and a musical supplement (pp.75-96) of *Seder* hymns and folksongs as compiled by music educator Harry Coopersmith (1902-1975).
Music lines only. Hebrew romanized.

982
COVICH, EDITH, comp./arr. *The Jewish Child Every Day.*
Cincinnati/New York:U.A.H.C.,1947; x,51pp., illus., music.
Collection of 13 songs for young children, ages 4 to 6.
With simple piano accompaniment, arranged by educator
Edith Covich. English song texts and narrative.

983
DEUTSCH, BEATRICE L. comp./arr. *So We Sing - Holiday and
Bible Songs for Young Jewish Children.* New York: Bloch,

1950; 63pp., illus., music.
   Collection of 39 selections — melody lines, with simple
   piano accompaniments — for Sabbath, High Holy Days,
   Festivals, *Hanukkah*, *Purim*, and other celebrations,
   and tunes with Bible texts. Musical arrangements by educator Beatrice Deutsch utilize Judaic motifs. Some original poetry by writer Sara G. Levy. English texts.
   984

DEUTSCH, MORITZ, comp./arr. *Breslauer Synagogen Gesaenge*
("Breslau Synagogue Chants"). Leipzig,Ger.:Breitkopf u
Haertel, 1880; iii,102pp., music. *Vorbeterschule ("Cantor's
Hymnal").* Breslau,Ger.:Hanover, 1871; viii,124pp., music.
   Two collections of liturgical chants, hymns and anthems
   — cantorial solos with SATB choir parts. Music for Sabbath and other year-round religious services. Compiled
   by cantor and music educator Moritz Deutsch (1818-1892),
   founder of a training school for cantors and choir directors in Breslau. German texts. Hebrew romanized.
   985

DEUTSCH, MORITZ, comp./arr. *Deutsche Synagogen und Shul
Lieder.("German Synagogue and School Hymns.")* Breslau,Ger.:
Schlitter, 1867; 29pp., music.
   Collection of hymns for Sabbath and other services —
   cantorial solo, SATB choir voice, with organ (or flute,
   ad libitum). Compiled by cantor and music educator
   Moritz Deutsch (1818-1892), who served at Great Synagogue of Breslau. German texts. Hebrew romanized.
   986

DONIACH, SHULA, comp./arr. *Rhymes from Carmel — Children's
Part Singing.* Tel Aviv,Isr.:I.M.P., 1953; 54pp., music.
   Collection of 12 selections — arranged in two (SA) and
   three part (SSA) choirs, rounds and canons, with simple
   piano accompaniments — for children's choruses. Arranged
   by educator Shula Doniach, using traditional Jewish musical motifs. Texts by Israeli writer A.L. Yaron treat
   various religious and Bible subjects. Hebrew romanized.
   987

EDEL, YITZHAK and JOACHIM STUTCHEWSKY, comps./eds. *Zemer
Am — Jewish Folksongs.* Tel Aviv, Brit.Mand.: Yuval Naaman,
1945; 160pp., music.
   Collection of 76 selections — melody lines only — of
   children's classroom songs for study of Hebrew language.
   Prepared by two notable musicians active in music education and in development of creative artistry in the
   emergent State of Israel: Yitzhak Edel (1896-1973) and
   Joachim Stutchewsky (1891-1983). Includes range of traditional hymns and Zionist Hebrew folksongs, as well as
   some children's tunes. Hebrew for melodies romanized.
   988

EISENSTEIN, JUDITH KAPLAN, comp./arr. *Festival Songs.* New
York: Bloch, 1943; 64pp., music.
   Collection of 36 selections — English hymns, Hebrew
   liturgicals and Jewish holiday folksongs — with piano
   accompaniments. Arranged by music educator Judith Kaplan
   Eisenstein for use by youth groups at clubs and camps.
   English annotations. Hebrew romanized.

989
EISENSTEIN, JUDITH KAPLAN, comp./arr. *The Gateway to Jewish Song.* New York:Behrman House,1948;x,172pp.,illus.,music
    Collection of 104 selections — melodies with simple piano accompaniments — arranged by music educator Judith K. Eisenstein for use with early grade levels at Jewish religious schools. Songs for children's synagogue services and holiday celebrations, musical settings of Bible texts and poetry describing daily Jewish life and customs. Adaptation of traditional melodic motifs. English translations and annotations. Hebrew romanized.

990
EISENSTEIN, JUDITH KAPLAN, comp./arr. *Seder Music Section: The New Haggadah.* New York:Behrman,1942;176pp.,illus.,music
    Collection of melody lines for *Seder* (Passover ritual meal) hymns and folksongs. Prepared by music educator Judith K. Eisenstein, for edited version of *Haggadah*, or prayer service book of *Seder*, as intended for use by members of Jewish Reconstructionist Foundation movement. English texts. Hebrew for music romanized.

991
EISENSTEIN, JUDITH and FRIEDA PRENSKY, comps./eds. *Songs of Childhood.* New York:United Synagogue of America, 1955; xxx,321pp., illus., music.
    Collection of 252 selections — melody lines with simple piano accompaniments — prepared for very young children at Jewish play-schools. Creative approach by compilers — music educators Judith Eisenstein and Frieda Prensky — presenting materials for: Sabbath; all religious occasions in calendar year; Jewish customs and folksongs; Hassidic songs; Yiddish, Hebrew and Ladino melodies; music of Israel — various groups ingathered and their cultures. Prefatory materials include pedagogical guidelines and background information on this wide-ranging music collection for children. English annotations and translations. Song index. Hebrew and Yiddish romanized.

992
EISIKOVITS, MAX, comp./arr. *Songs of the Martyrs; Hassidic Melodies of the Marmures.* New York: Sepher-Hermon, 1980; 61pp., illus., music.
    Collection of 20 selections with piano accompaniments — materials of particular Hassidic groups in special area of Eastern Europe. Compiled by musician Max Eisikovits, survivor of Holocaust and member of that Hassidic sect, as tribute to those who perished and to their musical legacy. English introduction by historian Moshe Carmilly and English annotations. Hebrew and Yiddish romanized.

993
ELIAS, WILLIAM, comp./ed. *Pa-amonit.* Tel Aviv,Isr.:Ohali/I.M.I., 1967; 32pp., music.
    Songster for very young children. Melody lines for 15 selections prepared by Israeli music editor/educator William Elias. Simple Hebrew song texts romanized.

994
ENGEL, JOEL, comp./arr. *Juedisher Kinder Lieder ("Jewish Children's Songs").* Berlin,Ger.:Juwal, 1923; 43pp., music.

Collection of 50 Hebrew and Yiddish selections — melody
lines only — adapted and arranged "for kindergarten
school and home" by composer, writer and music editor
Joel Engel (1868-1927). Melodies based upon traditional
East European Jewish folksong elements, with settings of
folk poetry. Trained in Russian music conservatories and
active in musical circle of "Russian Five," Engel turned
his energetic talents to Jewish music — collection, arrangement, performance and publication. He composed the
incidental music for *The Dybbuk*, Jewish play by Shlomo
Ansky (1863-1920). Engel settled in Berlin in 1920 and
established Jewish music publishing enterprise — Juwal/
Yuval. From 1924 to his death, he lived in Tel Aviv.
For songs in collection, Hebrew and Yiddish romanized.

995
EPHROS, GERSHON, comp./arr. *Children's Suite.* New York:
Bloch, 1944; 38pp., music.
Compilation of 16 selections — musical arrangements with
piano accompaniments, setting the Hebrew poetry of Haim
Nahman Bialik (1873-1934). Compiled and arranged by
cantor, liturgical anthologist and composer Gershon
Ephros (1890-1978). Jewish traditional musical motifs
used. English texts by Harry Fein. Hebrew romanized.
996
EPHROS, GERSHON, comp./arr. *Jewish Folk Songs.* New York:
Bloch, 1946; 14pp., music.
Collection of 4 traditional melodies, arranged with
piano accompaniments, by liturgical anthologist, cantor
and composer Gershon Ephros (1890-1978). Some English
annotations. Hebrew and Yiddish romanized.
997
FICHANDLER, WILLIAM, comp. and JOSEPH RUMSHINSKY, arr.
Selected Songs of Eliakum Zunser (1836-1913). New York:
Zunser/Metro Music, 1928; 236pp., music.
Collection of 49 selections — ballad-poetry and melodies
written by notable Jewish minstrel (*Badkhen*) Eliakum
Zunser. Music arranged with piano accompaniments by
prolific popular Yiddish song writer Joseph Rumshinsky
(1881-1956), and compiled by Yiddishist William Fichandler. Foreword by Abraham Cahan (1860-1951), a founder
and editor of *The Jewish Daily Forward*, Yiddish newspaper in New York City. English annotations for songs.
Yiddish texts under music lines romanized.
998
FRIEDLANDER, DANIEL H. and Committee, comps./eds. *Yehi
Shir - Let There Be Song.* New York:N.F.T.Y./U.A.H.C.,
1981; 32pp., music.
Collection of 21 selections — melody lines with chord
symbols — hymns for congregational singing on Sabbath
and Festivals. English annotations. Hebrew romanized.
999
FRIEDMAN, DEBBIE, comp./arr. *Songbook.* New York: Trans-
continental/U.A.H.C., 1980; 44pp., music.
Collection of 11 selections — melodies with guitar symbols and piano accompaniments — annotated with perform-

ance directions by compiler, Jewish music educator Debbie Friedman. English translations. Hebrew romanized.

1000
FRIEDMAN, MAURICE and SUSIE MICHAEL FRIEDMAN, comps./eds.
Beloved Jewish Songs. New York:Metro Music,1964;60pp.,music
Collection of 12 selections — melodies with piano accompaniments — Jewish folksongs and art music as performed
in the repertoire of dramatic singing duo (baritone and
and soprano), the Friedmans. English translations and
annotations. Yiddish and Hebrew romanized.

1001
FROMM, HERBERT, comp./arr. *Hymns and Songs for the Syna-*
gogue. New York:A.C.C./S.M.P., 1961; 19pp., music.
Collection of 12 melodies presented in a symposium on
Jewish hymnology at the 7th annual convention of the
American Conference of Cantors (Reform Judaism). Traditional liturgical music for congregational singing at
services, arranged with simple piano (or organ) accompaniments. English translations. Hebrew romanized.

1002
GEBIRTIG, MORDECAI (MORDKHE), comp./arr. *Mayne Lider - My*
Songs. New York:Workmen's Circle, 1942; 87pp., music.
Collection of melody lines of songs composed or arranged
by Yiddish minstrel-poet (*Badkhen*) Mordecai Gebirtig
(1877-1942), whose creativity reflected East European
Jewish life, until Holocaust era when he was hunted out
and shot by nazis. Music originally compiled by him in
in this form in Poland, and then republished in America.
English annotations. Yiddish song texts romanized.

1003
GELBART, MICHL, comp./ed. *Gezang Buch - Song Book.* New
York: Workmen's Circle, 1938; 100pp., music.
Collection of 62 selections, compiled as songbook for
early grades of Yiddish schools by music educator Michl
Gelbart (1889-1962). Yiddish songs — melody lines only —
presented in sections for grade levels 1, 2, 3 and 4.
Also group of holiday folksongs for *Hanukkah, Purim,*
Passover and other calendar celebrations, with some
Hassidic and folk dance melodies. Yiddish romanized.

1004
GELBART, MICHL, comp./ed. *Lider - Songs.* New York: Workmen's Circle, 1942/43; 20pp., music.
Collection of 23 Yiddish songs — melody lines — compiled
by music educator and choral leader Michl Gelbart (1889-
1962) for use at Yiddish schools. Children's tunes on
topics of Jewish life and learning. Yiddish texts only.

1005
GELBART, MICHL, comp./ed. *Mir Zingen - We Sing.* New York:
Workmen's Circle, 1952; 160pp., music.
Collection of 78 Yiddish songs — melody lines — compiled
by music educator and choral leader Michl Gelbart (1889-
1962) for use in Yiddish schools. Combines materials
of some previous songbooks issued 1933-1945: *Zingen*
Kinder, Gezang Buch, Lider, and *Zing Mit Mir.* This
edition prepared in honor of 100th anniversary of birth
of notable East European Yiddish writer and educator

Isaac Loeb Peretz (1852-1915). Yiddish texts only.
1006
GELBART, MICHL, comp./ed. *Zing Mit Mir - Sing With Me.*
New York:Workmen's Circle, 1945; 95pp., music.
  Collection of 130 Yiddish songs — melody lines — compiled for Yiddish schools by music educator and choral
  leader Michl Gelbart (1889-1962). Topics of home, school
  and holiday celebrations. Yiddish texts only.
1007
GELBART, MICHL, comp./ed. *Zingen Kinder - Children Sing.*
New York: Metro Music, 1933; 40pp., music.
  Collection of 40 Yiddish songs — melody lines, some
  choir parts (SSA) and with simple piano accompaniments.
  Popular folksongs and children's tunes for use in Yiddish school language classes. Prepared by music educator
  Michl Gelbart (1889-1962). Yiddish song texts romanized.
1008
GIDEON, HENRY LOUIS, comp./ed. *Jewish Hymnal for Religious*
Schools and Congregations. New York:Bloch,1909;99pp.,music.
  Collection of hymns and anthems for American Reform congregations — melody lines only — compiled by musician
  Henry L. Gideon (1877-19?). English and Hebrew prayer
  texts for calendar year of Jewish observances. This
  hymnal was widely used and reprinted many times by publisher. Last issue (11th — 1941) had appended supplementary section of children's hymns, selected by educator Rudolph Grossman. Hebrew romanized.
1009
GIDEON, HENRY and CONSTANCE RAMSEY GIDEON, comps./arrs.
From the Cradle to the Chuppe: Songs of Jewish Life. Boston: A.P. Schmidt, 1923; 64pp., music.
  Collection of 15 selections — melodies with piano accompaniments — compiled by organist of Temple Israel in
  Boston Henry Gideon (1877-?) and music educator and performer Constance R. Gideon ([?]). Prepared in two parts:
  1. 8 songs of childhood and love (36pp.); 2. 7 songs of
  meditation, festivals and weddings (28pp.). English annotations and translations. Hebrew/Yiddish romanized.
1010
GOLDBERG, ITCHE and Committee, comp./ed. *Let's Sing a Yid-*
dish Song. New York:Jewish Music Alliance,1960;212pp.,music
  Collection of 245 Yiddish songs — melody lines only —
  for use by Yiddish language schools and singing clubs,
  compiled under direction of educator Itche Goldberg.
  Traditional folksongs, broadside ballads of East Europe,
  anthems, children's tunes, melodies of Jewish life and
  customs, songs of year-round holidays and celebrations.
  Some annotations. Yiddish romanized.
1011
GOLDFARB, ISRAEL, comp. and SAMUEL GOLDFARB, arr. *Friday*
Evening Melodies. New York: B.J.E., 1918; 105pp., music.
  Collection of 21 selections — melodies, some two part
  (SA) lines for children's choir, with simple piano accompaniment — prepared as educational hymnal for religious schools by rabbi and educator Israel Goldfarb
  (1879-1956) and his brother, music educator Samuel E.

Goldfarb (1884-1967). When the Bureau of Jewish education of New York City was organized in 1910, Samuel
Goldfarb became its first music director. The Bureau
changed its name for a time to "Jewish Education Committee" (J.E.C.), but then resumed its original organizational title (B.J.E.) in 1960. Contents of this collection: 15 hymns for Friday evening services; 6 table
hymns (*Zemirot*) for Sabbath evening meal, including
Grace blessings. Booklet was reissued several times, the
last in 1948. English annotations. Hebrew romanized.

1012

GOLDFARB, ISRAEL, comp. and SAMUEL ELIEZER GOLDFARB, arr.
The Jewish Songster - Part One. Brooklyn, N.Y.: Goldfarb,
1925; 221pp., music.

Collection of 124 selections — melodies with some SATB
choir parts and simple piano accompaniments — prepared
by rabbi and educator Israel Goldfarb (1879-1956) and
music educator Samuel E. Goldfarb (1884-1967). (Rabbi
Goldfarb trained composer Aaron Copland for his *Bar
Mitzvah.*) Music collection presents hymnody and folksongs for *Hanukkah, Hamisha Asar, Purim, Pesah, Lag
B'omer, Shevuot, Sukkot* and the Sabbath. English annotations. Hebrew romanized. 1925 edition incorporated all
holiday materials which these educators had prepared in-
formally in pamphlets for religious school use during
years 1918-1924. This publication, and its subsequent
companion work *Jewish Songster - Part Two*, were reissued several times through 1948.

1013

GOLDFARB, ISRAEL, comp. and SAMUEL E. GOLDFARB, arr. *The
Jewish Songster - Part Two.* Brooklyn, N.Y.: Goldfarb, 1929;
250pp., music.

Collection of 113 selections — melodies with simple piano accompaniments — prepared by rabbi, cantor and educator Israel Goldfarb (1879-1956) and music educator
Samuel E. Goldfarb (1884-1967). Serves as supplementary
volume of folksongs for earlier songster-hymnal *The
Jewish Songster - Part One* (1925), which contained
hymns and anthems for Sabbath, Festivals and other religious occasions of year. Contents of *Part Two* include: Hebrew and Zionist folksongs, children's tunes,
table hymns (*Zemirot*) for Sabbath meals, Yiddish folksongs, and English Jewish anthems. Some English annotations. Hebrew romanized. Songbook reissued several times
through 1948, with its companion hymnal/songster.

1014

GOLDFARB, ISRAEL, comp. and SAMUEL E. GOLDFARB, arr. *Synagogue Melodies for High Holy Days - Shirim L'yomim Noraim.*
Brooklyn, N.Y.: Goldfarb, 1926; 63pp., music.

Collection of 115 prayer chants and hymns for *Rosh Hashana* (New Year) and *Yom Kippur* (Day of Atonement)
services — melody lines only — presented in order of
liturgy for High Holy Days. Compiled by rabbi and educator Israel Goldfarb (1879-1956), who was instructor in
cantorial training at Jewish Theological Seminary of A-
merica, and his brother Samuel E. Goldfarb (1884-1967),

trainer of music teachers for B.J.E. of New York. Hymnal
intended for use in religious school classes and at services for congregational singing. Hebrew romanized.
1015

GOLDFARB, ISRAEL and ISRAEL H. LEVINTHAL, comps./eds. *Song
and Praise for Sabbath Eve.* rev.ed. Brooklyn, N.Y.:Brooklyn
Jewish Center,1935; 96pp.,music.(orig.ed. 1920;64pp.,music)
Collection of 23 hymn selections — melody lines and
some part voice lines — with prayers and Psalm texts,
for use at synagogue gatherings for late Friday evening
sermons and discourses. Expanded edition of earlier in-
formally issued compilation also prepared by rabbi and
educator Israel Goldfarb (1879-1956) with his rabbinical
colleague, community leader Israel Herbert Levinthal
(1888-1982). Some English translations and annotations.
Hebrew romanized. This edition was popularly used by
Conservative tradition congregations and was reissued
several times, through an 8th printing in 1941.
1016

GOLDFARB, SAMUEL ELIEZER, comp./ed. *Jewish Songs for Ha-
bonim Jewish Youth.* New York:B.J.E.,1925; 32pp., music.
Collection of Hebrew folksongs — melody lines only — for
use by youth clubs and camps, compiled by music educator
Samuel E. Goldfarb (1884-1967). Hebrew romanized.
1017

GOLDFARB, SAMUEL ELIEZER, comp./ed. *Popular Jewish Melodies.* New York: B.J.E., 1927; 64pp., music.
Collection of 38 hymns and folksongs — melody lines only — compiled by music educator Samuel E. Goldfarb
(1884-1967) for use in religious school classrooms and
children's services. Two sections: 1. 16 hymns for Sabbath, holidays and festivals; 2. 22 folksongs in Hebrew,
Yiddish and English. Hebrew and Yiddish romanized.
1018

GOLDFARB, THELMA, comp./arr. *Echoes of Palestine.* Brooklyn,N.Y.: Goldfarb, 1929; 159pp., music.
English narrative and illustrative materials, with collection of various popular Hebrew and Zionist folksongs
— melodies with piano accompaniments — compiled by music
teacher and performer Thelma Goldfarb. Hebrew romanized.
1019

GOLDMAN, MAURICE, comp./arr. *New Songs for Jewish School.*
Los Angeles: B.J.E., 1959; 39pp., music.
Collection of 20 selections — melody lines only — of
hymns for daily services, Sabbath and holidays. Prepared
by music educator and choral director Maurice Goldman
for children in early grades of religious schools. Some
English texts and annotations. Hebrew romanized.
1020

GOLDSTEIN, MORITZ (MAURICE), comp./arr. *Kol Zimrah - Hymn
Book for Temple and Religious School; Adapted for Choirs and
Congregational Singing.* Cincinnati:Bloch,1885;144pp.,music.
Hymnal collection for Reform congregation Sabbath services — melodies with some part voice lines — compiled
by cantor and choral leader Moritz Goldstein (1840-1906)
for his liturgical duties at Temple B'nai Israel in Cin-

cinnati. Goldstein wished to restore traditional motifs
and melodies of synagogue to American Reform services,
and utilized materials from Sulzer and Lewandowski, with
his own arrangements. English texts. Hebrew romanized.
1021
GOLDSTEIN, MORITZ (MAURICE), comp./arr. *Temple Service -
New Year and Day of Atonement; Music for Union Prayer Book
of Jewish Worship.* Cincinnati:Bloch, 1895; 102pp., music.
   Collection of 80 hymns — melodies with some SATB choir
   parts and piano (or organ) accompaniments — for High
   Holy Days services at Reform congregations. Prepared by
   cantor and music educator Moritz Goldstein (1840-1906),
   as companion hymnal for his collection of Sabbath hymns
   Kol Zimrah (1885). English texts. Hebrew romanized.
1022
GOLDSTEIN, ROSE, comp. and REUVEN KOSAKOFF, arr. *Songs To
Share.* New York:United Synagogue of America,1949;64pp.music
   Collection of 24 selections — melodies with simple piano
   accompaniments — for youngsters in Jewish play-schools.
   Prepared by educator Rose Goldstein with Jewish musician
   Reuven Kosakoff. Includes songs for "every day" and for
   Sabbath and holidays. English texts. Hebrew romanized.
1023
GORALI, MOSHE, GIL ALMAGOR and MOSHE BIK, comps./eds. *Die
Goldene Pave ("The Golden Peacock").* Haifa, Isr.:Haifa Mu-
sic Museum and AMLI Library,1978; xiv,141pp.,illus.,music.
   Includes section of Yiddish folksongs from East Europe,
   pp.134-41. Some English annotations. Yiddish romanized.
1024
GORALI, MOSHE and DAVID SAMBURSKI, comps./arrs. *Sepher
Shirim U'manginoth - Songster for School and Home.* Jeru-
salem,Isr.:Kiryat Sepher, 1955; 128pp., music.
   Collection of 122 selections — melody lines and some
   parts for choir, with simple piano accompaniments — compiled by music editor Moshe Gorali and music educator
   David Samburski. Intended for use in Hebrew language
   primary schools for instruction, and for celebrations of
   Sabbath and holidays. Hebrew texts only.
1025
GOTTHEIL, GUSTAV, comp. and A.J. DAVIS, arr. *The Music to
Hymns and Anthems for Jewish Worship.* New York: S. Kakeles,
1887; 108pp., music.
   Collection of hymns for Reform congregational singing —
   melody lines only — for calendar year of religious observances. Prepared for use at Temple Emanu-El in New
   York City by cantor and choral leader Gustav Gottheil
   (1827-1903) with organist A.J. Davis (fl.19th cent.).
   Hymnal based upon earlier (1875) informal compilation
   for the Temple. English texts. Hebrew romanized.
1026
GOTTLIEB, JACK and Committee, comps./eds. *Songs and Hymns
- Shirim V'zimrot.* New York:C.C.A.R.,1977; xii,121pp.,music
   Collection of hymns — melody lines with guitar symbols —
   prepared as musical supplement to Reform synagogue service prayer book *Gates of Prayer.* Compilation by music
   educator and composer Jack Gottlieb and committee of

cantors and rabbis. Publication sponsored by American
Conference of Cantors and Central Conference of American
Rabbis. English translations and texts. Hebrew romanized
1027
GRAETZER, GUILLERMO, comp./ed. *Canciones Hebreas - Hebrew
Songs.* Buenos Aires,Arg.:Ricordi Americana,1946;40pp.,music
    Collection of 26 selections - melodies and simple piano
    accompaniments -- in Hebrew and Yiddish, with Spanish
    translations. No English texts. Contents: 8 Jewish holi-
    day folksongs; 3 liturgical hymns; 10 Hebrew songs; and
    4 Yiddish songs, including Holocaust anthem *Zog Nit
    Keinmol - Canto Guerrilleros.* Yiddish/Hebrew romanized.

    1028
GRAUMAN, MAX, comp./ed. *Music Service for New Year and Day
of Atonement, According to Union Prayer Book.* New York:
Behrman, 1937; 245pp., music.
    Posthumous publication of collection of hymns, chants
    and anthems for High Holy Day services of Reform congre-
    gations - cantor, SATB choir and organ accompaniments.
    Compiled by cantor and music director Max Grauman (1871-
    1933). English texts. Hebrew romanized.
    1029
GRIMM, CARL HUGO, comp./arr. *Sabbath Morning Service, According to Union Prayer Book.* Cincinnati:J. Church, 1916;
60pp., music.
    Collection of liturgical selections - cantorial solos,
    SATB choir parts with organ accompaniments. Prepared by
    Temple organist Carl Hugo Grimm (1890-?). English texts
    and annotations. Hebrew romanized.
    1030
**GROSS-LEVIN, M., M. DAFNA, SH. HOFMAN, E. AMIRAN-PUGATCHOV
and A. OMER-GRIMER,, comps./eds.** *Shiron - Songster.* Tel
Aviv,Isr.: Histadrut, 1963; 64pp., music.
    Collection of 62 selections - melody lines only - Sab-
    bath, festivals and other religious observances, com-
    munal celebrations and customs, and general Hebrew folk-
    songs. Prepared by group of music educators for music
    department of Israeli Ministry of Education and Culture,
    and to be used in primary school classes. Hebrew only.
    1031
GROSSMAN, LOUIS, comp./ed. *Responses, Psalms and Hymns for
Worship in Jewish Congregations and Schools.* Detroit: J.F.
Eby, 1894; 75pp., music.
    Collection of liturgical selections - melody lines only
    - for Reform congregational services and children's
    groups. Prepared by cantor and educator Louis Grossman
    (fl.19th cent.). English texts. Hebrew romanized.
    1032
HADAR, JOSEPH, comp./arr. *Negen Choral Series.* Tel Aviv,
Isr.:Negen/Schreiber, 1959; 31pp., music.
    Collection of 20 selections - melodies in two parts (SA/
    ST) - of Hebrew folksongs and musical settings for poems
    and Bible passages. Compiled by Joseph Hadar, Israeli
    music educator, for choral groups. Hebrew romanized.

1033
HALPERN, MAX, comp./arr. *Zemirot U'tefillot Yisrael - Syn-*
agogue Hymnal for Sabbath and Festivals. Boston: Boston
Music, 1915; 190pp., music.
Collection of 162 hymns and religious anthems - melodies
with SATB choir parts, *a cappella* - for congregational
singing at adult and children's religious services of
calendar year of Jewish observances. Prepared by cantor
and choir leader Max Halpern ([?]) utilizing traditional
liturgical melodies for his pulpit at Temple Adath
Jeshurun in Boston. English texts. Hebrew romanized.

1034
HAST, MARCUS, comp./ed. *Collection of Sacred Jewish Hymns*
and Prayers. London,Eng.:Davison, 1879; 64pp., music.
Hymnal for congregational singing - melody lines with
some SATB choir parts - for Sabbath, Festivals, chanting
of Psalms. Prepared by scholar and cantor Marcus Hast
(1840-1911). Polish born and trained, Hast brought those
particular East European Ashkenazic liturgical traditions to London, where he held cantorial pulpit 1871-
1911. This hymnal was used by many English synagogues.
English, German and Hebrew texts. Hebrew romanized.

1035
HECHT, SIMON, comp./arr. *Jewish Hymns for Sabbath Schools*
and Families. Cincinnati:Bloch,1878; 55pp., music.
Collection of 52 hymns and anthems - melody lines with
some two (SA) and three (SAT) parts for choir - for use
in Reform congregational services and religious schools.
Prepared by Simon Hecht (fl.19th cent.), rabbi and cantor in Indiana. This hymnal was reissued in 1888, 1893
and 1896, and used by many congregations in American
Mid-West. Though musically interesting, it was rejected
for sponsorship by U.A.H.C. on grounds that its music
materials were far too generalized and did not utilize
any traditional Jewish liturgical themes or motifs. Contents: 43 English hymns; 9 German anthems.

1036
HECKER, WOLF and FREDERICK PIKET, eds./arrs. *Songs of*
Prayer of Eliezer Gerowitsch. New York:Sacred Music Press/
H.U.C.-J.I.R., 1954; 56pp., music.
Collection of synagogue chants and hymns - melody lines
with some SATB choir parts and optional organ accompani-
ments. Music materials of cantor and liturgical composer
Eliezer Gerowitsch (1844-1913). Edition prepared by two
cantors and music educators - Wolf Hecker and Frederick
Piket (1902-1974). Some annotations. Hebrew romanized.

1037
HEMSI, ALBERTO, comp./arr. *Coplas Sefardies - Sephardic*
Songs. Alexandria,Egypt:Hemsi, 1933; 30pp., music.
Collection of 12 Ladino (Judaeo-Spanish) folksongs, arranged - voice with piano accompaniments - by Sephardic
liturgist and composer Alberto Hemsi (1896-1975). French
and Ladino texts only.

1038
HERZOG, AVIGDOR, comp./ed. *Renanot - Songster of Sacred*
Music. Jerusalem,Isr.:Institute for Sacred Music, 1962;

35pp., music.
   Collection of 29 selections — melody lines, some two
   part choir voices. Music for Sabbath, holidays, festive
   celebrations, and general folksongs. Originally prepared
   as separate songsheets. Compiled by music educator Avigdor Herzog, incorporating various liturgical traditions.
   English annotations. Hebrew romanized.
1039
HERZOG, AVIGDOR, comp./ed. *Rinatyah — Canticles and Songs.*
Jerusalem,Isr.:Inst. for Sacred Music,1963; 27pp., music.
   Collection of 14 liturgical selections — melody lines
   only. Compilation of various settings of prayer texts,
   according to different Jewish traditions. Prepared by
   Israeli liturgist and scholar Avigdor Herzog. With annotations and source notes. Hebrew romanized.
1040
HOFMAN, SHLOMO, comp./arr. *El Artzi — To My Land.* Tel A-
viv,Isr.:Yibneh/Yavneh, 1947; 24pp., music.
   Collection of 14 selections — melody lines, with two,
   three and four parts for chorus, *a cappella* — for use
   by children and amateur choral groups. Prepared by musicologist, educator and choral director Shlomo Hofman.
   Compilation of popular folksongs. Hebrew texts only.
1041
HOFMAN, SHLOMO, comp./arr. *Tzili Nof — Ring Out in Song.*
Tel Aviv,Isr.:Yavneh, 1936; 28pp., music.
   Collection of 7 selections — in two, three and four
   part music lines for chorus, *a cappella* — compiled by
   Israel music educator and choral director Shlomo Hofman.
   Settings of poetry to folktunes. Hebrew texts only.
1042
HORVITZ, ERNEST, comp./ed. *Min Ha-metzar; Mi Shirim Ha-
getos — Out of the Depths; From the Songs of the Ghettos.*
Tel Aviv,Isr.:Histadrut, 1949; 77pp., music.
   Collection of 31 selections — melody lines, some piano
   accompaniments — of songs from Holocaust era, translated
   from Yiddish into Hebrew. Original texts appended. Includes best known materials. Hebrew annotations only.
1043
IDELSOHN, ABRAHAM ZEBI comp./arr. *Sepher Ha-shirim — Book
of Songs.* Berlin/Jerusalem: Ezra Society of Germany, 1911;
xii, 112pp., music.
   Collection of 100 selections — melody lines only — of
   liturgical hymns and Hebrew folksongs, for use in classrooms of children at Ezra School and by teacher trainees
   at Ezra Academy in Jerusalem, and at Jewish religious
   schools in Germany. Prepared by musicologist and music
   educator A.Z. Idelsohn (1882-1938) during his years in
   Jerusalem (1906-1921), period of his ethnomusicological
   collections among Oriental, Sephardic and Hassidic Jews
   residing there. This compilation of hymns and folksongs
   for Jewish calendar year, also includes specially composed or arranged music for teaching of Hebrew language,
   including adaptation of Hassidic melody (Rabbi of Sadigora's *Nigun*) into lively Hebrew song *Hava Nagila*.
   Foreword in German, as endorsement by philanthropic Ger-

man Jewish Society (Ezra) which supported education in
Jerusalem. Hebrew introduction by Idelsohn, who called
himself "Ben-Yehuda" in tribute to his colleague at the
schools Eliezer Ben-Yehuda (1858-1922), considered as
"father" of modern Hebrew development. No English texts.

1044
**IDELSOHN, ABRAHAM ZEBI, comp./arr. and BARUCH JOSEPH COHON,
ed.** *Jewish Song Book for Synagogue, School and Home.* repr.
ed. Cincinnati:Publications for Judaism, 1961; xi,552pp.,
music. (rev.enl.ed. - B.J. Cohon, ed. - Cincinnati, 1951;
orig.ed. Cincinnati:Bloch, 1928/1929; 279pp., music.)
  Collection of 395 selections - melodies with piano accompaniments - of hymns, benedictions and liturgical
  chants for Sabbath, High Holy Days, Festivals and other
  religious celebrations in Jewish calendar year. Enlarged
  edition was prepared and musically edited by former pupil of Idelsohn, rabbi and educator Baruch J. Cohon, and
  is augmentation of original compilation made by music
  educator and musicologist A.Z. Idelsohn (1882-1938) for
  students of liturgical music at H.U.C.-J.I.R. in Cincinnati. Those materials, in turn, had been adapted by
  Idelsohn from his earlier hymnal publication *Sepher
  Shirim* (Jerusalem, 1911). Cohon prepared edition as
  tribute to Idelsohn, and for practical use in religious
  schools and for congregational singing. Piano, or organ,
  parts elaborated. English translations and annotations.
  Song index. Hebrew and Yiddish song texts romanized.

1045
**ISAACS, LEWIS MONTEFIORE and MATHILDE S. SCHECHTER, comps./
eds.** *Kol Rinah; Hebrew Hymnal for School and Home.* Cincin-
nati/New York:Bloch, 1910; 61pp., music.
  Collection of Sabbath and Festival hymns - melody lines
  only - for use by Conservative/traditional synagogues.
  Compiled by rabbi and educator Lewis M. Isaacs (1817-
  1944) and Jewish educator Mathilde S.Schechter (1859-
  1924). English translations. Hebrew romanized.

1046
IVKER, MOISES (MOSES), comp./ed. *Canciones Traditionales y
Populares - Lichvod Shabbat ("Traditional and Popular Melodies of Sabbath").* Mexico City,Mex.:Collegio Israelita de
Mexico, 1963; 96pp., illus., music.
  Collection of 89 selections - melody lines only. Sabbath
  melodies: hymns, table songs (*Zemirot*) and adaptations
  of traditional liturgical chants. Music for observances
  from Friday Eve to conclusion (*Havdalah*) at Saturday
  evening. Prepared by music educator and liturgist Moses
  Ivker for use by Ashkenazic congregations and religious
  schools in Mexico and Central America. Spanish texts and
  translations. Hebrew and Yiddish romanized.

1047
JEWISH CHAPLAINS: U.S.MARINES - Committee, comps./eds.
Chapel Jewish Songbook; Sing and Be Joyful. Wash.,D.C.: U.
S. Marine Corps/Chaplains, 1976; 90pp., music.
  Collection of 81 selections - melody lines only - of
  hymns and benedictions for Sabbath and other Jewish de-
  votional services. Prepared for military personnel. Eng-

lish texts and annotations. Hebrew romanized.
1048
JEWISH FRATERNALISTS — Committee, comps./eds. *Jewish Youth Sings.* New York:Jewish Music Alliance,1960; 38pp., music.
> Collection of 38 selections — melody lines only. Songs compiled for group participation. English translations and texts. Hebrew and Yiddish romanized.

1049
JOCHSBERGER, TZIPORA, comp./arr. *Bekol Zimra — Collection of Jewish Choral Music.* repr.ed. Cedarhurst, N.Y.: Tara, 1981; 117pp., music. (orig.ed. New York:Mercury, 1966)
> Collection of 16 selections — melodies arranged for solo voice and SATB choir, *a cappella* — of liturgical hymns for Jewish services. Piano part given for rehearsal use. Compiled by music educator and choral director Tzipora Jochsberger. English annotations. Hebrew romanized.

1050
JOCHSBERGER, TZIPORA, comp./arr. *Hava N'halela; Songbook with Recorder (Hallil).* New York:Jewish Agency/W.Z.O., 1952; 62pp., music.
> Collection of 133 Israeli folksongs — melodies with recorder/wind instrumentation — compiled and arranged by music educator Tzipora Jochsberger, for development of recorder playing skills with group singing. Guidelines in English and Hebrew. Hebrew song texts romanized.

1051
JOCHSBERGER, TZIPORA, comp./arr. *Melodies of Israel.* New York:Hebrew Arts/Shengold, 1961; 50pp., music.
> Collection of 48 selections — melodies, arranged in two and three parts for choirs and for recorder (*Hallil*) consorts, or other melody instruments. Hebrew hymns, festival and Israeli folksongs. Prepared by music educator Tzipora Jochsberger as songster and recorder music book. Guidelines for instrumental playing. English translations and annotations. Hebrew texts romanized.

1052
JOCHSBERGER, TZIPORA, comp./arr. and VELVEL PASTERNAK, ed. *A Harvest of Jewish Song.* New York:Tara,1980;144pp.,music.
> Collection of 74 selections — melodies with simple piano accompaniments and guitar symbols — of Hebrew, Yiddish and Ladino folksongs. Prepared by music educator Tzipora Jochsberger and music editor Velvel Pasternak. English annotations. Hebrew and Yiddish romanized.

1053
KAMMEN, JACK, comp./ed. *Jewish Nostalgia.* Carlstadt,N.J.: J. & J. Kammen, 1963; 78pp., music.
> Collection of 45 selections — melodies with piano or organ accompaniments, and with guitar or accordion symbols. Yiddish theatrical "hits" of 1920's and 1930's, written by popular composers and lyricists in heyday of Yiddish theater in New York City. Also includes some arrangements of East European folksongs. Compiled by music publisher. English translations. Hebrew romanized.

1054
KAPLAN, SHLOMO, comp./ed. *B'mitzad — Songs of the Israeli Army.* Tel Aviv,Isr.:Histadrut, 1948; 88pp., music.

Collection of 42 songs of Israeli Defense Army (*Z'va Haganah L'Yisrael*) - melody lines, with some guitar symbols - compiled by music educator Shlomo Kaplan (1909 -1979) for use by military personnel. Contains songs of land and people, liturgical hymns and holiday folksongs, and several marching tunes. Collection "designed to provide Israeli soldier with a book of popular songs of musical value." Some English texts. Hebrew romanized.

1055
KARTSCHMAROFF, EDWARD, comp./arr. *Ten Choice Hebrew Song Classics.* New York:E.B. Marks, 1920; 32pp., music.

Collection of traditional melodies - voice with piano accompaniments. Selections for high Holy Days, Sabbath and *Hanukkah*. Compiled by pianist and music educator Edward Kartschmaroff. Hebrew and Yiddish romanized.

1056
KATZ, AVNER, comp./ed. *Ha-tsoadim Ba-rosh; Shirim U'pizmonim - Hit Parade; Songs and Ballads.* Tel Aviv, Isr.: Subar, 1969; 114pp., illus., music.

Collection of 45 selections - melody lines with guitar symbols. Popular Israeli songs by current songwriters and lyricists (c.1965/69). Photographs. Hebrew only.

1057
KAUFMANN, FRITZ MORDECHAI, comp./ed. *Die Schoenster Lieder der Ostjuden ("Loveliest Songs of East European Jewry").* Berlin,Ger.:Juedischer Verlag, 1920; vii,100pp., music.

Collection of 47 selections - melody lines only. Music of traditional liturgy, hymns, Hassidic tunes and some secular folksongs. Compiled by pianist and music educator Fritz M. Kaufmann (1888-1921). German texts. Hebrew and Yiddish romanized.

1058
KIPNIS, MENAHEM, comp./ed. *Folkslider - Collection of Yiddish Folksongs.* repr.ed. Buenos Aires,Arg.:Central Union of Polish Jews in Argentina, 1949; 90pp., music. (orig.ed. Warsaw,Pol.,1918/1929)

Collection of 100 folksongs - melody lines only - compiled by choral conductor Menahem Kipnis (1878-1942), who perished in the Holocaust. Songbook reissued in his memory by his colleagues who survived and resettled in South America. Some Spanish text. Yiddish romanized.

1059
KISSELGOF, SUSSMAN, ALEXANDER ZHITOMIRSKI and PESACH LVOV, comps./arrs. *Lieder Sammelbuch ("Folksong Collection").* repr.ed. Berlin,Ger.:Juwal,1923; 136pp., music. (orig.ed. St. Petersburg,Russia:Engel, 1912).

Collection of 62 selections - SAA voice parts with piano accompaniments - "for Jewish school and family." Compiled by Jewish educator Sussman Kisselgof (1876-19?), music collector Alexander Zhitomirski (1881-1937) and composer/arranger Pesach Lvov (1881-1913). Includes liturgical cantillations, chants and hymns, Hassidic melodies, secular folksongs and some "art-song" materials. Originally prepared and published under sponsorship of St. Petersburg Society for Jewish Folk Music (1908-1920) and reprinted by music editor and composer Joel Engel

(1868-1927) for his roster of Juwal publications. Hebrew, Yiddish and Russian texts for music romanized.
1060
KITZIGER, FREDERICK EMIL, comp./arr. *Hymns for Jewish Wor-*
ship. New Orleans,La.:Kitziger, 1894; 60pp., music.
Collection of 20 selections - melody lines with SATB
choir and organ (or piano) accompaniments - of hymns for
Reform congregational services. Arranged by Frederick E.
Kitziger (1844-1903), organist and music director of
Judah Touro Synagogue in New Orleans. Issued as supplement for his earlier hymnal collection *Shire Yehudah*
(New Orleans, 1888). English texts only.
1061
KITZIGER, FREDERICK EMIL, comp./arr. *Shire Yehudah - Songs*
of Judah. New Orleans:Kitziger, 1888; 155pp., music.
Collection of 106 selections - melody lines, with SATB
choir and organ (or piano) accompaniments - of hymns for
Jewish worship services. Prepared for congregational use
at Judah Touro Synagogue in New Orleans by its organist
and choral director Frederick E. Kitziger (1844-1903),
according to 19th century Reform *Union Prayer Book*.
His hymnal was popular among Jewish congregations in the
South and was reprinted in 1891, 1892, 1895 and 1899.
English texts. Hebrew romanized.
1062
KLOTZMAN, LAZARO, comp./arr. *Canciones Hebreas Modernes -*
Yidishe Lider. Buenos Aires,Arg.:Ricordi,1954;26pp.,music.
Collection of 8 Yiddish folksongs - melodies with piano
accompaniments. Spanish texts and annotations, as well
as Yiddish (romanized). Compiler music performer.
1063
KON, HENECH, comp./arr. *Kedoshim - Martyrs.* New York:
Machmadim, 1947; 32pp., illus., music.
Collection of 10 selections - melody lines only - poetry
and music inspired by and dedicated to those who perished in Holocaust. Compiled by musician Henech Kon
(1890-1972), who escaped from nazis in 1940 and came to
America. He gathered a legacy of poetry and arranged the
music of Ghettos, Concentration Camps and of Partisans
who fought and died. Yiddish song texts romanized.
1064
KON HENECH, comp./arr. *More Songs of the Ghetto.* New
York:Congress for Jewish Culture(CYCO), 1972; 32pp., music.
Collection of 20 selections - melodies with piano accompaniments. Songs of Holocaust era, settings of poetry
and adaptations of folk music. Prepared by musician
Henech Kon (1890-1972) who had been associated with Warsaw Polish Yiddish theatricals before he escaped to A-
merica in 1940. This is companion book for his earlier
collection *Songs of the Ghetto*, issued in 1960. Some
English annotations. Hebrew and Yiddish romanized.
1065
KON, HENECH, comp./arr. *Songs of the Ghetto.* New York:
Congress for Jewish Culture (CYCO), 1960; 64pp., music.
Collection of 30 selections - melodies with piano accompaniments. Songs of Holocaust era, settings of poetry

and adaptations of folk music. Prepared by East European
born and trained musician Henech Kon (1890-1972) who
fled to America in 1940. Some English annotations for
songs. Hebrew and Yiddish romanized.
1066
KOTYLANSKY, CHAIM, comp./ed. *Folks Gezangen - Folksongs.*
Los Angeles:Farband/YKUF, 1944; 152pp., music.
Collection of Jewish folksongs - melodies with piano accompaniments, as arranged by various musicians. From
performance repertoire of singer/actor Chaim Kotylansky.
English translations. Hebrew and Yiddish romanized.
1067
KRAUSKOPF, JOSEF, comp./arr. and RUSSELL KING MILLER, arr.
The Service Hymnal. repr.ed. Phila.:E.Stern, 1922; 170pp.,
music. (orig.ed. Phila.:Keneset Israel Temple, 1904)
Collection of 100 hymns - melody lines only - for Jewish
services in Reform congregations. Prepared by rabbi,
cantor and educator Josef Krauskopf (1858-1923) with
organist R.K. Miller ([?]). See pp.35-165 in this hymnal
and prayerbook of Congregation Keneset Israel in Philadelphia. Mostly English texts. Hebrew romanized.
1068
KREMER, ISA, comp./arr. *Album of Jewish Folk Songs; The
Jewish Life in Song.* London,Eng.:Chappell,1930;48pp.,music.
Collection of 24 Yiddish songs - melodies with piano accompaniments. Popular and traditional music of Eastern
Europe. Compiled from her performance repertoire by
singer/actress Isa Kremer (1885-1856). Songs of love and
marriage, home and family, religion and human struggles.
Some English annotations. Yiddish and Hebrew romanized.
1069
LAZOVSKI, CHAIM and JOSEPH RAMBAM, comps./arrs. *L'Shabbat
Mizmor - Sabbath Songs.*Tel Aviv,Isr.:Sinai,1948;42pp.,music
Collection of 26 selections - melody lines only - for
Sabbath, from Friday eve through afternoon *Oneg Shabbat*
(celebration), to conclusion (*Havdalah*) ritual. Pre-
pared by two cantor/music educators. Hebrew texts.
1070
LEFKOWITCH, HENRY, comp./arr. *Jewish Songs - Folk and
Modern.* New York:Metro Music, 1935; 114pp., music.
Collection of 35 Yiddish folksongs and Hassidic chants
(*Nigunnim*) - melodies with piano accompaniments. Com-
piled by musician/music editor and publisher Henry Lef-
kowitch (1892-1959). English texts. Yiddish romanized.
1071
LEFKOWITCH, HENRY, comp./arr. *Yiddishe Lieder - Shirim -
Yiddish Songs by Solomon Golub.* repr.ed. New York:Metro
Music,1936;103pp.,music.(orig.ed. New York:Metro Music,1928)
Collection of 27 selections - melodies with piano accom-
paniments. Works of folk composer and Yiddish minstrel
(*Badkhen*) Solomon Golub (1889-1952). Compiled by music
arranger and publisher Henry Lefkowitch (1892-1959).
English annotations. Hebrew and Yiddish texts romanized.
1072
LEFKOWITCH, HENRY and WILLIAM SCHER, comps./arrs. *Metro
Album of Selected Palestinian Hebrew, Hassidic and Yiddish*

Songs. New York:Metro Music, 1951; 49pp., music.
    Collection of 36 selections - melody lines, with guitar
symbols and piano accompaniments. Compiled by musician
and publisher Henry Lefkowitch (1892-1959) with pianist
William Scher. Traditional "favorites" included. Some
English annotations. Hebrew and Yiddish romanized.
  1073

LEVIN, NEIL, comp./arr. *A Bicentennial Presentation; Songs
of the American Jewish Experience.* Chicago: B.J.E., 1976;
214pp., illus., music.
    Collection of 108 selections - melody lines, with some
part voices for chorus and guitar symbols. Songs in Yiddish, Hebrew, Ladino (Judaeo-Spanish) and English. Topically grouped to reflect American Jewish life from early
Colonial times through 19th century, mass immigration of
East European Jews at turn of century, and events during
20th century. Song texts deal with society and family,
religious expression, economic and social issues, celebrations and commemorations. Music of varied styles and
origins. Historical annotations. Materials highlighted
with photographs and facsimile illustrations. Introduction gives background on music and documentations.
Prepared by music educator Neil Levin for celebration
of American Bicentennial year 1976. English translations
and annotations. Index. Hebrew and Yiddish romanized.
  1074

LIMUD, ORAH, comp./ed. *Zemirot; Shirim L'makhela - Songs
for Chorus.* Jerusalem,Isr.:Histadrut, 1975; 65pp., music.
    Collection of 31 popular Israeli folksongs - melodies,
with two and three part choral lines, *a cappella*. Compiled by music educator Orah Limud and intended for use
in Hebrew language schools and for children's choirs.
Hebrew song texts romanized.
  1075

LOEWE, HERBERT M.J., comp./ed. and ROSE L. HENRIQUES, arr.
*Mediaeval Hebrew Minstrelsy - Songs for the Bride Queen's
Feast.* London,Eng.:J. Clark,1926; iii,134pp., illus.,music.
    Collection of 16 Sabbath table-hymns (*Zemirot*) - tra-
ditional melodies, with two, three and four part voice
lines, *a cappella*. Compiled by cantor and music educator Herbert M.J. Loewe (1882-1940), with musician Rose
L. Henriques ([?]). Foreword by Chief Rabbi of Great
Britain Joseph H. Hertz (1872-1946). Introduction and
explanatory notes by Loewe provide information on this
musical heritage from Central and East Europe. English
annotations and translations. Hebrew romanized.
  1076

MAYEROWITSCH, HERMAN, comp./arr. *Oneg Shabbat; Ancient Hebrew Table Songs, or Zemirot.* repr.ed. London,Eng.:E.Gold-
stone, 1951; xiii,42pp., music. (orig.ed. E.Goldstone, 1937)
    Collection of 39 Sabbath hymns, folksongs and Hassidic
chants - melody lines, with some solfege symbols for use
by choir, *a cappella* - with traditional Grace blessings at meals and *Havdalah*, concluding Sabbath ritual.
Compiled as companion hymnal to Sabbath services prayerbook by cantor and educator Herman Mayerowitsch (1882-

1945), who served pulpit of London's Great Synagogue, an
Ashkenazic congregation. Prefaces by scholar Cecil Roth
(1899-1970) and Chief Rabbi of British Empire Joseph
Herman Hertz (1872-1946). Also, English annotations and
translations. Hebrew song texts romanized.
1077
MILLGRAM, ABRAHAM E., comp./ed. *Beth Israel Hymnal.*
Phila.:Cong. Beth Israel, 1937; 145pp., music.
    Collection of 44 hymns — melody lines only — for tra-
ditional liturgical services and congregational singing,
especially at late Friday evening gatherings in synagogues. Hymnal with special prayer texts for Sabbath.
Compiled by rabbi, educator and literary anthologist
Abraham E. Millgram. Some English. Hebrew romanized.
1078
MIRON, ISSACHAR, comp./ed. *Great Songs from Israel.* New
York:Mills Music, 1965; 63pp., music.
    Collection of popular Israeli selections — melodies with
piano accompaniments and guitar symbols. Includes Zionist and general Hebrew folksongs. Compiled by music educator Issachar Miron (Michrovsky). English annotations
and translations. Hebrew romanized.
1079
MIRON, ISSACHAR, and Committee, comps./eds. *Garlands of
Melodies - Songs of the Israeli Arab Communities.* Jerusalem,Isr.:A.I.C.F./Cultural Ministry,1961;60pp.,illus.,music.
    Collection of 33 Arabic folksongs — melody lines with
rhythm-percussion symbols. Prepared by composer and music educator Issachar Miron (Michrovsky) with editorial
committee of Arab and Jewish musicians. Intended for
Israeli school use and includes traditional materials as
well as more recent musical adaptations, such as Arabic
version of Israeli folksong *Hava Nagila.* Introduction
and annotations in Arabic, Hebrew and English. Guidelines for music structures and styles and Arabic pro-
nuciation. Arabic and Hebrew song texts romanized.
1080
MIRON, ISSACHAR, and YOSEF KARIV, comps./eds. *Zemirot Shi-
ronim - Songster Booklet Series.* Jerusalem,Isr.:W.Z.O.,
1956-1961; 38 issues (16-32pp. each), music.
    Songster collections — melody lines, some part voices —
offering broad range of music for Jewish calendar year
of religious observances and communal celebrations, and
with some secular folksongs. Compiled by music educators
Issachar Miron (Michrovsky) and Yosef Yariv, for use by
schools, community groups, choirs, and for general study
of Hebrew language. Each booklet with topical contents,
annotations in English, French and Spanish, and with Hebrew romanized. Total 370 songs.
1081
MLOTEK, ELEANOR (CHANA) GORDON, comp./arr. *Mir Trogn a Gezang - The New Book of Jewish Songs.* enl.ed. New York:Work-
men's Circle, 1977; 240pp.,illus.,music. (orig.ed. New York:
Workmen's Circle, 1972; 202pp., illus., music.)
    Collection of 107 selections — melody lines with guitar
symbols — of "favorite Yiddish songs of our generation."

Prepared by ethnomusicologist Eleanor G. Mlotek, as an
enlarged edition of her earlier collection of 90 Yiddish
folksongs. Introduction on historical background of this
music, and English annotations for songs. Preface by
actor and folksinger Theodore Bikel. Contents include
folksongs of childhood, courtship and family life, holiday celebrations, work and communal events, economic and
social issues, immigration to America and rebuilding of
Israel. Also section of 16 songs by East European folk
balladist and minstrel (*Badkhen*) Mordecai Gebirtig
(1877-1942). Hebrew and Yiddish song texts romanized.
1082

MLOTEK, ELEANOR G. (CHANA) and MALKE GOTTLIEB, comps./eds.
*25 Ghetto Songs.*New York:Workmen's Circle,1968;58pp.,music
Collection of 25 selections - melody lines only - of
songs from Holocaust era, compiled and issued in commemoration of 25th anniversary of Warsaw Ghetto Uprising
(April 1943). Prepared by musicologist Eleanor G. Mlotek
with music educator Malke Gottlieb. Introduction and annotations in Yiddish and English. Yiddish romanized.
1083

MLOTEK, ELEANOR GORDON and MALKE GOTTLIEB, comps./eds.
Songs of the Holocaust; We are Here. New York: Workmen's
Circle, 1983; 104pp., illus., music.
Collection of 40 selections - melody lines with guitar
symbols. Music of Ghettos and Concentration Camps, as
created and sung during Holocaust era. Compiled by musicologist Eleanor G. Mlotek and musician Malke Gottlieb
for use at commemorative gatherings. Singable English
translations. With foreword in Yiddish and English by
writer Elie Wiesel. Annotations for all songs. Source
notes and bibliographic details. Yiddish romanized.
1084

**MLOTEK, ELEANOR GORDON (CHANA) and MALKE GOTTLIEB, comps./
eds.** *Yomtovdike Teg - Festive Days.* repr.ed. New York: B.
J.E., 1980; 105pp.,music. (orig.ed. New York: B.J.E., 1972)
Collection of 40 Yiddish songs - melodies with simple
piano accompaniments - for Jewish holidays year-round.
Prepared by musicologist Eleanor G. Mlotek and music
educator Malke Gottlieb, to be used at Yiddish language
schools of Workmen's Circle, sponsored by B.J.E. of New
York City. English annotations. Yiddish romanized.
1085

MOSES, ISAAC SALOMON, comp./arr. *Hymns and Anthems for
Jewish Worship.* 2nd rev.ed. New York:Bloch,1921/1923;352pp.
music. (rev.ed. Cincinnati/New York:Bloch, 1904/1907/1909/
1911/1914; 218pp., music; orig.ed. Cincinnati: Bloch, 1894/
1896/1897; 194pp., music.)
Collection of 200 hymns, anthems and congregational responses - melody lines only. Enlarged edition of one of
most popular Jewish hymnals of late 19th and early 20th
century America. Compiled by rabbi, cantor and educator
Isaac S. Moses (1847-1926). First edition (1894) had
German and English hymn texts. Revised edition (1904)
included several Hebrew hymns, and many more were added
to second revised version (1921). That edition was used

by numerous congregations, for Sabbaths and all other
services year-round. Hebrew romanized.
1086
MUSHKES-SAUBEL, BLUMA, comp./ed. *Coletanea de Cancoes Ju-
daicas - Collection of Jewish Songs.* New York: C.Y.C.O.,
1968; 64pp., illus., music.
>   Collection of 24 selections - melody lines only. Musical
>   settings of Yiddish poetry compiled by Brazilian Jewish
>   performer Bluma Mushkes-Saubel. Introductory materials
>   in Yiddish and Portuguese. Yiddish song texts romanized.
1087
NARDI, NAHUM, comp./arr. *An Album of Jewish Songs.* New
York: Edward B. Marks, 1952; 40pp., illus., music.
>   Collection of 15 selections - melodies with simple piano
>   accompaniments. Hebrew songs for children, as composed
>   or adapted by Nahum Nardi (1901-1977), Russian born and
>   trained composer and pianist. He settled in Palestine
>   during 1920's and devoted his talents to creation of
>   children's songs, and to concert-style arrangements of
>   Oriental-Yemenite folksongs, for performances by notable
>   folksingers. English annotations. Hebrew romanized.
1088
NARDI, NAHUM, comp./arr. *Nardi's Collections of Children's
Songs.*Tel Aviv,Isr.:Nardi,1960/61;6 issues(each 8pp.),music
>   Collection of 73 selections - melody lines only - of
>   Hebrew songs composed or arranged by Israeli pianist and
>   music educator Nahum Nardi (1901-1977). Intended for use
>   by schools, camps and communal groups. Issued by Nardi
>   in 6 booklets: Sabbath; High Holy Days; Three Festivals;
>   *Hanukkah; Purim*; and, Israel Independence Day. Some
>   English annotations. Hebrew song texts romanized.
1089
NARDI, NAHUM, comp./arr. *Songs for Children.* Tel Aviv,
Isr.:Negen/Schreiber, 1958; 28pp., music.
>   Collection of 35 selections - melody lines only - of
>   children's Hebrew songs, composed or arranged by Israeli
>   Nahum Nardi (1901-1977). Hebrew song texts romanized.
1090
NATHANSON, MOSHE, comp./arr. *Jewish Liturgy and Ritual;
Benedictions.* New York:C.A.A./Hebrew Pub.,1954;87pp.,music.
>   Collection of liturgical chants, blessings and hymns -
>   melody lines only - for use by Conservative and Recon-
>   structionist congregations. Compiled by cantor and music
>   educator Moshe Nathanson (1899-1981), upon commission of
>   Cantors Assembly of America. Nathanson served at Society
>   for Advancement of Judaism/Reconstructionist synagogue
>   in New York City. English annotations. Hebrew romanized.
1091
NATHANSON, MOSHE, comp./arr. *Manginoth Shireynu - Hebrew
Melodies, Old and New, Religious and Secular.* New York:
Hebrew Publishing, 1939; 96pp., music.
>   Collection of 226 selections - melody lines only - folk-
>   songs for religious schools, camps and communal singing
>   groups. Compiled by cantor and music educator Moshe
>   Nathanson (1899-1981), who was music director of B.J.E.
>   in New York City, succeeding Samuel Goldfarb (1879-1967)

and Gershon Ephros (1890-1978) in that position. Nathanson, who had trained in Jewish music in Jerusalem with
A.Z. Idelsohn (1882-1938), also served as cantor/music
director for the Reconstructionist Synagogue in New York
City from 1941 to his death. He was followed at B.J.E.
by Harry Coopersmith (1902-1975). This songbook includes
liturgical chants, hymns and tunes for all calendar Jewish observances, Sabbath table-songs (*Zemirot*), Hassidic melodies, Yiddish and Hebrew folksongs. Some English
annotations. Song index. Hebrew and Yiddish romanized.
    1092

NATHANSON, MOSHE, comp./ed. *Zamru Lo: Volume One - Congre-*
gational Melodies and Zemirot (Hymns) for Friday Evening
Service. repr.ed. New York:C.A.A., 1974; 151pp., music.
(orig.ed. New York: C.A.A., 1955)
    Collection of 261 selections - melody lines only - in-
    cluding liturgical hymns and chants of the Ashkenazic,
    Sephardic and Yemenite traditions for Friday evening
    (Sabbath eve) services, with congregational singing.
    Prepared by cantor and music educator Moshe Nathanson
    (1899-1981). Materials arranged in order of prayers and
    rituals. Some English annotations. Hebrew romanized.
    1093

NATHANSON, MOSHE, comp./ed. *Zamru Lo: Volume Two - Congre-*
gational Melodies and Hymns (Zemirot) for Sabbath Day. New
York: C.A.A., 1960; 185pp., music.
    Collection of 412 selections - melody lines only - of
    traditional liturgical chants and hymns of Sabbath, from
    morning service through *Oneg Shabbat* (afternoon cele-
    bration), with music for various ceremonial meals of day
    and concluding service (*Havdalah*). Extra materials for
    special Sabbaths during Jewish calendar Year. Prepared
    by cantor and music educator Moshe Nathanson (1899-1981)
    as commissioned by Cantors Assembly of America, for use
    at Conservative synagogues. Music in order of rituals.
    English annotations and translations. Hebrew romanized.
    1094

NATHANSON, MOSHE, comp./ed. *Zamru Lo: Volume Three - Con-*
gregational Melodies for Sh'losh Regolim (Three Festivals)
and High Holy Days. New York:C.A.A.,1974;xvi,239pp.,music.
    Collection of liturgical chants, hymns and religious
    folksongs - melody lines only - for services of Three
    Festivals (*Sukkot/Simhat Torah; Pesah; Shavuot*) and
    for High Holy Days (*Rosh Hashana; Yom Kippur*). Pre-
    pared by cantor and music educator Moshe Nathanson (1899
    -1981), as commissioned by Cantors Assembly of America,
    for use by traditional Conservative synagogues. Some
    English annotations and translations. Hebrew romanized.
    1095

NETZER, EFFI, comp./arr. *Hava Nashira; Let us Sing.* Tel
Aviv,Isr.:Subar Music, 1970; 111pp., illus., music.
    Collection of 44 selections - melody lines with guitar
    symbols - of favorite Israeli songs, many composed and
    balance arranged by popular performer Effi Netzer. Only
    Hebrew texts. For music lines, Hebrew romanized.

1096
NEUMANN, RICHARD, comp./ed. *Shiron L'Yisrael - Songs for Israel.* New York:B.J.E., 1973; 40pp., music.
  Collection of 25 selections — melodies with some two part voice lines, and guitar symbols. Hebrew folksongs reflecting rise of State of Israel and dedicated to "celebration of Israel's 25th anniversary." Compiled for schools and communal groups by music educator Richard Neumann, who succeed Harry Coopersmith (1902-1975) as music director of B.J.E./N.Y.C. Early Zionist songs included. English texts and annotations. Hebrew romanized.

1097
NEUMANN, RICHARD and Committee, comps./eds. *Israel Sings.* New York: B.J.E., 1983; 40pp., music.
  Collection of 35 selections — melody lines with guitar symbols — of Hebrew folksongs "celebrating 35 years of State of Israel." Prepared by music educator and pianist Richard Neumann, with advisory committee. Music reflects history of country. English texts. Hebrew romanized.

1098
NEWMAN, HAROLD, comp./arr. *Music of Hebrew People - Israel and Jewish Songs.* (Hargail Folk Anthology Series) New York: Hargail Music, 1960; 20pp., music.
  Collection of 26 selections — melodies, with music lines for alto recorder, and guitar symbols. Compiled by music educator Harold Newman for school use. Includes Israeli and Jewish holiday folksongs, and version of *Kol Nidre.* English annotations. Hebrew and Yiddish romanized.

1099
NISSIMOV, NATAN, comp./ed. *Pirkey Zimra - Portions of Melody.* (Series of 45 Booklets) Jerusalem,Brit.Mand./Isr.: Tarbut/Histadrut, 1940-1950; 20-50pp. each, music.
  Over decade, series of 45 songsters prepared and issued with 15 to 30 selections in each edition — melody lines and some part voices for chorus, *a cappella.* Includes liturgical chants and hymns, holiday music, Hebrew folksongs and works of modern folk composers. Contents of booklets topically sorted reflecting calendar year of Jewish observances, "cycle of life" materials and events of 20th century Jewish history. Prepared by music editor and educator Natan Nissimov. Heb. and Yid. romanized.

1100
NULMAN, MOSHE (MACY), comp./ed. *Sabbath Chants.* New York: C.T.I./Yeshiva Univ., 1958; v,55pp., music.
  Collection of 77 liturgical selections — melody lines for cantorial solos with congregational responses, *a cappella* — for Sabbath morning services, including special hymns for Sabbaths of *Hanukkah* and New Month (*Rosh Hodesh*). Compiled by cantor and music educator Moshe Nulman for Cantorial Training Institute of Yeshiva University, and for use at traditional Orthodox synagogues. English prefatory materials, annotations and musical sources. Hebrew romanized.

1101
OKUN, MILT, comp./arr. *The Shlomo Carlebach Songbook.* New York:Zimrani Records, 1970; 75pp., illus., music.

Collection of 60 Hassidic selections — melody lines with
guitar symbols — from repertoire of liturgical singer
and folk performer Shlomo Carlebach. Compiled by music
arranger Milt Okun. English annotations and translations
for religious text materials. Hebrew romanized.
1102

OREN, EITAN, comp./ed.*"If I Forget Thee, O Jerusalem" -
Songbook With Programs.* New York:A.Z.Y.F.,1977;18pp.,music.
Songster collection of 10 Israeli folksongs — melody
lines with guitar symbols — as part of program "package"
which includes English script, cassette of music and
song lyrics slides. Prepared by music educator Eitan
Oren. English translations. Hebrew romanized.
1103

OREN, EITAN, comp./ed. *"Israel Alive and Singing" - Celebration of 30 Years in Song, Pictures and Drama.* New York:
A.Z.Y.F., 1978; 36pp., illus., music.
Songbook for multi-arts presentations. Collection of 10
selections — melody lines with guitar symbols — as part
of program "package" which includes pictorial and song
text slides, English script and cassette of music. Prepared by music educator Eiten Oren. English annotations
and translations. Hebrew romanized.
1104

OREN, EITAN and MORDECAI NEWMAN, comps./eds. *"From the
East I Will Gather You" - The Eastern Jewish Heritage Presented in Song, Story, Drama and Pictures.* New York: A.Z.Y.
F., 1979; 36pp., illus., music.
Songbook of 8 selections — melody lines with guitar symbols — as part of program "package" including English
script, pictorial and song text slides and cassette of
music. Materials relating to Jewish cultural heritage of
Spain, Balkans and North African areas. English annotations and translations for songs in Ladino (Judaeo-
Spanish) and Hebrew (romanized).
1105

PASTERNAK, VELVEL, comp./arr. *Hassidic Favorites; Best
Loved Hassidic and Israeli Songs.* Cedarhurst,N.Y.:Tara,
1972; vii,72pp., illus., music.
Collection of 125 selections — melodies, with some two
part voice lines, and guitar symbols. Compiled by music
editor and publisher Velvel Pasternak. Hassidic liturgical folksongs (*Nigunnim*), devotional chants and several Israeli songs based upon Hassidic music. Materials
from among Hassidic groups of East European origins, who
are now settled in America and Israel: Lubavitch, Ger,
Modzitz, Bobov, Skul, Melitz and Sadigora — named for
their European rabbinical roots. English introductory
materials, with background information on this music,
as well as annotations and translations for songs. Song
index. Hebrew and Yiddish romanized.
1106

PASTERNAK, VELVEL, comp./arr. *Hassidic Hits.* Cedarhurst,
N.Y.:Tara, 1977; 60pp., illus., music.
Collection of 56 selections — melodies with guitar sym-
bols — of Hassidic-style music by various contemporary

writers or adapters of that traditional liturgical folksong genre (*Nigunnim*). Settings of liturgy and Bible
texts, especially of Sabbath prayers and poetry. Compiled by music educator and editor Velvel Pasternak.
English prefatory materials, annotations and translations. Hebrew and Yiddish romanized.
1107
PASTERNAK, VELVEL, comp./arr. *Hassidic Style Songs of the*
70's. Cedarhurst,N.Y.:Tara, 1975; 60pp., illus., music.
Collection of 56 selections — melodies with guitar symbols — of newer songs created in style of Hassidic folksongs (*Nigunnim*). Settings of liturgical and Biblical
texts. Compiled by music educator and editor Velvel Pasternak. English prefatory materials, annotations and
translations. Hebrew and Yiddish romanized.
1108
PASTERNAK, VELVEL, comp./arr. *New Children's Songbook.*
New York:B.J.E./Tara, 1982; 80pp., illus., music.
Collection of 110 selections — melody lines with guitar
symbols. Jewish holiday music and folksongs for use with
very young children in religious schools and camps. Compiled by music educator Velvel Pasternak. With activity
"aids" and other prefatory materials. English translations. Hebrew romanized.
1109
PASTERNAK, VELVEL, comp./arr. *"Rejoice" – Songs in Modern*
*Hassidic Style.*Cedarhurst,N.Y.:Tara,1973;72pp.,illus.,music
Collection of 68 selections — melody lines with guitar
synbols — of Hassidic liturgical folksongs (*Nigunnim*).
More recent creativity among groups of East European
origins: Bobov, Skul, Kalev. Also includes materials in
this genre by American and Israeli adapters. Compiled by
music educator and editor Velvel Pasternak. English prefatory materials, annotations and translations. Song
index. Hebrew and Yiddish romanized.
1110
PASTERNAK, VELVEL and RICHARD NEUMANN, comps./arrs. *Great*
Songs of Israel. New York:B.J.E./Tara, 1976; 108pp., music.
Collection of 90 selections — melodies, some two part
voice lines and guitar symbols. Songs of more recent
creativity in Israel, including Hebrew secular and music
for Sabbath and other religious observances, and with
"rounds" and other simple choir arrangements. Compiled
by music editor Velvel Pasternak and music educator
Richard Neumann, for school and camp use. Companion
songster to their earlier publication *Israel In Song*
(1974). English preface and annotations. Heb. romanized.
1111
PASTERNAK, VELVEL and RICHARD NEUMANN, comps./arrs. *Hanuk-*
kah Melodies. New York:B.J.E./Tara, 1977; 20pp., music.
Collection of 16 selections — melody lines with guitar
symbols. Hymns, folksongs and candle-lighting blessings
for Hanukkah celebration. Compiled by music editor Velvel Pasternak and music educator Richard Neumann, for
use in school and home. English texts. Hebrew romanized.

1112
PASTERNAK, VELVEL and RICHARD NEUMANN, comps./arrs. *High Holy Days (Rosh Hashana and Yom Kippur) and Sukkot/Simhat Torah Melodies.* New York:B.J.E./Tara, 1977; 16pp., music.
> Collection of 19 selections – melody lines with guitar symbols – of traditional East European Ashkenazic liturgical chants and hymns. Compiled by music editor Velvel Pasternak and music educator Richard Neumann, for use at religious schools. Hebrew romanized.

1113
PASTERNAK, VELVEL and RICHARD NEUMANN, comps./arrs. *Israel In Song.* New York:B.J.E./Tara, 1974; 104pp., illus., music.
> Collection of 91 selections – melodies, with some two part voice lines and guitar symbols. Songs from Israel: Hebrew secular and liturgical; simple "rounds" and part tunes for children's choirs. Compiled by music editor Velvel Pasternak and music educator Richard Neumann. Includes many popularly known folksongs. English prefatory materials and annotations for songs. Hebrew romanized.

1114
PASTERNAK, VELVEL and RICHARD NEUMANN, comps./arrs. *Seder Melodies.* New York:B.J.E./Tara, 1977; 16pp., music.
> Collection of 20 selections – melody lines with guitar symbols – for entire *Seder* (Passover ritual meal) service, from candle-lighting blessings to concluding *Had Gadya*, folk hymn. Compiled by music editor Velvel Pasternak and music educator Richard Neumann, for school lessons and home use. English texts. Hebrew romanized.

1115
PASTERNAK, VELVEL and RICHARD NEUMANN, comps./arrs. *Shabbat Melodies.* New York:B.J.E./Tara, 1978; 36pp., music.
> Collection of 26 selections – melody lines with guitar symbols – of liturgical chants and hymns for Sabbath, from Friday eve, through Saturday morning services, including table-songs (*Zemirot*), and concluding music for *Havdalah.* Compiled by music editor Velvel Pasternak and music educator Richard Neumann, for school and home use. English annotations. Hebrew romanized.

1116
PASTERNAK, VELVEL and RICHARD NEUMANN, comps./arrs. *Tu B'shvat and Purim Melodies.* New York:B.J.E./Tara,1978;20pp.
> Collection of 20 selections – melody lines with guitar symbols. Songs for celebration of "New Year of Trees" or *Tu B'shvat*, and for "Feast of Lots" or *Purim.* Compiled by music editor Velvel Pasternak and music educator Richard Neumann. English annotations and other background information. Yiddish and Hebrew romanized.

1117
PAUER, ERNST, comp./arr. *Traditional Hebrew Melodies Chanted in Synagogue and Home.* London,Eng.:Augener, 1896; iv,33pp., music.
> Collection of hymns and anthems for Sabbath and festival services – melodies with organ accompaniments – for English Liberal, or Reform, congregations. Compiled by organist and music director Ernst Pauer (1826-1905). Preface by liturgist and educator Francis Lyon Cohen

(1862-1934). English texts. Hebrew romanized.

1118
POOL, DAVID de SOLA and TAMAR de SOLA POOL, comps./eds.
Liturgy and Ritual - Haggadah of Passover. New York: J.W.B.
/Jewish Chaplains, 1943; viii,139pp., music.
> Collection of traditional blessings, hymns and folksongs
> in both Ashkenazic and Sephardic traditions, for *Seder*
> ritual meal of Passover observance - melody lines only.
> Intended for use by Armed Services personnel during
> World War II. Compiled by rabbi and scholar David de
> Sola Pool (1885-1970) and his wife, Jewish educator
> Tamar de Sola Pool (1893-1981). English annotations and
> translations for ritual texts and music. Heb. romanized.

1119
RAVINA, MENASHE, comp./arr. *Shirim L'yeladim - Songs for*
Children. Tel Aviv,Brit.Mand.:Hanigun, 1932; 15pp., music.
> Collection of 9 selections - melodies with piano accom-
> paniments. Compiled by music educator and composer Me-
> nashe Ravina (1899-1968), for school use. Edition spon-
> sored by "World Society for Promotion of Jewish Music."
> Hebrew texts only.

1120
RINDER, REUBEN R., comp./ed. *Music and Prayer for Home,*
School and Synagogue. New York:H.U.C.-J.I.R./Sacred Music
Press, 1959; ix,308pp., music.
> Collection of 266 selections - melody lines with some
> SATB choir parts, and organ (or piano) accompaniments.
> Chants, hymns and anthems for weekdays, Sabbath, High
> Holy Days, Three Festivals, and other religious services
> in Jewish calendar year. Also, music for family and home
> celebrations - table songs (*Zemirot*) for Sabbath meals
> and hymnology of Passover ritual meal (*Seder*). Broad
> range compilation of materials prepared by cantor and
> music educator Reuben R. Rinder (1887-1966). English
> translations and annotations. Indexes and source notes.
> Hebrew romanized. In 1913, Reuben R. Rinder succeeded
> Edward J. Stark (1856-1918) as cantor of Temple Emanu-El
> in San Francisco. Rinder helped secure financial subsi-
> dy during years 1930-33 for composer Ernest Bloch (1880-
> 1959), as well as the commissioning of Bloch for his
> Sacred Service - *Avodath Ha-kodesh*, according to the
> Reform *Union Prayer Book*. Rinder also arranged for
> commissionings of Jewish liturgical services from Darius
> Milhaud (1892-1974) and Marc Lavry (1903-1967).

1121
RITTERBAND, CHAIM, comp./ed. and ABRAHAM SLEP, arr. *Yid-*
dishe Melodier ("Yiddish Melodies"). Vilna,Lith.:Grininke
Beimelekh, 1935; 56pp., music.
> Collection of 45 Yiddish folksongs - melody lines with
> some part voices for choir. Compiled for use in Yiddish
> language schools, by Jewish educator from Copenhagen
> Chaim Ritterband (?-1943), with Vilna music educator and
> choral director Abraham Slep (?-1943). Both perished in
> the Holocaust - Slep at a slave labor camp in Esthonia,
> and Ritterband among those massacred at Ponar, near
> Vilna. Yiddish song texts romanized.

1122
ROCKOFF, SEYMOUR, comp./arr. *Songbook.* Cedarhurst,N.Y.:
Tara, 1977; 50pp., illus., music.
    Collection of 36 selections - melodies with guitar sym-
bols. Liturgical hymns, holiday tunes, Hebrew and Yiddish folksongs. Compiled by music educator Seymour Rockoff, for use in primary grades of religious schools.
Some English annotations. Hebrew romanized.
1123
RON, HENECH and Committee, comps./eds. *Zemirot:Educational
Songbooks.* (Series of 16) Jerusalem,Isr.:W.Z.O., 1960-1973;
each booklet 8pp., music.
    Collection of Hebrew liturgicals, holiday hymns and se-
cular folksongs - melody lines only - sorted topically
into 16 booklets. Prepared by Israeli educator and music
advisory committee, for use in elementary grades of
schools in Israel and for Hebrew language courses
abroad. Some annotations. Hebrew song texts romanized.
1124
ROSENBAUM, SAMUEL, comp./arr. *Sabbath and Festival Songs.*
New York: Mills Music, 1959; 48pp., music.
    Collection of hymns and liturgical chant materials -
melodies with piano accompaniments - as performance arrangements of traditional music. Compiled by cantor,
concert performer and music educator Samuel Rosenbaum.
English translations. Hebrew romanized.
1125
ROSENBAUM, SAMUEL, comp./ed. *Songs from Jewish Folklore.*
New York:C.A.A., 1967; 32pp., music.
    Collection of 8 selections - melodies with piano accom-
paniments. Yiddish songs in artistic arrangements, from
concert repertoire of cantor, performer and educator
Samuel Rosenbaum. English translations. Yid. romanized.
1126
ROSMARIN, JOSEPH and SAMUEL CHAIT, comps./eds. *Jewish Folk
Songs.* New York:Bloch, 1929; 34pp., music.
    Collection of 32 selections - melody lines only. Com-
piled by two music leaders for members of their Young
Judea organization in Montreal. Includes materials from
"Goldfarb" and "Binder" songsters, with due acknowledge-
ments. English texts. Hebrew and Yiddish romanized.
1127
ROSS, ISRAEL, comp./arr. *New Hebrew Rounds.* Cedarhurst,
N.Y.: Tara, 1977; 22pp., music.
    Collection of 21 selections - melody lines with "round"
parts. Hymns for Sabbath, Passover and *Hanukkah*, and
some general Hebrew folksongs. Compiled by music educator Israel Ross, for use in religious schools. English
translations and annotations. Hebrew romanized.
1128
ROTHENBERG, ANNA SHOMER, comp./ed. *The Songs Heard in
Palestine.* New York:Bloch, 1928; xv,89pp., music.
    Collection of Yiddish and Hebrew selctions - melodies
with piano accompaniments - from repertoire of singer
and lecturer Anna Shomer Rothenberg (1885-1960). With
explanatory notes and suggestions for interpretations.

English translations. Hebrew and Yiddish romanized.
1129
RUBIN, RUTH, comp./ed. *Jewish Folksongs in Yiddish and*
English. New York:Oak, 1965; 96pp., illus., music.
   Collection of 50 selections - melody lines with guitar
   symbols. Folksongs of East European life, and of immigration and settlement in America. Compiled by ethnomusicologist Ruth Rubin. English texts. Hebrew romanized.
1130
RUBIN, RUTH, comp./ed. and RUTH POST, arr. *A Treasury of*
Jewish Folksong. repr.ed. New York:Schocken, 1964; 224pp.,
illus., music. (orig.ed. New York:Schocken, 1950)
   Collection of 110 selections - melodies with piano accompaniments. Jewish folksongs, Sabbath and holiday
   hymns, songs of Holocaust and State of Israel. Compiled
   by folksinger and writer Ruth Rubin, with musician Ruth
   Post. Informative introductory materials. English annotations and translations. Hebrew and Yiddish romanized.
1131
RUMSHINSKY, JOSEPH, comp./arr. *Album of Songs.* New York:
Metro Music, 1938; ii,57pp., music.
   Collection of music for voice and piano - Yiddish songs
   composed or arranged by theatrical musician Joseph Rumshinsky (1881-1956). English texts. Yiddish romanized.
1132
SALOMON, KAREL, comp./arr. *Shirey Yisrael-Songs of Israel,*
1/2. TEl Aviv,Isr.:I.M.P., 1960; 36pp./37pp., music.
   Two collections of Hebrew hymns, holiday melodies and
   secular folksongs - music with piano accompaniments and
   guitar, or accordion, symbols. Compiled by Israeli composer and music director Karel Salomon (1897-1974). Book
   1 - 29 selections: Sabbath, general and Yemenite music;
   Book 2 - 30 selections: *Hanukkah* and Passover, general
   and Sephardic music. Eng. translations; Heb. romanized.
1133
SAMBURSKI, DANIEL and MOSHE BRONZAFT, comps./eds. *Sefer*
Shirim U'manginot - Book of Songs and Poetry. Jerusalem,
Isr.:Kiryat Sefer/Histadrut, 1948; 120pp., music.
   Collection of 122 selections - melody lines, some part
   voices. Children's songs for classroom music activities
   and other educational uses. Music for entire calendar
   year of Jewish observances, in roster by months, seasons
   and topics. Prepared by Israeli composer Daniel Samburski, with music educator Moshe Bronzaft. Heb. romanized.
1134
SAMINSKY, LAZARE, comp./arr. *Hebrew Folksongs.* New York:
Carl Fischer, 1924; 29pp., music..
   Collection of 10 Hassidic and other Jewish folk melodies
   with piano accompaniments. Arranged by composer, conductor and writer Lazare Saminsky (1882-1959), who was
   music director of Temple Emanu-El in New York City. English translations. Hebrew and Yiddish romanized.
1135
SAMINSKY, LAZARE, comp./arr. *Hebrew Sacred and Traditional*
Songs. New York:Bloch, 1946; 55pp., music.
   Collection of various hymns and anthems for Sabbath and

other liturgical services in Reform congregations. Arranged by music director and composer Lazare Saminsky
(1882-1959) for cantorial solo, SATB choir with organ
accompaniments. English translations. Hebrew romanized.
1136

SAMINSKY, LAZARE, comp./arr. *Song Treasury of Old Israel.*
New York:Bloch, 1951; 42pp., music.
Collection of 27 selections - melody lines, some SATB
voices, with organ (or piano, or harp) accompaniments.
Compiled by Russian-born music director and composer
Lazare Saminsky (1882-1959), who collected Jewish folk-
songs in Caucasus and Turkey, 1913-1919. Some of those
materials arranged here. Songbook includes cantorial and
Hassidic chants, songs of Georgian and Persian Jews, and
Sephardic groups. English annotations. Hebrew romanized.
1137

**SCHACK, SARAH PITKOWSKY, comp./ed. and ETHEL SILBERMAN
COHEN, arr.** *Yiddish Folksongs.* repr.ed. New York:Bloch,
1947; 104pp., music. (orig.ed. New York:Bloch, 1924)
Collection of 50 Yiddish folksongs - melodies with piano
accompaniments. Prepared by two music educators. Wide
range of materials: Hassidic music; ballads of folk min-
strels (*Badkhonim*); popular songs of 19th century life
in Eastern Europe. English prefatory materials, annotations and translations. Yiddish romanized.
1138

SCHAEFER, JACOB, comp./ed. *Gezang un Kamf; Songs of Struggle.* New York:Jewish Music Alliance, 1932; 90pp., music.
Collection of Yiddish songs and narrative ballads, or
scripts with music - melodies with SATB choral lines and
some piano accompaniments. Compiled by choral leader and
music educator Jacob Schaefer (1888-1936). English annotations for music and texts. Yiddish romanized.
1139

SCHREIBER, JOEL, comp./ed. *Shirim - Folksongs of a People.*
Tel Aviv,Isr.:Negen/Schreiber, 1958; 28pp., music.
Collection of 20 selections - melody lines with guitar
symbols. Group of generally-known Israeli folksongs and
ballads. Compiled by music editor and publisher Joel
Schreiber. English texts. Hebrew romanized.
1140

SCHROGIN, JOSEPH, comp./ed. *Gezangen - Songs.* New York:
Jewish Music Alliance, 1972; 324pp., illus., music.
Collection of 60 selections - melodies and piano accompaniments - with other Yiddish poetry, ballads and dramatic materials. Compiled by musician Joseph Schrogin.
No English texts. Yiddish for music romanized.
1141

SEARLES, SUSAN CLAIRE, comp./ed. *Hebrew Songs for all Seasons, vols. 1 and 2.* Toledo,Ohio: B.J.E., 1978/1979; 64pp./
78pp., illus., music.
Two collections of music - melody lines with guitar symbols. Jewish liturgicals and hymns, holiday and general
folksongs. Compiled by music educator for use with young
children in religious schools. Vol.1 - 48 songs; vol.2 -
54 songs. With descriptions of educational activities.

English translations. Hebrew romanized.
1142
SEGAL. ROBERT, comp./arr. *Responsive Singing; A Sabbath Morning Service for Congregational Participation.* New York: United Synagogue of America, 1960; 184pp., music.
    Collection of hymns and liturgical chants — melody lines only — for Sabbath morning traditional Conservative synagogue service. Compiled by cantor and music educator Robert Segal, especially for use with children's congregations. Some English. Hebrew for music romanized.
1143
SELTZER, DOV, comp./arr. *Daber Elay B'shirim - Speak to Me With Songs.* Tel Aviv,Isr.:Subar,1970; 112pp.,illus.,music.
    Collection of 44 selections — melody lines with guitar symbols. Music composed or arranged by Israeli popular song composer and entertainer Dov Seltzer. Settings of contemporary lyric poetry. Hebrew print text only.
1144
SHEMER, NAOMI, comp./arr. *Sing Along.* Tel Aviv,Isr.: Yediot Ahronot, 1975; 84pp., music.
    Collection of 77 selections — melody lines with guitar symbols. Songs written or arranged by popular Israeli musician Naomi Shemer. Includes her "Jerusalem of Gold." Hebrew song texts romanized.
1145
SHUR, YEKUTIEL comp./ed. *Zimriyah - Program for Israeli Song Festival.* New York:A.Z.Y.F.,1970; 44pp., music.
    Collection of 17 selections — melodies with some two and three part voice lines. Songs suitable for group participation at Israeli song fests. Preliminary section of materials, including program guides and resources. Prepared by educator. English translations; Heb. romanized.
1146
SILBERMINTZ, SEYMOUR and Committee, comps./eds. *Songs of Israel.* New York:Z.O.A., 1949; 168pp., music.
    Collection of 178 selections — melody lines only. Comprehensive songster of wide musical scope, including Hebrew liturgicals and hymns, holiday songs, Hassidic tunes, secular folksongs and varied styles of Zionist music. Materials from Ashkenazic, Sephardic and Near Eastern/Oriental Jewish traditions. Settings of Biblical texts and Jewish poetry. Prepared by music educator. English annotations. Hebrew and Yiddish romanized.
1147
SILVERMAN, JERRY, comp./arr. *The Yiddish Song Book.* Briarcliff Manor,N.Y.:Scarborough/Stein and Day, 1983; xvi,204pp +2n.p., illus., music.
    Collection of 114 selections — melody lines with guitar symbols. Compilation of better known Yiddish songs, arranged in topical sections: Love; Children; *L'chayim* (To Life); It's Hard to be a Jew (Songs of Work and of Struggle); *Amerike* (Jewish Immigrant Experiences in America); and, Holocaust Songs. Prepared by guitarist, folksinger and educator Jerry Silverman, based upon his repertoire for performance and teaching. With prefatory materials and annotations for each song. Supplementary

diagrams of basic guitar chords as instructional aid.
Singable English texts. Photographs. Yiddish romanized.
1148
SOCIETY OF AMERICAN CANTORS — Committee, comps./eds.
Anthems, Hymns and Responses for Union Prayer Book. New
York(?):C.C.A.R., 1894; vii,63pp., music.
Hymnal materials — melody lines only — for Sabbath and
holidays. Prepared for services of Reform congregations
by committee of cantors and music educators, with spon-
sorship of Central Conference of American Rabbis. Mostly
English texts. Hebrew romanized.
1149
SOCIETY OF AMERICAN CANTORS — Committee, comps./eds. *The*
Union Hymnal. New York:W.C. Popper,1897; 218pp., music.
First official *Union Hymnal* of Central Conference of
American Rabbis (Reform Judaism). Contains 129 hymns and
anthems — melody lines with some two part choir voices —
for Sabbath and other Jewish religious observances of
year, according to edition of *Union Prayer Book* then
in American congregational use. Includes materials from
19th century hymnal collections of various synagogues.
Mostly English texts. Hebrew romanized.
1150
SPECTOR, JOHANNA, comp./ed. *Geto Lider Aus Littland und*
Littauer — Songs from Lithuania and Latvia. Vienna,Aus.:
J.D.C., 1947; 59pp., music.
Collection of poetry and songs from Holocaust era — melody lines only. Compiled by ethnomusicologist Johanna
Spector, herself a survivor who settled in America after
World War II. Yiddish romanized.
1151
SPICKER, MAX and WILLIAM SPARGER, comps/eds. *The Synagogue*
Services for Sabbath. New York:G.Schirmer,1901;2vols.,music
Collection of anthems and hymns for Sabbath, according
to Reform congregation *Union Prayer Book* — SATB choir
voices with organ accompaniments. Compiled by choral
director Max Spicker (1858-1912), with cantor and music
educator William Sparger (1860-1904), both of Temple
Emanu-El in New York City. Vol.1 — *Sabbath Eve*, 43pp.;
11 selections. Vol.2 — *Sabbath Morning*, 87pp.; 19
selections. English texts. Hebrew romanized.
1152
STAJNER, MIRJAM and Committee, comp./ed. *Shiron/Pesmarica/*
Songster. Belgrade,Yugo.:Jewish Society,1971; 24pp., music.
Collection of 18 selections — melody lines with guitar
symbols. Israeli Hebrew songs and Yiddish folksongs.
Prepared by musician Mirjam Stajner. Slovakian annota-
tions for songs. Translations into Slovakian and Cro-
ation of such selections as "Jerusalem of Gold" and of
"*Rozhinkes Mit Mandlen.*" Yid. and Heb. romanized.
1153
STARK, EDWARD JOSEF, comp./arr. *Sefer Anim Zemirot:Musical*
Services, According to Union Prayer Book for Jewish Worship,
New York:Bloch, 1909-1913; 5 vols., music.
Collection of chants, hymns and anthems — cantor, SATB
choir with organ accompaniments. Compiled by cantor,

composer and music educator Edward J.Stark (1856-1918)
for Reform congregational services. Vol.1 – *Sabbath
Morning*, 1909; 180pp. Vol.2 – *New Year*, 1910; 120pp.
Vol.3 – *Sabbath Eve*, 1911; 80pp. Vol.4 – *Festivals:
Sukkot/Pesach/Shavuot*, 1912; 140pp. Vol.5 – *Day of
Atonement*, 1913; 180pp. English texts; Heb. romanized.
1154

STARK, EDWARD JOSEF, comp./arr. and JACOB VOORSANGER, ed.
Services for Children – A Hymnal. San Francisco: Emanu-El,
1900; 56pp., music.
   Collection of hymns, with prayer texts, for use on Sabbath and holidays by children's congregations at Reform
   Temple Emanu-El of San Francisco. Compiled by cantor,
   composer and music director Edward J. Stark (1856-1918),
   with rabbi and educator Jacob Voorsanger (?-1908). With
   English texts and hymn translations. Hebrew romanized.
1155

SYNAGOGUE RITUAL BOARD, and Committee, comps./eds. *Hymns
Written for Use of Hebrew Congregation.* Charleston,S.C.:
Beth Elohim, 1856; 210pp., music.
   Collection of 65 hymns – melody lines only – for use
   with associated prayer texts. Compiled by Congregation
   Beth Elohim of Charleston, South Carolina. Mostly Eng-
   lish text materials. Hebrew hymn words romanized.
1156

URSTEIN, CARL, comp./arr. *Sefer Limud Ha-hazzanut.* New
York: C.A.A., 1974; 148pp., music.
   Collection of liturgical selections – melody lines only
   – for Sabbath services, from Friday evening, through
   Saturday morning and afternoon, to concluding service of
   Havdalah. Compiled by cantor and music educator Carl
   Urstein for children's congregations of Conservative
   synagogues. English annotations. Hebrew romanized.
1157

WAREMBUD, NORMAN H., comp./ed. and ZALMEN MLOTEK, arr.
Great Songs of the Yiddish Theater. New York:New York Times
/Quadrangle/Ethnic Music, 1975; 256pp., illus., music.
   Collection of 57 selections – melodies with piano accompaniments and guitar symbols. Yiddish theater songs,
   "favorites" of 1920's and 1930's. Compiled by music editor Norman Warembud (1917-1978) with pianist Zalmen Mlotek. Foreword by Yiddish theater actress/singer Molly
   Picon. Illustrations and annotations provide background
   on heyday of Yiddish theatricals in New York City. Song
   and composer/lyricist indexes. Yiddish romanized.
1158

WEINBERG, JACOB, comp./arr. *Five Hebrew Melodies.* New
York:Transcontinental, 1947; 15pp., music.
   Folksongs – melodies with piano accompaniments – adapted
   for children's use. Compiled by educator and composer
   Jacob Weinberg (1879-1956). Yid. and Heb. romanized.
1159

WEINBERG, JACOB, comp./arr. *Six Hebrew Songs.* New York:
Transcontinental, 1948; 9pp., music.
   Collection of folksongs and liturgical chants – melodies
   with piano accompaniments. Compiled by music educator

and composer Jacob Weinberg (1879-1956). Heb. romanized.
1160
WEINBERG, JACOB, comp./arr. *Ten Palestinian Songs.* New
York:Bloch, 1941; 15pp., music.
   Collection of 10 selections – melodies with piano accompaniments. Early Zionist folksongs. Compiled by music
   director and composer Jacob Weinberg (1879-1956). Some
   English annotations. Hebrew romanized.
1161
WEINBERG, JACOB, comp./arr. *Thirty Hymns and Songs for
Congregation, School and Home.*New York:[?],1947;64pp.,music
   Collection of hymns, anthems and religious folksongs –
   melodies with organ, or piano, accompaniments – for use
   in Reform services and rituals. Compiled by composer,
   conductor and music director Jacob Weinberg (1879-1956).
   Some English translations. Hebrew romanized.
1162
WISE, JAMES WATERMAN, comp./ed. *Synagogue Songs: Personal,
Social and National – for Synagogue and Extra-Congregational
Services.* New York:Bloch, 1924; 44pp., music.
   Collection of 34 hymns – melody lines only – for various
   religious observances of Jewish calendar year. Compiled
   by James W. Wise (1901-1983). Eng. texts; Heb. romanized
1163
WEINER, LAZAR, comp./arr. *Five Yiddish Songs: Settings of
Yiddish Poetry.* New York:Transcontinental, 1953; 19pp.,
music. (orig.ed. Vienna,Aus.:Jibneh, 1936)
   Collection of songs – voice with piano accompaniments.
   Compositions of Lazar Weiner (1897-1982), who devoted
   his talents to art-song settings of Yiddish poems. Some
   English and German texts. Yiddish romanized.
1164
WEINER, LAZAR, comp./arr. *Fourteen Songs:Settings of Yid-
dish Poetry.* New York:Transcont./U.A.H.C.,1980; 57pp.,music
   Collection of songs – voice with piano accompaniments.
   Compositions by choral director and music educator La-
   zar Weiner(1897-1982). English texts. Yiddish romanized.
1165
WEINER, LAZAR, comp./arr. *Song Cycle:Settings of Poetry by
Heschel.* New York:Transcontinental, 1974; 19pp., music.
   Collection of musical settings – voice and piano accompaniments – of five Yiddish poems by Jewish philosopher
   and educator Abraham Joshua Heschel (1907-1972). Compositions of Lazar Weiner (1897-1982). Yiddish romanized.
1166
WEINER, LAZAR, comp./arr. *Songs for Chorus.* New York:
Workmen's Circle, 1955; 112pp., music.
   Collection of 15 selections – SATB choral lines, some
   a cappella and others with piano accompaniments. Compiled by choral cirector and music educator Lazar Weiner
   (1897-1982). English annotations. Yiddish romanized.
1167
WEINER, LAZAR, comp./arr. *Songs of the Concentration Camps*
New York:Schaver/Weiner, 1948; 14pp., illus., music.
   Collection of 4 selections – melodies with piano accompaniments. Songs from Holocaust era. Arranged by pianist

and composer Lazar Weiner (1897-1982), with singer Emma
Schaver. English translations. Yiddish romanized.
1168
WEINER, LAZAR, comp./arr. *Twelve Songs:Settings of Yiddish*
Poetry. New York:Metro Music, 1948; 48pp., music.
     Collection of songs — voice with piano accompaniments —
     compositions by pianist, music educator and composer
     Lazar Weiner (1897-1982). English texts; Yid. romanized.
1169
WEINER, LAZAR, comp./arr. *Twelve Songs:Settings of Yiddish*
Poetry. New York:Transcontinental/U.A.H.C.,1978;51pp.,music
     Collection of songs — voice and piano accompaniment.
     Compositions of pianist and music educator Lazar Weiner
     (1897-1982). English translations. Yiddish romanized.
1170
WEISGALL, HUGO, comp./arr. and ALBERT WEISSER, ed. *The*
Golden Peacock:Seven Popular Songs from the Yiddish. Bryn
Mawr,Pa.:Presser, 1980; 28pp., music.
     Collection of 7 Yiddish folksongs — melodies with piano
     accompaniments. Prepared by composer and music educator
     Hugo Weisgall, with choral director and educator Albert
     Weisser (1918-1982). English texts. Yiddish romanized.
1171
WEISSMAN, JACKIE, comp./arr. *Shiru Yeladim — Sing Children*
Overland,Kan.:Jackie, 1978; 24pp., illus., music.
     Collection of ten Jewish melody lines, with activity
     ideas, for use with pre-school children. Prepared by
     music educator. English texts. Hebrew romanized.
1172
WERNER, ERIC and C.C.A.R. Music Committee, comps./eds.
Union Songster; Songs and Prayers for Jewish Youth. New
York:C.C.A.R., 1960; xii,448pp., illus., music.
     Collection of 193 selections, for use at assemblies and
     liturgical services by religious schools of Reform con-
     gregations. Melody lines, with SATB choral parts (or
     simple piano/organ accompaniments). Music for Sabbath,
     High Holy Days, Three Festivals (Passover, *Sukkot* and
     Shavuot), *Hanukkah, Purim* and other celebrations.
     Also with Israeli and Bible songs. Editorial direction
     by scholar and educator Eric Werner. Section of prayers.
     English translations. Hebrew for music romanized.
1173
WOHLBERG, MAX, comp./arr. *Shirei Zimrah: Sabbath Morning*
Hymns. New York: Bloch, 1947; 43pp., music.
     Collection of 125 prayer chants, motifs and hymns — me-
     lody lines only — for Sabbath morning services, accord-
     ing to prayerbook of United Synagogue of America: Con-
     servative tradition. Prepared by cantor and music edu-
     cator Max Wohlberg. English annotations. Heb. romanized.
1174
WOHLBERG, MAX, comp./arr. *Yachad B'kol; Cantorial Recita-*
tives for Sabbath, With Congregational Refrains. New York:
C.A.A., 1975; 51pp., music.
     Collection of 24 selections — melody lines only — for
     use by Conservative congregations. Compiled by cantor
     and music educator Max Wohlberg. Introductory informa-

tion and annotations in English. Hebrew romanized.
1175
WOHLBERG, MAX, comp./arr. *Yalkut Z'mirotai; New Settings of the Sabbath Zemirot.* Elkins Park,Pa.:Ashbourne, 1981; xxiii,42pp., music.
   Collection of 40 selections — melody lines only — of Sabbath table songs and home celebration hymns (the *Zemirot*) for observances from Friday eve to conclusion on Saturday evening (*Havdalah*). Compiled by cantor and music educator Max Wohlberg. Introductory information on historical background and traditional customs of this music. English annotations. Hebrew romanized.
1176
YARDEINI, MORDECAI and Editorial Board, comps./eds. *Fifty Years of Yiddish Song in America.* New York: Jewish Music Alliance, 1964; 236pp., illus., music.
   Collection of various types of folksong materials — melody lines only — compiled with other Yiddish texts and illustrations, all reflecting 20th century Jewish life in America. Prepared by choral director M. Yardeini with committee. English annotations. Yiddish romanized.
1177
YARDEINI, MORDECAI and Editorial Board, comps./eds. *Yiddish Poets in Song.* New York: Jewish Music Alliance, 1966; 348pp., illus., music.
   Collection of 70 selections — melody lines, some choir voice parts, all with piano accompaniments. Musical settings of Jewish poetry in Yiddish, Hebrew and English. Biographical studies of poets and musicians, with photographs. Compiled by choral director M. Yardeini, with advisory committee. Hebrew and Yiddish romanized.
1178
YOUNG PIONEERS — Committee, comps./eds. *Shirey Ma-avak - Songs of Struggle.* Brooklyn,N.Y.:Hechaluts/Hatsair, 1950; 66pp., illus., music.
   Collection of 31 selections — melody lines only. Hebrew songs by modern folk composers of Israel and America. English annotations/translations. Hebrew romanized.
1179
YOUTH DEPARTMENT — Committee, comps./eds. *Classified Palestine Songs.* (Series of 6 Booklets) Jerusalem,Brit. Mand.:Jewish National Fund,1946; 50pp. each, music.
   Series of 6 collections, 40 selections in each — melody lines with some voice parts for choir. Hebrew folksongs topically sorted: 1. Camping tunes, general songs and dance melodies; 2. *Hanukkah, Purim* and songs of Jewish struggle; 3. Children's melodies; 4. New Year and other commemorations; 5. Festivals: *Sukkot, Pesach, Shavuot;* 6. Sabbath. Prepared for Jewish schools and camps. Some English texts and annotations. Hebrew romanized.
1180
YOUTH DEPARTMENT — Committee, comps./eds. *Hava Nashira - Let Us Sing.* Jerusalem,Isr.:Keren Hayesod,1949;64pp.,music.
   Collection of 27 selections — melody lines only. Songs of seasons and land, with various poetical materials. Compiled for members of Israeli cooperative farms, or

Kibbutsim. English annotations. Hebrew romanized.
  1181
YOUTH FOUNDATION — Committee, comps./eds. *Songs of the*
Thirty Years. New York:A.Z.Y.F., 1978; 30pp., music.
      Collection of 39 selections — melody lines with guitar
      symbols. Hebrew folksongs reflecting three decades of
      Statehood of Israel (1948-1978). English annotations and
      translations. Hebrew romanized.
  1182
ZEIRA, MORDECAI, comp./arr. *Shirim-Songs.* Tel Aviv,Isr.:
Histadrut, 1960; 186pp., music.
      Collection of 94 songs — melody lines only — as composed
      or arranged by Israeli folk composer and music educator
      Mordecai Zeira (1905-1969). Born in Russia, he settled
      in Palestine in 1924 and worked on a farm, taught chil-
      dren and wrote or adapted many Hebrew songs. Zeira was
      a Hebrew minstrel (*Badkhen*), whose prodigious talents
      reflected times and events in songs, set Biblical and
      folk poetry, and celebrated nature and life in renascent
      Israel. No English. Hebrew song texts romanized.
  1183
ZIM, SOL, comp./arr. *The Joy of Israel.* Cedarhurst,N.Y.:
Tara, 1980; 88pp., illus., music.
      Collection of liturgical chants and secular folksongs —
      melodies with guitar symbols. Compiled by performer and
      music educator. English annotations. Hebrew romanized.

8.
Dance with Jewish Music

1184
BAHAT, AVNER and NOEMI BAHAT. "Some Notes on Traditional
Scriptural Reading Hand Movements as Source to the Dance of
Yemenite Jews." *World of Music*, vol.23,no.1. (W.Berlin,
Ger.:I.M.C./UNESCO, 1981), pp.20-5, illus.
   Summary of basic text materials for a series of lectures
   given by authors. Information on Biblical accents in
   general Jewish traditions, and as specifically performed
   in religious observances of Yemenite Jews. Singing and
   dancing viewed as arising from those cantillation chants
   as music and also as motion, determining body movements.
1185
BENNETT, ELSIE M., comp./arr. *Hebrew and Jewish Songs and
Dances.* New York:Metro Music, 1951; 38pp., music.
   Collection of 36 Yiddish and Hebrew folksongs - melody
   lines with accordion symbols - with suggestions for appropriate folk dances. Music for holidays and general
   Jewish celebrations. English annotations and transla-
   tions. Hebrew and Yiddish romanized.
1186
BERK, FRED, comp./ed. *Guide for the Israeli Folk Dance
Teacher.* New York:A.Z.Y.F., 1977; 16pp.
   Collection of information and source materials prepared
   by dance educator Fred Berk (1911-1980). Originally ap-
   peared in issues of *Hora - Dance Newsletter* (New York:
   A.Z.Y.F., 1970-77). Includes details on suitable music.
1187
BERK, FRED, comp./ed. *Ha-rikud - The Jewish Dance.* New
York:A.Z.Y.F./U.A.H.C., 1972; 100pp., illus., music.
   Collection of brief articles and other materials on
   Jewish dance, compiled by dance specialist Fred Berk
   (1911-1980). Contents: Part 1 - "History" (articles):
   "Beginnings of Jewish Dancing" by Benjamin Zemach, pp.3-
   9; "Treasure Out of Yemen" by Sara Levi-Tanai, pp.10-14;
   "Hassidic Dance" by Dvora Lapson, pp.15-20; "Jewish

Dance Activities in America" by Fred Berk, pp.21-25;
"Folk Dance in Israel" by Gurit Kadman, pp.26-33. Part 2
- "Leader's Guide to Israeli Folk Dances" by Fred Berk,
pp. 35-59. Including dance information, resources and
recording sources for music, as well as details of terminology. Part 3 - "Twenty-Five Popular Israeli Folk
Dances in America" by Fred Berk, pp.61-100. Dance notations and music references. Photographs. Heb. romanized.
1188

BERK, FRED, comp./ed. *The Hassidic Dance.* New York:A.Z.Y.
F./U.A.H.C., 1975; xii,64pp., illus., music.
   Compilation of brief articles and other materials on
   development and performance of Hassidic dances. Prepared
   for Israel Folk Dance Institute by educator and choreo-
   grapher Fred Berk (1911-1980). Part 1 - (articles):
   "Hassidism" by Haim Leaf, pp.3-6; "A Hassidic Wedding"
   by Lois Bar Yaacov, pp.7-12; "Wedding Dances" by Marsha
   Seed, pp.13-15; "With Body and Soul" by Jill Gellerman,
   pp.16-21; "Hassidic Dances at the Festivities of Rabbi
   Simon bar Yohai in Meron" by Zvi Friedhaber, pp.22-33;
   "Hassidic Dances in the Jewish Theater" by Lillian
   Shapiro, pp.34-36. Part 2 - "Ten Hassidic Dances in
   Israeli Style" by Fred Berk, pp.47-64. Instructions and
   music resources. Photographs. Hebrew texts romanized.
1189

BERK. FRED. comp./ed. *New Israel Folk Dances.* New York:
A.Z.Y.F., 1962; 31pp., illus., music.
   Dances with instructions and suitable music. Compiled,
   edited and notated by performer and dance educator Fred
   Berk (1911-1980). Introductory materials, including explanation of terms. Twelve dances and songs - melody
   lines with guitar symbols. Sources for recordings of
   music. English translations of songs. Hebrew romanized.
1190

BERK, FRED, BARBARA TAYLOR and SUSIE HOFSTATTER, comps./eds
One Hundred Israeli Folk Dances. New York:A.Z.Y.F., 1977;
108pp., illus.
   Compilation of folk dance choreography, with suggestions
   of suitable music available on recordings or performance
   scores. Notations by dance educator and performer Fred
   Berk (1911-1980), with editing assistance of two folk
   dance specialists: Taylor and Hofstatter. Each of 100
   different dances described and graded, with references
   to folk songs, as integral part of entire presentation.
   Introduction, with explanation of terminology for instructions. Hebrew romanized. Photographs of Israeli
   folk dance festivals held in New York City 1970-77.
1191

CHOCHEM, CORINNE, comp./ed. and TRUDI RITTMAN, arr. *Jewish
Holiday Dances.* New York:Behrman, 1948; 87pp.,illus.,music.
   Detailed instructions for 14 Jewish holiday dances -
   Sabbath, Three Festivals, *Hanukkah, Purim.* Music se-
   lections for each dance - melody lines with simple piano
   accompaniments. Prepared by performer and dance educator
   Corinne Chochem, with pianist Trudi Rittman. Prefatory
   information and annotations. English translations of

song texts. Hebrew romanized. Photographs and drawings.
Foreword by composer Darius Milhaud (1892-1974).
1192

CHOCHEM, CORINNE, comp./ed. and MURIEL ROTH, arr. *The*
Palestine Dances. New York:Behrman,1941;64pp.,illus.,music.
Collection of 17 folk dances, including 5 versions of
the *Hora.* With two-part music lines (SB) and simple
piano accompaniments. Prepared by choreographer and educator Corinne Chochem, with pianist Muriel Roth. Prefatory materials and annotations, as well as dance instructions. English translation of song texts and Hebrew
words romanized. Photographs and drawings.
1193

DELAKOVA, KATYA and FRED BERK, comps./eds. and SYLVIA
MARSHALL, arr. *Jewish Folk Dance Book.* New York:J.W.B.,
1948; iv,45pp., illus., music.
Introductory materials and instructions for 14 holiday
and general Jewish folk dances. With discussion of performance styles and types of group participation. Music
for each dance - melodies with simple piano accompaniments. Prepared by dance educators Katya Delakova and
Fred Berk (1911-1980) with pianist Sylvia Marshall. English translation of song texts. Hebrew words romanized.
Photographs and drawings.
1194

DELAKOVA, KATYA and FRED BERK, comps./eds. and SYLVIA
MARSHALL and HARRY ELLSTEIN, arrs. *Dances of Palestine.*
New York:B'nai B'rith/Hillel, 1947; 32pp., illus., music.
Introductory materials and instructions for 10 folk
dances. With appropriate music selections - melodies
and piano accompaniments. Prepared by performers and
dance educators Katya Delakova and Fred Berk (1911-1980)
with pianists Sylvia Marshall and Harry Ellstein. English translations of songs. Hebrew romanized. Drawings.
1195

FRIEDHABER, TZVI. *Dances of Israel.* Haifa,Isr.: Haifa
Music Museum and AMLI Library, 1969; 52pp., illus.
Scholarly discussion of Israeli folk dances - origins,
styles, modes of performance and musical associations.
Mostly Hebrew texts, with some English materials.
1196

GERSON-KIWI, EDITH. "Wedding Dances and Songs of the Jews
of Bokhara." *Journal of I.F.M.C.,* vol.2 (Cambridge, Eng.:
I.F.M.C., 1950), pp.17-18.
Summary of scholarly paper presented at conference of
International Folk Music Council. Israeli scholar and
educator Edith Gerson-Kiwi treats aspects of folk dance
and folk music traditions among Near Eastern/Asian Jews.
1197

INGBER, JUDITH BRIN, comp./ed. *Dance Perspectives 59:*
Shorashim - Roots of Israeli Folk Dance. Jerusalem,Isr.:
Ingber, 1974; 60pp., illus.
Collection of materials on Israeli folk dances - origins
and descriptions, information on various performers and
choreographers, and some musical resources. Compiled by
performer and educator J.B. Ingber. Photographs.

1198
KADMAN, GURIT. *The New Israel Folk Dance.* Tel Aviv,Isr.:
I.M.I., 1968; 18pp.
    Resource information on current folk dance expressions
    in Israel, with associated music materials. Prepared by
    scholar and dance educator. Hebrew and English texts.
1199
KADMAN, GURIT. "Yemenite Dances and Their Influence on the
New Israel Folk Dances." *Journal of I.F.M.C.*, vol.4 (Cam-
bridge,Eng.:I.F.M.C., 1952), pp.27-30.
    Summary of scholarly paper presented at conference of
    International Folk Music Council by enthnomusicologist
    and educator Gurit Kadman. Consideration of musical ele-
    ments and qualities of dance expression, as adapted in
    contemporary Israel.
1200
KAPLAN, SHLOMO and YEHUDAH HODES, comps./eds. *Zemer U'-
machol - Songs for Dances.* Tel Aviv,Isr.:Histadrut/
Nissimov, 1957; 42pp., music.
    Collection of 25 selections - melody lines only - of
    folksongs for particular dances. Identification of
    dances, without instructions. Compiled by music educator
    and choral director Shlomo Kaplan (1909-1979) with dance
    educator Yehudah Hodes. Hebrew song texts romanized.
1201
KINKELDEY, OTTO. *A Jewish Dancing Master of the Renaissance - Guglielmo Ebreo.* repr.ed. Brooklyn,N.Y.:Dance Horizons,1966; 46pp., illus. (orig. pub. in collection of essays
by various authors: *Studies in Jewish Bibliography - In
Memory of Abraham Solomon Freidus.* New York:Alexander Kohut
Memorial Found.,1929; on pp.329-372.)
    Monograph reprint of informative study by musicologist
    and educator Otto Kinkeldey (1878-1966), treating legacy
    of manuscripts on dance by Guglielmo Ebreo of Pesaro
    (fl.15th cent.). Discussion of that art - as created,
    taught and performed during the Renaissance period in
    North Italy communities. Writings by "William, the Jew
    of Pesaro," with information concerning contemporaries
    and influences, provide details on practical as well as
    theoretical aspects along with descriptions of dance
    patterns and music styles. Facsimiles and source notes.
1202
LAPSON, DVORA, comp./ed. *The Bible in Dance.* New York:
B.J.E., 1980; 147pp., illus., music.
    Collection of 23 dances based upon Biblical materials,
    with annotations, instructions and suitable music -
    melody lines with roster of recordings. Including other
    varied resources and details on topic of "Bible and
    Dance." Compiled by educator and authority on Jewish
    dance Dvora Lapson. Glossary of terms. Source notes.
    English translation of song texts. Hebrew romanized.
1203
LAPSON, DVORA, comp./ed. *Dances of the Jewish People -
Israeli and East European Dances.* New York:J.E.C./B.J.E.,
1954; 58pp., illus., music.
    Collection of 27 dances, with instructions and suitable

music - melody lines and roster of recordings. Compiled
by choreographer and dance educator Dvora Lapson, who
served as dance consultant for J.E.C./B.J.E. in New York
City from 1940 to 1980. Explanation of dance terms. English translation of song texts. Hebrew romanized.
    1204
LAPSON, DVORA, comp./ed. *Folk Dances for Jewish Festivals.*
New York:J.E.C./B.J.E.,1961; viii,163pp., illus., music.
    Collection of 45 dances, created or adapted by various
    Israeli and American choreographers. Graded, with in-
    structions and suitable music - melody lines and roster
    of recordings. Dances for Sabbath, *Hanukkah, Purim,
    Pesach, Sukkot, Shavuot* and Israel Independence Day.
    Compiled by dance educator Dvora Lapson. Glossary of
    dance terms. Sources and index. English translation of
    song texts. Hebrew romanized.
    1205
LAPSON, DVORA. "The Jewish Dances of Eastern and Central
Europe." *Journal of I.F.M.C.*, vol.15. (Cambridge,Eng.:I.F.
M.C., 1963), pp.58-61.
    Summary of scholarly paper presented by performer and
    dance educator Dvora Lapson at conference of Inter-
    national Folk Music Council.
    1206
LAPSON, DVORA, comp./ed. *Jewish Dances the Year Round.*
New York:J.E.C./B.J.E., 1957; 96pp., illus., music.
    Collection of original dances, expressive of Israeli and
    general Jewish themes, by educator and performer Dvora
    Lapson. With annotations, instructions and suitable
    music - melody lines and roster of recordings. Costume
    suggestions. English translations. Hebrew romanized.
    1207
GOODMAN, PHILIP, comp./ed. *The Hanukkah Anthology.* Phila.
:J.P.S.A., 1976; xxxiii,465pp., illus., music.
    See Chapter 20 - "Dances for *Hanukkah*" by Dvora Lapson
    and Sara Levi, pp.405-411. Collection of 5 dances with
    instructions and suitable music - melody lines only.
    Compiled by two dance educators. Annotations and source
    notes. English translations of texts. Hebrew romanized.
    1208
GOODMAN, PHILIP, comp./ed. *The Passover Anthology.* Phila.
:J.P.S.A., 1961; xxiii,496pp., illus., music.
    See Chapter 22 - "Dances for Passover" by Dvora Lapson,
    pp.414-419. Three dances with instructions and suitable
    music - melody lines only. English translation of song
    texts. Hebrew romanized.
    1209
GOODMAN, PHILIP, comp./ed. *The Sukkot and Simhat Torah An-
thology.* Phila.:J.P.S.A.,1973; xxxiii,475pp., illus.,music.
    See Chapter 22 - "Dances for *Sukkot, Simhat Torah*" by
    Dvora Lapson and Corinne Chochem, pp.426-433. Collection
    of dance materials, with instructions and suitable music
    - melody lines only. English texts. Hebrew romanized.
    1210
MANOR, GIORA and JUDITH BRIN INGBER, comps./eds. *Israel
Dance.* Tel Aviv,Isr.:Kushner, 1976; 96pp., illus.

Collection of 10 brief articles, in Hebrew and English, on aspects of contemporary Israeli dance — folk and art, amateur and professional. Historical and biographical information, reports on dance companies and schools, performances and general activities. References to music for dance. Compiled by educators. Numerous photographs.

1211
OESTERLEY, WILLIAM OSCAR EMIL. *The Sacred Dance: A Study in Comparative Folklore.* repr.ed. Brooklyn,N.Y.:Dance Horizons,1968; x,234pp. (orig.ed. New York:Macmillan, 1923)
See following sections: Chapter 3 — "The Sacred Dance Among the Israelites," pp.31-43; Chapter 4 — "The Old Testament Terms for Dancing," pp.44-53; Chapter 5/part 1 — "The Sacred Processional Dance Among the Israelites," pp.54-55; Chapter 6/part 1 — "Ritual Dance Round a Sacred Object Among the Israelites," pp.88-93; Chapter 7/part 1 — "Ecstatic Dance Among the Israelites," pp.107-114; Chapter 8/part 1 — "The Sacred Dance at Israelite Feasts," pp.140-143; Chapter 9/part 1 — "Dances in Celebration of Victory Among the Israelites," pp.159-166; Chapter 10/part 1 — "Sacred Dance as a Marriage Rite Among Israelites," pp.177-183; Chapter 11/part 1 — "Dancing as a Mourning and Burial Rite in the Old Testament," pp.194-197; Chapter 11/part 2 — "The Rite Among Mediaeval and Modern Jews," pp.198-201. Extensive treatment of topic by liturgist, scholar and educator W.O.E. Oesterley (1866-1950). Source notes and index.

1212
RABINOWICZ, HAIM. "Music and Dance in Hassidism." *Judaism* vol.8,no.2. (New York:J.T.S.A./A.J. Cong.,1959), pp.252-7.
Theoretical consideration of some elements of Hassidic religious expression, as reflected in their male dance movements with liturgical chants and folksongs.

1213
RICHARDSON, J.F., comp./ed. *A Selection of Folk Dances — Volume 5:Israel.* Oxford,Eng.:Pergamon,1977; 36pp., illus.
Collection of 10 Israeli dances — instructions, annotations and suggestions of suitable music with sources. Part of series on international dance traditions.

1214
SACHS, CURT. *World History of the Dance.* (trans. from German by Bessie Schonberg) New York:Seven Arts/W.W. Norton, 1937; 469pp., illus.
Scholarly consideration of dance as significant art form and folk expression by musicologist, music curator and educator Curt Sachs (1881-1959). Consult index for many topical references to aspects of Jewish dance, in wide range of creative modes and cultural traditions.

1215
SAGI, YAACOV and SHLOMO KAPLAN, comps./eds. *Festive Israel Dances.* Tel Aviv,Isr.:Tarbut, 1968; 14pp., illus., music.
Cycle of 5 folk dances, as performed by Karmon Dance Company of Israel. With suitable music — melody lines only. Compiled by choreographer Yaacov Sagi with music educator Shlomo Kaplan (1909-1979). Hebrew romanized.

1216
SHOSHANI, MICHAL, comp./ed. *Folk Dances of Israel.* Tel
Aviv,Isr.: I.M.I., 1970; 111pp., illus., music.
Collection of various types of dances, with annotations,
instructions and suitable music – melody lines, with
roster of recordings. Includes resource information on
dance in Israel. Compiled by dance leader Michal Shoshani. English song texts translated. Hebrew romanized.
1217
SORELL, NORMAN. "Guglielmo Ebreo, Co-founder of Ballet."
Menorah Journal, vol.42,nos.1/2.(New York,1954), pp.79–95.
Information on "William, the Hebrew of Pesaro" and on
other Jewish artists – musicians and dancing masters –
in North Italy during Renaissance. Guglielmo (c.1450–?)
left legacy of manuscripts on dance forms and styles of
that time. He appears to have been notable dancer and
teacher/leader at prominent courts, for which he created
new dance steps. Some of those innovations are described
by scholar Norman Sorell as early formulations of the
ballet. Source notes.
1218
TATCHER, TZAFRAH, comp./ed. *Israel Folk Dances.* New York:
W.Z.O., 1959; 40pp., illus., music.
Collection of 16 dances, with annotations, instructions
and suitable music – melody lines only. Compiled by
group dance leader. English song texts. Heb. romanized.
1219
VIZONSKY, NATHAN. "The Evolution of the Jewish Folk Dance"
Chicago Jewish Forum, vol.13,no.1.(Chicago,1954),pp.45–50.
Some historical perspectives on origins and practices of
Jewish folk dance expression, by scholar and educator.
1220
ZAHAVA, RUTH, comp./ed. and GERSHON KINGSLEY, arr. *Jewish
Dances.* Los Angeles:B.J.E., 1950; 55pp., illus., music.
Collection of 10 dances for Yiddish folksongs, with an-
notations, instructions and music – melodies with simple
piano accompaniments. Prepared by educator Ruth Zahava
with composer Gershon Kingsley. Glossary of dance terms.
English translations of song texts. Yiddish romanized.

Glossary of Judaica

Aramaic Hebraic vernacular of Jews from time of Second
Holy Temple through centuries of Talmudic Era. Some Near
Eastern Jewish groups have retained elements of this folk
language into modern times. Aramaic liturgical texts, such
as Kaddish and Kol Nidre, are important Jewish prayers.

Ashkenazic Jews ("Franco-Germanic") Settled in Rhineland
area during Roman Era. Over centuries communities flourished
in Western, Central and Eastern Europe. Folk vernacular of
Eastern European Jews — Yiddish (Juedisch).

Ba'al Kore Bible chanter — "master of cantillation" who
is responsible for Biblical intonations at service.

Ba'al Tefillah Prayer leader — "master of prayer chant"
for daily services and first sections of Sabbath and holiday liturgies. May be assistant cantor or volunteer member
of religious congregation.

Ba'al Toke'a Shofar (ram's horn) blower — "master of
sounding Shofar" as significant ritual for High Holy Days.

Badkhen (pl. Badkhonim) Folk minstrel/bard for weddings
and other communal festivities, especially in areas of
Eastern Europe. Often was composer/poet in addition to performer. Some achieved notability and left legacy of Yiddish
folksongs and poetry.

Bar/Bas Mitzvah Son/daughter of "blessed commandment"
formally inducted into adult congregational participation by
his/her chanting of benedictions and cantillation of Bible
passages, during a regular religious service.

Bible, Jewish Consists of Torah (Five Books of Moses),
Haftarah (Prophetic Books) and Ketuvim (Holy Writ/Scrolls).

Cantillation   Intonation of Bible portions according to 28 designated melodic/motival accent patterns. Historical and traditional purposes: grammatical punctuation; textual interpretation; reader and listener concentration; and, content remembrance. Associated terminologies: Biblical Accents; Cheironomy; Ekphonetics; Masoretic Notation; Neumes; Te'amim (Heb.); and Tropes/Trop (Yid.).

Cantorial Art   see: **Hazzanut.**

Conservative Judaism   Modified traditional ritual practices, developed as branch movement in America early in this century.

Diaspora   World-wide Jewish communities, except in Holy Land. Jewish dispersion dates from destruction of First Temple of Solomon in Jerusalem 586 B.C.E.

Dissident Judaic Sects   Non-rabbinic traditions: Essenes; Falashas; Karaites; Samaritans; and Therapeutae.

Festivals   Shalosh R'golim (Heb.) — "Three Pilgrimage Festivals" — Sukkot, Passover/Pesach, Shavuot. These holidays date from First Holy Temple Era, at which time they also were observed as "harvest celebrations" and journeys were made to attend the Levitical services in Jerusalem.

Geniza   Formal "burial chamber" for old Hebrew manuscripts and prayerbooks. Valuable Geniza was rediscovered in Cairo early in this century.

Haftarah/Haftorah   Bible: Prophets. Early: Joshua, Judges, Samuel, Kings. Later: Isaiah, Jeremiah, Ezekiel. Minor (12): Hosea, Joel, Amos, Obadiah, Jonah, Micah, Nahum, Habakkuk, Zephaniah, Haggai, Zechariah, Malachi.

Haggadah   Religious book of benedictions, historical narrative, prayers, poetry and folksongs. Text constitutes the Seder ("order") of the Passover ritual home meal service in celebration of freedom and Exodus from Egyptian bondage. The food — including matzoh (unleavened bread), wine, egg, roast lamb, greens, bitter herbs, and charoses (chopped apples and nuts) — is intrinsic to this ritual. Religious texts are chanted in learning/study musical style, and Seder includes singing of traditional folksongs.

Hallel   Liturgical reference to Psalms 113-118, which form special section of Festival services.

Hanukkah   Feast of Lights. Celebration of rededication of Holy Temple (Second Commonwealth) by Maccabees (Judas Maccabaeus with the Hasmoneans). Observed eight days, with kindling of Hanukkiah Menorah (nine-branch candelabrum). Biblical Apocrypha: Book of Maccabees.

Hassidism   Eastern European movement of Jewish Pietism,

which arose in 18th century out of earlier Judaic Kabbalah/
mysticism and spread throughout area, flourishing until the
Holocaust. Some Hassidic sect groups now reside in Israel
and America. Hassidim ("Pious Ones") ascribe particular significance to music as an active means of communion with God.
Their spiritual melodies (niggunim) are often wordless and
improvisationally elaborated. Hassidic dance movement (male)
is an aspect of this musical inspiration in behalf of faith.

Havdalah Ritual of chanted benedictions and religious
folksongs concluding Sabbath (Saturday after sundown).

Hazzan (pl. Hazzanim) Cantor. Liturgical music leader of
Jewish congregations.

Hazzanut "The Cantorial Art" — Prayer leadership by means
of: recitation and recitative/parlando; chanting of traditional mode patterns and melodic formulas; strict and free
musical improvisation; antiphonal singing with congregation;
renditions of musically arranged or composed liturgical
works.

Hebrew Language of Jewish prayer and Judaic studies.
Modern Hebrew is official language of State of Israel.

High Holy Days Most solemn season of Jewish calendar.
Rosh Hashanah (Jewish New Year) and Yom Kippur (Day of
Atonement).

Hora Popular Jewish circle dance.

Hymnody, Jewish Poetic songs of Praise to God, with set
melodies. Associated with particular holidays and special
liturgical services.

Improvisation Cantorial artistry of intoning prayers,
utilizing specified synagogue modes and traditional melodic
motifs in extensive musical elaboration. Two forms: strict
improvisation (Tefillat Ha-seder) according to orderly set
patterns; and free improvisation (Tefillat Ha-regesh) of
on-the-spot inspiration, associated with coloratura flights
and performances by virtuoso cantors of Eastern European
customs. Generally cantors have been expected to improvise
vocally upon prayer texts. Such spontaneous musical interpretations have been considered as "outpourings of the soul"
deeply inspirational to congregants in their own devotions.

Kabbalah Movement of religious mysticism among Jewish
poetic liturgists of 12th to 16th century, resulting in
elaboration of poetry and musical celebrations especially
for Sabbath. see: **Zemirot**.

Kabbalat Shabbat Welcoming the Sabbath (Friday eve) with
singing of Psalms, hymns and folksongs.

Kaddish Jewish Doxology-Sanctification. There are five

versions, including mourner's prayer.

Ketuvim   Bible: Scriptural Writings — Psalms, Proverbs, Job; and Scrolls — Song of Songs, Ruth, Lamentations, Ecclesiastes, Esther, Daniel, Ezra, Nehemiah, Chronicles.

Kiddush   Benediction for wine at Sabbaths, holidays and special occasions.

Kinot   Lamentations, chanted at Tisha B'av services in memorial for destruction of Holy Temple in Jerusalem.

Klezmer   (pl. Klezmorim) Folk instrumentalist of Eastern European/Ashkenazic Jewry. Ensembles were often called Kapelyeh (Yid.).

Kol Nidre   Opening Hebrew-Aramaic prayer for Yom Kippur (Day of Atonement) eve. Generally known melody for this ancient text belongs to Ashkenazic tradition. Sephardic and Oriental Jews chant prayer to other melodic formulas.

Ladino/Judezmo. Spaniolic vernacular of Sephardic Jews, based upon 13th century Spanish dialects blended with He-brew elements and other vocabulary ingredients derived from Diaspora communities of Mediterranean area.

Lag B'omer   "Holiday of the Scholars" honoring Rabbi Akiva, Simeon bar Yohai and leader Simon bar Kokhbar ("Son of a Star"), heroic figures in rebellion against tyranny of Rome early in Common Era.

Liberal Judaism   see: **Reform Judaism.**

Ma-ariv/Arvit   Evening service for every day.

Mahzor   Traditional prayerbook for High Holy Days.

Megillah   Scroll. see: **Ketuvim.**

Meshorer   (pl. Meshorerim) Liturgical choir singer.

Minha   Afternoon service for every day.

Minhag   (pl. Minhagim) Customary tradition.

Minyan   Quorum for Jewish prayer service — ten adult males for strict traditional observances.

Missinai (Holy) Melodies   Oldest, most treasured melodic elements of Ashkenazic synagogue musical traditions.

Modes of Synagogue Music   Traditional melodic patterns for particular prayers and services. Primary modes are: Adonoy Moloch/Adonay Malakh — a modified Mixolydian, with ambiguity of major-minor; Ahavo Rabbo/Ahava Rabba — an altered form of Phrygian; Mogen ovos/Magen Avot — an Aeolian minor. Secon-

dary modes are: Mi Sheberach/Ukrainian Dorian — character-
ized by interval of augmented 2nd; Yishtabach — combined
qualities of Ahavo Rabbo and Mogen Ovos; Yekum Purkan — a
variant of Adonoy Moloch; Selicha — a modified Ahavo Rabbo;
Viddui — a form of major.

Musaf Additional morning service (after Shaharit) for
Sabbath, High Holy Days and Festivals.

Neilah Additional afternoon service (after Minha) for
conclusion of Yom Kippur.

Niggun (pl. Niggunim) Hassidic spiritual melodies. Religious folksongs, often wordless and with male dance movements, serving devotional purposes beyond liturgical services. Hassidim (Pious Ones) adapted ("ennobled") tunes and
developed a unique reservoir of music for various occasions,
Sabbath and holiday celebrations. Different Hassidic groups
have musical themes reflecting their own special styles.

Nusah Ha-tefillah "Melodies of Prayer" — Jewish liturgical chant.

Oberkantor Chief cantor of a congregation.

Oriental Jews Diaspora Jewish communities located east of
Jerusalem. Near East/Middle East; Asia Minor; Asia. Vernacu-
lars include Aramaic, Judaeo-Arabic, Judaeo-Persian.

Orthodox Judaism Strict traditional ritual observances.
Liturgical services without any instrumentation. Male choir.

Passover/Pesach "Freedom Festival" — Celebrating Exodus
from Egyptian slavery. Seder ritual home feast. Bible readings during holiday include Song of Songs.

Piyyut/Pizmon (pl. Piyyutim/Pizmonim) Sacred poetry which
has entered into liturgy as prayer, especially for High Holy
Days. Chanted with special motives and modal elaborations.

Purim "Feast of Lots" — Holiday of deliverance from
oppression. Liturgical service includes Bible portion of
Scroll of Esther as focal aspect of observance.

Psalmody, Jewish Chanting of Psalms in daily, Sabbath and
holiday services. Sephardic and Oriental Jewish traditions
have preserved special cantillation formulas. Ashkenazic
tradition favors free chant allied to musical motives for
the particular service. Psalms are also chanted parlando
in private devotions.

Reform Judaism Modified ritual practices with revised
prayerbooks. Services with organ or other instrumentation
and mixed choir. Branch movement arose in Germany early in
19th century, and soon afterwards was brought to America.

Rosh Hashanah   Jewish New Year of High Holy Days season.
Sounding of Shofar is significant aspect of liturgical
services.

Rosh Hodesh   First day of each Jewish month, liturgically
observed with special prayers. Approximate analagous calen-
dars: Nisan (April); Iyar (May); Sivan (June); Tammuz (July)
Av (August); Elul (September); Tishrei (October); Cheshvan
(November): Kislev (December); Tevet (January); Shevat
(February); Adar (March); Adar II (for Jewish leap years).

Sabbath   "Seventh Day of Rest" - Observed from Friday eve
sundown to Saturday night twilight.

Saegerin   Term refers to female leader of women in prayer,
as common practice especially among Ashkenazic groups
during earlier centuries.

Scrolls   see: **Ketuvim.**

Seder   Passover holiday home ritual meal, conducted according to religious text and order of Haggadah, special
prayerbook. see: **Haggadah.**

Selichot   "Penitential Days" - Season of spiritual preparation for High Holy Days.

Sephardic Jews   ("Spaniolic") Commenced with settlements
in Iberia during 2nd century and flourished in Spain and
Portugal and their territories. Following Inquisition era
and expulsion in 1492, Sephardic Jewry and its traditions
resettled in Western, Central and Southern Europe, and in
Mediterranean areas. Folk vernacular is Ladino/Judezmo.

Shaharit   Morning service for every day.

Sheliah Tsibbur/Shatz   "Congregational Messenger of the
Prayers" - Early title for office of liturgical leader,
dating from rise of communal synagogue services. Duties then
were voluntary and were assumed as an honorary obligation.
Well into Talmudic Era, religious services began to require
musical and intellectual skills, in addition to personal
devotion and piety. Thus a formal office of Hazzan evolved.

Shavuot/Shevuoth   "Festival of Pentecost/Weeks" - Holiday
celebrating Ten Commandments, as time of revelation. Bible
portions include Book of Ruth.

Shofar   Ram's horn. Ancient wind instrument which was used
in Biblical times for numerous ritual purposes, and has
remained the singular musical instrumentation for traditional Judaism. Undecorated, it is blown without any mouthpiece;
and its musical sounds conform to specially designated
"Shofar calls" in a very particular pattern of blasts. The
sounding of the Shofar is intrinsic to devotional observance of the High Holy Days.

Shul Yiddish term for synagogue.

Siddur Traditional prayerbook for weekdays, Sabbath and Festivals.

Simhat Torah "Holiday of Torah" — Celebration of Bible reading annual cycle. At this service, the final portion and first portion are read, thereby affording a continuity.

Sukkot "Festival of Tabernacles/Booths" — Holiday of thanksgiving and renewal, following soon after High Holy Days. Bible portions include Ecclesiastes.

Synagogue House of religious assembly for prayer and study. Arose during time of Second Holy Temple/Commonwealth Era among Jews already in Diaspora, as well as those remaining in the Holy Land.

Tanzfierer Yiddish term for dance leader/entertainer in Eastern Europe.

Tefillah (pl. Te'fillot) Prayer.

Tisha B'av Memorial holiday, commemorating destruction of Holy Temple in Jerusalem. Bible portions are Lamentations, or Kinot (Heb.).

Torah Bible: Pentateuch/Five Books of Moses — Genesis, Exodus, Leviticus, Numbers, Deuteronomy.

Tu B'shvat/Hamisha Asar "Jewish Arbor Day" — Holiday of trees and agriculture.

Vorbeter/Vorsinger Precentor; cantor.

Yiddish ("Juedisch") Ashkenazic folk vernacular which was developed from 12th century onward. It is composed of Germanic, Romance and Slavic elements as well as Hebrew. Yiddish has flourished as a vital intellectual, social and cultural medium of expression for Jewish life, especially in the communities of Eastern Europe.

Yom Kippur Day of Atonement of High Holy Days season. Solemn fast day, concluded with sounding of the Shofar.

Zemirot Sabbath table hymns and folksongs for festive home meals and communal synagogue celebrations. Many are melodic settings of poetic liturgy written by Kabbalist/mystic religious leaders of 12th to 16th centuries. Among Ashkenazic groups, certain specific Zemirot are associated with each of the three special meals (Shalosh Se'udot) for the Sabbath day, as well as the greeting of the Sabbath as a "bride" (Kabbalat Shabbat) on Friday eve and the farewell to the "bride" (Melave Malke) on Saturday night. Hassidic music is particularly rich in these materials.

Author Index

Topical Index

441,467,487,513,520,523,550,551,
559,565,567,587,594-596,664,666,
673,680,693,707,717,725,727,739,
747-750,753,754,838,843,871,
1075,1211.
Milhaud, Darius 285,302,323,329,
749,856,906,977,1120,1191; also
see: France.
Milner, Moses 196; also see: Folksongs, Yiddish; Russia; U.S.S.R.
Mirandola, Pico della 421.
Missinai (Holy) Melodies 3,161,
176,184,199-201,203,232,409,692,
693,737,744,745,815; Collections
of 841,846,873; also see: Cantorial Art; Liturgical Chant;
Synagogue Music.
M. Levi of Wuettemburg 120; also
see: Germany.
Modena, Leon da 161,184,203,230,
392; also see: Italy; Renaissance Era; Rossi, Salomone.
Modes, Synagogal 3,99,127,140,166,
171,184,200,201,203,224,226,255,
267,298,332,369,370,371,410,416,
417,430,431,434,437,448,471,485,
494,519,529,531,550,625,701,740,
741,744,747,749,753,754,766,768,
774,815,873,879; also see: Adonoy Moloch/Adonay Malakh; Ahavo
Rabbo/Ahava Rabba; Ashkenazic
Musical Traditions; Cantorial
Art; Liturgical Chant; Mogen
Ovos/Magen Avot; Synagogue Music
Mogen Ovos/Magen Avot 3,161,184,
203,437,625,873; also see: Can-
torial Art; Liturgical Chant;
Modes; Synagogue Music.
Monteverdi, Claudio 740.
Morocco, Jews of 407,445,592,873,
899,900; also see: North Africa.
Moscheles, Ignaz 500.
Moses (Moshe) ibn Ezra 440,520,
754; also see: Rabbinical
Writings.
Moslem Music 283,369,443; also
see: Arabic Literature; Islam;
Israeli Arabic Music.
Mozart, Leopold and Wolfgang Ama-
deus 490.
Museum Exhibitions of Jewish Music
76; also see: Iconography.
Musorgsky, Modest Petrovich 209,
593; also see: Russia.

Nadel, Arno 97,377,462; also see:

Cantorial Art; Germany; Synagogue Music.
Najara, Israel 127,161,184,263;
also see: Piyyutim/Pizmonim;
Zemirot.
Nathan, Isaac 143,324,581; also
see: England.
Naumbourg, Samuel 90,139,141,154,
157,159,161,171,176,879; also
see: Cantorial Art; Cantors
(Historical Figures); France;
Liturgical Chant; Rossi, Salomone; Synagogue Music.
Near East/Middle East, Jews of 34,
152,164,179,184-186,199,200,220,
222,223,225,226,233,258,259,288,
292,298,320,331,332,335,342,343,
350,362,411,416,419,430,443,444,
448,450,454,459,480,494,519,524,
529,530,550,592,670,693,749,753,
835,836,840,842,871,873,874,
1146,1196; also see: Asia Minor;
Mediterranean Area; Oriental
Jews.
Nebel (Psaltery) 183,234,422,753;
also see: Bible, Musical Instruments of; Temple (Ancient).
Netherlands (Amsterdam), Jews of
125,475,740,741,744,752,883;
also see: Western and Central
Europe.
Netzer, Effi 930,931; also see:
Israel (Modern), Composers and
Their Works.
Neumes 184,200,201,203,227,535,
548,565,567,596,639,654,703;
also see: Biblical Accents; Cantillations; Cheironomy; Ekphonetics; Masoretic Notation; Te'-
amim; Tropes.
New Testament/Gospels 183,184,200,
201,306,578,694; also see:
Christian Liturgy, Early Development of.
Nigun/Niggun (Spiritual Melody)
3,99,176,184,199,203,209,413,
472,753,754,868,870,873,901,909,
912-914,916,917,1043,1070,1101,
1105-1107,1109,1187,1188,1212;
also see: Hassidism, Musical
Expression of.
Nineteenth Century, Jewish Music
During 34,40,50,90,91,111,113,
116,120,121,126,138,154,159,161,
171,176,195,249,274,276,309,314,
326,364,400-402,409,466,489,503,

About the Compiler

IRENE HESKES is the founder and director of the American Yiddish Theater Music Restoration and Revival Project. She has contributed to *Musical Theater in America* (Greenwood Press, 1984) and the *Encyclopedia Judaica* and is the author of *The Cantorial Art*, *Studies in Jewish Music*, *Jews in Music*, and *Ernest Bloch: Creative Spirit.*

DATE DUE